GREAT OPERAS

ERNEST NEWMAN

THE DEFINITIVE TREATMENT OF THEIR HISTORY, STORIES, AND MUSIC

VOLUME

I

VINTAGE BOOKS

NEW YORK

A DIVISION OF RANDOM HOUSE

Contents

Orfeo ed Euridice

CHRISTOPH GLUCK [1714–1787]

PRINCIPAL CHARACTERS

ORFEO	*Contralto*
EURIDICE	*Soprano*
AMOR	*Soprano*

1

LUCK had already more than thirty works to his credit when, in 1762, he produced his *Orfeo*. This is the work with which he began his famous "reform of the opera"; and it is the oldest opera now in the repertory.

The poem is by Ranieri Calzabigi, an Italian who managed to combine culture with business in a way peculiar to his century. Born at Livorno in 1714, he settled in Paris, where he attracted attention not only by his writings on music and poetry and the arts in general but by a scheme for a lottery that was intended to restore health to the ailing French finances. Nine years later he was in Vienna, in the capacity of "Chamber Councillor to the Exchequer of the Low Countries." There he came into close contact with the Austrian Chancellor, Prince Kaunitz, through whom he met Count Durazzo, the director of the Vienna theatres. As Calzabigi was known to hold advanced views on the subject of opera libretti, Durazzo seems to have invited him to give them practical shape; whereupon Calzabigi wrote the poem of *Orfeo*. He must have met Gluck shortly after his arrival in Vienna, as the pair collaborated in the ballet *Don Juan,* which was produced in October 1761. According to Calzabigi's own account, written some years later, at a time when his relations with Gluck were a little clouded over, it was he who suggested Gluck as the composer of *Orfeo*. The question who began the rapprochement is, however, of no more than academic interest today. The two men had for some time been approaching the same problem along different but converging lines; and it was inevitable that as soon as they found themselves side by side at Durazzo's dinner table they should plan to co-operate in a solution of that problem, which was none other than to substitute a "return to nature" for the formalities and frigidities that had been weighing on opera seria for so long.

Calzabigi alleged that he "consented" to the production of his drama on the sole condition that the music to it should meet with his approval; whereupon Durazzo "sent" Gluck to him. This is no doubt an exaggeration: Gluck's reputation and official position in Vienna just then were not of the kind that would make it likely that Durazzo would "send" him to Calzabigi; nor would a man of his tough fibre allow himself to be "sent." According to Calzabigi, he read his poem to the musician, repeated several sections of it for him in order to show him how he wished his lines to be "declaimed," and generally indicated the procedure the composer was to follow. No doubt he did something of that kind; but the respect in which *Orfeo* is held today, and consequently the very survival of Calzabigi's poem, are due not to the composer having "declaimed" the text as the poet would have had him do — on his copying, as Calzabigi says, "the nuances I put into my declamation, the suspensions, the slackening of the pace, the rapidity, the greater or less intensity and emphasis of the voice, which I desired him to employ in his composition" — but to the quality of the *music* written by Gluck. The most correct declamation in the world would not have saved the score from oblivion, and with it would have vanished the poem had the music not been what it is. Calzabigi certainly owes as much to Gluck as Gluck did to him. Even without Calzabigi, indeed, Gluck would still have been a great figure in the history of opera, whereas but for his association with Gluck, Calzabigi would today be almost forgotten. Who, apart from students who specialise in the subject, is aware even of the existence of the libretti the Italian wrote for certain other composers?

Gluck, for his part, frankly acknowledged his indebtedness to his collaborator in the famous preface to a later opera of his, *Alceste*, in 1769, in which he says that Calzabigi had "conceived a new type of lyric drama, in which flowery descriptions, futile similes, and cold, sententious moralising were to be replaced by strong passions, interesting situations, the language of the heart, and a constantly varied spectacle." Four years later, in a letter to the Paris *Mercure,* he paid still more generous tribute to his former colleague.

Ever since the middle of the seventeenth century the feeling against certain deficiencies or absurdities in the dramatic basis of opera had been growing in more than one European country. But the immense literature on the subject would have been impotent to effect any substantial reform without the musical genius of Gluck: the poets and the aestheticians might have talked till they were black in the face had the *musician* not arrived just at the right time to achieve in practice what they could no more than aspire to do in theory. The situation was exactly paralleled half a century later in the case of Wagner. In the very year of Wagner's birth one Ignaz Franz Mosel published a book in which he suggested most of the later Wagnerian reforms; but had Wagner died in his childhood we should still, in all probability, be theorising very much as Mosel did, and still awaiting the coming of the great practician.

Orfeo was first given in Vienna on the 5th October 1762, under Gluck himself; Calzabigi "produced" it on the stage. The text used, of course, was the original Italian one. The Orfeo was the male contralto Gaetano Guadagni, the Euridice Marianna Bianchi, the Amor Lucia Gelbero-Claverau. Twelve years later Gluck recast the work for Paris, the French version being made by Moline. As the French stage did not use male soprani or contralti, Gluck rearranged the part of Orfeo for the tenor voice, besides making a few further alterations in, and additions to, his score.

It is an endless subject for debate whether the part of Orfeo should be sung today by a female contralto or a tenor. The advocates of the latter course insist that the drama becomes more human when the Orfeo is a man, and that the ear, as well as the eye, finds an opera with the three principal characters in it women a little monotonous. Besides, they say, did not Gluck's willingness to recast the part for a tenor show that he was not inseparably wedded to the idea of a contralto Orfeo? To this it is rejoined that if Gluck had preferred a tenor to a contralto in the Vienna production he had only to cast the part for a tenor when writing his original score: the fact that he wrote it for a contralto suggests that he saw the character in terms of contralto colour, and consequently to substitute the tenor colour for this is to alter the whole scheme of psychological as well as musical values. To this argument, in turn, it is replied that the timbre of the female contralto voice is a different thing altogether from that of the male contralto, in which the eighteenth century took such keen delight. No final solution of the problem is, or will ever be, possible.

In its new form the work was given in Paris on the 2nd August 1774, with Legros as Orfeo,[1] the brilliant, witty Sophie Arnould as Euridice, and Rosalie Levasseur as Amor. In the ballets there figured not only the two famous Vestris, père et fils, but the Mlle Guimard who was the victim of some of Sophie Arnould's brightest *mots*. Sophie seems to have regarded Mlle Guimard as more a statuesque *poseuse* than a dancer. The lady once had the misfortune to break her arm. " What a pity it wasn't her leg," said Sophie: " then it wouldn't have prevented her from dancing." It is interesting also to note that among the dancers mentioned in the French playbill of the 2nd August 1774 were the brothers Gardel. Mlle Guimard, it seems, was rather long and lanky; and Sophie Arnould said that whenever she saw her dancing a pas de trois with Gardel and another male dancer, Dauberval, it reminded her of two dogs disputing with each other the possession of a bone. We can only hope that the lady cut a better figure in Gluck's Elysian Fields than she does in the biographies of Sophie Arnould.

2

The multiform legend of Orpheus has been dealt with by Calzabigi in a way of his own; and though, while in conscious revolt against the conventions of his day, he has not been able entirely to free himself of them subconsciously, his poem is on the whole admirably planned for both musical and dramatic effectiveness. As the opera is always given today with a contralto Orfeo it is the original Italian version of it that we shall analyse here, with an

---

[1] As Legros insisted on something "effective" for his exit at the end of the first act he was given a bravura aria, " L'espoir renaît dans mon cœur," that was at one time believed to be the work of one Bertoni, but is now known to have been written by Gluck himself for a performance of *Orfeo* in Frankfort-on-the-Main in 1764.

occasional reference to the changes made in the French score.

The short overture is not one of Gluck's most distinguished efforts in this line: it merely plays the opera in, in the most general terms, without any specific reference to the drama, and without having very much to commend it musically. The real *Orfeo* begins when, after an expressive orchestral preamble of fourteen bars:

the curtain rises, showing the tomb of Euridice in a vale in Thessaly: nymphs and shepherds are adorning it with flowers, while at the foot of an adjacent tree Orfeo abandons himself to his grief. From time to time he ejaculates a mournful " Euridice! ":

which does not interrupt the chorus but blends with it, taking on itself the harmonic aspect of the particular moment; for example:

The orchestral colouring is at once sweet and sombre. Here, at the very commencement of the work, we can see how much greater Calzabigi's debt is to Gluck than Gluck's to him. We can visualise the poet reading this opening chorus of his to the composer and indicating, as he says, the proper scansion of the words. Gluck does indeed follow the prosodic values in the melody he puts into the mouths of the nymphs and shepherds:

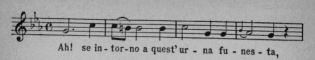

Ah! se in-tor-no a quest'ur - na fu - nes - ta,

This is the soprano part: in the other three parts the composer's fidelity to the poet's prosodic pattern is still more manifest:

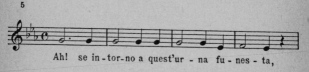

Ah! se in-tor-no a quest'ur - na fu - nes - ta,

But throughout virtually the whole movement Gluck maintains in the *orchestra* the syncopated rhythmic scheme:

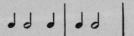

shown in example No. 1; and it is these cross-beats — a purely musical effect, beyond the powers of poetry — that before everything else give the episode its accent of grief.

Orfeo, in a short recitative, bids his companions be silent, continue their work of bedecking the tomb with flowers, and leave him undisturbed in his sorrow. They circle in solemn antique fashion about the tomb in what was called in the eighteenth century a "pantomime":

Before leaving they repeat their first strain (No. 1, etc.) in a curtailed form, and Calzabigi and Gluck show their fine sense of style by omitting this time the distracted cries of Orfeo to the beloved dead; for he is now about to make a longer, more stylised, and still more moving lament over the lost Euridice. "I call on my loved one at dawn of day and at fall of even," he sings:

(The melody is said to be an adaptation of a Czech popular song: Gluck, it may be recalled, had spent his youth in Bohemia). "But vain is all my grief: my love responds not to me." The tender cadences of his phrases are echoed softly by a few instruments behind the scenes. Orfeo continues his complaint in an expressive recitative, which also has its echo effects — it is as if all nature were listening sympathetically to him. The aria (No. 7) is repeated to other words; then there follows a third recitative, in which once more the woods and streams repeat his dolorous cries of "wretched Orfeo" and "loved Euridice," and after this comes another repetition of the aria. The whole lay-out of this opening scene of the opera is admirable in the way it preserves the one fundamental note of overwhelming grief and pain through the many variations of technical device.

A more agitated recitative follows, in which Orfeo bitterly reproaches the gods for their cruelty: he will pursue Euridice to where she now is, he says, and tear her from their keeping. Whereupon Amor (Eros) appears, to tell him that the gods, in their pity for him, will allow him to descend to Lethe; and if there he can overcome the Furies with his song, Euridice shall return to the light of day with him. But the gods impose a hard condition: until the pair have left the shores of the Styx behind them he is not to turn his eyes on her, on pain of losing her for ever. In the French version this scene is more spun out than in the Italian. In the former, Amor has two arias, in the latter only one, in which, in the "galant" musical style of the period, he exhorts Orfeo to be of good cheer:

9

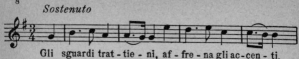

Gli sguardi trat - tie - ni, af - fre - na gli ac - cen - ti,

and the act ends with a vigorous and varied recitative, in which Orfeo affirms his resolve to dare the great adventure, and a brief orchestral postlude (*presto*) that underlines his resolution.

3

The second act takes place at the entrance to Tartarus, with the river Styx in the distance. A majestic orchestral prelude depicts at once Orfeo's resolution:

and his grief:

There follow three bars of sharp arpeggios that announce the singer's coming; then the chorus of the Furies — the four voices in a hard unison — asks who is the mortal that thus dares to brave the terrors of their abode:

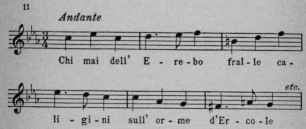

Chi mai dell' E - re - bo fral - le ca -

li - gi - ni sull' or - me d'Er - co - le

A short dance of the Furies follows this: then the chorus is repeated, with a new phrase hinting at the horrible fate of the intruder if he be not a god:

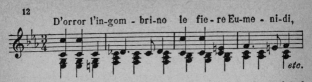

Against these harsh harmonies and colours the pleading of Orfeo and its harp accompaniment stand out in complete contrast:

Between the broken phrases of his appeal to them to have pity on his misery the Furies thunder an uncompromising " No! " — for example, at the points represented by minim rests in the foregoing quotation. In the orchestral basses we hear also the growling and barking of Cerberus. The next ensemble of the Furies, however, suggests that some spark of pity is already beginning to show itself in them. He appeals to them in still more urgent accents:

And so it continues, with further solos of Orfeo:

and a further softening of the Furies, until at last they confess themselves vanquished by his song: their ranks divide, and the victor passes through. (In the French score Gluck inserts at this point a "pantomime" of the Furies, the music of which is drawn from his *Don Juan* ballet of 1761).

The scene changes to the Elysian Fields, which are bathed in the purest of light; some of the happy shades are dancing to a tranquil melody:

To the Paris score Gluck added for this scene a long melody for a single flute, with string accompaniment, that is without parallel for its romantic beauty in all Gluck's music, and may fairly claim to be still the loveliest of all solos for the flute. Berlioz quoted the movement in full in his treatise on the orchestra. He shows with what consummate art Gluck has exploited the peculiar timbres of the instrument. No other instrument, as Berlioz says, would be adequate to express "this very sublime lament of a suffering and despairing departed spirit." "It is at first," he continues, "a voice scarcely audible, which seems to fear to be overheard; then it laments softly, rising into the accent of reproach, then into that of profound woe, the cry of a heart torn by intolerable wounds, then falling little by little into complaint, regret, and the sorrowing murmur of a resigned soul. What a poet!"

An aria by Euridice depicts in soft lines and colours the felicity of these blest spirits:

the chorus joining in from time to time.

Orfeo enters. He is dazzled by the clearness of the light, intoxicated by the sweetness of the air, ravished by the song of the birds, in this place where all is pure contentment. Shall he find his Euridice here? he asks. His long scena, which commences with a melody in the oboe:

18 *Andante*

flows along suavely, unhurriedly, the orchestra supplying, in the eighteenth century manner, all kinds of pictorial touches suggested by the images aroused by the words. (This music was taken over by Gluck from a couple of his earlier works and adapted to the present situation. In the French version it underwent further modifications).

The happy spirits, in a tender chorus, lead Euridice to the impatient Orfeo: and the general joy finds expression in a dignified ballet. The act ends with a repetition of the previous chorus.

4

At the commencement of the third act we see the re-united pair in a wild region of dubious light, somewhere between the Elysian Fields and the world of men. Orfeo holds Euridice by the hand, but, true to his compact with the gods, keeps his eyes averted from her. Gluck sets the emotional tone of the long dialogue between them (in recitative) in a few preliminary bars in the orchestra that convey clearly to us that the time for the happiness of the pair is not yet. Euridice can hardly believe that she is with her lover again, and asks how this good fortune has come about: Orfeo, anxious and fearful, begs her to think of nothing but pressing on until the end of the journey is reached. After a while she begins to wonder why he is so scant of speech, why he does not embrace her, why he keeps his eyes turned away from her. Has she changed? she asks him. Is she less beautiful than of old? She implores at least one glance from him: he tells her that it would bring evil on them. She reproaches him for his coldness: it is for this, then, that the deceiver has torn her from the bliss of Elysium!

The psychological cross-currents continue in the duet that follows, in which Orfeo in vain begs Euridice to have faith in him and to hasten with him to their goal:

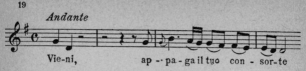

Death, she tells him, would be preferable to life with one so heartless.

The misunderstanding grows until Euridice can bear no longer the thought of having exchanged death and its serene oblivion for this living misery. She so works upon him that his resolution at last breaks down: in sheer desperation he turns his eyes on her, and at once the gods exact the penalty — she sinks dead in his arms. Orfeo pours out his grief and despair in one of the most famous of operatic arias, " Che farò senza Euridice? ":

It is the tendency nowadays to regard this aria as having been overrated by its contemporaries. The truth probably is that our singers no longer possess the style for music of this kind; and we may take it as certain that the way they sing it was not the way of Guadagni.

His aria concluded, Orfeo is on the point of slaying himself in order to follow Euridice when Amor enters, to tell him that his constancy is to have its reward. Euridice is forthwith restored to him, and while the lovers are expressing their satisfaction at this happy conclusion in brief exchanges of recitative we cannot help feeling that Calzabigi has managed the *dénouement* of his opera none too well, and that Gluck, with nothing vital to work upon here, has failed to give us the musical climax we had a right to expect. All that he and his poet can do now is to stage a brilliant ballet in a temple dedicated to Eros, — in which the happy ending of the adventure is celebrated by all the participants in the drama — and dismiss us with a final chorus in praise of Eros himself.

Don Pasquale

GAETANO DONIZETTI [1797–1848]

PRINCIPAL CHARACTERS

DON PASQUALE	*Buffo Bass*
DOCTOR MALATESTA	*Baritone*
ERNESTO	*Tenor*
NORINA	*Soprano*
A NOTARY	*Bass*

1

ISTORIANS speak respectfully, as in duty bound, of Paisiello's *The Barber of Seville* (1780); but the fact remains that of the enormous repertory of Italian comic opera in the last quarter of the eighteenth century and the first half of the nineteenth only three works still keep the boards intact, not merely respected as museum pieces but admired as masterpieces that seem, for all the changes that have taken place in music since their day, to be perennially young. These three works are Rossini's *The Barber of Seville* (1816), Donizetti's *L'Elisir d'Amore* (1832), and his *Don Pasquale* (1843), which was nearly the last of its composer's sixty-odd operas. Already in 1843 he showed signs of exhaustion and a tendency to morbid melancholy: he was, in fact, suffering from a cerebro-spinal disease.[1] In 1845 he became paralysed. Almost the whole of 1846 and the first six months of 1847 he spent in an asylum at Ivry. In October of the latter year he was re-

---

[1] The cause of his malady does not seem to have been determined beyond question. That the seeds of it had been in him since his youth seems to be suggested by the fact that of his three children (born respectively in 1829, 1836 and 1837) the first lived less than a fortnight and the other two were stillborn.

moved to his native town, Bergamo, where he died on the 8th April 1848.

The libretto of *Don Pasquale* is from Donizetti's own pen. He seems, indeed, to have had a decided gift for this kind of thing: the book of more than one of his early operas is his own work, and one at least of these, *Il Campanello di Notte*, is a little gem of humorous inventiveness, even if, as is probable, he derived the fundamental idea of it from a farce he had seen in Paris. For the general idea of *Don Pasquale* he was indebted to a comic opera produced in Milan in 1810, *Ser Marcantonio*, the composer of which was one Stefano Pavesi and the librettist Angelo Anelli. The plot of this hinges upon two eternally popular themes of the Italian comic theatre, that of the anxiety of the relatives of a rich man as to the dispositions he may have made in his will, and that of an elderly bachelor who suddenly decides to plunge into matrimony, and is given reason to regret it later.[2] Old Marcantonio perturbs his expectant relations by informing them that he intends to marry and hopes to become a father. The news is particularly unwelcome to his nephew Medoro and his niece Norina: the former is engaged to a milliner named Bettina, the sister of one Tobia, a stockbroker, who, as the laws of theatrical symmetry demand, is in love with Norina. Together they hatch out a plot by which Bettina is passed off on Marcantonio as the very wife for a man like him, she being an exceptionally inexperienced and modest girl: the mock marriage ceremony is performed by Tobia made up as a notary. Bettina, however, quickly reveals a shrewish temper and a passion for domestic extravagance that frighten the old gentleman out of his wits; so that he is easily persuaded to let Medoro take her off his hands in consideration of a handsome annuity, while Tobia, of course, marries Norina.

In construction, as will be seen, the play ran true to a well-established type: there were two hopeful young relatives, two other lovers, and two servants, one attached to Medoro, the other to Norina. Donizetti wisely rid this traditional pattern of its superfluities. He made shift with only one relative — old Pasquale's nephew Ernesto, — and consequently a single love interest. This

[2] The latter of these two themes is probably of great antiquity. A variant of it is found in Ben Jonson's comedy *Epicœne, or The Silent Woman*. Richard Strauss's opera *Die schweigsame Frau* (1935) is based on this.

left him room to treat more extensively the character who hatches the ingenious plot against the old bachelor; Tobia now becomes Dr. Malatesta, the trusted friend of Don Pasquale. This drastic simplification and condensation of the too crowded canvas of *Ser Marcantonio* gave Donizetti, of course, more opportunity to expand his simple musical forms and to extract the last ounce of humorous expression out of each situation. The chorus is equally skilfully and economically handled: it appears only twice in the three acts, and on each occasion with perfect appropriateness, consisting as it does of Don Pasquale's house servants.

2

The wit and humour of the music, the composition of which is said to have occupied Donizetti no more than eleven days, ensured popularity for the work from the beginning. It was first performed in Paris on the 4th January 1843, with a cast that sends our thoughts back wistfully to the great days when singing *was* singing: Lablache was the Pasquale, Tamburini the Malatesta, Mario the Ernesto, and Grisi the Norina. Mario must have made a handsome and sympathetic Ernesto; he not only looked but was a gentleman, by birth as well as training — something of a rarity on the Italian operatic stage of that period. The charming Grisi was his wife. Tamburini was a baritone of unique quality, both as a singer and as an actor. As for Lablache, opera has perhaps never seen or heard his like before or since. He was equally great in serious and in comic rôles. Henry Chorley, who knew something about opera singing, and had heard again and again all the finest artists of the first half of the nineteenth century, described him as " taking him all for all the most remarkable man whom I have ever seen in opera. . . . An organ more richly toned or suave than his voice was never given to mortal." He was " gifted with personal beauty to a rare degree. A grander head was never more grandly set on human shoulders." He was of gigantic stature, " yet one never felt on the stage how huge he was. His shoe was as big as a child's boat. One could have clad the child in one of his gloves; and the child could almost have walked on his belt. But every article of his dress was so excellently fitted to its wearer, was worn so unconsciously, and was so thoroughly in agreement with all that it accompanied, that there was neither time nor temptation for comparison. . . .

This handsome young French-Neapolitan had got an amount of general and genial and solid musical culture . . . which, for a singer, has been something with too little precedent . . . Lablache's perfect acquaintance with the great Roman style, his marvellous voice and, little less marvellous, his power of sustaining and animating his comrades without bearing them down, afforded a distinct idea of how such music might be sung, and how, when well sung, it might move, impress and exalt those who heard it as a portion of a rite."

The reader might do worse than to try to picture to himself, the next time he hears some ill-trained, weary, wobbly victim of the modern mania for pushing people on to the stage before they have acquired much more than the rudiments of a technique, how the recitatives and melodies of Don Pasquale used to be *sung* by Lablache. And when, as is more than likely, he sees some lubberly lout of a bass, who has never been taught anything better, laying on the humour in the grossest fashion, the reader should try to visualise Pasquale as Donizetti conceived him and as Lablache represented him — " the farce of fatness," as Chorley says, " trying to make itself seductive," " the dear silly hero of the farce-opera " wearing a coat " which stuck to him with as terrible a closeness as the outside garment of a sausage does to its contents within," yet, for all that, never for a moment angling for the horse-laugh of the mob. " Throughout the entire farce of Lablache's performances nothing was more admirable than his entire avoidance of grossness or coarse imitation. There was, with him, that security which belongs only to persons of rare and admirable tact; and, with that security, the highest power of expressing comedy, tragedy or grotesque — because it belongs to one who will risk nothing hazardous, but who is not afraid of daring anything extraordinary. When I hear of this person's style, and that person's high note, and when I think of Lablache, I am tempted to feel as if I had parted company with real comic genius on the musical stage for ever."

The part of Don Pasquale should never be clowned. The work was at first performed in what was then contemporary costume, an innovation in opera which, however, did not appeal to every spectator. But the very fact that Pasquale, as did Norina, Ernesto and Malatesta also, looked precisely like someone in real life is of itself a proof that the part was never intended by Donizetti as a vehicle for conventional clowning. Pasquale, for all his amorous foolishness, was a gentleman in an epoch when good breeding still counted for something.

3

The gay overture passes in review two or three of the many delightful melodies with which the work is strewn, without any attempt at arranging them in such a sequence or developing them in such a way as to summarise the story of the opera. After a few bars of quick preamble we hear in the clarinet the melody of Ernesto's serenade in the third act (See No. 21 below); the theme is then continued in turn by horn and flute. It is succeeded by the gay melody of the second part of Norina's cavatina in the first act (No. 6), which, with some lively connective tissue between its several returns, dominates the remainder of the overture.

The setting of the first act is the frequent stage one of a room with a door at the back and one at each side. Don Pasquale is seen walking impatiently up and down with his watch in his hand. A brief orchestral introduction of no more than a dozen bars indicates as conclusively that he is plunged in thought as the prelude to *Siegfried* suggests the profound cogitation of Mime. Then a pleasant melody steals out in the orchestra:

as Don Pasquale complains that it is nine o'clock and Dr. Malatesta is still not here to keep his appointment. Pasquale is preparing, he lets us know, a nice little pill for his nephew. While the orchestra continues with the strain of No. 1, Malatesta enters; as always, he is the soul of self-assurance and hearty humour. He is able to assure the impatient old bachelor that the bride he has commissioned him to procure for him has been found. Malatesta sings her praises in an aria every word of which Pasquale drinks in as the thirsty soil drinks in a shower of rain: it appears that the maiden is beautiful as an angel, fresh as a lily opening its petals to the morning sun; she has eyes that slay at night, hair blacker than ebony, and a smile that is pure enchantment. So much for the person of this paragon; as for her moral qualities, she is blessed with a soul so innocent, so ingenuous, that it is ignorant even of itself; she is of a modesty without its parallel on earth; she is beloved by all for her goodness, her gentleness, her sympathy; heaven, in fact, created her purely and simply to make some super-fortunate man or other uniquely happy:

Bel - la sic-co-me un an - ge-lo in ter - ra pel - le - gri - no, ___

Pasquale swallows it all, licks his lips, and asks for more. Her family, he next learns, is well off, and her name is Malatesta — she is none other, in short, than the sister of the Doctor, who has to implore his old friend to control his ardour just a trifle longer, for he will bring the maiden to him this same evening. With that he leaves him. Don Pasquale, in a lively 3/8 rhythm, gives vent to his enthusiasm over this news:

Ah! un fuo-co in - so - li-to mi sento ad - dos - so, o - mai re - si-ste-re io più non pos - so.

The burden of his more than sixty years, he says, has fallen from him; he feels a mere twenty again; already he hears the patter of baby feet about the house. And now he will put that obstinate nephew of his in his place.

Ernesto enters at that very moment, and Don Pasquale at once becomes the man of affairs again. He looks severely at the young man. Is it true or isn't it, he asks him, that two or three months ago he gave him the chance to marry a certain rich, noble and beautiful maiden, promising him a handsome allowance if he obeyed, and threatening to disinherit him if he refused. Quite true, replies Ernesto; but he loves his Norina, he is pledged to her, and he cannot give her up: she may be poor, but she is virtuous. Thereupon Pasquale tells him that he will have to keep himself in future, for as for him, he is going to get married. Ernesto is at first incredulous and inclined to be satirical; his uncle must surely be joking. Pasquale assures him that he is not; and to a tripping melody in the orchestra:

he tells his nephew that " I, Pasquale da Corneto, here in the flesh before you, being of sound mind and body, have the honour to inform you that I am going to marry, and that immediately."

Ernesto's amusement evaporates when he realises that the old gentleman really means what he says; and in a melancholy little aria, punctuated by the unfeeling comments of his uncle, he bids eternal farewell to his own dream of love:

Too poor now to marry his Norina, he nobly renounces her for ever. He warns Pasquale, however, not to take so rash a step without consulting Dr. Malatesta, a man of proved judgment and probity. His uncle triumphantly assures him that he has already done so, and that so far from trying to dissuade him the Doctor himself has found him a bride in the person of his own sister. At the revelation of this perfidy on the part of Malatesta, whom he had always

looked upon as a friend, poor Ernesto breaks down utterly: he has
lost faith in everyone and everything. He gets no sympathy from
Pasquale, whose only comment is that he has brought it all on himself through his pigheadedness. The curtain descends with Ernesto still bewailing his martyrdom and his uncle still chuckling
over his discomfiture.

The scene changes to a room in Norina's house, where the pretty
young widow is reading aloud, from a book she has in her hand,
an episode in which a cavalier transfixed by a glance from his lady
falls on his knees before her and vows eternal and undivided homage. Norina laughs merrily: she too, she says, knows all the arts and
crafts — smiles, tears, and all the rest of it — by which men are enslaved:

6 *Allegretto*

So anch'io la virtù ma-gica d'un guardo a tempo e lo-co,

She is capricious, fond of a jest, she admits, a trifle hasty, and inclined to fly into a temper, but for all that the best-hearted creature
in the world; when it comes to managing men no one can teach her
anything; and as she is not only a young woman of the world but a
heroine of Italian comedy opera she says all this with an abundance
of sparkling coloratura.

She is impatient for the coming of Malatesta with news of how
his little scheme for some good joke or other at Don Pasquale's expense is going. Just as Malatesta enters and begins the gay story
of how beautifully the fish rose to the bait, a servant enters with a
letter for Norina. After a glance at this she tells Malatesta that she
washes her hands of the business: she has more serious things to
think of now. She hands him the letter, which he reads aloud: "My
Norina, I write to you with death in my heart. Don Pasquale,
worked upon by that two-faced Doctor, is going to marry the
scoundrel's sister; he has turned me out of his house and has cut
me out of his will. Out of love for you I must renounce you: I shall
leave Rome this very day, and Europe itself as soon as I can. Farewell. That you may be happy is the ardent prayer of your Ernesto."
Malatesta tells Norina not to take the young donkey too seriously:
he will disclose the plot to him, and then there will be no fear of

his leaving. But what precisely is the plot? she asks. She knows already that Don Pasquale has talked about getting married to punish his nephew for his disobedience; but what else is there? She now learns that Malatesta, having been consulted by the old bachelor, has concocted a plan for doing her and Ernesto a good turn. If *he* doesn't plant a bride on Don Pasquale, someone else will — someone with an axe of his own to grind. Pasquale knows that Malatesta has a sister in a convent; the Doctor accordingly proposes that Norina shall impersonate her. His cousin Carlotto will pose as the notary and draw up the marriage contract: once they have that they can do what they like with the old man. Norina is willing to do anything that will not involve infidelity to her lover. Her lively and humorous imagination at once begins to run riot, to the accompaniment of an impish figure in the orchestra:

at the thought of the tricks she will play on Don Pasquale. Dr. Malatesta takes up the congenial theme: now, he hopes, she can see that he is a real friend of Ernesto, and that the sole purposes of his stratagem are to help the lovers and to have a bit of fun at Don Pasquale's expense.

Norina at once begins to practise her part, under the tuition of Malatesta. Is she to act the haughty dame? she asks him. No! Melancholy? No! Tearful? Shrewish? No, no! that isn't the idea at all. She must be the timid simpleton, the shrinking female, looking as if butter wouldn't melt in her mouth. Easy! she says; and she gives Malatesta a few specimens of her art of playing the simpering ingénue. Each is now eager to get to work on the victim:

They will fool Don Pasquale to the top of his bent: already they taste the sweets of vengeance. The duet, from start to finish, is of an irresistible vivacity, of a type and in a tempo only possible with a language so liquid as Italian and a music so purely melodic as that of Italian comedy. Incidentally we realise, from some of the passages that Donizetti gives Malatesta to sing, that in that epoch even a baritone or a bass was occasionally expected to be something of an expert in coloratura.

4

The second act also is played in Don Pasquale's house. Ernesto is alone, indulging himself in the luxury of a little Donizettian self-pity before he carries his broken heart with him to a foreign land. The main melody of his aria (No. 9 below) is first of all given out in full in an orchestral prelude. It is one of those melodies for which Donizetti had a curious aptitude — melodies that bring gravity enough into a comedy to make us take the character immediately concerned quite seriously for the time being, but still not too seriously: never do we feel that we have been snatched out of the comedy atmosphere of the work as a whole. Sorry as Ernesto is for himself, we know all along, though as yet he does not, that all will come right with him in the end. Meanwhile we listen sympathetically to his sad assurance that he is going into banishment, there to mourn to the end of his days his lost Norina, whose sweet image will never fade from his heart:

9 Larghetto

Cer-che - rò lon -ta-na ter-ra do - ve
ge - mer sco - no - sciu - to;

Even should Norina, in his absence, find consolation elsewhere, he will not reproach her, but be glad that she is happy:

10 Moderato

E se fia che ad al - tro og -

get-to   tu   ri - volga un gior - no il co - re,

to which handsome sentiment he makes his exit.

Don Pasquale now enters with a servant, to whom he gives instructions that he is not at home except to Dr. Malatesta and whoever may accompany him. When he is alone he struts up and down, pluming himself on being in such good condition for a man of his years; but all the same, when he hears his visitors approaching he nervously commends himself to the protection of the god of matrimony.

Malatesta enters, leading a veiled, very shy, and almost fainting "sister" by the hand and exhorting the poor little thing to keep up her courage. Don Pasquale makes to approach her, but at a sign from the Doctor he retires to a corner. "For pity's sake do not leave me, dear brother," begs Norina. Malatesta goes to Don Pasquale and apologises for his sister; fresh from the convent as she is she is naturally a little scared on such an occasion, and Pasquale must be very gentle with her. While the men are colloguing in this fashion Norina completes the trio with a malicious aside:

11

Larghetto

Sta a ve-de-re, si sta a vede-re, o vecchio mat-to,

that bodes no good to Don Pasquale. Then, the clinging female of the species once more, she turns to her brother with a new appeal for protection. To reassure her he points out that she is not alone: *he* is with her, as well as Don Pasquale. Norina, horrified at this discovery that there is another man in the room, wants to run away. The trio is repeated, with Norina reiterating her sotto voce warning to the old bachelor, Pasquale lost in admiration of her simplicity and modesty, and Malatesta chuckling over the perfection of the little slut's acting.

Don Pasquale, he informs his sister, is the last man in the world of whom she need be afraid; he is a friend of his, and the best of men. She makes him a curtsey, but does not dare raise her eyes to him. The three of them sit down, Malatesta in the middle. At his

suggestion Pasquale asks his bride a few questions bearing on their
future married life. No doubt she will want company in the evenings? "Not at all," she replies: "in the convent I was always
alone." "A theatre occasionally?" The modest creature does not
know what a theatre is, and does not want to know. "An admirable
sentiment!" says Don Pasquale, "but all the same one must pass
one's time in some way or other." But the prospective bride asks for
no better way of passing the time than sewing, knitting, cooking
and embroidering. Just what he would have ordered in the way of
a bride! thinks Pasquale. But when Norina, after much pressing, is
persuaded so far to overcome her modesty as to raise her veil in the
presence of a man, the conquest of the old bachelor is complete.
Words fail him; he can only stammer out a request for Malatesta
to speak for him. Very timidly Norina accepts Pasquale's hand.
Malatesta goes into the next room and returns with the pseudo-
notary — "This Doctor thinks of everything!" says Don Pasquale to
himself — and the masterly scene of the final fooling of Pasquale
begins.

The four having seated themselves at a table, the notary — a
familiar Italian comedy figure — takes down from the dictation of
Dr. Malatesta, repeating, in his thin, high, nasal voice, the last word
or syllable as he gets it on paper. The melodies mostly sing out in
the orchestra, the voices speaking through them in the way so favoured by the composers of the old comic opera: Donizetti in particular has an inexhaustible supply of these charming tunes on tap.
We begin with an insinuating orchestral melody:

to the accompaniment of which the Doctor dictates the terms of
the marriage contract between "Sofronia Malatesta, etc., etc., of
the one part, and Pasquale da Corneto, etc., etc., of the other part,
both here present and willing." Don Pasquale continues the dictation: the bridegroom settles on the bride half his property, mov-
able and immovable; she is further to be absolute mistress of the
household. When Don Pasquale has signed, and as Norina is about
to do so, the notary points out that another witness besides Mala-

testa is necessary. Just then the voice of Ernesto is heard without, expostulating with the servants who are trying to bar his entrance. Norina lays down the pen, a trifle scared. Malatesta also is for the moment worried, for it seems that he has not yet had time to communicate the plot to Ernesto, and, as he says under his breath, "It looks as if the whole thing is going to be ruined." Here, then, are all the materials for a fresh comic imbroglio.

Ignoring the others, Ernesto goes straight to Don Pasquale to bid him good-bye. His uncle tells him he has arrived in the nick of time to witness the marriage contract; and Ernesto nearly collapses when he sees that the bride is Norina. This is more than he can be expected to stand! Dr. Malatesta takes him aside, and in agitated tones that are a test of the coloratura technique of the best baritone:

13 *Allegro moderato*

Ah! fi - gliuol, non mi far

sce - ne, fi - gliuol, non mi far sce - ne,

implores him not to make a scene, as all that is happening is purely for his benefit. Although he feels he is going mad under the intellectual and emotional strain he is induced to sign after Norina; and the notary, joining the hands of Don Pasquale and Norina, solemnly declares them to be man and wife. Instantly Norina's manner changes from timidity to audacity: "Now," she says sotto voce, "the battle begins." The notary leaves.

Pasquale tries to embrace his Sofronia, but she tells him to wait for her permission to do that. Ernesto laughs loudly. His uncle orders him out, but Norina asks him what he means by manners so countrified and clownish as these. The orchestra plays lightly and humorously round the characters all the time, especially when Pasquale, hardly able to believe his ears, says to Malatesta, "Doctor, she's not the same!" He has good reason to think this, for Norina tells him that an old gentleman like him, fat, heavy, decrepit, must not treat a young man in this fashion: Ernesto shall be her cavalier.

Pasquale protests in vain: Norina reminds him that she has been given absolute command of the household, and gives him to understand that she will tolerate no nonsense from him.

Malatesta takes the lead:

in a slow emphatic quartet in which each of the characters comments on the situation after his own fashion, Malatesta, like the good friend he is, urging the abashed Pasquale not to be discouraged by this unexpected turn of events, and some notion of what it all means beginning to soak at last even into Ernesto's brain.

Norina snatches up a bell from one of the tables, rings it violently and orders the whole of the domestic staff to be brought in. A major-domo and two servants appear. She laughs this meagre ménage to scorn. Promptly she doubles the astonished major-domo's wages, and, to a merry little theme in the orchestra:

orders him to engage a new staff of bright young people, to buy a couple of new carriages at once, together with the necessary horses, to clear out the rubbishy old furniture, which is fit only for a museum, and replace it by something smarter and more modern, and to engage such necessaries for her as a hairdresser, a tailor and a jeweller. When Don Pasquale begins to protest against the cost of all this she rounds on him in good earnest, calling him by every unpleasant name she can think of. He is now pretty well sure that she is out of her mind. Ernesto is delighted by the storm she has raised, while the artful Malatesta begs his dear sister not to try his old friend too far.

All is now set for the grand finale. Don Pasquale realises at last that Norina has fooled him:

Son   tra - di - to, son tra - di - to, son tra - di - to, bef - feg - gia - to, bef - feg - gia - to.

and swears he will not tolerate any more. Ernesto sees how mistaken he has been about Norina; and Dr. Malatesta advises his over-heated old friend to go to bed, leaving him to deal with this spitfire sister of his, whose conduct is as much a surprise to him as it is to her husband. The curtain comes down with them still arguing it out among themselves.

5

The setting of the third act is once more a room in Don Pasquale's house. Tables, chairs and floor are strewn with every species of female finery — costumes, hats, furs, scarves, lace, and so on. The unhappy Don Pasquale is sitting at a table that is hardly visible for tradesmen's bills. New servants stand all around. From a neighbouring room — that of Norina — comes a hairdresser carrying all the apparatus of his profession: he crosses the stage and goes out by another door.

The servants sing the liveliest of choruses as they try to cope with the mass of goods in the room, while poor Don Pasquale sits examining one account after another and lamenting over the madhouse that his once quiet home has suddenly become. When the servants have left, Norina enters hurriedly, magnificently dressed, with a fan in her hand: she takes no notice of her husband, but makes to go out by another door. He detains her, and asks with studied politeness where she is going. To the theatre, she says, and without him. His temper rising, he orders her to go at once to her room; but she only laughs at him and advises him to go to bed and have a nice sleep. They get to calling each other " coquette " and " impertinent fellow " respectively; and the climax comes when she slaps his face. "It's finished, it's finished; Don Pasquale, you have got yourself into a pretty mess!" he says sadly, the orchestra pointing his words with a melancholy motive of its own:

17

There is nothing to be done now but to go and drown himself. Norina, in a quiet aside, agrees that the old man is being rather severely tried, but it had to be done, and the scheme must be carried through to victory. The little duet, with its clear differentiation of the two characters, is one of the best things in the opera: there is a tenderness in Norina's phrases:

18

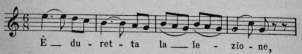

that shows she is not bad at heart, and that she is really sorry for the old simpleton.

At the end of the duet he tells her she can leave the house if she likes, but she need never return. She assures him amiably that she will be back again next day; to which he replies that if she does she will find the door bolted. In the most dulcet of tones:

19

like a mother talking to a naughty and somewhat backward child, she advises the old man once more to be good and go to bed and sleep well; his wife will come and wake him in good time. "Divorce!" he cries. "Bed? Wife? A worse union there never was in this world! Wretched fool that I have been!"

When she has finished teasing and exasperating him she goes
out; as she does so she lets fall a piece of paper, which Pasquale
picks up, imagining it at first to be a bill. He reads: " Adored Sofronia, Between nine and ten this evening I shall be in the garden,
in the part looking north. For extra security try, if you can, to admit me by the secret gate. We shall be in the shade of the grove.
I forgot to tell you that you will know when I am there by my serenade. Your faithful one." This is the last straw: almost out of his
mind he rings for a servant and sends him to Dr. Malatesta with
orders to come to him at once.

When he has left the room the servants comment in a charming
chorus on the strange goings-on in the house. None of them can get
a moment's peace for the incessant ringing of bells; all the same it's
a fine place, where money is poured out like water. Those who had
heard the altercation between the master and the mistress give a
full report of it to those who had not; others hint darkly at there
being a nephew somewhere in the offing. After they have filed off
the stage the Doctor appears on the threshold of the room, making
the last arrangements with Ernesto, who goes down into the garden
to play his own part in the coming comedy. Malatesta, hearing Don
Pasquale approaching, composes his features in the best professional style.

Don Pasquale pours into his ears his long tale of woe, with the
letter of assignation as the climax. Malatesta finds it hard to believe
that his sister could have done any of the things of which Don Pasquale accuses her. Don Pasquale unfolds his plan for catching the
faithless one. He and Malatesta will go into the garden; the servants will surround the grove:

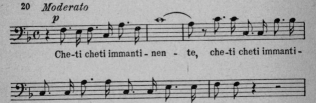

20 Moderato

Che-ti cheti immanti-nen - te, che-ti cheti immanti -

nen - te nel giar-di - no di - scen-dia-mo;

the couple will be caught and taken before the magistrate. But
Malatesta, also to the strain of No. 20, counsels quieter and subtler

31

methods: he and Pasquale alone will surprise the pair, and get all they want without a scandal, by the mere threat of exposure; after all, Sofronia is his sister. After some argument he gets Don Pasquale to agree to *his* plan — they two will conceal themselves in the grove, and if what they overhear proves Sofronia's guilt, Pasquale will get rid of her there and then. Gloating over his coming revenge, Pasquale pours out his words in such profusion and at such a pace that one wonders how he can articulate them at all: the effect is irresistibly comic, and again one that is possible only in Italian. Malatesta follows his example in this respect as he remarks, sotto voce, that Pasquale is going to be caught in his own net.

The scene changes to the grove adjoining the house: on the left is a flight of steps leading from the house to the garden: on the right is a terrace: in the distance a gate. Ernesto is heard singing his serenade:

21

Andante mosso

Com'è gen-til ____ la notte a mezzo A-pril!

to an accompaniment of chords on the guitar, and with a small chorus behind the scenes joining in occasionally. Norina enters from the right, and goes cautiously towards the gate to admit Ernesto, who now lets fall the cloak that has enveloped him. The lovers sing a tender duet, mostly, as Italian opera tradition dictated, in intertwining sixths and thirds. Seeing Pasquale and Malatesta creeping along with dark lanterns from the direction of the gate they conceal themselves behind some trees. Pasquale flashes the light in Sofronia's face and demands to know where her lover is. She denies that anyone is with her; she has been taking the air alone, she swears. While the two men are groping about in the wood, Ernesto slips into the house.

Don Pasquale orders Sofronia to leave him, but she refuses to go, as the house is hers. The Doctor now takes charge of the imbroglio, Pasquale having given him carte blanche. Malatesta tells his sister that tomorrow another woman will be settling in the house — Norina, the bride of Ernesto. "This is your cue for flying into a temper," he whispers to her. The sister passionately refuses to live a single day under the same roof as this Norina, a coquette whom she despises. ("Splendid, Doctor!" says Pasquale: nothing will please him better than for Sofronia to go). Turning next to Pasquale, the Doctor advises him to consent to his nephew marrying Norina. Ernesto having been sent for, Malatesta informs him that Don Pasquale is not only willing that he shall marry his Norina but will settle on him an annuity of four thousand scudi. Ernesto joyously assents, but Malatesta's " sister " opposes the idea, which fact, of course, is of itself sufficient to recommend it to Don Pasquale. The latter tells Ernesto to send for his Norina and he himself will marry them there and then. " No need to go far for that," says Malatesta; " this lady is Norina. Sofronia is still in the convent, and your ' marriage' was only a scheme of mine to stop you from getting really and truly married." Delighted at his escape and profiting by his lesson, Don Pasquale forgives the conspirators; and led by Malatesta they join in singing the moral of it all, which is that matrimony is an adventure which it is better for a man of Don Pasquale's age not to embark upon:

22   *Allegretto moderato*

Bra-vo, bra-vo— Don Pa - squa-le! —

The Barber of Seville

GIOACCHINO ROSSINI [1792–1868]

PRINCIPAL CHARACTERS

COUNT ALMAVIVA	*Tenor*
FIGARO	*Baritone*
ROSINA	*Mezzo-soprano*
DOCTOR BARTOLO	*Bass*
FIORELLO	*Tenor*
AMBROSIO	*Bass*
BERTA	*Soprano*

1

THE CARON DE BEAUMARCHAIS to whom we owe *The Barber of Seville* and *The Marriage of Figaro* began life in a humble way in January 1732 as Pierre Augustin Caron, the son of a Paris clockmaker. The boy was trained in his father's profession, and at twenty invented a new watch escapement. His idea was stolen by a rival: a lawsuit followed: the young Caron saw to it that the affair received plenty of publicity, and it all ended very much in his favour. The incident was symbolic and prophetic: all his long life he was at variance with someone or other, and practically always victor by virtue of his superior adroitness and his satiric tongue and pen.

By now he had attracted the attention of the Court. He was appointed clockmaker to Louis XV, and before long we find him, rather surprisingly, teaching the guitar and harp to his Majesty's daughters and organising the Court musical entertainments and ballets. In 1755 he married a rich widow, eleven years his senior, who died after some eighteen months of wedlock. Much of the money he inherited from her was lost in lawsuits with her relations. There remained in his hands, however, a small landed property of hers that carried with it the title of de Beaumarchais, by which he chose to be known for the rest of his life. In 1768 he married another widow, who also died within a couple of years.

A born adventurer, cool, audacious, infinitely resourceful and none too scrupulous, for the next thirty years or so he was ready to try his hand at anything that looked like turning out profitably and at the same time attracted him by a spice of difficulty and danger in it. He was equally happy gun-running for the American insurgents (or, during the Terror, for the Dutch), acting as a royalist spy and purloiner of secret documents in London, or insinuating his plays into the Paris theatres and fighting the actors for his author's fees. (Literary men should remember him with gratitude as the founder of the Société des auteurs dramatiques, the prime object of which was to see that the actors at the Comédie Française did not bamboozle playwrights out of their royalties.) He was a man who would have come to the front in any age and any milieu: today he would no doubt be equally notorious, equally successful, as a dealer in armaments, a secret service agent, a Hollywood magnate, a playwright and a smuggler of Swiss watches, nylons or foreign currency.

His excursions into serious drama were not a success; sentimentality did not sit well on him. His literary fame rests today almost entirely on three works—the two immortal Figaro comedies and the *Mémoires*; [1] and the last is as great in its way as the two stage works by which he is mostly known now. In his late thirties he had become closely associated with one of the big financiers of the day, a certain Pâris-Duverney, who had no doubt found him very useful in some of his business transactions and was appropriately grateful. Beaumarchais soon found himself sufficiently in funds to buy for 50,000 livres an appointment as royal secretary that carried with it a title to nobility: when detractors ventured to throw doubts on his claim to be one of the aristocracy he would reply, with a frankness rare among recipients of titles, "If you don't believe me I'll show you the receipt." On the 1st April 1770 he and Pâris-Duverney had a final settlement of

[1] Not "mémoires" in the autobiographical sense of the term, but "documents relating to . . ."; the full description of the work in question is *Mémoires dans l'affaire Goezman*.

accounts, the financier acknowledging in writing that he owed Beaumarchais 15,000 livres. Four months later Pâris-Duverney died. His nephew and general heir, Count de la Blache, reluctant to let this ripe plum slip out of his hands, accused Beaumarchais of having falsified the books, and alleged him to be indebted to the estate to the tune of 139,000 livres. The case was decided legally first against Beaumarchais, then in his favour; but he had been imprudent enough just then to incur the hostility of the powerful Duke de Chaulnes by filching the latter's mistress from him, and there was a quarrel that ended in both the Duke and Beaumarchais being placed under arrest.

This gave La Blache an opportunity to reopen his case. When, in the second act of *The Barber*, Bartholo hints at getting Count Almaviva out of the way by attacking him in a night ambuscade, the wily Basile cries "Fie!" on him for the crudity of his technique. Basile knows a better way of ruining the Count's chances with Rosine—by means of calumny, a subject on which he grows eloquent. "Calumny, monsieur! You do wrong to despise it. I have seen the most respectable men pretty well annihilated by it. Take my word for it, there is no stupid vileness, no horror, no absurdity that you can't get the loungers of a big town to believe; —and here in Madrid we have some real experts in that line!" La Blache, with his adversary temporarily out of the way, renewed the battle for the precious livres, and found calumny his best weapon. Forged letters from and to Beaumarchais were put into circulation, and he was accused of having got rid of both his wives by poison. The upshot of it all was that La Blache won his case on a re-trial, and Beaumarchais, at the age of forty-one, was wellnigh ruined.

2

But, as usual, disaster and conflict brought out all that was best in him; his genius needed rough friction to develop all its latent light and heat. The climax in the Pâris-Duverney dispute had come in April 1773. A legal councillor named Goezman had been entrusted with the preparation of a report on the case, which was to come before the tribunal on the fifth of that month. On the first, Beaumarchais, who was, of course, seriously hampered in both defence and attack by the circumstances of his imprisonment, obtained permission to leave the jail on each of the next few mornings on the conditions that he would be accompanied everywhere by a certain M. Santerre, that he would not occupy himself in his free time with anything but the coming lawsuit, and that he would return to the prison each day at nightfall. The person who mattered most to him was of course Goezman, who, he feared, was not as well acquainted with the financial details of the Pâris-Duverney matter as he would have liked him to be; so Beaumarchais's first, indeed only, care was to have a little confidential talk with this influential gentleman.

Friends had told him that his judge Goezman's young wife took an interest of her own occasionally in the cases that came before her husband: as Beaumarchais puts it ironically in his first *Mémoire*, she had assured his chief informant that if a litigant's nature was generous and his cause just, and he asked of her nothing that was inconsistent with her honesty, she would not resent the offer of a little private gift as an outrage on her delicacy. The friend who was acting for Beaumarchais learned that Mme Goezman was so anxious to do all a poor weak woman could do to further the interests of justice that for a trifle of a hundred louis d'or she would arrange for her husband to grant Beaumarchais an audience before the case came on. On the 3rd April the latter did indeed manage to see the judge, but only for a few minutes before the great man's supper. A promise of a longer talk the next day was made, but not kept. Thereupon Mme Goezman guaranteed him an interview on the following morning—the 5th April —in return for a further disinterested transfer of a hundred louis; but as Beaumarchais did not possess that sum she was content with a watch set with diamonds—plus fifteen louis, intended, so she said, for her husband's secretary. But again Beaumarchais was refused the door, making the ninth time in all; the case was heard on that fateful fifth, and, after an all-day sitting of the court, judgment was given against him.

His adversaries were sure he was for ever down and out: but little did they know their man. It had been one of the conditions of the understanding with Mme Goezman that if the promised interview with her husband did not materialise and Beaumarchais lost his case she would return the gifts. This she did, so far as the hundred louis and the watch were concerned, but not as regards the fifteen louis for the secretary—which the latter denied ever having been offered him. Thereupon Beaumarchais began to make trouble. The details of the affair having become public property—Beaumarchais had seen to that—Goezman was forced to come into the open with a charge that the litigant, having tried to suborn one of his judges and failed, was now calumniating the latter's innocent wife. The old intrigues, machinations and chicaneries began all over again, but now on a much larger scale, more and more people being dragged into the affair. Beaumarchais took bold aggressive action: since the courts would not give him justice as he conceived it he would appeal to the public. This he did in four *Mémoires*, masterpieces of wit, humour, gay argument and urbane malice that were the delight of a town always appreciative of good rapier play. The full story of his own conduct in the affair was told with irresistible vivacity. Mme Goezman cut a sorry figure in court under his relentless examination. He had turned her inside out, made her contradict herself—in a moment of flurry she was indiscreet enough to deny that she had ever received the fifteen louis—showed her up in all her feminine silliness, disarmed her at times with flattery—gallantly declining to believe that a women who looked, as he assured her, no more than eighteen could possibly be thirty, as she said—goaded her into threatening him with personal violence, worked her up at one moment into a wild-cat fury and the next baffled her by his imperturbable politeness, so that on one occasion, after a particularly devastating handling of her, she smilingly accepted his arm as they left the court. Beaumarchais had everyone on his side: Voltaire, no mean controversialist himself, was enchanted with the *Mémoires*: "Don't tell me," he chuckled, "that this man poisoned his wives; he's much too gay and amusing for that."

3

Everyone on his side—except his judges, who had lost their heads completely. Their verdict, delivered on the 26th February 1774 after an all-day sitting, was worthy of one of his own comedies. The *Mémoires* were condemned to be burned by the public executioner as defamatory, scandalous, and heaven knows what else; Mme Goezman was censured and ordered to refund the fifteen louis; Goezman, an awkward episode in whose private life Beaumarchais had unkindly dragged into the open, was so discredited that he had to give up his post; and both Beaumarchais and Mme Goezman were ordered to appear before the tribunal and beg its pardon on their knees.[1] Beaumarchais must have enjoyed the whole thing immensely; he had become overnight the most popular man in Paris, for every one of his opponents and judges was hated for some reason or other by some one or other from the King down to the man in the street,[2] so that the butchery gave general satisfaction. But the King, who thought the scandal had gone far enough for public safety, had a hint conveyed to Beaumarchais that he did not wish him to develop it any further: meanwhile, till a new trial of the case could be ordered, he was entrusted with a confidential mission in London.[3] *L'affaire Goezman* is of particular importance to us today because so much of the actual Beaumarchais went straight into the making of the immortal Figaro, and something of the acid fun he had poked at French administrators of justice finds its echo in the scene in the third act of *The Marriage of Figaro*, in which the breach of promise case of Marceline v. Figaro, Bartholo intervening, is solemnly tried by that moral pillar of society, Count Almaviva.

Le Barbier de Séville had been written in 1772: it was then an opéra-comique, that is to say a mixture of spoken play and music, which accounts for the relatively large proportion of the latter still surviving in the present form of the work. The play was intended for the Comédie-Italienne, but was refused there because the actor who was to play the barber Figaro jibbed at the part, he having been at one time a barber's apprentice. Recast as an ordinary play, *Le Barbier* was accepted by the Comédie-Française and actually put into rehearsal; but the theatre closed down on it when Beaumarchais was committed to prison at the same time as the Duc de Chaulnes. In 1774, when the Comédie-Française was willing to take it up again, the police forbade a production, for

[1] Beaumarchais was spared this ignominy, however.
[2] The King's favourite, Mme Dubarry, had the episode of Beaumarchais's public tussle with Mme Goezman dramatised and staged at the Court.
[3] We cannot follow the remainder of his busy and varied life in detail here. He got into trouble with the French revolutionaries in 1792, but somehow survived the Terror. After three years in Holland, still active in the business of gun supplies, he returned in 1796 to Paris, really ruined at last, and died on the 18th May 1799.

the Goezman affair was then in full swing and it was rumoured that the comedy contained attacks on the magistrature. It was not until February 1775 that *Le Barbier de Séville, ou la Précaution Inutile*, in five acts, appeared on the stage. It failed decisively on the first night. Beaumarchais, always the realist, saw where he had gone wrong and at once proceeded to put things right. He cut a large quantity of dead wood out of the overgrown tree, suppressed a whole act that had been added to the original opéra-comique, and shortened the action and the speeches at several points. The second performance was a complete success; and when he printed the play he added a long and brilliant "Letter" to his critics in which he anticipated the publicity technique of Bernard Shaw.

4

Figaro, as the author introduces him to us in the opening act of the play, was essentially Beaumarchais himself. Like the latter, he had tried his hand at everything. In Madrid he had been in the service of the rich young grandee Count Almaviva, who, while admiring his remarkable talents, obviously would not trust him any further than he could see him: the Count's first words on recognising him at dead of night outside Rosine's house in Seville are "Why, it's that rogue Figaro!" The latter gives him an account of his vicissitudes since the pair had last met. Almaviva had recommended him for government employment: he had been given a medical job, not, however, in the hospitals, as he had expected, but in the Andalusian stables, where, he now claims, by dosing human beings with the medicines intended for the horses he had not only put money in his pocket but effected some remarkable cures: if occasionally his human patients had died, well, as he philosophically remarks, "there's no universal remedy." He had been dismissed, according to his own account, from sheer jealousy and stupidity on the part of the Minister concerned, who held that literary ambitions were incompatible with a talent for business—for Figaro, it appears, had been writing madrigals and contributing to the papers. But he had taken his dismissal philosophically, maintaining—and here it is the actual Beaumarchais who is speaking from experience—that an exalted personage is doing a poor man like him all the good he can when he refrains from doing him any harm. When the Count smilingly remarks that he remembers quite well what Figaro was when in his service—a bit of a rascal, a good-for-nothing, lazy, disorderly—he gets the biting riposte, "Ah, Monseigneur, with your high ideal of the virtues necessary to a servant, how many masters, would you say, are fit to be valets?" a fencing pass that wins the admiration of the broadminded young grandee.

Figaro, on the occasion of that meeting, resumes the story of his life. He had gone back to Madrid, where he had attempted dramatic authorship. In this he had failed, though he could not understand why, for, as he admits, he had done everything possible to ensure success, employing all the arts of the paid claque and getting himself and his piece talked about in advance in the cafés. But the cabals had beaten him; his play had been hissed, and if ever he sees a chance to get his own back—! The Count interrupts him: "Don't you know that in the law courts one has only twenty-four hours in which to call down curses on his judges?", to which Figaro replies grimly, "In the theatre one has twenty-four years."

Having found it impossible to make any headway in Madrid against the butting animals and stinging insects that everywhere made the literary man's life a burden to him, and being out of funds and very much in debt, he had decided that the honourable emoluments of the razor were preferable to the empty honours of the pen; so he had travelled across Spain, practising his new profession of barber, "made much of in one town, jailed in another, but always superior to events . . . laughing at the fools, defying the rascals, taking my poverty light-heartedly and shaving all and sundry." At last he had come to Seville, where he still is, ready to do anything that Count Almaviva may demand of him. His gay philosophy of life, he assures the Count, is the product of his misfortunes: he forces himself to laugh at everything to keep himself from weeping. He is at every point Beaumarchais himself to the life.

There let us leave him and Beaumarchais for a moment and turn to Rossini.

5

He was in his twenty-fourth year when he wrote *Il Barbiere di Siviglia*. Young as he was he already had several operas to his credit. To some of these, in whole or in part, the Rossini lover still turns with delight, particularly *La Cambiale di Matrimonio* (*Marriage by Bill of Exchange*, 1810), *La Pietra del Paragone* (*The Touchstone*, 1812), *Il Signor Bruschino* (1812), *Tancredi* (1813) and *L'Italiana in Algeri* (*The Italian Girl in Algiers*, 1813); while the sparkling overture to *La Scala di Seta* (*The Silk Ladder*, 1812) has won for itself a secure place in our concert rooms. With the Barber of Seville subject he had had more than one predecessor: in addition to the well-known work of Paisiello (1782) there had been at least four French or German treatments of the theme. Morlacchi, the Italian director of the Dresden Opera from 1810 to 1841, had produced a *Barbiere di Siviglia* there in 1814.

Rossini had been commissioned in December 1815 by Duke Francesco Sforza-Cesarini, the director of the Argentina Theatre in Rome, to provide an opera buffa in which a notable Spanish tenor, Garcia, was to "star." The libretto having been found unsatisfactory, Rossini himself, it is conjectured, suggested the Beaumarchais comedy to his librettist Sterbini, who made a very good job of it. (It is astonishing how naturally and easily both *The Barber* and *The Marriage of Figaro* adapt themselves to the purposes of the musical stage.) As Paisiello still had his fanatical admirers, Sterbini and Rossini thought it diplomatic to call their own work, in the first place, not *The Barber of Seville* but *Almaviva, or the Vain Precaution,* and to make it known that they did so out of deference to the older composer. But their own precaution proved to be in vain; the partisans of Paisiello, joining forces with the personal enemies of the impresario, saw to it that the first performance, on the 20th February 1816, failed miserably. Presumably these gentry, satisfied with their victory, did not turn up on the second night, when the general Roman public, left to itself, welcomed the new work warmly. The Figaro was Zamboni, the Almaviva Manuel del Popolo Garcia,[1] who, on the opening night

[1] He had been born, appropriately enough, in Seville. His daughter Maria was the famous Malibran; another, Pauline, was the still more famous Mme Viardot. His son Manuel Patricio Garcia began as a bass singer but

(though not afterwards) was allowed to substitute for Rossini's music for the serenade to Rosina some arrangements of his own of Spanish folk-melodies, which, he had no doubt thought, supplied a local colour that was lacking in the score.

According to the legends, Rossini dashed off the music of the opera in anything from eight days to a fortnight; his own account of the affair in later years varied from twelve days to thirteen. The score was certainly completed within about three weeks at the most. Verdi's summing up of the matter in one of his letters says the sensible thing—Rossini had certainly lived with the characters for some time previously, and they must have taken musical shape in his mind before ever he put pen to paper. Donizetti's dry comment when he was told that the score had been completed in thirteen days was "Yes, but then Rossini always was a lazy fellow."

The nineteenth century German and English writers on music managed to persuade themselves, and did their best to persuade the world, that Mozart, in his *Marriage of Figaro*, had raised what had been in Beaumarchais a mere "sordid comedy of intrigue" to a loftier ethical sphere—a signal example of the moral sense, as Oscar Wilde put it, intruding where it is not wanted. But whatever we may think of the Beaumarchais-Mozart case there can be no doubt that the one and only *Barber of Seville* in music is and always will be Rossini's. The subject had gone, so far as the music was concerned, to the right man at the right time; Rossini alone had the sprightliness of spirit, the combination of lightness and certainty of touch, and the southern vivacity appropriate to the mercurial Figaro; and the *Barber*, as Verdi said, with its copiousness of genuine musical ideas, its comic verve and its veracity of declamation, remains to this day the best of all Italian opere buffe. It was a young man's work, something that even its creator could achieve to the same degree only once in his life. Weber rightly pointed out that in *The Seraglio* was incarnated "what every man's joyous youthful years are to him, the bloom of which he will never recapture": as Mozart grew in experience of life he was bound to write a *Figaro* and a *Don Giovanni*, "but with the best will in the world he could never have written another *Se-*

ultimately settled down to teaching. He died in London in July 1906 at the age of 101. He was the inventor of the laryngoscope.

raglio." Rossini still had a rich comic vein to explore, but a *Barber*
he would never accomplish again; there is in it an enjoyment of
the absurd comedy of the world, a delight in a coltish kicking up
of the heels, that comes to an artist only once in life, and that
when he is young and the sap of life in him rich and abundant.

6

The overture to *The Barber of Seville* is a pleasant enough piece
of work, but has no particular bearing on the opera: it could
hardly be expected to, seeing that it had begun life as the overture to *Aureliano in Palmira* in 1813, and had been used again in
1815 to introduce *Elisabetta, Regina d'Inghilterra*. It opens with
a short andante sostenuto section, not without distinction, the
most salient feature of which is a melody in the violins:

1

that would be in place in almost any Rossini overture. With a
change of tempo to allegro the strings give out quietly a typical
Rossini theme:

2

which, after a brief development, runs on into a second theme
in the oboe:

3

Repetitions of these two main themes, together with the first
example in the work of a favourite device of Rossini—a long
crescendo gradually working up from pianissimo to fortissimo:

44

4

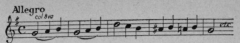

suffice to keep the overture on its feet until the curtain rises.

The scene is a square in Seville, the time, very early morning. On the left is the house of Doctor Bartolo, the windows of which are barred and the blinds closed. Fiorello, a servant of Count Almaviva, steals in cautiously, shepherding a number of musicians with their instruments: they are shortly joined by the Count himself, wrapped in a cloak.[1] He is about to serenade old Bartolo's ward, the fair and young Rosina. They all congratulate themselves, quietly, it is true, but none the less audibly, on the complete silence that reigns in the square, a silence highly propitious to their purpose. Telling each other that they must not speak a word, they keep on speaking, for there is nobody about, Fiorello remarks sagely, whom their performance can disturb, and presumably when the playing and singing begins they will be heard by no one in the adjacent houses but the young person for whose ears the music is intended. We accept the operatic convention, and note with approval the skill with which the composer conveys a suggestion of secrecy and caution: "Keep silence, all; piano, piano, let no one speak," the Count, imitating Fiorello, enjoins on them.

The musicians, having tuned their instruments, preludise for a minute or two on the theme of the coming aria of the amorous Count, which he then launches in full:

5

[1] Beaumarchais, who had been in Spain, specifies in detail the costumes he desired for his characters. For Almaviva, in the first act, a large brown Spanish cloak with cape; a turned-down black hat with a coloured ribbon round the crown. For Figaro, the general get-up of a Spanish *majo*; a snood on his head; a white hat with a coloured ribbon round the crown; round his neck a loose kerchief; satin waistcoat and breeches, with silver-mounted buttons and silver-fringed button holes; a broad silk sash; garters with tassels; a coat of brilliant colour, with large facings of the same colour as the waistcoat; white stockings; grey shoes.

Behold, the dawn is breaking, he informs the sleeping world, yet his fair one is still wrapped in slumber; and he implores her to awake and show herself and take pity on her adorer; "Oh happy moment that has no equal!" he concludes. His vocal line becomes more and more exuberant and technically difficult as it proceeds, drawing more and more on the resources of early nineteenth century coloratura, and the aria concludes with a rousing fortissimo flourish on the part of the orchestra.

7

To his chagrin there is no response from the house, and after a brief colloquy with Fiorello, who draws his attention to the rapid oncoming of the morning light, he dismisses the musicians with thanks and a cash donation so liberal that Fiorello can hardly get the grateful creatures to leave. They crowd round the Count, kissing his hands and the hem of his cloak, and it is a long time before Fiorello, getting more and more annoyed with them, can induce them to terminate a chorus of thanksgiving that threatens to be interminable and depart. If they hadn't stopped their noisy chatter, Fiorello remarks acutely, they might have awakened the whole neighbourhood. He retires into the background, where he will await his master's further orders. The Count is disappointed that his fair one had not yet appeared at the window, for she is generally visible on the balcony about this time, inhaling the morning air. He will wait a little longer, for he is so deeply in love that he, a grandee of Spain, is actually prepared to make the lady his Countess, though as yet he does not know her station, or even her name.

His musings—in recitative—are broken in upon by a hearty voice off-stage trilling a gay "La, la, la." The Count decides to see who the newcomer is without himself being seen; so he conceals himself beneath the portico, thus leaving the ground clear for Figaro and his immortal aria. The mental key of this is set in the racy orchestral prelude:

6

and its pendant:

7

The prelude having run its course Figaro enters, with a guitar suspended from his neck. He is in the highest spirits: dawn has come, and he is off to his shop to start the serious business of the day—for apparently Seville cannot really get going till the great Figaro is at his post, ready for action. Is there any better life conceivable, he asks, than that of a barber of quality? "Bravo, Figaro, bravissimo, fortunatissimo!" He is prepared for anything, by night or by day:

No. 8

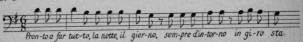

Pron-to a far tut-to, la notte, il gior-no, sem-pre d'in-tor-no in gi-ro sta.

There is no better profession in the world than his for a man like him; what can't he do with his razors, his combs, his lancets, his shears? He is equally indispensable to ladies and cavaliers, old and young. He is rushed off his feet with orders or appeals—here a cry for a wig, there a demand to be shaved; this client wants bleeding, another sends him off somewhere with a billet-doux; the air is thick with impatient cries of "Figaro! Figaro! Figaro! Figaro!" In vain does he appeal, for heaven's sake, for one call at a time upon his services; it's "Figaro here!", "Figaro there!", "Figaro everywhere!" He has to move like lightning, for he is the factotum of all the town. The aria ends with a breathless apostrophe of himself as the best and most fortunate of mortals:

9

Ah bra-vo, Fi-ga-ro, ah bra-vo Fi-ga-ro, bra-vo, bra-vis-si-mo, a te for-
bra vo, bra-vis-si-mo.

tu-na, a te --- for-tu--na

For energy and gusto the aria has not its equal in all comic opera; for anything to compare with it we have to go to the racy tarantella of Rossini's later years—*La Danza*—which here and there still defeats the technique and the breath control of the best singers, Caruso not excepted.

Figaro continues his catalogue of his own virtues and of the delights of his profession in a recitative. Truly a fine life! Little to do, plenty of fun, and always a doubloon or two in his pocket. Does a Seville girl want to marry and settle down? She sends for Figaro. Is a nice little widow anxious to find another husband? She calls for Figaro. With his comb he can go anywhere by day, with his guitar everywhere by night; the great things are tact and discretion, and Figaro can always be counted on for these. Once more he congratulates himself on his choice of a profession, and his profession on possessing such an ornament to it as the incomparable Figaro. He will have still more reason to be pleased with himself before the opera is over, for henceforth the whole action springs from and depends on him. The others are puppets whose wires he jerks this way and that for his own amusement and profit, for he has more brains, more audacity than the whole of them put together. He is, in fact, Beaumarchais.

8

As Figaro is going off Almaviva emerges from his concealment, and the pair recognise each other. The scene that follows is carried on in recitative. The Count is surprised, and at first none too pleased, to find here in Seville the rapscallion of a Figaro who had been in his service in Madrid, and he asks him a few questions. Figaro assures him that he has not been in any particular trouble with the magistrates, and accounts for his looking so plump and well to his poverty. The Count in his turn explains why *he* is in Seville, of all places. It appears that on the Prado in Madrid [1] he had seen and instantly fallen head over heels in love with a beautiful girl, the daughter, he had been told, of some old doddering Doctor.[2] The pair had left Madrid for Seville. He had followed them thither, and had spent his days and nights recently parading

[1] According to Beaumarchais, six months ago.
[2] In Beaumarchais, Almaviva assumes Rosina to be the Doctor's young wife.

up and down in front of the balcony which he points out to Figaro.

The barber congratulates him on his extraordinary good luck —as he puts it in his own idiom, the cheese has fallen straight on to the macaroni.[1] For in that very house he, Figaro, happens to be *persona grata*, barber, wig-maker, surgeon, herbalist, apothecary, veterinary, and general handy-man. The young lady in question is not the old Doctor's daughter, as the Count imagines, but only his ward. But before he can get any further with his explanation Rosina and Bartolo appear on the balcony, and Figaro retires into the background.[2] Rosina is wondering why her unknown admirer has not put in an appearance as usual. She has brought with her a letter intended for him, but does not know how to convey it. Bartolo asks what the paper is she is holding in her hand; she blandly assures him that it is simply the words of an aria in the new opera, *The Vain Precaution*, that has just appeared with such great success in Seville. The Count is delighted with her feminine artfulness: "the vain precaution!" he repeats with a chuckle. Figaro too is pleased; he recognises a fel-

---

[1] The opera libretto does not in general preserve the fine distinction between the manners and the speech of the two characters, an indication of their different social standing, that Beaumarchais had done: perhaps by 1816 the sense of these distinctions had been lost. We know, however, that they were very real in the 1770's, and that more than one cool observer foresaw the social dangers implicit in the two Beaumarchais dramas, in which the lackey of low degree is so obviously the superior of his aristocratic master in intelligence, wit and resource. In *The Barber* Beaumarchais seems to have been at pains to emphasise the difference between the social milieu of the two chief characters. He puts low-class expressions and idioms into the barber's mouth of which the Count would have disapproved as severely as Lord Chesterfield would have done. When Figaro, having persuaded Almaviva to get access to Bartolo's house in the guise of a tipsy soldier, is coaching him for the part, he criticises the Count's acting of it. He would like a little more realism, especially in the legs; and his own demonstration of how *he* would play the part draws from the Count the disgusted comment, "Faugh! that's the drunkenness of the people!" But to these and many other skilful touches in the plays the modern opera audience is of course quite insensitive.

[2] Beaumarchais's description of Bartolo is "a doctor; Rosina's guardian; short black coat, buttoned up; a large wig; a black sash; for out-of-doors, a long scarlet cloak."

low-craftsman in this innocent-looking young Rosina. Bartolo
pours out his scorn on operas in general—long-winded, melancholy, tiresome things, suited only to the barbarous taste of a
civilisation run to seed.

9

Rosina lets the paper fall, apparently by accident, and sends the
grumbling Bartolo out to retrieve it; and when he has left the
balcony she tells the Count, *sotto voce*, to pick the letter up
quickly. Just as he does so Bartolo appears in the square. He has
his doubts as to Rosina's suggestion that the wind must have carried the paper away, and begins to suspect that he is being fooled.
He roughly orders her back into the house and swears that he will
have the balcony walled up. At the Count's bidding Figaro reads
out the letter: "Your assiduous attentions have piqued my curiosity. My guardian is just going out; as soon as he does so, find
some ingenious method of letting me know your name, your
condition, and your intentions. It will be impossible for me to
come out on the balcony again without my tyrant accompanying
me; but rest assured that everything will be done to break her
chains that can be done by the unfortunate ROSINA." [1]

"She'll break them all right!" the Count remarks to Figaro;
"but tell me, what sort of a fellow is this guardian of hers?" "An
old man who seems to have the devil in him," is the reply, "a
miser, suspicious, an inveterate grumbler, about a hundred years
old but ambitious to play the gallant, who wants to marry Rosina
to get her money." Bartolo, as he quits the stage, barks his final
instructions at the invisible Rosina; until he returns she is not to
admit anyone except Don Basilio, who is to be detained until
Bartolo returns. The best thing he himself can do, he mutters as

[1] All this had been managed rather better by Beaumarchais: Rosina's letter
is written on the *music* of a song from *The Vain Precaution*, to which Rosina
bids Almaviva improvise words that will inform her who he is, etc. He is
to sing it in a "casual" sort of way, the implication being that the tune is so
well known that anyone might be warbling it at that or any other hour in
Seville, and therefore it will not attract any particular attention. This, when
the time comes for the song, leads to an amusing episode in which Figaro
forces his guitar on the Count, in spite of the latter's protests that he is at
best an indifferent performer on that instrument, and coaches him in his
stanzas.

he goes off, is to speed up the arrangements already in progress for the marriage.

His parting words have been overheard by the Count, who asks again who is this dotard who proposes to marry Rosina, and who is this Don Basilio? "A solemn fellow," is the answer, "who manages to have a finger in every matrimonial pie, a hypocrite, a veritable down-and-out, with never a farthing in his pocket— and Rosina's music teacher." (Beaumarchais adds another touch that bears on the future—"a poor creature whom it will be easy to twist round our fingers.")

Almaviva explains to Figaro that he wants to woo Rosina without her knowing his name and rank, to make sure that she loves him solely for himself. While they are discussing this matter Figaro gets a glimpse of Rosina behind the shutters, and urges the Count to get to work at once. Almaviva does so, in a little song with guitar and pizzicati strings accompaniment:

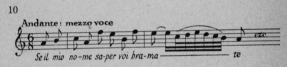

10

Andante: mezzo voce

Se il mio no-me sa-per voi bra-ma— te

in which he manages to inform her that his name is Lindoro:

11

Io son lin-do-ro, che fi-do v'a-do-ro, Che spo-sa vi bra-mo,

and that he is madly in love with her. Encouraged by Figaro's approval of his musical technique he embarks on a second stanza, in which he confesses, with regret, that he is not rich, but assures her of the constancy of his passion. She begins a reply of equal ardour, but after a few notes breaks off suddenly in the middle of the word "Lindoro" and disappears from the watchers outside, who surmise that someone must have entered the room. The distracted Almaviva swears he must somehow get into the house that very day, and calls vehemently on Figaro to provide a means. The shrewd barber exacts an assurance that all the money required will be forthcoming, and then breaks into a lively song in praise of gold, the very thought of which stimulates his mental faculties, he says.

10

Then the dialogue, starting with a carefree melody in the orchestra:

12

drops into the vivacious conversational tone that Italian opera buffa always had at its command as Figaro reveals the brilliant plan of campaign that has occurred to him. This very day a regiment is arriving in the town the colonel of which happens to be a friend of Almaviva's. The Count is to impersonate a soldier who has been billeted on Doctor Bartolo. To the accompaniment of the jolly No. 12, Figaro, whose invention has been tuned to the highest pitch by the thought of easy money, suggests an attractive nuance in this technique. The supposed soldier shall be half-drunk; and the versatile barber gives the Count an imitation of the thick speech and awkward movements of such a one. The conspirators bubble over with joy at the ingenious idea, which will certainly take the Doctor in. (Unfortunately the libretto omits the best reason of all, which had been supplied by Beaumarchais, for Bartolo's being duped by the stratagem; as Figaro points out, the Doctor will argue that a drunken soldier will be more anxious to go off somewhere to sleep off his potations than to meddle in the urgent affairs of the household.)

The pair are about to separate, in the highest glee, when they remember that Figaro has not told the Count where he can find him. This affords the barber a pretext for a patter song over a lively tune in the orchestra:

13

in which he explains where his shop is—just round the corner, number fifteen on the left, four steps up, the shop with the white front, with five wigs and some pots of pomade in the window, and so on: the Count can't mistake it. They can hardly bear to bring the scene to a close, so full are they of the rich humours and the possibilities of the coming intrigue, Almaviva, to the melody of No. 13, singing with exuberant coloratura of his love for Rosina, and Figaro already hearing in imagination the tinkle of the gold that will pour into his pockets soon. At last, after much repetition of their respective sentiments, they manage to tear themselves away; Figaro goes into Bartolo's house; Almaviva hurries away to obtain a soldier's uniform. One naturally expects the curtain to fall here; but before this can happen, Rossini and his librettist, for no discoverable reason, bethink themselves of Fiorello, whose existence we had forgotten. Suddenly coming to life, he indulges, Leporello-like, in a short recitative grumble about this master of his, who keeps him glued to the same spot for two long hours while *he* indulges himself in amorous adventures. He can put up with this sort of life no longer, he vows. As we are incapable, however, of feeling any interest now in Fiorello's little problems we raise no objection if the producer omits the trifling episode.

Sterbini and Rossini chose to regard all that has happened until now as constituting only the first scene of the first act of their opera, but today we feel justified in following Beaumarchais and taking it as the first act; the cards have been laid on the table, and now the game is ready to begin.

11

A certain parallelism runs through the comedy. It extends further than the simple fact that Almaviva and Bartolo have concentrated on the pursuit of the same object. Each of them relies on the brains of a clever hireling to pull him through, and each of them has to make it worth the hireling's while to cooperate; "money," Figaro tells the Count, "c'est le nerf de l'intrigue," while the musician Basilio warns Bartolo not to be niggardly where he is concerned, for the dissonances to be expected in any business partnership "are best prepared and resolved by the perfect consonance of gold." The next stage of the action is a matter less of a struggle between the two main forces than of one between the two instruments. Beaumarchais could handle all this in much livelier fashion, not merely because he was a Beaumarchais and Sterbini merely a Sterbini, but because spoken drama can move more swiftly than opera and therefore find room for more of the complexities of intrigue and the agile give-and-take of dialogue; though it must be conceded that Sterbini has been dexterous in general in his condensation of the French original.

It is now a matter of trickster against trickster, ruse against ruse, rogue Figaro against rogue Basilio. In the end, of course, the ruses of the barber will prove superior to those of the pimping music master, though here and there even Figaro can trip up and the race look for a moment like going to his and Almaviva's opponents. Figaro's immediate problem is how to get himself and Almaviva into a strategic position in the Bartolo household, in face of the Doctor's orders to the servants that no one but Basilio is to be admitted while he is out. Beaumarchais shows in humorous detail how this problem has been solved. Bartolo is Figaro's landlord; as the barber explains to the Count, his business premises are the property of the Doctor, who allows him the use of them *gratis,* while he, for his part, shows his gratitude by a promise to Bartolo of ten gold pistoles per annum, also *gratis.* One of his ways of covering his rent is to act not merely as the Doctor's barber but as apothecary, consultant and surgeon to the household. In Beaumarchais' second act we see how he has just applied his medical science—derived from his veterinary practice—to the problem of making all clear for the intrusion of Almaviva into the house: having persuaded one of the servants, humorously named L'Éveillé, that he is ill, he has given him a sedative so potent that he is incapable of anything but yawning for the next few hours. To another, a tottering old fellow with the equally humorous name of La Jeunesse, he has administered a sternutatory that keeps him perpetually on the sneeze; so that, Figaro having thoughtfully left the front door open, there will be nobody there to keep the pseudo-soldier out when he arrives.

Bartolo, whatever his faults may be, is no fool. He is, of course, a stock figure of the comedy of the period, the elderly guardian who wants to marry his rich and pretty young ward. But in brains he is superior to the average of his stage type, as he could hardly help being, seeing that his creator is Beaumarchais. We learn casually that he had become aware in Madrid that a gallant of the name of Count Almaviva had been trying to make Rosina's acquaintance. The incident of the sheet of paper containing an extract from *The Vain Precaution*, which had so mysteriously disappeared after it had fallen into an apparently empty square, has made him very suspicious, though it does not occur to him to associate it in any way with the Count, whom as yet he does not know to be in Seville. His strategy is now determined by recent events. There is no time to be lost; during the day that has now opened he must make arrangements for his marriage to Rosina on the morrow. At this very moment his tool Basilio is engaged in making those arrangements—which is why Bartolo has told his servants that if Don Basilio calls while he is out he is to stay there till he returns.

12

In the next stage of the opera the action has to be condensed and the talk curtailed because of the necessity of giving the characters scope to demonstrate their musical talents. Rosina is the first to do so. The setting is a room in Bartolo's house; we observe that the Venetian blinds have been closed. Rosina, taking advantage of her guardian's absence, has been writing a letter, which she now holds in her hand, to Lindoro.[1] Her great display aria, "Una voce poco fa," [2] so beloved of coloratura sopranos in the concert room as well as in the theatre, begins seriously enough with a declaration of her resolve to be Lindoro's, no matter what her guardian may say or do. Then, quickening her tempo a little, she embarks, like her parallel Norina in a similar situation in *Don Pasquale,* upon a eulogy of her own good qualities. She is a thoroughly good girl, she assures us, respectful, obedient, sweet-natured, affectionate:

[1] Beaumarchais's specification for the costuming of Rosina is simply "a young lady of noble descent, dressed in Spanish fashion."

[2] The listener with no Italian who knows nothing more of the words than these four manages fairly well with "Una voce" but is gravelled by the "poco fa." This is simply an Italian idiom for "a little while ago." What Rosina is saying in her opening words is that a little while ago a voice had resounded in her heart with electrifying effect: it was Lindoro's serenade.

14

easy to lead and to govern:

15

(Note the pert little stresses on "reggere"; these continue to be
a feature of the melody.) But if anyone thinks he can take advantage of these amiable weaknesses of hers, she continues, let him
look out; in defence of her rights she can be a little devil, a viper,
the mistress of a hundred wiles. Poor Doctor Bartolo will discover
before long what she is capable of in the way of feminine artfulness, especially with the ingenious, unscrupulous Figaro to back
her up.

After the lively aria the action is carried on for some time in
recitative. Having sealed her letter Rosina regrets she has no
trusty messenger, watched as she is by Bartolo, to send it by. Then
she remembers that when she had caught a glimpse of Lindoro
in the square he had been accompanied by the barber, and this
Figaro is a good sort of fellow who might be on her side. At this
point Figaro himself enters, and she bewails her sad situation to
him; sealed up within four walls as she is she might as well be in
a tomb! He is about to tell her something it will do her good to
hear when Bartolo is heard approaching; so the barber conceals
himself where he can get a view of whatever may happen, while
Rosina retires into the background.

Bartolo, muttering to himself, is full of grievances—that cursed
rascal of a barber, for some reason the Doctor cannot fathom, has
turned the house into a hospital with his bleedings, doses of
laudanum and what not: when Bartolo calls in the servants Berta
and Ambrosio to ask them if Figaro has been there talking to

Rosina the one can only sneeze, the other only yawn. Rosina, however, has boldly admitted that she has seen Figaro and has found him very sympathetic. While Bartolo is cursing the barber, Basilio enters.[1] He is invariably smooth, unctuous, deferential towards his employer, and obviously a bit of a knave. He has important news for Bartolo—he has discovered that Count Almaviva is in Seville; and now the Doctor divines who the unknown is who has been hanging about his house lately. The first thing to do, Basilio assures him, is to invent some story about the Count that will put him in bad odour in the town and force him to leave it. The Basilio way of getting rid of an enemy, he explains, is a technique of his own invention that never fails. He launches his famous aria: "Calumny! There's nothing to beat it!" The orchestra is hushed to a *sotto voce* as he begins. Calumny, he says, starts as a gentle breeze, that imperceptibly grows in force as the slander passes from mouth to mouth, from ear to ear, what was no more than an almost inaudible hiss in the first place becoming in time a horrifying roar that rends the air like the firing of a cannon, till the wretched victim finds himself crushed under the weight of public opprobrium and hatred. To depict the gradual swelling of the calumny from a breath to a gale, Rossini employs effectively a device that was always a favourite of his (though not his invention), a slow crescendo beginning almost inaudibly in the strings:

16

and piling up to a fortissimo; but at the words "The miserable wretch, calumniated, bespattered, collapses under the public scourging" the orchestra drops to a pianissimo again as a sinister phrase makes a chromatic descent in the strings and bassoon: [2]

[1] Beaumarchais's description of him is "an organist, Rosina's singing teacher; wears a black turned-down hat, a cassock, and a long cloak without frills or ruffles."

[2] Beaumarchais, of course, took his cue for his description of calumny, either at first or fifty-first hand, from Vergil's famous description, in the fourth book of the *Aeneid*, of the gradual spread of Rumour in Dido's

17

PP

Bartolo agrees with Basilio in principle, but as time is pressing he prefers his own plan—to push on with the marriage; once Rosina is his wife he will put a stop to her amorous escapades; and Basilio says under his breath that to him it's all one so long as there is money in it for him. The pair go into an inner room to talk about the marriage contract, whereupon Figaro emerges cautiously from his hiding-place. Now he understands exactly what is afoot, and he has his plan to help Rosina. When she comes into view again he tells her what he has just overheard—a scheme for a wedding on the morrow. She replies grimly that they will have to reckon with her before that happens! She artfully turns the conversation to the subject of the young man whom she had seen with Figaro under her balcony early that morning—a cousin of his, he assures her, a fine young fellow who has come to Seville to complete his studies and make his fortune if he can. He has only one fault—he is in love. Rosina's eager enquiries elicit the teasing information that the object of this love is a beautiful young creature remarkably like Rosina in appearance, and, in fact, bearing the same name. She breaks into a cascade of coloratura at the welcome news, and Figaro takes up the gay strain. To a delightful chattering melody in the orchestra they discuss their future plan of action. First of all, says Figaro, Rosina is to write a letter to Lindoro. She protests that maidenly modesty would not let her go as far as that—and then, greatly to the barber's admiration, produces the already written letter. Then they unite their voices in a duet, Rosina congratulating herself on the way things have turned out for her—for she has been promised a meeting soon with her Lindoro—Figaro marvelling quietly at the unsuspected depths of artfulness in women in general and this pretty little kitten of a Rosina in particular.

Carthage—Fama, surpassed in swiftness by nothing else that is evil, enlarging herself and gathering strength by her own motion, etc.

13

Figaro having left—presumably to re-establish connections with the Count—Bartolo re-enters. He tackles Rosina boldly on the subject of "the vain precaution," and succeeds in throwing her into some confusion. He demands to know what she and the barber had been talking about. She lies fluently—it was only this trifle and that, the Paris fashions, Figaro's sick little daughter Marcellina, and what not. Not believing a word she says, for she is not yet sufficient of an expert to lie without blushing, Bartolo goes straight to the point. Did Figaro bring her a reply to the letter she had let fall from the balcony? How is it that there are ink-stains on her finger? She can parry that one; she had burnt her finger, and had always been told that ink was the remedy for burns. There were six sheets of paper on the desk when he left, Bartolo continues, for he had counted them; and now there are only five. What has become of the other? Rosina explains that she had used it to wrap up some sweetmeats she had sent to Marcellina. But why the newly cut quill? continues the inexorable Bartolo. Her reply is that she had needed it to design a flower for her embroidery.

He loses patience and seeks relief for his feelings in a pompous aria, in which he asks her whether she really thinks she can impose on a man like him with such feeble tarradiddles, and recommends her to try to improve her technique; the vocal part is very difficult —giving us, as several other arias in Rossini's comic operas do, an idea of the agility expected of the basses in those days—while the orchestral chatter is rich in pointed characterisation. He ends by assuring her that the next time he goes out she will be locked up so effectually that not so much as a breath of air will be able to steal into the room. The aria would be excessively long were it not for the pounding pace at which it goes. Its very length and repetitiousness is the comic stroke; poor old Bartolo is too angry and at the same time too distracted to be able to pull up.

At last, however, quite out of breath, he storms out of the room, whereupon Rosina assures herself and us that the worse he behaves, and the more difficult her situation, the more reserves of feminine guile she has to draw upon. After this brief recitative she too goes out, and the maidservant Berta enters. She has heard knocking without, and, sneezing as she goes, she shuffles off to open the door to the Count. He is now disguised as a soldier and accompanied by a mock-martial motif in the orchestra:

18

Pretending to be tipsy he begins to throw his military weight about: why is there no one in the house to attend to a man of his importance? When Bartolo re-enters the soldier fumbles in his pocket for his billeting paper. (He exasperates Bartolo by never getting his name right—it is now Doctor Balordo, now Barbaro, now Somaro (mule).) He is delighted to hear that the man on whom he has been quartered is a doctor, for that, he explains, constitutes a professional bond between them, he himself being the regimental farrier. A pungently comic duet follows, Bartolo spluttering with rage, the Count puzzling him with his inane behaviour, a mixture of ironic patronage and camaraderie. Almaviva is really playing for time; his purpose is to see Rosina and convey a letter into her hands.

When she enters she is at first taken aback at seeing a soldier there, and stops in her tracks, for Figaro had not disclosed this part of his plan of campaign to her. The duet now becomes a lively trio, the Count frantically endeavouring to give her some idea of what is afoot, Rosina unable as yet to make head or tail of it all, and Bartolo fuming away without the others paying any attention to him. When Rosina comes forward he roughly orders her back to her chamber. Almaviva, who by this time has managed to whisper to her "I am Lindoro," suggests going with her to view his new quarters. This goads Bartolo beyond endurance. He plays his trump card: there will be no quarters for him or anyone like him in this house, for Bartolo happens to possess an official order exempting him from having soldiers billeted on him. This is something the Count had not expected, and for the moment he is completely thrown out of his stride. Still, when the Doctor goes to his desk to hunt for the exemption order Lindoro manages to get in a confidential word or two with Rosina.

Bartolo, having found and read out the order, flourishes it triumphantly in the Count's face, who contemptuously tosses the document in the air. When the Doctor threatens to throw him out the pseudo-soldier affects to take this as a challenge to mortal combat; and fighting, of course, is his trade, as he explains to the accompaniment of the martial No. 18. Pretending to make some preliminary passes with his sword he surreptitiously drops a letter and tells Rosina *sotto voce* to let her handkerchief fall on it, which she does. But as Bartolo has seen all this the Count's invention is once more strained to the utmost. He himself picks up the letter, which is no doubt, he informs Bartolo, a medical prescription. No, he is wrong; it is a letter, obviously the property of the young lady here; and he picks it up and hands it to her along with her handkerchief.

14

The fun becomes fast and furious, Bartolo angrily demanding to see the letter—which Rosina blandly assures him is only the laundry list—and the Count still trying to keep up the bluff. At the height of the imbroglio Berta enters to announce that Figaro and some other people have arrived. With her is Basilio. Bartolo is very glad to see him, for Rosina has stumped him again, the document she has dexterously fobbed off on him having really turned out to be just a laundry list. The Count is delighted with her cleverness; now, as he puts it, they have Bartolo in the bag. Basilio, not having as yet got the hang of it all, remembers that he is a music master and limits his part in the ensemble to a simple trolling of "Sol, Do, Re, Fa, Re, Sol" and so forth; for a big buffo finale of this kind is a sort of Christmas pudding into which anything can go.

Rosina, making the most of the tactical victory she has won with the laundry list, now thinks the time has come to turn on the tears: this she does as the mode of the music changes from major to minor, with a new motif in the oboe that is punctuated by sham sobs; the general tempo, however, remains unchanged:

19

(This short minor inset is admirably designed to obtain a little variety before the main current of the huge finale is resumed, as it will be at the entrance of Figaro.)

Bartolo, completely bluffed, is all contrition now: he apologises abjectly to his dear Rosina, while the Count draws his sword again and threatens him with bodily violence. The tension is broken by the arrival of Figaro with a barber's basin under his arm. What is the matter? he asks; for the hullabaloo is audible in the square, where a large crowd has now gathered. He whispers a word of caution to the Count, and, pushing his basin between him and Bartolo, orders the pseudo-soldier to have better manners. But still the shindy goes on, till at last there comes a knocking at the door that freezes them all into silence. It is the town guard, come to see what the uproar is about. Bartolo explains that this drunken lout of a soldier has threatened and maltreated him; and Basilio confirms the story. Figaro protests that he has come in merely to pour oil on the troubled waters. The Count blusters that he is in a rage only because this rascal of a Doctor has refused to obey a billeting order. Rosina apologises for the too demonstrative soldier, attributing his exuberance to too much wine.

The officer of the guard orders his men to arrest the soldier and take him away; but the Count takes him aside and shows him a document that evidently astounds him, for at once he bids the guards stand back. Rosina, Bartolo and Basilio (not knowing who the "soldier" is) cannot understand this sudden display of respect; but Figaro, who knows well enough that it is due to the Count having disclosed his rank, chuckles quietly over Bartolo's discomfiture, his ironic ejaculations of "Poor Doctor Bartolo!" always standing out clearly from the vocal texture. A big sextet is now built up by a series of imitations between the various vocal parts, in which all profess verbally their inability to understand the new turn that events have taken.[1]

When at last Bartolo and Basilio are able to make their expostulations audible to the guard they are roughly told to be quiet. Finally the six characters express once more, in a massive unison:

[1] There is no *dramatic* reason at all for Berta being on the stage in the finale; she has been brought there only to add an extra female voice to the predominantly male ensemble.

20

Mi——par d'es——ser col——la tes——ta

their complete incapacity to make head or tail of what is going on, so confused are they all by the noise the others are making; and after another thirty pages or so in the score, in which they repeat themselves *ad infinitum*—for Rossini has only about a fortnight in which to write his opera—the act comes at last to a rumbustious end.

15

When the curtain rises again we see the library in the Doctor's house; among the furniture is a clavecin on which stands some music. It is now evening; the tumult and the shouting have died, and Bartolo, in the grateful quiet of his room, is thinking things over. Though he has got rid of the blusterous and inconvenient soldier he is still worried. He has had enquiries made in the town about that soldier, and discovered that the regiment concerned knows no such person. A light breaks upon him—the fellow had probably been sent by Count Almaviva to get information about Rosina. No man is safe in these days, he muses, even within his own four walls.

Almaviva and Figaro, though the first round has gone against them, have still not given up the fight. A knocking is heard at the house door, and soon the Count turns up again, this time disguised as a music teacher, and accompanied by an insinuating, hypocritical tune in the violins:

21

The newcomer is all deference and unction. He calls down on Bartolo and his household peace and joy for the next thousand years. The Doctor has a dim feeling that he has seen this face somewhere or other already, but he keeps his thoughts to himself; Almaviva, for his part, is hoping that his present ruse will have more success than his first. The Doctor keeps begging the newcomer to make an end of compliments and declare his business, but to no effect, the sly, oily No. 21 twining itself endlessly round the conversation of the pair. The duet is Rossini and opera buffa at their best.

At last Bartolo manages to persuade his visitor to come down to earth, introduce himself, and explain his presence there. From the dialogue that follows (in recitative) we learn that this is Don Alonso, a teacher of music, studying with Don Basilio, who, having been suddenly taken ill, has sent his pupil in his stead. Alonso has some difficulty in dissuading the Doctor from rushing off at once to see the sick Basilio, who is of so much importance to him just now. Pretending to be angry, and raising his voice in the hope that Rosina may hear him, the intruder tells Bartolo that, happening to be lodged where Count Almaviva is staying, he had that morning lighted on a letter from the Doctor's ward to his lordship. Don Basilio knows nothing of this letter, but he, Alonso, had brought it with him believing that it would make it easier for him to gain access to the young lady in order to give her her lesson. A glance at the letter makes it clear to Bartolo that the handwriting is really Rosina's. (It is, as a matter of fact, the missive we saw her writing in an earlier scene.) The Count, not having Figaro to back him up, becomes more and more confused both inwardly and outwardly as he gabbles on; but he wins the complete confidence of the Doctor when he argues that if he is given access to the ward he can easily persuade her that the letter had been given to him by another of the naughty Count's ladyloves, thus proving him to have been merely playing with the affections of Rosina. "Bravo!" Bartolo chuckles. "Calumny! Now I recognise you for a worthy pupil of Don Basilio!" He thanks Alonso effusively, embraces him, assures him that he himself will see that the letter gets into his ward's hands, and shuffles off into the inner room. Left to himself the Count realises that this plan of his, which had been devised by him on the spur of the moment, is not as clever as he had thought; still, it was the only way he could think of to prevent Bartolo from turning him out of the house as an irresponsible fool. However, when he gets an opportunity to speak to his Rosina he will be able to explain it all to her satisfaction.[1]

16

Bartolo returns with Rosina, to whom he introduces this Don Alonso who has come to give her her music lesson. At the unexpected sight of Lindoro she is staggered for a moment, but accounts for her choked cry of alarm by alleging a spasm of cramp in her foot. Lindoro assures her, with a grave professional air, that the best cure for a thing of that sort will be the music lesson he is going to give her in the place of Don Basilio. She quite agrees, and artfully elects to sing the rondo from *The Vain Precaution.* Bartolo breaks out with "What is this 'Vain Precaution' that she is always talking about lately?", and she patiently explains once more that it is the title of the new opera that is the rage of the town. The Count (who now seems to have developed a musical accomplishment the possession of which he had disclaimed in a previous talk with Figaro), seats himself at the clavecin to play the accompaniment, while Bartolo settles himself in a chair to listen. The subject of the aria is the powerlessness of any tyrant to influence the heart that is feeling its first love; and of course it is to "Lindoro" that the reassuring confession is made, and "Lindoro" to whom she appeals for help. The "lesson," therefore, containing as it does responses in which Lindoro assures her that he will not fail her, plays, or should do, a vital dramatic part in the intrigue; but all this goes for nothing in a modern production, where the "singing lesson" consists merely of whatever showpiece the prima donna and the producer may elect to insert in the score.

Bartolo does not think much of the aria from *The Vain Precaution:* in *his* young days music was music, not the fiddle-faddle modern stuff served up to them nowadays; and the old donkey

[1] Some points in the rather tangled intrigue are made clearer in Beaumarchais than in the opera; for instance, in the former Bartolo thinks it will be all the easier to get Rosina to take her music lesson from Alonso because she has already told her guardian that she will take no more music lessons from Don Basilio now she knows him to be acting as Bartolo's matrimonial agent. On the other hand, mere words could never achieve and sustain such finesses of ironic comedy as we get in the duet that commences with our No. 21.

proceeds to show them how Cafferelli, according to him, used to sing a gallant little ditty to one Giovanna, a name which, he explains, he is altering to Rosina to suit the present company. While this grotesque exhibition is going on Figaro enters with his basin under his arm, stands behind Bartolo, and mimics him. When the Doctor turns on him he explains that he has come to shave him. Bartolo is for putting this off until tomorrow; but Figaro, producing a doubtfully authentic notebook from his pocket, protests that this is impossible, so many pressing engagements has he the next day—all the regimental officers to be shaved, the Marchioness Andronica's wig to be fitted, Count Bombe's toupet to be fixed, the lawyer Bernadone's dyspepsia to be dosed, and so on: tomorrow is quite out of the question. His whole morning had been wasted, he complains, for when he had come there expressly to shave the Doctor he had found the house in an uproar; now the man wants to put it off again! Does he think Figaro is just a country barber? If so, let him choose another artist, for *he* has had about as much as he can stand; and he takes up his basin as though he were going to throw up his part and walk out of the show.

The bluff works. Bartolo, handing him his bunch of keys, tells him to go into his private room and bring the necessary towels and things, then immediately changes his mind and decides to go himself. This gives Figaro the opportunity to tell Rosina that if only he can get those keys in his hands the game will be won, for among them is the vital key to the balcony. But the suspicious Bartolo is back again in a moment, feeling that it is not wise to leave his rebellious ward with "that devil of a barber." He sends Figaro out with the keys, telling him where he will find everything—"straight down the corridor, above the cupboard, and see that you don't touch anything else." "The trick is won!" Figaro whispers exultantly to Rosina as he goes off, Bartolo explaining complacently why he can't trust this rogue of a barber any further then he can see him, for it was he who had carried Rosina's letter to Count Almaviva, and he, Doctor Bartolo, is too wise an old bird to be caught twice in the same snare.

17

But just then a fearful clatter is heard from within. Bartolo
rushes out and returns with Figaro, wailing that all his dishes,
eight wine-glasses and a bowl have been smashed to atoms. The
barber turns the tables on him by pointing out that it is his own
fault for keeping the place in darkness as he does: it was only by
the mercy of Providence that he had escaped having his head
smashed against the wall; and at the same time he gleefully shows
the Count the key of the balcony, which he has detached from the
bunch. All now seems to them for the best in the best of all possible worlds as Bartolo seats himself in the chair and orders the
barber to begin. But Beaumarchais still has some cards up his
sleeve, some as yet unforeseen hurdles for the conspirators to get
over.

Almost before Figaro can get to work the recitative in which
the foregoing scene has been carried on comes to an abrupt end
with a crashing E flat chord in the orchestra as, to everyone's
amazement, Don Basilio appears in the doorway: it is one of the
most effective entrances in all opera. "Don Basilio!" ejaculates
Rosina. "What on earth is this?" asks the Count. Figaro mutters
(in effect) "That's torn it!" Bartolo can only babble "What, you
here?" To a characteristically unctuous Basilian motif in the
orchestra:

22

the unsuspecting Basilio greets the company: "Your servant,
good people one and all." He is frankly astounded when ·the
Doctor enquires anxiously about his health, and still more flabber-
gasted by the next question, "And the court?" [1] The first concern
of the conspirators now is to prevent Basilio from expressing
more surprise and asking any questions. The Count takes charge.
·"I have told Doctor Bartolo," he assures the music master, "that
everything is now settled"; and Bartolo confirms this. The pseudo-

---

[1] i.e. the legal body concerned with the marriage.

Alonso keeps gabbling on to Basilio, at the same time urging Bartolo to get rid of the man before he can blurt out something indiscreet: "He knows nothing of the letter," he reminds the Doctor, whereupon the latter orders Basilio to take himself off at once. Figaro backs him up; the worthy man shouldn't be out of his bed with such a fever on him. So it goes on, in a delightful give-and-take of talk that is held together musically by the oily No. 22. But the more the others explain, the less Basilio comprehends. Alonso assures him that he is as yellow as a corpse; Figaro, feeling his pulse, is horrified at its irregularity and diagnoses scarlatina. The Count is more practical; while also advising the bewildered Basilio to go home and take some medicine he slips a purse into his hand. The cumulative weight of testimony as to his being mortally ill had already begun to impress him: the purse brings final conviction. The richly comic scene ends with a "Good night!" from all in turn as they manœuvre him out of the room, Almaviva leading off with a charming melody:

23

that is worked up into a grand quintet.

With Basilio out of the way Figaro can get on at last with the lathering of Bartolo, managing it in such a way that he obscures the Doctor's view of the lovers. While Rosina appears to be absorbed in the study of the music, Almaviva, to the accompaniment of a new motif in the orchestra:

24

contrives to tell her hurriedly that all is going nicely: now that Figaro has the balcony key they will be there at the stroke of midnight to carry her off. She promises to be ready. Figaro does his best to help them by pretending to have got something in his eye and asking Bartolo to examine it. But the Doctor chances to overhear Almaviva trying to account to Rosina for the use of that letter of hers and for his present disguise; and now he realises how he has been duped. Leaping angrily from his chair he turns on Figaro and "Alonso" and orders the latter out of the house. To a new tune in the orchestra: [1]

25

the others affect to regard him as half-demented and exhort him to calm himself, while he keeps cursing and threatening them. The lively quartet ends with Rosina, Figaro and the Count quitting the scene, leaving Bartolo still fuming. He rings for his servants. Ambrosio he orders to go at once to Don Basilio's house over the way and bid him to come to him at once. Not trusting to Berta to guard the door he rushes out to attend to it himself, thereby leaving the stage clear for what, dramatically considered, is the weakest episode in the opera—an aria in which Berta complains at great length about the trials of being in service in a house like this, and enlarges on the absurdity of crack-brained old men falling in love. Yet the complaint, she admits, is universal, she herself, mature as she is, not being immune from it. The long aria is unnecessary; the only functions it can be said to perform are to give the second soprano an opportunity to distinguish herself and to fill up the interval of time and space between this scene and the next.

18

On the rising of the curtain we see the Doctor's room again as in the first act, with the Venetian blinds closed as before. The time is later the same evening. Bartolo and Basilio are in earnest confabulation in recitative; Basilio has disclaimed all knowledge of "Alonso," whom Bartolo now suspects to be an agent of Count Almaviva, though the shrewder Basilio believes him, on the evidence of the purse, to be none other than the Count himself. If that be so, Bartolo rejoins, the need is all the more pressing to

[1] As is so often the case in Italian opera buffa the main musical line in the *Barber* is frequently entrusted to the orchestra, the voices confining themselves to a rapid patter that is sometimes hardly more than a monotone.

have the marriage business concluded today; he himself will hurry
off to the notary and have the contract drawn up. Basilio pours
cold water on this idea: for one thing, it's raining cats and dogs;
for another, the notary won't be available that evening because
he has already been engaged by Figaro for the marriage of the
latter's niece. "But the barber has no nieces!" says Bartolo; "I
smell a rat! The scoundrel means to play some trick on me tonight!" Giving Basilio the key to the outer door he sends him
off with orders to bring the notary to him at once.

Left alone, the worried Doctor thinks things over: by hook or
by crook, by love or by compulsion, Rosina must be made to
yield, and quickly. An idea strikes him. That fool of an Alonso
has unintentionally put in his hands the ideal weapon for his
purpose—Rosina's letter to her lover. She comes in just then,
and he unmasks his battery. She has put her innocent trust, he
tells her, in a pair of rogues (Figaro and Alonso) who are conspiring to throw her into the arms of Count Almaviva, in proof of
which he shows her her own letter to her supposed lover, which
has providentially come into his hands. (The spectator must always bear in mind that Rosina still does not know that the humble
"Lindoro" to whom she had given her heart is the great Count
Almaviva.)

Naturally believing she has been befooled, and being a girl of
spirit, she decides to wreak vengeance on the faithless Lindoro.
She not only assures Bartolo that she will marry him out of hand
but tells him of the Lindoro-Figaro plan to carry her away that
night. Bartolo is going off at once to bar the door; but Rosina
tells him this will be useless, as they will enter by the window,
they having got possession of the key of the balcony. Bartolo is
afraid the ruffians may be armed; so he advises Rosina to lock
herself up in her room while he runs off to inform the police that
according to information received two thieves are going to break
into his house. Bewailing her sad fate, she decides to do as he has
told her.

Basilio's passing allusion to the bad weather has not been without its dramatic significance. A storm has evidently been brewing,
and now it breaks over the house.[1] Rossini throws himself with

---

[1] For this storm music Rossini drew upon an earlier opera, *La Pietra del
Paragone* (1812).

delight into the painting of an orchestral picture of a tempest, beginning with a far-off rumble of thunder in the lower strings, hints of lightning flashes in the flute, and the staccato pattering of the first raindrops. Soon the storm is in full fury; then it subsides and gradually dies away in the distance, and we see Figaro and Almaviva stealthily entering from the balcony. Their conversation is carried on in recitative. As Figaro strikes a light Rosina becomes visible. The Count would take her in his arms, but she repulses him with indignant reproaches; she has discovered, she tells him, that he is only a perfidious deceiver, merely feigning love for her in order to get her into the clutches of the vile Count Almaviva. That little misunderstanding is soon cleared up, the Count being delighted to find that she really had' loved him as "Lindoro," in ignorance of his rank and name. Opening his cloak and throwing himself at her feet he discloses himself as not Lindoro but Count Almaviva, Grandee of Spain.

19

This happy dénouement brings on, of course, a severe attack of coloratura that racks Rosina for quite a while, the Count kindly aiding and abetting her; and once again we get some idea of the vocal technique expected in those days of male as well as female singers. Figaro has for some time been trying to persuade the happy pair to limit their transports and fix their minds on the business before them, but in vain. At last he manages to make an impression on them; in agitated tones he tells them that he sees two people outside with a lantern. This sobers them, if not to the extent of making them take action, at any rate to that of singing about the necessity of doing so. The Count begins with an exhortation to silence and flight:

26

the theme of which is taken up in turns by the others in character-istically Rossini fashion.[1] Frenziedly, at great length, they entreat each other to lose no time but fly while the flying's good, remaining all the while, as is the operatic way, glued to their respective spots. When at last they decide to move they find, to their dismay, that the ladder by which they had hoped to escape is no longer there and that someone is stealing in on them. They retire into the background, Almaviva wrapping his cloak round him once more and exhorting Rosina to have courage.

Basilio comes in stealthily, with another man whom Figaro soon recognises, to his delight, as the notary. So he comes for-ward and reminds the lawyer that he had been engaged to draw up the marriage deed between his (Figaro's) niece and one Count Almaviva. Here the couple are, he continues, pointing to the lovers; and the man of law produces the necessary document. The bewildered Basilio asks where on earth Doctor Bartolo can be; but the Count, drawing a ring from his finger with one hand and a pistol from his pocket with the other, gives the music master his choice between a bribe and a couple of bullets in his head. Basilio, always open to reason, has no difficulty in making his choice; more than that, he signs as one of the witnesses to the marriage, the other being Figaro.

As the barber locks the music master in a derisive embrace Bartolo enters with a military patrol. He orders the officer to arrest Figaro and his accomplice as criminals, but the Count once more easily settles the matter by revealing his identity and rank. In a vigorous aria he imperiously puts Bartolo in his place, and the Doctor, unable to bear up against such a combina-tion of moral indignation and tenor coloratura, soon gives up the fight.

Almaviva's joy is so overwhelming that it sweeps him off for a moment into a key signature of five flats as he turns to congratu-late Rosina on her escape from the clutches of her tyrant:

---

[1] The writer of the article on Rossini in *Grove's Dictionary* informs us that "the eight opening bars of the trio 'Zitti, zitti' are notoriously taken note by note from Simon's air in Haydn's *Seasons*." This is not strictly true, however, as the reader can discover for himself by the simple process of comparing the two melodies.

27

E tu in-fe-li-ce vit-ti—ma

But the key of B flat is soon restored, with the soldiers—who
have come in most opportunely for the musical purposes of the
composer—adding their felicitations in chorus. The Count continues to pour out the happiness of his heart:

28

Ah il più lie-to,il più fe——li-ce e il mio cor de' co-ri a—man-ti,

the chorus still joining in from time to time, and the solo part
proliferating into increasingly difficult coloratura.

By this time Bartolo has recovered his breath, and he uses it in
the first place to round on Basilio for going over to the enemy;
but Basilio blandly points out that he has merely followed the
dictates of reason, Count Almaviva having produced arguments
that were really irresistible. Then the Doctor turns to cursing
himself for his stupidity in removing the ladder, thus facilitating
the marriage. This gives Figaro the opportunity for a suave reminder of the vanity of precautions, whereupon Bartolo retires
to his last line of defence; it is quite impossible, he protests, for
him to pay Rosina her dowry. The Count cuts him short: he
would not in any case accept anything of that sort with his bride;
which provokes the cynical comment from Figaro that rogues
have the best of it in this world. So everyone has won something
and is satisfied. Figaro extinguishes his lantern, as a symbolic way
of indicating that all's well that has ended well:

29

Di si fe-li-ce in-ne————sto,

a sentiment taken up by Berta, Bartolo, Basilio and the chorus, followed eventually by the rest of the company. The vista before the lovers, they all declare, is one of pure and endless affection and felicity. If they could foresee the future they would realise that they were being over-optimistic; but the sequel to *The Barber of Seville, or The Vain Precaution* was probably unthought of at this time even by Beaumarchais.

Rigoletto

GIUSEPPE VERDI [1813–1901]

PRINCIPAL CHARACTERS

Rigoletto	*Baritone*
Duke of Mantua	*Tenor*
Gilda	*Soprano*
Maddalena	*Contralto*
Sparafucile	*Bass*
Monterone	*Baritone*
Marullo	*Baritone*
Borsa	*Tenor*
Count Ceprano	*Bass*
Countess Ceprano	*Mezzo-soprano*

1

Verdi's "middle period" may be said to have extended from the *Luisa Miller* of 1849 to the *Don Carlos* of 1867. The latter part of this long period comprises the *Simon Boccanegra* of 1857 (afterwards revised), *Un Ballo in Maschera* (1859) and *La Forza del Destino* (1862), all of which still keep their place in the repertory. The early part of the period saw the creation of three works in which Verdi can be said to have first truly found himself—*Rigoletto* (1851), *Il Trovatore* (1853) and *La Traviata* (also 1853). The popularity of these three works has been uninterrupted from their day to ours.

In March 1850 the Fenice Theatre, Venice, commissioned an opera from Verdi for production during Lent of the following year. The composer's mind was about that time full of plans and ideas of all sorts, among them a *King Lear*, a *Hamlet*, and the

Spanish drama that ultimately became *Il Trovatore*; but in the end he decided on Victor Hugo's play *Le Roi s'amuse*, which had been produced in Paris some seventeen years earlier without establishing itself, the public finding it hard to follow the poet in his bold contention that drama, and indeed art in general, was as capable of dealing with the "ugly" as with the "beautiful," with thoroughly repulsive characters as with attractive or borderline ones. Hugo had indeed set himself a formidable task—to win his audience's sympathies for a leading character not only physically but mentally and morally deformed, having only one redeeming trait, his love for his daughter. (Other considerations, such as the cynical immorality of the King in the case, were subordinate to this.)

When he published his play Hugo prefaced it with a *pièce justificative* that revealed what had been at the back of his mind when he created the character of his Triboulet. He had imagined, he said, a man labouring under a triple disadvantage—he was physically deformed, he was unhealthy, and fate had allotted him the rôle of a buffoon at a corrupt court. Under these stresses his nature had gone to pieces. He had become hate incarnate, hating the King because he was the King, the noble courtiers because they were courtiers, "and men in general because they do not have a hump on their backs." His dominant passion is to bring them all down to ruin by playing them off against each other: the King he encourages in his vices, off the courtiers he scores by making even them the victims of his master's villainies, incessantly pointing out to him "some wife to seduce, some sister to abduct, some daughter to dishonour." All are puppets in his hands; the viler he makes them the more voluptuous is his sense of triumph over them; till the day comes when, as he imagines, the arch-criminal of them all, the self-indulgent, unscrupulous King himself, having committed his worst crime—the seduction of the buffoon's daughter—unconsciously delivers himself into his hands for vengeance.

2

The conception is admirable, and the threads of the action are cunningly interwoven; but the stage realisation is not altogether successful. What might have become drama of a very fine kind tends to become in Hugo's hands merely melodrama. Later generations, unable to take the violences of the French romantics as seriously as they did, are inclined to see the personages as puppets rather than flesh-and-blood characters: the late nineteenth century view of the play in general seems to have been voiced by the dramatic critic William Archer, who described it as "a nightmare of a play, in which changes are rung upon cynicism, lust and cruelty until exhausted nature cries 'Hold! too much!'. In Triboulet [the Rigoletto of the opera] we have an instance of that 'system of predetermined paradox' (to use Mr. Myers's phrase) which has vitiated so much of Victor Hugo's work. He has told us how he determined to take the vilest of beings, a physical monstrosity placed in the most despicable of situations, and then to give him a soul, and place in that soul 'the purest sentiment known to man, the paternal sentiment' . . . This sublime sentiment . . . will transform before our eyes this degraded creature; the small will become great, the deformed will become beautiful."

Turning later to Hugo's actual handling of his characters and his theme, Archer remarked that "Melodrama [in which category he places *Le Roi s'amuse*] is illogical and sometimes irrational tragedy. It subordinates character to situation, consistency to impressiveness. It aims at startling, not at convincing, and is little concerned with causes so long as it attains effects. Developments of character are beyond its province, its personages being all ready-made, and subject at most to revolutions of feeling. Necessity and law it replaces by coincidence and fatality, exactitude by exaggeration, subtlety by emphasis."

What is true of Hugo's drama is equally true of the opera libretto; one finds it hard to sympathise entirely with the misshapen thing of evil that is the Rigoletto of the opening of the work, even when his love for his daughter is thrown into the scales in his favour. Under the seductive influence of music, however, we are more charitably inclined towards him than we can be towards the Triboulet of Hugo; and anyhow opera audiences have never been as exacting psychologists as the students of dramatic literature are. Verdi himself was over head and ears in love with his subject. It was a drama, he wrote to one friend and another, with some terrific situations, full of vitality, variety and pathos. He rather loved violence in a story, for he aimed, he said, before everything at "passion." He did not mind very much whether people found his music "beautiful" or "ugly" so long as he felt it to be true to the character and the situation of the moment; why then should he shrink from trying to make "a repulsive and ridiculous hunchback" *sing* melodiously with the best of them? He was convinced that the Rigoletto subject was the best he had so far come upon in his search for an opera libretto.

3

After the unfriendly reception *Le Roi s'amuse* had had in France, Verdi and his librettist Francesco Piave expected a certain amount of trouble with the censorship and perhaps with the Italian public, but they were hardly prepared for all the difficulties that sprang up in their path. The Austrian censor jibbed, as high circles in Paris had done years before, at the stage presentation of no less a personage than a king as an out-and-out immoralist. Verdi offered to make simply a prince of him, but in the end had to reduce him to the rank of a mere sixteenth-century Italian duke. The very title of the opera stuck in the censor's maw. Verdi had wanted to entitle it *La Maledizione*, for was not the curse laid on the brutal, cynical jester by the wronged Monterone the very core of the tragedy? [1] They took curses very seriously in those days, and the censor feared that religious susceptibilities might be deeply wounded by seeing one of them in actual operation on the stage. Finally the opera was named after the hunchback himself, at first *Triboletto* (an Italianisation of Triboulet) then *Rigoletto*. The music was written in quite a short time, and the opera produced at the Fenice on the 11th January 1851 with enormous success.

Verdi has his gloomy drama well in hand from the beginning. The orchestra opens with the vital motif of the Curse in the solemn tones of the brass:

---

[1] As Hugo himself said in his polemic against his critics, "The real subject of the drama is *The Malediction of M. de Saint-Vallier.*"

1

Andante sostenuto ♩=66

It swells for a moment to fury, then subsides into a descending wailing figure of a type frequently employed by Verdi to express anguish, becomes its ominous self again for a few bars, and finally leaves us with an imposing gesture; thirty-five bars of slow music have sufficed to place us at the core of the tragedy.

The pace changes to allegro con brio as the curtain rises, showing the foremost of a series of splendid apartments in the palace of the young Duke of Mantua, with cavaliers and ladies passing to and fro, some talking, others dancing. A succession of lively tunes in the orchestra, which are repeated again and again, depicts the carefree gaiety of the company. Against this gay background the Duke enters from an inner room with Borsa, one of the gentlemen of his court, telling him complacently that soon he hopes to bring to a happy ending one of the latest of his amorous adventures—the pursuit of a maiden, as yet unknown to him, whom he has seen at her devotions in the church each day for the last three months, though his pursuit of her has so far brought him no further than the discovery that she lives in a remote quarter of the town, in a humble house that is visited every night by a man about whom the Duke has been able to learn nothing.

These two, we surmise already, are the court buffoon Rigoletto and his daughter Gilda. We hear, however, no more of them for some time, for the Duke has several other amorous affairs on his hands. In the well-known ballata "Questa o quella":

2

Allegretto ♩=80

Quest-a o quel-la per me pa-ri so-no, A quant' al——tre d'in-

tor—no—— d'in-tor-no mi ve——do.

he sings to Borsa of the delights of promiscuity in affairs of gallantry; to him, as to Don Giovanni, all women are attractive, and to pursue and take them is a law of his nature. At the court he is mainly interested at the moment in the Countess Ceprano, the wife of one of his courtiers; with her he now has a brief surreptitious colloquy, during which the lady's husband watches him suspiciously, while some of the other guests comment amusedly on the familiar situation. The brief furtive episode ends with the Duke taking the Countess out on his arm, while Rigoletto insults Ceprano with a word or two of mock sympathy. Then he turns to the courtiers with a cynical shrug of the shoulders: it is always thus with the Duke, he says, who spends his time between gaming, drinking and lovemaking—in this latest instance with Count Ceprano's wife—while the rest of them enjoy the fun. Some of the company dance a perigodino (a piquant dance in 6/8 time), and when this is over another courtier, Marullo, enters with a piece of news which the others swallow eagerly, the orchestra playing round the conversation with the lively tunes with which the opera had opened. The news is certainly startling: Marullo believes he has discovered that the ugly, deformed, misanthropic court buffoon secretly plays the gallant like the rest of them. The courtiers are highly diverted by this metamorphosis, as they express it, of the hunchback into a Cupid. But for the moment this new dramatic motif recedes into the background as the Duke re-enters with Rigoletto, whom he is consulting as to the best way of getting rid of the inconvenient Count Ceprano. The buffoon reveals his evil nature in almost the first words he utters: he advises the Duke to put Ceprano in prison, or, failing that, to exile him, or, if that is impracticable, to settle the matter once and for all by having him beheaded. The cynical advice is overheard by Ceprano and some of the other courtiers, who turn angrily on Rigoletto. The latter is complacently sure of his master's protection in whatever rascality he may devise for him, but the Duke, who evidently despises his servile minion as heartily as the others do, bids him not to be too sure of that. The long-smouldering hatred of the courtiers for the evil-natured buffoon finds spirited expression in a big ensemble in which they call for vengeance on him. The light-hearted Duke, however, who takes nothing seriously but his own pursuit of pleasure, manages in time to make them all forget their grievance against the jester.

The atmosphere of gaiety that has enveloped the drama until now is suddenly dissipated by the entry of an elderly nobleman, Count Monterone, who forces his way into the company in spite of the efforts of the servants to restrain him. With his entry we find ourselves at once under the shadow of the Curse (No. 1). The old man has come to vent a personal grievance: the Duke has abducted and outraged his daughter. Before the Duke can say a word, Rigoletto takes it on himself to impersonate him. To the accompaniment of various orchestral figures that are meant to suggest the tortuosities of his own evil soul, such as:

3

and

4

he insults the old man, who, turning from him contemptuously, warns the Duke that even if he sends him to the scaffold his curse will pursue him to the grave and beyond it. And in that curse he includes Rigoletto: "it was not well done, Duke," he declares, "to set your hound upon the dying lion; and as for you"—turning to Rigoletto—"viper that could mock the sorrow of an old man, my malediction be on you!" The buffoon recoils in horror; and in an agitated ensemble the Duke and the courtiers, half in fear, half in anger, warn Monterone of the consequences of his audacity. At a sign from the Duke the old Count is led out between two halberdiers, and the remainder of the company follow them.

4

The scene now changes to a deserted alley in which stands the humble home of Rigoletto, the retreat in which he tries to conceal the one being he loves, his daughter Gilda, from the world he despises and hates so bitterly. A wall runs round a small court-yard, to which a door in the wall gives access, while above it some arches support a verandah, which can be approached from a door on the first floor of the house. On the other side of the street is a high wall, over which we have a view of an angle of the Ceprano palace. It is now night.

Rigoletto comes in slowly, closely wrapped in a great cloak. A sombre bit of tone-painting in clarinet, bassoon and lower strings:

5

shows him stealthily and thoughtfully making his way through the darkness to his home. From his opening words it is evident that he is still brooding superstitiously over the recent events in the ducal palace: "that old man laid a curse on me!", he mutters:

6

(The operatic world of the first half of the nineteenth century attached great importance to curses, and, for some reason or other, particularly to those of a father. The curse of a mother, a sister, a brother, a son, a daughter or even an aunt never attained the same high level of dramatic potency; it was from a father's curse alone that the best horrific results could be obtained.)

Rigoletto has been followed at a little distance by someone who now draws level with him and accosts him—a sinister figure also wrapped in a cloak, from beneath which a long sword pro-jects. It is Sparafucile, by profession an assassin, and by operatic

convention a cavernous bass. Verdi limns him for us convincingly
in a sinister theme that winds its way slowly through the orchestra as if, like Sparafucile himself, it was cautiously feeling its way
in the uncanny dark:

7

To the accompaniment of this theme the pair dialogue for a
moment. The bravo—his name, he tells Rigoletto, is Sparafucile—
places his professional services at the disposal of this stranger
should he ever require them. Everyone, he suggests, has some rival
or other whom he would gladly see removed from his path. "How
much would you charge for a nobleman?" Rigoletto asks tentatively. "More, of course, than for a common man," is Sparafucile's
reply. His terms, he says, are reasonable—half down before the
murder, the balance after it. His methods are as safe as they are
simple: either he disposes of his victims quickly in the town, or
his lovely sister lures them to their conveniently secluded house,
where his good sword—which he draws for his interlocutor's in-
spection—does the deed smoothly in no time. But to his regret
Rigoletto declines his services for the present. Sparafucile informs
him that he is to be found in this neighbourhood every night
should his new friend have need of him; and the pair part company.

5

Left alone, the buffoon, considerably chastened by his recent
encounter with Monterone, makes, in a long recitativo accompa-
gnato, a bitter comparison of himself with the assassin who has
just left him: "I murder with my tongue and my laughter, he
with his sword!" Suddenly he recalls the Curse (No. 6), and he
breaks into a passionate lament over his unhappy lot in life.
Nature and men have between them made him base and vile,
deformed in soul as in body. Each day his young, handsome,
tyrannic master demands a new amusement from his buffoon, and

he is compelled to obey. How he despises and hates humanity in general and these courtiers in particular! "Come what may, I must laugh: the tears that are the solace of other men are denied me. If I am vile, it is you who have made me so." (For the first time in the opera he becomes sympathetic to us.) But here in his humble home, he continues while a gentle figure steals out timidly in the flute, he can generally be another man; tonight, however, he cannot rid his tortured mind of the curse that the old man had laid on him. "Is it an augury of woe?" he asks.

As he goes into the courtyard his daughter—who must be assumed by the spectator to be much younger and more prepossessing than the average prima donna player of the part—runs to meet him, and the whole character of the music changes: it is now all childlike joy:

8

as Gilda throws herself into the arms of this mysterious father whose name, even, she does not know; her mother she has never known. In mournful tones he tells her of that good woman who, deformed and poor though he was, had loved him and thrown in her lot with his; too soon death had taken her from him, leaving him only this dear child to console him in his loneliness. Gilda pours out her love for him in rather florid phrases:

9

Oh quan-to do-lor, quan-to do-lor! che spre—me-re—si a-ma-ro pian-to può?

for she is a coloratura soprano as well as an affectionate daughter. Once more he refuses to tell her who and what he is, but warns her that he has many enemies, some of whom fear him, while others curse him.

It is three months since they came to this house, Gilda reminds him, and all that time he has kept her in strict seclusion, for his constant fear is that some man or other, perhaps one of those whom he has derided and injured, will rob him of her. She assures him that she never goes into the town in his absence. Rigoletto calls out his servant, Giovanna, and passionately demands assurance from her that no one has ever observed him entering the house and that the door is always kept locked; and he begs her piteously to watch unceasingly over his child.

At the conclusion of this perhaps over-long scene Rigoletto opens the courtyard door and goes into the street for a last look round. As he does so the Duke slips into the courtyard, throws a purse to Giovanna with a gesture that commands silence, and conceals himself behind a high tree. Returning after this rather naïve piece of byplay Rigoletto asks the servant if anyone has ever followed his daughter on her way to and from the church, and is falsely assured that no one has. He bids Giovanna see that the door is opened to no one in his absence. "Not even to the Duke?", she asks. "To him least of all" is the reply. Meanwhile the Duke, from his place of concealment, has recognised Rigoletto, and from the buffoon's parting words to Gilda—"Good night, my child"—he makes the surprising discovery that she is his hireling's daughter. Gilda and Rigoletto wish each other a fond good night, she all affection, he in accents in which tenderness is shot with anxiety.

6

When he has left the scene Gilda reproaches Giovanna and herself for having concealed from her father that a young man has been in the habit of following her from church—a young man whom she confesses that she already almost loves. The worldly-minded servant points out that one so generous with his money as this stranger is perhaps noble birth; but Gilda, in simple words and music that contrast markedly with her former coloratura, vows that she would prefer a lover who is as poor as herself. On this cue the Duke, having dismissed Giovanna with a gesture, comes forward, throws himself at Gilda's feet, and declares his love; and she recognises him as the man she had first seen in the church. He bears down her maidenly resistance in a passionate aria:

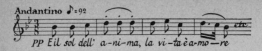

Andantino ♪=92

PP E il sol dell' a-ni-ma, la vi-ta è a-mo-re

to the later strains of which she contributes a florid counterpoint.
(Gilda is not consistently drawn throughout; Verdi's music for
her alternates between childlike simplicity and showy coloratura,
seldom achieving an organic unity of the two).

She longs to know his name, she tells him; and just as he is
informing her that he is Gualtier Maldé, and only a poor student,
Giovanna enters in great agitation, for she has heard footsteps
without. (They are those of Borsa and Ceprano.) Gilda fears
that her father has returned, and the Duke is hastily ushered
out *via* the house, his voice and that of Gilda joining in a final
feverish duet. Left alone, Gilda muses fondly upon the supposed
name of her lover, that is now so dear to her—"Dear name that
first awakened my heart to love": this is the famous "Caro nome"
aria, a remarkable combination of psychological expression and
vocal exhibitionism.

As she slowly makes her way from the verandah into the house
to a final rapturous sighing of her lover's name the prowling
courtiers enter stealthily, to phrases that unintentionally acquire
a somewhat comic air by their regular alternations of forte and
pianissimo:

11

Andante assai mosso

Rigoletto, still brooding on the Curse (No. 6), runs into them in
the dark, and they at once recognise him. The abduction scene
that follows was evidently taken by Verdi with the utmost
seriousness, but it is often undesignedly comic in its effect on the
spectator. Revealing themselves, in reply to Rigoletto's enquiries—
for he has not been able to identify them in the dark—as Marullo
and his court associates, they carry out their heartless jest at

the expense of the detested buffoon. Their design, they say, is to carry off Ceprano's wife, a project that at once appeals to the evil element in Rigoletto's nature. The problem will be, he says, to get admission to the Count's house, which stands on the other side of the road. Ceprano, whom the jester has not recognised, hands over his key, the crest on which Rigoletto manages to decipher with his fingers. He consents to being masked, like them, and without his knowing it he is blindfolded in addition; then he is allotted the task of holding the ladder while the conspirators climb the wall not into Ceprano's house, as he imagines, but into his own. (They, of course, are still under the impression that the girl in the jester's house is his inamorata.) We dimly see them entering the house, the chorus to which they accomplish their purpose once more bringing a disturbing note of the comic into the scene. Next we vaguely see them emerging from the house carrying a protesting Gilda calling distractedly on her father. Rigoletto apparently does not hear her, and this jest in the dark now begins to pall on him. Realising that he is blindfolded as well as masked he tears off the bandage, picks up a lantern which one of the conspirators has left behind him, and by its light recognises on the ground a scarf that had become detached from Gilda in her struggle with her captors. He runs wildly into the house, and comes out again dragging with him a bewildered Giovanna. At last the truth dawns on him. "The Curse! the Curse!" he cries despairingly, and falls down in a faint.

7

At the beginning of the second act, which is staged in an ante-chamber in the palace, we find the Duke, in great agitation of soul, lamenting the misfortune that had befallen him the night before—the loss of the girl who for the moment had become the guiding star of his life. Who were the abductors? Where had they taken her? They shall suffer for it when he discovers them! He has hardly concluded an invocation—one that sits none too convincingly on his lips—to this lost angel of purity when the courtiers, headed by Borsa, Marullo and Ceprano, break in upon him, bursting with the news that they had taken possession of the buffoon's lady-love. Mightily pleased with themselves, they tell the diverting story of the abduction in an ensemble that is of a type rather too frequent in the Verdi of the second period: the intention is half-serious, half-humorous, but the realisation somewhat ludicrous; one sees the circling handle of the barrel-organ rather too plainly:

12

The Duke, remembering Rigoletto's "Good night, my child!" of the night before, realises that his new love is not the mistress but the daughter of his jester; and when he learns that the girl is now actually in the palace he expresses his joy, and avers his willingness to give up his kingdom for her, in some lyrical strains that do not ring quite convincingly; while the courtiers, to music equally lacking in distinction, comment surprisedly, as well they might, that they have never seen their ruler in such a state as this before. Rigoletto enters, vainly endeavoring to conceal his anxiety under a façade of indifference:

13

His eyes wander about the room, probing for a clue to what has happened since the abduction of the night before. The courtiers play heartlessly with him. He lights upon a handkerchief at the back of the salon, but soon satisfies himself that it is not Gilda's. A page appears with a message that the Duchess would like to speak with her husband; and from the evasive replies of the courtiers Rigoletto gathers that his master, ostensibly out hunting, is in the palace but does not wish to be disturbed. The buffoon senses now that Gilda is somewhere in the palace, and throwing off the mask, he tells the courtiers that the girl they had carried off is his daughter, and passionately demands their help in finding her. They bar his exit from the room, and he breaks out into a savage denunciation of them and all they stand for: then his tone changes to one of heartfelt love for his child.

Before the others can say anything in reply Gilda bursts into the room in a state of wild agitation, throws herself despairingly into the arms of her father, and tells him that the Duke has dishonoured her. Rigoletto impetuously orders the courtiers out, declaring that even if his master himself should come now he would bar his entry. His fury cows them and they depart, muttering among themselves, leaving the stage free for a long duet in which Gilda tells her father of her first encounter with a stranger youth in the church:

of his intrusion upon her last night, proclaiming himself to be a poor student who loved her ardently, and of her abduction. In spite of the coloratura into which she cannot help breaking towards the end, her music is sincere and moving. Rigoletto becomes once more wholly sympathetic to us as he speaks of the pains he has been at to preserve her from the world's harm, but Gilda's tearful praise of his love is too liberally festooned with coloratura to impress the modern opera-goer as much as it was meant to do. "Thus," laments Rigoletto, "has the world about me changed in a single day!" He and she will leave this dreadful place at once, he assures her.

Just then Monterone passes across the stage, being conducted to prison by some halberdiers; he is accompanied in the orchestra by one of those volleying rhythmic figures, rising from pianissimo to a mighty fortissimo, which Verdi knew so well how to handle. A portrait of the Duke on the wall catches the old man's eye: he pauses before it and ejaculates, "So my curse was laid on you in vain! No thunderbolt has struck you down! You will live on, happy as before!" As the halberdiers take him out, Rigoletto springs forward with a cry of "No, old man! You shall be avenged! Vengeance, direst vengeance, is all I live for now! Heaven's thunderbolt shall strike through me!":

15

Allegro vivo ♩:138

Si, ven—det—ta, tre-men-da ven~det—ta

In vain does Gilda implore him to spare the wrongdoer for whom she already feels love; there is no room in Rigoletto's heart now for any thought but that of revenge. He hurries away, taking his daughter with him, and the curtain falls.

8

The third act shows us the fulfilment of Monterone's curse on the buffoon who had jibed at him in his moment of misery.

No information is vouchsafed to the spectator of what may have happened in the interval between the second and third acts, and for a little while no hint is afforded him why any of the characters should be just where they are when the curtain rises again. The scene is a deserted spot on the Mincio, a glimpse of whose waters we catch over a ruined parapet in the background. On the left of the stage stands a dilapidated two-storeyed house, the front of which has to be non-existent for operatic purposes, so that we see that the ground floor is a sort of inn, from which a rickety staircase leads up to a loft in which is a rough couch. This is evidently the secluded lair to which, Sparafucile had told Rigoletto in the first act, his sister was in the habit of decoying the men of whom the hired assassin had to dispose. When the curtain rises Sparafucile is seen sitting at a table in the lower room, polishing his belt. It is night.

To the accompaniment of some sombre preludial phrases in the subdued strings Rigoletto and Gilda come into sight on the road that runs by the side of the building. Their conversation (in recitative) runs thus:

Rigoletto: And you love him!
Gilda: Always.
Rigoletto: But I have given you time enough to cure yourself of that.
Gilda: I love him.
Rigoletto: Poor woman's heart! Ah, the base villain! But you shall be revenged on him, my Gilda.
Gilda: Have pity, father.

Rigoletto: But if you had proof that he is false to you, would you love him still?

Gilda: I do not know; but he adores me.

Rigoletto: He!

Gilda: Yes.

Rigoletto: Well then, observe.

    Leading her to the house he bids her look through a fissure in the wall.

Gilda: I see a man.

Rigoletto: Wait a while.

    The Duke appears in the inn, disguised as a cavalry officer.

Gilda: Oh, my father!

The spectator may reasonably feel that he is entitled to a little more explanation than this. Verdi and his librettist, however, scorn detailed elucidation; their sole concern is to get to grips at once with the main tragic action.[1]

Addressing Sparafucile, the Duke orders two things—a room and some wine. Sparafucile, scenting profitable business of the kind he likes, goes out, while Rigoletto remarks cynically to Gilda, "This is the way with him!" Left alone, the Duke sings his famous canzone, "La donna è mobile"—"Woman is as variable as a feather in the wind, false to the marrow, yet the man who does not love does not know what felicity is"; it is an expanded version of the famous dictum—"Souvent femme varie"—of King François the First of France, who has obviously sat as a model for the Duke of Mantua:

> *Souvent femme varie,*
> *Bien fol est qui s'y fie.*
> *Une femme souvent*
> *N'est qu'une plume au vent!*

9

At this point we must digress for a moment to throw a little more light on the situation than, as has been remarked above, Verdi and his librettist have done. In the opera no information is vouchsafed us as to anything that may have happened between acts two and three: and it is only after the third act has been running for a little time that we begin to understand just why

[1] On this point see *infra.*

Rigoletto and Gilda happen to be outside Sparafucile's inn when the curtain rises. For elucidation of it all we have to turn to the fourth act of Victor Hugo's play. There we discover, from the opening colloquy between the father (Triboulet) and the daughter (Blanche), that some time has elapsed and much has happened between the end of the third act and the beginning of the fourth. It appears that Blanche had settled down quite comfortably in the palace as the mistress of the King, with whom she had fallen deeply in love: only yesterday, we learn from her own lips, he had assured her once more that he adored her, and her present considered opinion of him is that he is an excellent King, brilliant and handsome. Triboulet had given her ample time to think it over and change her mind, but she had seen no reason to do so; and latterly she had thought that he too was now kindly disposed towards the King. She assures Triboulet, however, that her love for him is as great as ever, and that in fact she would be ready to lay down her life for either her father or her lover—a remark that becomes of considerable dramatic significance later.

Triboulet, however, declares that if he had seemed to have forgiven the King he had only been feigning: he is as resolved as ever on revenge. What would she say if she were to discover that her lover is deceiving her? he asks tentatively. She refuses to believe that this is possible. What would you say, he continues, if before your own eyes you had evidence of his perfidy? He bids her look through a crevice in the wall of the inn; and she sees the King, in the costume of a simple officer, entering from an inner room. It now becomes clear to us that Triboulet had already worked out with Saltabadil (Sparafucile) a plan for the murder of the King in the hut, the assassin's sister Maguelonne (Maddalena) being used as a decoy. A week ago, we and Blanche soon learn, Triboulet had taken the King to some hostelry or other where he had been introduced to Maguelonne; he had fallen in love with her at first sight, and agreed to an assignation with her at the miserable inn kept by her brother; and there he intends to spend the night with her.

While the scene of amorous ardour on the one side and coy refusal on the other is being played out inside the inn, Saltabadil has a brief conversation with Triboulet outside. "Your man is inside there," he says: "is he to live or die?" "Come back in a little while," replies Triboulet, and sends him away. Blanche, as in the opera, becomes the horrified witness of the long scene between the King and Maguelonne. When her father rejoins her she bids him, in a moment of bitter revulsion, to proceed with his plan for revenge. This rejoices him, but he will not disclose to her yet what his plan is; he merely tells her to hasten back to their house, dress herself as a man, take money and a horse,[1] and make with all speed to Évreux, where he will rejoin her the day after tomorrow: on no account is she to return to the inn, "for here something terrible is about to happen."

10

We can now return to the opera, from which, for clarity's sake, we had to digress at the point where, having dismissed Sparafucile with orders to prepare a room and bring him wine, the Duke launches his nonchalant "La donna è mobile." Sparafucile, adopting no doubt what is his regular technique on these occasions, returns with a flask of wine and a couple of glasses, then knocks at the ceiling twice with the hilt of his great sword, whereupon a handsome, smiling girl of gipsy aspect comes down the staircase. The Duke tries to embrace her, but she makes a coy pretence of eluding him. Sparafucile slips out of the house for a quick dialogue with Rigoletto: "Your man is inside there. Is he to live or die?" to which the hunchback replies, "I will return later, and the job can be finished then."

Verdi now gets fairly into his musical stride. In a gay conversational strain the Duke assures Maddalena that he has loved her ever since he first met her, and, having learned that it is here she lives, he has made bold to follow her. She fences with him dexterously—no doubt, she says, he has told the same tale already to many another woman. He goes so far as to promise to marry her, but she still declines to take him seriously. Their dialogue is heard by Gilda and Rigoletto outside, who comment on the situation each according to character. All is now set for the great quartet,

[1] The costume, he tells her, he has already had made expressly for her; she will find it in the chest near the portrait of her mother. The horse stands ready saddled. Triboulet, we see, has thought of everything; the plan for the murder of the King and the disposal of his body has evidently been worked out in careful detail with Saltabadil.

one of the marvels of the Italian opera stage. The core of it is a splendid continuous melody for the tenor—a declaration of his love for Maddalena—upon which each of the other three characters embroiders his or her reactions, Maddalena laughing it all off ironically, Gilda bemoaning her lover's perfidy and her own sad lot, and Rigoletto assuring her with grim persistence that she shall soon be avenged. Victor Hugo, when he heard the opera, commented wistfully on the advantages music sometimes has over poetry or prose, opera over spoken drama: what would the ordinary dramatist not give, he asked, to be able to make four people animated by different sentiments speak all at the same time, each in character, and each fully intelligible to the audience!

The superb ensemble over, Rigoletto bids the protesting Gilda return to their house, dress herself as a boy, and make for Verona, where he will rejoin her on the morrow. Inside the house the Duke and Maddalena are still laughing and drinking. Sparafucile returns, and in a scene of sinister orchestral suggestion Rigoletto pays the bravo, as arranged, half his money in advance, the remainder to follow when the deed is done. He will return, he says, at midnight. Sparafucile assures him that there is no need for that—he himself will throw the body into the river; but Rigoletto insists on having that pleasure himself. "Who is the victim?" Sparafucile asks. "His name," replies the buffoon, "is Crime, and mine, Punishment." With that he leaves his confederate, going off in the night alone. Within the house the ardent Duke would press matters to their logical conclusion with Maddalena, but she fends the prospective victim off with the warning that her brother is coming.

11

She remarks to him that a storm is brewing; thunder and lightning, indeed, roar and flash in the orchestra, while the soughing of the wind is suggested by a chorus of tenors and basses behind the scenes, singing with closed lips a phrase:

16

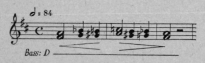

which will be employed frequently later to convey the sense of storm in the air all the while the human tragedy is working itself out. As the moment for the murder approaches, Maddalena feels a pang of pity for this handsome young gallant and—quite unprofessional conduct on her part—urges him to leave. He refuses to do so in such a torrent of rain as is now falling, whereupon Sparafucile obligingly places the upper room at his disposal until the storm shall have died down. The Duke, who is very tired, accepts the ominous offer, and soon we see him in the upper room divesting himself of his hat and sword and singing a phrase or two of his "La donna è mobile" before sleep overcomes him. Thither Maddalena goes and contemplates him pityingly, a brief colloquy with her brother having convinced her that the ruffian is inexorably bent on earning the money he has been promised for the murder.

Gilda's love and pity for the Duke have made her disobey, in part, her father's orders. Instead of going to Verona she has returned, now in male costume, booted and spurred, and once more, as the storm rages in the orchestra and in the choral figure, with closed lips, seen in example No. 16, we see her again peering through the fissure. She sees Sparafucile seated drinking, and Maddalena returning to the lower floor and placing the Duke's sword on the table: Gilda also hears her pleading with her brother for the life of this agreeable young man, handsome, as she says, as Apollo, who apparently loves her and with whom she is now in love. Sparafucile's only reply to this is to throw a sack at her and bid her mend it; it will do excellently, he says, for her Apollo, who, after he has had his throat cut, will find his grave in the river.

Maddalena continues her pleadings and suggests an alternative plan. Her brother, she reminds him, has already received ten pieces of silver; why not kill the hunchback, then, and so secure the remaining ten while sparing the life of the stranger? This kindles Sparafucile's anger; his professional pride is hurt, his professional honour impugned. Does she take him for a thief, he asks her reproachfully, a mere bandit? When has she known him to betray a client's trust? The hunchback is paying him, and it is the job entrusted to him by the hunchback that he means to do. Maddalena makes to run up the stairs to warn the victim, an âct which draws an approving comment from the listening Gilda outside. Sparafucile begins to weaken; while still reluctant not to keep the money he already has and earn the remainder in a way of which his conscience can approve, he now consents to a compromise—if someone else happens to come to the inn before midnight he shall die for the young Apollo, and his body be palmed off on the hunchback:

17

Se pria ch'ab-bia il mez-zo la not-te toc-ca-to

But who is likely to come on such a night as this? Maddalena asks distractedly; and the voices unite in a short tense trio, with Gilda's voice soaring above the other two in a wild appeal to heaven for pity:

18

Allegro

ff Oh —— cie — lo! pie —— tà!

Maddalena, now in tears, is not consoled by her brother's reminder that they have only half an hour before them. With No. 16 still wailing in the orchestra a clock strikes: the sands are running out. Gilda's resolution has already been half-taken. Touched by the pity that even this woman in the inn seems to feel for the destined victim—for Maddalena has again implored her brother piteously to wait a little longer—she decides to offer herself up as a sacrifice.

As the storm rises to its height she knocks twice at the door of the inn, to the great astonishment of the couple inside. In answer to Sparafucile's cry of "Who's there?" she declares herself to be a beggar seeking shelter for the night. Another trio follows, launched by Maddalena to the strain of No. 17: feverishly she exhorts her brother to do at once the deed that shall spare the life of the gallant, while Gilda once more appeals frantically to heaven as in our No. 18. The storm in the orchestra rises to its height as Gilda, in response to Sparafucile's invitation, enters the hut, where he is waiting for her behind the door with a raised dagger. Darkness closes in as the bravo shuts the door, and the rest is left to our imagination.

12

For a little while after, the storm continues to rage in the orchestra, but it begins to abate as Rigoletto appears outside the inn, closely wrapped in a cloak. The gateway, he sees, is still fastened, so presumably the murder has not yet been done. But he can wait, he says, and he savours voluptuously the completeness of his coming revenge on his master and on the world that has so long misused him. He knocks at the door, and Sparafucile appears, dragging a sack. A hurried colloquy ensues: Rigoletto, having discharged the remainder of his debt, will not allow the assassin to throw the body into the river; that last exquisite satisfaction he reserves for himself. Sparafucile directs him to a spot where the river is deeper, bids him good night, and re-enters the inn.

Rigoletto places his foot on the sack and revels in his triumph; it is the Duke, without a doubt, for he can feel his spurs! He invokes the courtiers to behold the victory of the poor buffoon over the powerful prince who had lorded it over him so long. And now for the river! But just as he is about to drag the sack away the voice of the Duke is heard, singing once again his "La donna è mobile" as he crosses the stage at the back.[1] As the song dies away in the distance Rigoletto realises that the Fates have played their last and cruellest trick on him. But whose, then, is the body before him? Frenziedly he tears the sack open and discovers the still-

---

[1] Some producers show him accompanied by Maddalena. This is quite nonsensical. In Hugo everything is perfectly lucid. Some time has elapsed between the murder of Blanche and the scene of Triboulet with the body, and at the climactic moment, just as the buffoon is about to throw it into the Seine, we get the following stage directions; "just as he places the sack on the parapet the lower door of the inn is cautiously opened. Maguelonne comes out, looks anxiously round her, makes a gesture signifying that there is no one about, goes into the inn again, and returns in a moment with the King, to whom she explains by signs that the coast is clear for his departure. She re-enters the inn and closes the door, while the King makes his way across the strand in the direction she has indicated." Triboulet is about to tip the sack into the Seine when he hears the King, at the back of the stage, singing his "Souvent femme varie."

living Gilda, who has only just strength enough to tell her broken-hearted father how she had deceived him and died to save the man she loved too much. She is going to rejoin her mother in heaven, she says:

19

Andante ♩=66

Las-sù in cie — lo, vi-ci-na al-la ma-dre

where they will pray for him together and wait for him. She dies, and Rigoletto throws himself in grief and despair upon her body, with a wild cry of "Gilda! Gilda! Dead! The Curse is fulfilled!"

Falstaff

GIUSEPPE VERDI [1813–1901]

PRINCIPAL CHARACTERS

FALSTAFF	*Baritone*
FENTON	*Tenor*
FORD	*Baritone*
DR. CAIUS	*Tenor*
BARDOLPH	*Tenor*
PISTOL	*Bass*
MISTRESS FORD	*Soprano*
ANNE FORD	*Soprano*
MISTRESS PAGE	*Mezzo-soprano*
MISTRESS QUICKLY	*Mezzo-soprano*

1

NEVER what one would call the sunniest of men, Verdi became decidedly gloomy in his last years. As he looked back on his life, he said in 1895, he could see little more than an immense number of notes, and unfortunately he had his doubts whether the notes were worth very much. This was merely the exaggerated self-criticism of a sincere and modest artist. *Otello,* produced in 1887, when Verdi was in his seventy-fourth year, would have been an honourable enough ending to the career of any composer. But the old warrior was not finished even yet. Six years after *Otello* came *Falstaff;* and one of the most serious and seemingly least humorous of men bade farewell to the world of art with a comedy of a light-fingeredness unique in that or any other epoch. And after *Falstaff* the grand old man had still eight years to live.

Held in universal admiration as it is among musicians, *Falstaff* does not appear in the general operatic repertory as often as one could desire. The exact reason for this is not easy to discover. It may be that its very lightness of touch and its delicacy of texture go against it in our large opera houses, with their too-long intervals between the acts: the sparkle, the aroma of each of the first two acts is lost by the time the audience reassembles for the next. It has to be admitted, too, that the final scene as a whole is neither musically nor dramatically on the same level as the other two. For here Falstaff, who has so far been the life and soul of the work, passes, at times, almost unobserved; and a *Falstaff* scene without Falstaff is as lame as *Hamlet* without the prince. A lover of the delightful work may perhaps be allowed to suggest that as Verdi's librettist Boïto has dealt so freely in the first two acts with the Shakespearean — or pseudo-Shakespearean —material presented to him by tradition, he might have exercised his rights in this respect still more fully, and invented an ending of his own for the opera. " Reverence for Shakespeare " is all very well in its way; but what if we are asked to fall down on our knees to something that is not Shakespeare at all?

Neither Boïto nor Verdi could be expected to be *au fait* with even the Shakespeare scholarship of their own and an earlier day; still less could they have anticipated that of a generation or two after their time. Perhaps they did not even know that *The Merry Wives of Windsor* has always been a stumbling-block to Shakespeare scholars. The older perplexity with regard to the work, and the vague older doubts about it, were frankly expressed by Professor A. C. Bradley in 1909: " Falstaff," he said, " was degraded by Shakespeare himself ":

" The original character is to be found alive in the two parts of *Henry IV*, dead in *Henry V*, and nowhere else. But not very long after these plays were composed, Shakespeare wrote, and he afterwards revised, the very entertaining piece called *The Merry Wives of Windsor*. Perhaps his company wanted a new play on a sudden; or perhaps, as one would rather believe, the tradition may be true that Queen Elizabeth, delighted with the Falstaff scenes of *Henry IV*, expressed a wish to see the hero of them again, and to see him in love. Now it was no more possible for Shakespeare to show his wn Falstaff in love than to turn twice two into five. But he could rite in haste . . . a comedy or a farce differing from all his other lays in this, that its scene is laid in English middle-class life, and aat it is prosaic almost to the end. And among the characters he ould introduce a disreputable fat old Knight with attendants, and ould call them Falstaff, Bardolph, Pistol and Nym. And he could epresent this Knight assailing, for financial purposes, the virtue of wo matrons, and in the event baffled, duped, treated like dirty nen, beaten, burnt, pricked, mocked, insulted, and, worst of all, epentant and didactic. It is horrible. It is almost enough to convince one that Shakespeare himself could sanction the parody of Ophelia in *The Two Noble Kinsmen*."

All which means, in somewhat franker language, that Professor Bradley, like a great many other people before and after him, thought, although he did not like to say so outright, that *The Merry Wives of Windsor* is for the most part so poor a piece of work that it is difficult to believe that Shakespeare in his prime could have been responsible for very much of it. Nor is this the only difficulty in connection with the play. No one has ever yet succeeded, for example, in bringing sense into the chronology of it, particularly where the ages of Falstaff and Mrs. Quickly are concerned. Other incongruities abound.

The truth of the matter is in all probability that set forth by the late Mr. John M. Robertson in a paper on *The Problem of 'The Merry Wives of Windsor,'* read before the Shakespeare Association in 1917. Although the legend that the Queen, having been delighted with the robust humours of *Henry IV*, said that she would now like to "see Falstaff in love" is not met with earlier than the eighteenth century, it need not be summarily rejected. The Queen may quite possibly have been referring to an *already existing* play in which the fat Knight *was* shown in love — an earlier form, in fact, of the play which now figures among the works of Shakespeare as *The Merry Wives of Windsor*. This play, in which, as Mr. Robertson shows by means of verbal fingerprints, Chapman in all probability had a hand, was apparently touched up here and there by Shakespeare about 1593: it is as certain that some strokes of humour and certain felicities of style in it are from his hand as it is that he was never capable of turning out such poor stuff as much

of it unquestionably is, and more especially of grinding out suc
wretched blank verse as that of the final act.[1]

Now Boïto never hesitates to play fast and loose with the tissu
of *The Merry Wives of Windsor* when it suits his purpose to do s
He resorts, whenever it suits him, to the character-drawing and th
actual words of *Henry IV*. He transfers to Dr. Caius, in the openin
scene, the episode of the robbery which in the play is associate
with Justice Shallow. He abolishes Page. He dispenses altogethe
with Slender, making Fenton the only lover of Anne, apart fror
Caius. He makes Anne herself (Nanetta) not Page's daughter bu
Ford's. He reduces the number of duperies of which Falstaff is th
victim at the hands of the wives and Mrs. Quickly; and so on. A
other liberty or two on the top of all these would have made n
difference, and there are two in particular which one could wis
Boïto had taken. The first would have been to devise a better enc
ing to the opera than is afforded by the fifth act of the play. Th
other would have been to reduce the age of Falstaff.

In the play, as Bradley mournfully pointed out, Falstaff is nc
only treated most despitefully but hatefully: particular malice
imported into some of the references to the advanced age of th
would-be seducer — "Old, cold, withered, and of intolerable er
trails" is one of Page's descriptions of him, while Mrs. Page wor
ders that "one that is well-nigh worn to pieces with age" shoul
try "to show himself a young gallant." But, as Mr. Robertson wa
the first to show, of the six references to Falstaff's age in the firs
Folio, from which our present text is derived, five are "entirel
absent" from the earlier Quarto, which represents, apparently, th
play in something like its original form. (In the Folio it is nearl
double the length of the version in the Quarto). In the latter, Fa
staff himself asks "Ah, Jack, will thy old body yet hold out?"; bu
"old" is no more necessarily to be taken in its literal sense her
than in a thousand other uses of the word in colloquial speech; an
whereas the Folio makes him say "I'll make more of thy *old* bod
than I have done," in the Quarto the corresponding passage run
"*Good* body, I thank thee, and I'll make more of thee than I ha
done." No stage performance of the play ever takes the text quit
literally in this matter of Falstaff's age; that is to say, it stops shoi

[1] For further light on these and other points the reader who is intereste
in the subject must be referred to Mr. Robertson's paper.

of making the man "old, cold, withered" and "well-nigh worn to pieces," so as not to alienate the sympathies of the audience. There seems no good reason why producers should not go a step further and reduce the Knight's age still more: he can be made as fat and as fatuous as you please, of course. From every point of view it is a pity that Boïto did not adopt a still freer attitude towards "Shakespeare" than he has actually done.

Verdi's correspondence shows that he embarked with a certain reluctance on this final opera of his, fearing that the labour of it would put too great a strain on the health of a man of his advanced age. He seems, however, to have allowed himself to be persuaded by Boïto somewhere about 1889; and by the summer of 1892 the score was finished.

The first performance was given at the Scala, Milan, on the 9th February 1893, under the conductorship of Mascheroni. Maurel was the Falstaff. With this gentleman Verdi had had a little trouble. True to the traditions of his type, the famous singer had tried to secure for himself in advance the sole right to play Falstaff for a certain number of performances. Verdi refused: his view was that in an opera of his no one part, and therefore no one singer, was more important than another. Couldn't the man see, he wrote to his publisher, Giulio Ricordi, that all he had to do was to play the part in superior style and it would be his by artistic right, without their needing to offend other people? He resented the intrusion of Madame Maurel into the matter: "I simply ask to be allowed to be owner of my own belongings, without ruining anyone. Let me add that if I were confronted with the alternatives — 'Either accept these conditions or burn your score' — I would at once get the fire ready and myself throw on it Falstaff and·his paunch." Fortunately it never came to that!

2

The curtain rises on a room in the "Garter" Inn at Windsor. That it is occupied by Falstaff is indicated by the number of bottles on the table; and apparently he has not long finished breakfast. At the moment when he comes into view he has Bardolph and Pistol for company. He himself is sealing a couple of letters: that done, he stretches his limbs luxuriously and drinks deeply, to the accompaniment of a bustling orchestral phrase:

1 *Allegro vivace* ♩ = 116

coll' 8va

which runs through a good deal of the present scene.

Falstaff orders the landlord to bring him another bottle of sherry, taking no notice for a little while of Dr. Caius, who comes in in a great hurry and angrily accuses the Knight of having broken into his house, beaten his servants, and ridden his bay mare. Falstaff calmly admits it all, but advises Caius not to make a public fuss about it unless he wants to become a public joke. Caius then turns on the other two. He had drunk copiously, it appears, with Bardolph and Pistol the night before, and when he was fuddled they had picked his pocket. Each of the rascals solemnly denies that he ever did anything of the kind: Bardolph opines that Dr. Caius must have dreamt it while he was drunk, and Pistol threatens personal violence. "You see," says Falstaff judicially, "the charge has been denied; depart in peace." Poor Caius swears, in the words of Slender in *The Merry Wives*, "I'll ne'er be drunk whilst I live again, but in honest, civil, godly company . . . if I be drunk, I'll be drunk with those that have the fear of God, and not with drunken knaves" — which looks, by the way, like a real Shakespearean touch. Even Verdi has found it impossible to convey the rich tang of the English words in music.

Bardolph and Pistol sing "Amen" to the pious sentiment, making quite a little canon of it in the approved ecclesiastical style; as they do so they ceremoniously escort Caius to the door, Pistol beating time, — a delicious burlesque effect that would be impossible, of course, in any other art but music. Falstaff, seemingly, does not think much either of their melody or their performance of it — one gathers that he imagines them to be unable to keep time, whereas what Bardolph is really doing is to take up and imitate Pistol's phrase at a half-bar's distance.[2] Falstaff bids the precious

[2] The idea and the text here are an ingenious embroidery on the original on Boïto's part. In *The Merry Wives*, Falstaff merely says of the stupid Bardolph,

pair cease their antiphon, as he calls it, and gives them the sage advice, equally good in music and in their particular profession, if they must steal[3] to steal gracefully and *a tempo*: as it is, they are mere crude artisans, not artists, he tells them contemptuously.

Having run his eye over the host's bill, he is shocked to discover how little there is in his purse to meet outgoings such as his. It is true that Bardolph saves him something, for that monstrous red nose of his serves the three of them as a lantern when they make their way from tavern to tavern at night:

So che se andiam, la not-te, di ta-ver - na in ta-ver-na

But what Falstaff economises in this way on lamp oil he spends, and more, on wine to light up this human beacon. And this has been going on now for thirty years! The pair of them are ruining him. The thought is so grievous that he has to call to the host for another bottle; for as to himself, were Falstaff to lose anything of that generous bulk of his he would no longer be Falstaff. "This is my kingdom," he says, stroking his paunch, "and I mean to extend it." But for that and other things money is necessary, and for the raising of money he has worked out a nice little scheme. In Windsor, it appears, there is a rich burgher of the name of Ford, rich in gold and fortunate in a handsome wife — what eyes! what a neck! what lips! he rhapsodises, to a suave, caressing phrase in the orchestra:

"I am glad I am so acquit of this tinder-box: his thefts were too open; his filching was like an unskilful singer; he kept not time"; to which Nym adds, "The good humour is to steal at a minute's rest." Boïto, being himself a musician, saw the opportunity this gave him and Verdi to make Bardolph and Pistol sing canonically "at [metaphorically] a minute's rest," and to make Falstaff imagine that they do so because they "cannot keep time."

[3] A neat allusion to *tempo rubato*.

And this pearl among women, this Alice, had set his heart on fire by smiling at him as he passed her window — yes, at him, with his fine figure, his ample chest, his well-turned leg; and her heart had so melted within her at the sight of him that she seemed to be sighing "I am Sir John Falstaff's." (He imitates the female voice in falsetto). But this is not all. There is another lady of Windsor, he tells his dazzled entourage — one Margaret Page (known to her intimates as Meg, Pistol interjects), who also has succumbed to his charm. Each of these desirable beauties has the key of her husband's money-box; and together they shall be his Golconda, his Gold Coast!

He gives Bardolph and Pistol the glowing letters he had just finished writing when the curtain rose, and bids them deliver them to Mistress Alice and Mistress Meg, whose virtue he means to put to the test forthwith. The myrmidons refuse, Bardolph pleading his honour, and Pistol swearing that he is a soldier, not a Pandarus. Falstaff thereupon sends the notes by little Robin, the page-boy of the hostelry, turns contemptuously on Bardolph and Pistol, and gives them an eloquent lecture on the subject of honour. Has not he himself to pawn his own occasionally? And yet these evil-looking, evil-smelling bundles of dirty rags, these pole-cats dare to prate about *their* honour! and he launches into an impressive catalogue of the things that honour cannot do, on the lines of the famous " catechism " in *I Henry IV*, Act V, — " Can honour set to a leg? no: or an arm? no: " and so on — which Boïto has paraphrased admirably and Verdi set incomparably. As for Bardolph and Pistol, the honest Knight has had enough of such rascals. He takes a broom and chases them round the stage and finally out of the room.

3

The second scene of this act shows us the exterior of Ford's house. The short and lively orchestral preamble:

introduces us to the two merry wives, Mistress Ford's daughter Anne, and Mrs. Quickly. Each of the wives has a letter which she is dying to show the other. Both missives prove to be from the same gallant wooer, the noble Knight Sir John Falstaff; and when the ladies come to compare them they find, to their vast amusement, that they are couched in identical terms; the burden of them is that Alice (or Meg as the case may be) is a gay gossip and Falstaff a merry fellow, and together they would make an ideal pair. The letters culminate in a grandiose lyrical outburst on the part of the amorous knight — " Let your face shed its refulgent rays on me like a star in the immensity of the night ":

E il vi - so tu - o su me ri-splen-de - rà

The four women make merry over the fat old fool in a lively, light-fingered quartet.

As they leave the stage — though they are still visible occasionally among the trees — Ford, Caius, Bardolph, Pistol and Fenton enter. Falstaff's quondam henchmen have been hinting to Ford that his domestic security is in danger; and being of a jealous nature he takes the suggestion seriously. Fenton does not like Sir John, Dr. Caius has grievances of his own against him, and Bardolph and Pistol are out for revenge for the indignity recently inflicted on them; so trouble seems to be blowing up for Falstaff from every quarter. They all express their feelings about him simultaneously in a quintet which every now and then becomes a nonet through the addition of the chatter of the women. The ensemble is most skilfully managed by Boïto, and Verdi's tripping music is a joy even if we do not understand a word of what is being said. But we enjoy the whole thing still more when we do understand, and the only way to do that is to get thoroughly familiar with the words apart from the music; for as the characters are all saying different things at the same time it is rarely possible for the listener to get the sense of a single sentence. Poor Ford seems to be in the same difficulty himself, for he complains that while the men talking to him are four, he is only one; and he wishes he could make up his mind which of the four to listen to — " If you would only speak one at a time," he remarks plaintively, " I might be able to hear you."

At last Pistol, speaking solo, makes it clear to him that Falstaff, meditating an attack on the virtue of Mistress Ford, has already written her a letter, of which he, Pistol, has nobly refused to be the bearer. Ford resolves to keep an eye on his wife. The women return for a moment, still cackling about the plan for Falstaff's discomfiture which they have evolved among themselves; then all leave the stage except Fenton and Anne, who seize the opportunity to sing a tender little love duet:

Lab-bra di   fo - co! Lab-bra di   fio - re!

Their love-making, charming as it is in its way, is perhaps more Boïtian and Verdian than Shakespearean; but that, of course, is equally true of many other things in the opera.

As the older women are seen approaching, Fenton hides among the trees. The two wives and Mrs. Quickly enter, and, to appropriately fussy music, begin to elaborate their scheme for dealing with Falstaff. It is decided that Mrs. Quickly shall take him a letter from Alice, making an assignation with him at her house. The three women are then shuffled off the stage on the rather clumsy pretext that they catch sight of someone spying on them among the trees, the truth being that the librettist and the composer want the stage free once more for a continuation of the duet between Fenton and Anne. The pair of love-birds bill and coo as prettily as before; then they too run off as they see someone approaching.

It is Ford, who is followed by Caius, Bardolph and Pistol; Fenton also insinuates himself among them. It is arranged that Falstaff's two former companions shall introduce Ford to him under another name; and as this is an opera, and we are now nearing the end of the act, the women are brought in to combine with the men in a delightful ensemble on the subject of Falstaff and what is coming to him before long. Here, as elsewhere, the women and the men preserve their own group-individualities within the frame of the choral texture as a whole, while Fenton, who can never think of anyone but Anne — and besides is a tenor — takes his own melodic course independently of the others. The men having left the stage, the women have a last chuckle among themselves over the fun in prospect, rolling over their tongues delightedly the quotation from Falstaff's amorous letter quoted as our No. 5.

4

The setting of the second act is once more the interior of the "Garter." Falstaff's porcine bulk is stretched out in an armchair: he has finished breakfast and is now drinking sack. Bardolph and Pistol stand before him, professing penitence, begging forgiveness, and beating their breasts in unison every now and then. The Knight regards them both with lofty indifference until Bardolph announces that a lady desires to see him. It is Mrs. Quickly. She approaches Falstaff with a phrase of mock humility that is one of the gems of the opera: it is a veritable genuflection in music:

After the exchange of many courtesies between them, she tells the "great seducer," as she calls him, that she comes from Mistress Alice Ford, who is crazy with love for him. Alice thanks him for his letter, and wishes him to know that her husband is always away from home between two o'clock and three:

He smacks his thick lips over this "dalle due alle tre" as he fatuously repeats it. But he has no sooner assured her that he will be there at the right time than Mrs. Quickly tells him that she has another message for him: the beautiful Mistress Page, an angel if ever there was one, has also succumbed to his charms, though unfortunately *her* husband is seldom away from home. The Knight, preening himself monstrously, dismisses the messenger with a reward, and breaks out into a song of triumph to an Italian version of the monologue in *The Merry Wives* — "Say'st thou so, old Jack? go thy ways; I'll make more of thy old body than I have done. . . . Good body, I thank thee." The scoring of the soliloquy admirably underlines the grossness of the fat fellow's self-satisfaction.

Bardolph now introduces Ford, under the name of Brook (in the Italian, Fontana). He commends himself to Falstaff straight away by his generosity in the matter of wine. He is rich, he says, and fond of pleasure, and he has come to solicit Sir John's help in a certain matter. Bardolph and Pistol, who are enjoying the joke, having been sent out, Brook offers Falstaff a bag of gold to help him win one Mistress Ford, of Windsor. He has squandered large sums on her, it appears, but alas, her virtue seems impregnable. He places his last hope in the diplomacy of a gentleman so distinguished, so gallant, so courtly, as Sir John Falstaff. The Knight promises him complete success, for he himself happens to stand high in the favour of this Mistress Ford, who only that morning had sent him word that her lout of a husband is always out between two and three. Master Brook has come to the right quarter for assistance; he, Falstaff, will see to it that this poor Brook is treated as he deserves.

In high exultation he goes out to dress himself, taking care not to leave the bag of gold behind him. In his absence Ford indulges in a long and passionate monologue, the subject of which is the faithlessness of women. He has just finished swearing that he will have revenge on Falstaff also when the latter returns, dressed in his best, to take a walk with Brook. The short scene that follows is perhaps the opera's high water mark of musical grace and wit. The pair ceremoniously yield each other the precedence for some time, but finally solve their problem by going through the door arm in arm, the orchestra giving out the while the theme of Falstaff's self-satisfaction ("Say'st thou so, old Jack? . . . I'll make more of thy old body than I have done. . . ."). A neater "curtain" has never been devised in comedy. Humpty-Dumpty is on the top of the wall; but the great fall is coming.

5

The next scene is played in Ford's house: we see a large room with three doors, two staircases, a large cupboard, a screen, etc.

Alice and Meg are in conversation, the subject, of course, being Falstaff. Mrs. Quickly and Anne enter: the latter, whose thoughts run on her hopeless love for Fenton, stands sadly apart from the others. Mrs. Quickly tells delightedly the story of her successful mission to Falstaff, mimicking her own hypocritical humility and the pomposity and condescending courtesy of the over-blown amorist. The scheme has succeeded to perfection; Falstaff will soon be there. At Alice's order, two serving-men bring in a huge buck basket full of dirty linen. The room in general is arranged for the reception of the chief actor in the coming comedy, the women keeping up a gay running commentary all the time:

Ga-je co-ma-ri di Vind-sor! è l'o - - ra!

Then, as Falstaff is seen from the window to be approaching, Mrs. Quickly, Meg and Anne hurry out.

When the Knight enters it is to find the love-lorn Alice pensively striking chords on her lute. He makes love to her in the most grotesque fashion, wishing that Ford were in the next world so that he might lay at her feet his ancient name and title. She responds simperingly that she has no taste for riches or splendours, to which he replies with the famous description of himself as he once was, the slender page of the Duke of Norfolk:

Quand' e - ro pag - gio del Du - ca di Nor -
folck, e - ro sot - ti - le, sot - ti - le

The precise bearing of this little monologue on the action is not quite clear; but as it gives Verdi a pretext for writing a couple of pages of his most delicate music we need not be too critical as to the way in which the episode is spatchcocked into the general tissue of the scene. But the last thing, surely, that a grossly corpulent and vain lover would do would be to add to the handicap of his fatness by describing to the lady he is trying to seduce how slender he was in the days *before* she knew him.

The dialogue is broken in upon by Mrs. Quickly, who announces that Mistress Page, who has arrived in great agitation, wants to speak with Mistress Ford. Falstaff hides behind the screen, where he hears, when Meg enters, just what he is intended to hear — that the jealous Ford is hot on the track of Alice's lover, whom he believes to be now in his house. Soon Ford comes in with Caius, Fenton, Bardolph and Pistol. The hunt is up. Some of the men search the room, others run into the corridors to cut off his retreat. Ford, who is beside himself with rage, after hurling an insult or two at his wife begins to throw the linen out of the basket. But Falstaff is not there, nor, apparently, anywhere else in the house; for no one thinks of looking behind the screen which Mrs. Ford has folded round him. He emerges when the coast seems to be clear, and the three older women stow him into the basket; while they are doing so, Anne and Fenton steal behind the screen for a bit of love-making.

The men return, and the search for Falstaff is resumed more frantically than before, and with an even greater abundance of comic touches. At last a suspicious sound from behind the screen is heard. It is only Anne and Fenton kissing; but the hunters think they have run their quarry to earth at last. While they are gathering stealthily round the screen, the women pile the clothes on to the protesting Falstaff, who looks like being stifled. Behind the screen the sound of billing and cooing increases: obviously it comes from Falstaff and Alice! The hunters are in no great hurry to pounce on their prey, for first of all they have to build up an animated musical ensemble. At long last, after a " one, two, three " from Ford, the screen is thrown down, only to disclose the embarrassed young couple. Ford rails at them both, swearing that they shall never marry; and at a fresh view-hallo from Bardolph, the men, with the exception of Fenton, who has already left the stage with Anne, run up one of the staircases. While they are following up this false alarm, Anne returns with four menservants, who, at an order from Alice, hoist the basket on their shoulders and heave it out of the window into the shallow river, just as

Ford and the others return. Shaking with laughter, Alice takes her husband to the window and shows him a spectacle that ought to rejoice his heart.

6

At the opening of the third act we see a very disillusioned Falstaff sitting meditating outside the " Garter." It is now evening. He intones his immortal comment on the wickedness of a world that can treat a good man as he has just been treated — pushed into a basket stuffed with foul linen and flung into the river like an unwanted kitten or puppy. Fortunately his roundness and cork-like substance had made it impossible for him to sink; otherwise the world would now be lamenting the passing of one of the best of men. He takes a deep draught of sack to dilute the Thames water he has swallowed. Wine is good, he muses; and as his spirits begin to revive we are treated to one of the most brilliant effects in the whole score — an orchestral trill that commences with the utmost quietness and gradually extends to a *fortissimo* in the whole orchestra; we seem positively to see the new life within the man rising from a faint trickle to a mighty flood.

Mrs. Quickly enters, greeting Falstaff once more with the hypo-critical No. 7. At first he sends her and her beautiful Mistress Alice to the devil: he has suffered enough on her account, he says. While he is fuming in this fashion, Alice, Meg, Ford, Anne, Caius and Fenton emerge from behind a house on the left, and, alternately peering out and hiding themselves, listen to the conversation that follows. Mrs. Quickly begs Falstaff to believe that Alice was not to blame for the regrettable little incident with the basket. She is, in fact, most unhappy about it: and the old go-between gives Falstaff a letter from her, making an assignation with him by Herne's Oak in Windsor Park at midnight. He is to disguise him-self as the Black Huntsman. (There seems to have been a tradition in Shakespeare's day that a certain Herne, one of the keepers of the royal Park, had hanged himself on an oak, which was con-sequently haunted by his ghost). Falstaff takes Mrs. Quickly into the inn, to talk the matter over in quiet; and the group outside naturally pounce on this opportunity to come into the open and settle, in the audience's hearing, the details of the new plot against Falstaff. Anne, dressed in white, is to be the Queen of the Fairies;

Meg, in green, will be a wo⸱ ʼland nymph, and Mrs. Quickly a goblin; while Alice will be in charge of a number of children made up as sprites and imps, who will gather round Falstaff and plague him:

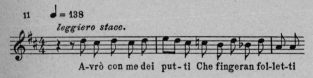

until, in due time, all the conspirators reveal themselves to him and leave him to profit by his lesson. As Mrs. Quickly comes out of the "Garter" again she overhears Ford assure Caius, sotto voce, that he shall marry Anne, who, he impresses on him, will be robed in white: at the proper moment Caius and she are to come secretly to him, and he will give them a matrimonial blessing. Darkness has by now set in. The stage gradually empties, and the last thing we hear as the curtain falls is the piquant No. 11 in the orchestra.

7

The setting of the final scene is Windsor Park, with Herne's Oak in the centre, showing up in the moonlight. Distant horns are heard, as of some spectral hunt. Fenton enters and sings a sensitive little aria in praise of love:

which ends with a refrain we have already met with in the duets between Fenton and Anne: it is completed by Anne herself in the distance.

Mrs. Ford enters, not masked, but carrying on her arm a black cloak and a mask, which she orders Fenton to put on. (She is bent on countering the trick of her husband to marry Anne to Caius with a trick of her own).

All of them make a hurried exit as some mysterious chords in the orchestra announce the approaching Falstaff, who, according to plan, is enveloped in a heavy cloak and carries antlers on his head. A distant clock strikes twelve. Falstaff, more than a little scared at the eeriness of the hour and the place, commends himself to the protection of the gods. Alice enters, and Falstaff makes love to her in his usual twopence-coloured fashion. He is pleased rather than otherwise when she tells him that Meg also is somewhere about: they can carve him up between them, he says, like a buck at table! Meg's voice is now heard, calling for help, and Alice runs away in pretended terror. The demons, it appears, are coming. Falstaff throws himself on the ground face downwards when he hears a voice (that of Anne) summoning the elves, goblins and what not, for, as everyone knows, it is death for a mortal to look on the fairies. Anne now enters, dressed as the Fairy Queen, with nine other fairies in white and nine in blue. Soon the whole force of those engaged in the masquerade are present — Fenton, Bardolph, Alice, Meg and Mrs. Quickly in one mask or another, Ford undisguised and not masked, and another crowd of fairies. Anne calls on the fays to come out and sing and dance in the moonlight:

This they do, afterwards advancing en masse to Herne's Oak. Bardolph halts them: he has stumbled over the prostrate body of Falstaff. As a man has no business there among their revels, they order him to get up; but he pathetically explains that this will be impossible for him without the assistance of a crane. Thereupon, at the instigation of Bardolph, goblins, demons and imps of all sorts descend on the Knight and pinch and flog and plague him.

Meanwhile, seeing Caius looking about for Anne, Alice removes her and Fenton to a little distance off, and soon the lovers and

Mrs. Quickly slip away among the trees. Falstaff is assaulted and tormented by almost everyone until he begs for mercy. Ford crows over him; Alice shows herself to him unmasked; Mrs. Quickly curtsies ironically to him as she had done in the tavern (No. 7); his humiliation is complete.

Ford now thinks it time to spring his great surprise on the company — the betrothal of the Queen of the Fairies. Caius, still masked, comes forward, leading, as he imagines, Anne by the hand; but in reality it is the red-nosed Bardolph, heavily veiled. Alice brings forward at the same time Fenton, cloaked and masked, and Anne, draped in blue; Alice asks for Ford's permission, which is readily given, to include "this other ardent young couple" in the ceremony. The two couples join hands, and, after being solemnly blessed by Ford, Fenton and Caius unmask, while Anne removes her veil. Mrs. Quickly snatches the veil from Bardolph, and all laugh at the discomfiture of Caius. Ford, when he has recovered from his astonishment, takes his defeat in good part, and he and Falstaff invite them all to join him in a chorus as the preliminary to a carouse. The whole company comes down to the footlights for the chorus, the text of which is to the effect that the world is just one huge joke, and man the greatest of jesters: everyone has his laugh at the expense of everyone else, and he laughs best who laugh last. This lively finale is an elaborate fugue on the following subject:

which, we note, is given out by Falstaff.

Il Trovatore

GIUSEPPE VERDI [1813–1901]

PRINCIPAL CHARACTERS

MANRICO (THE TROUBADOR)	*Tenor*
LEONORA	*Soprano*
AZUCENA	*Mezzo-soprano*
COUNT DI LUNA	*Baritone*
INES	*Soprano*
FERRANDO	*Baritone*
RUIZ	*Tenor*

1

VERDI's appetite for dramatic gloom had been far from sated in *Rigoletto*. Even before he decided to concentrate on that work, indeed, early in 1850, he had spoken of the fancy he had taken to a romantic play by a Spanish dramatist, Antonio García Gutiérrez (1813–1884), *El Trovador*, which had been highly popular in its own country since its first production in Madrid in 1836. (García Gutiérrez recast it in 1851.) It made an irresistible appeal to Verdi by reason of its abundance in "powerful" situations of the kind his sombre genius loved, and above all by the character of the gipsy woman Azucena, with the perpetual conflict raging in her bosom between, as he put it, maternal and filial love. His first idea was to name the opera after her; Leonora, in his view, was a secondary figure.

In April 1851 the poet Cammarano sent him a draft of a proposed scenario for an opera on the subject, in which Verdi made many changes. In September of that year we find him telling his librettist that for some time he had been unable to do any serious thinking about the new work because of an accumulation of misfortunes and griefs, chief among them being the death of his mother on the preceding 30th June. Rome and Venice, it appears, were both anxious to give the first performance of *Il Trovatore*, and of the two casts likely to be at his disposal Verdi perferred on the whole that of Rome, though just then he could not see his ideal Azucena in any mezzo-soprano there. A few weeks later, his health and spirits having returned, he was pressing his collaborator to finish the text with all possible speed; but apparently there was still some work to be done at it when Cammarano died in July 1852, and one Leone Emanuele Bardare had to be called in to add the final touches. The legend, for what it is worth, is that the music was "composed" between the 1st and 29th November 1852, but obviously Verdi must have done a good deal of preliminary work at it long before then. The orchestration was finished by the 14th December. The first performance—very successful in spite of the headshaking of the critics over some features of the opera—took place in the Apollo Theatre, Rome, on the 19th January 1853.

2

The course of events in the opera is not easy to understand at a first acquaintance, largely because Cammarano copied too closely at times the layout of the García Gutiérrez drama, in which stage narrative plays rather too large a part. The action takes place in Aragon, and García Gutiérrez specifies the fifteenth century as the period. There is no overture, twenty-seven bars of orchestral flourish serving as introduction to the first scene, which shows us the hall of the Queen's palace of Aliaferia. The hall is occupied by soldiers, for the loyalists live in constant danger of attack from insurgents led by the Count Urgel. There is also a bevy of servants, and all are awaiting the return of their master the Count di Luna, who, we learn, is at his usual nocturnal occupation of watching before the window of a lady of the palace, Leonora, on the trail of a rival—a troubadour who is in the habit of serenading her. As the company are finding it difficult to keep awake they entreat Ferrando, the Count's trusty retainer, to tell them a story which, one would imagine, must have been familiar enough by that time to the whole countryside—that of the tragedy of the Count's brother. However, we in the audience have to be made acquainted with it, so Ferrando tells it at considerable length.

It seems that the old Count, now gathered to his fathers, had two sons, one of whom had been confided when an infant to the care of a nurse, who, waking up early one morning, was startled to see a repulsive gipsy woman gazing intently at the child. The nurse's shrieks brought the servants to the spot; they drove away the intruder, who made the excuse that she had merely come to cast the child's horoscope. But from that day he fell into a decline; so the witch was pursued, captured, and burned at the stake. She left behind her, however, a daughter bent on vengeance. The sickly child disappeared, and later some still smoking remains, obviously of an infant, were found on the very spot where the gipsy's mother had been burned. The company listen to Ferrando's harrowing story with occasional interjections of horror.

His narrative is based on a phrase:

which typifies the manner of much of Verdi's writing in his middle period. The Italian audiences of that day required of a composer that no one of his melodies should remind them of any other; at a much later date, indeed, we find them abusing Puccini for his use of reminiscent motifs, which they took to be an indication of his inability to invent new melodies. Verdi had consequently to make it clear from the outset of a given "number" that it was based musically on a melody not to be met with elsewhere. To do this he had to give it an individuality of physiognomy and of gesture, as it were, that easily degenerated into an automatic *tic* of which he sometimes became the servant instead of the master. In our No. 1, for example, and its sequel:

119

we see him almost hypnotically constrained to repeat again and
again the semiquaver figure that is the outstanding feature of it:
this figure recurs no less than twenty times in the forty-odd bars
of Ferrando's narrative, and the final effect, as elsewhere when
Verdi became the victim of an obsession of this kind, is undesignedly comic—in some cases, indeed, downright ludicrous.

Ferrando goes on to inform his listeners (and us) that the old
Count had to the last been reluctant to believe that his child was
dead, and had laid on his surviving son the injunction to look for
him unceasingly; but not only has the search been in vain but the
spirit of the witch is said to haunt the scene of her crime. (Here
we find Verdi employing in the orchestra, for the expression of
horror, the wailing thirds of which he had already made such good
use in the final scene of *Rigoletto*: see Ex. No. 16 in our analysis
of that work.) The scene ends with the whole company calling
down curses on the sorceress.

3

The necessity for narrative elucidation of the plot being over
for the moment (though only for a moment), Verdi can now look
forward to a spell of more lyrical writing. The scene changes to
the garden of the palace, on the right of which a marble flight of
steps is visible. It is night, with the moon trying fitfully to pierce
the heavy clouds. We see the lady Leonora expressing to her
confidante Ines her perturbation at the non-appearance lately of
a knight who had been in the habit of serenading her. Once more
Verdi is reduced for a while to narrative, though now it takes the
loftier form that befits the heroine of the opera. Leonora tells Ines
how she had first met this knight at a tournament where she had
bestowed on him the meed of valour and victory: then she had
seen him no more for a time, and she had eaten her heart out in
silent grief, till one night she had heard beneath her window a
song of love and devotion and the calling of her name:

and looking out she had recognised in the singer the gallant
knight of long ago, and her soul had dissolved in ecstasy. Ines'
advice to her is to forget this disturbing stranger whose name,
even, she does not know; but this merely provokes her to a declaration of undying love for him:

the melodic outline, as was usual with Verdi at that period, becoming more and more exuberantly florid as it evolves:

Come life, come death, she swears, she is the Troubadour's alone.

As she and Ines make their exit to the palace by way of the
steps, the Count di Luna enters; he too, at this witching hour of
night, has come to commune with Leonora while everyone else
in the palace is deep in slumber. As he makes to ascend the steps
he hears the strumming of a lute, and ejaculates angrily "The
Troubadour!" It is indeed Manrico, singing softly:

of his lonely desolate heart and his one consolation in life—his
love for his lady. Leonora comes out of the palace, sees a figure
wrapped in a cloak, and, under the combined influences of her
agitation and the darkness, mistakenly assumes it to be that of her
Troubadour and rushes towards the Count with a rapturous cry;
to the great annoyance of the Troubadour, who, hiding among the
trees, naturally assumes her to be unfaithful to his memory. As
the moon shines out, revealing a knight with closed visor,
Leonora realises her mistake, and, running to the Troubadour

and throwing herself at his feet, assures him of her devotion. Raising his visor, he declares himself to be the knight Manrico, whom the furious Count at once denounces as the partisan, pro-scribed and condemned to death, of the rebel Urgel, whose blood he means to have:

Upon this theme a vigorous trio is constructed, the jealous Count vowing vengeance, Manrico replying in kind, and Leonora trying in vain to pour oil on the troubled waters of love and jealousy. As Manrico and the Count go off with drawn swords to fight their quarrel out in a more convenient spot, Leonora falls senseless and the curtain descends on the first act.

4

When it rises again we see an encampment of gipsies in a wild spot in the Biscayan mountains. Day is dawning. Azucena is seated by a camp fire, with Manrico, wrapped in his cloak, re-clining on a couch at her side, his helmet at his feet and his sword in his hand. A piquant orchestral introduction leads into a chorus in which the gipsies—the men striking their anvils with their hammers—sing the praises of the nomad life with its agree-able combination of work, drinking and love-making; it is the second of the two main phrases of the chorus:

that makes the strongest impression on us and is of most impor-tance in what follows.

Into this atmosphere of gaiety the brooding Azucena suddenly breaks with a sombre canzone that gathers the gipsies round her in rapt attention. Her mind is running reminiscently on the burning of her mother, which she describes in graphic detail—the crowd crazy with blood lust, the indignities heaped on the victim, the binding to the stake, the lighting of the fire:

Allegretto ♩.=60

Stri-de la vam——pa, la———fol-la in-do———mi—ta

But she has a further story to tell, for the ears of Manrico alone; so the gipsies obligingly replace their tools in their bags, and, to the melody of No. 8, go off nonchalantly to seek the day's provisions in the neighbourhood.

Left alone with Manrico, Azucena tells him what apparently his long absence at the wars has prevented him from learning until now—how her mother, accused by the old Count of magic arts, had been burned at the stake on the very spot on which Manrico now stands. (He recoils in horror.) Azucena, her son in her arms, had watched the whole terrible scene, and heard her mother's dying injunction to her to avenge her. Then Azucena had stolen the Count's child and brought him to the still burning pyre. For a moment she had been moved to pity by its crying; then, as the vision of her mother in her death agony stole over her again, reason deserted her; she had thrown, as she thought, the Count's child into the flames, only to discover later that it was her own son she had sacrificed. As she recalls it all, her hair stands on end in horror, she assures Manrico, in a sombre phrase:

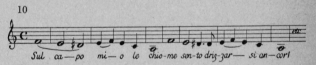

Sul ca—po mi—o le chio-me son-to driz-zar— si an—cor!

in which Verdi makes effective use of the darkest tones of the mezzo-soprano voice. The character of Azucena obviously made a profound appeal to Verdi; he generally finds for her a musical idiom less conventional than the one that comes almost too readily to his pen for the others.

Manrico is quite understandably puzzled by Azucena's revelation. "So I am not your son," he says; "who then am I?" She assures him that she is indeed his mother, and, apparently realising now that she has said more than was discreet, she puts an end to his questioning by saying that when her ancient wrongs take possession of her mind she is apt to wander. Has she not always been the tenderest of mothers to him? Was it not she who had nursed him back to life when he had been wounded in the battle at Pelilla? In a long lyrical outburst he recalls that combat with the forces of Count di Luna, and his own gallantry in it; he had had the Count himself at his mercy, but had spared him. And in return for his clemency, says Azucena bitterly, the Count has ever since pursued him with unrelenting venom; what had moved him to grant the man his life? Manrico does not know. He had beaten down his enemy's puny resistance, it appears:

and was about to deliver the death blow, when an irresistible, incomprehensible power within him had stayed his hand. Ferociously she implores him, should the Count ever be in his power again, to slay him without mercy; and this he promises to do.

Off-stage a horn call is heard, and soon a messenger from Manrico's henchman Ruiz enters with the tidings that the fortress of Castellor has been taken. For its defence, however, the Prince orders the immediate return of Manrico. Ruiz too bids him lose no time, for the Lady Leonora, having received false news of her lover's death, is about to enter a convent. The distressed Azucena implores him not to leave her, but he wildly declares that nothing will shake his resolution to fly to the rescue of the woman he loves:

5

The scene changes to a convent garden; it appears that Count di Luna also has heard of Leonora's decision to take the veil, and he has come with Ferrando and others of his men at dead of night to abduct her before she can take the fatal step. An aria being by this time no more than the leading baritone's due, Verdi decides to indulge him in it here: the result is the famous "Il balen" ("The light of her smile dims the radiance of the stars"):

13

that had an almost unparalleled vogue in the concert room and on the barrel organ during the second half of the nineteenth century.

From inside the convent comes the solemn tolling of a bell announcing that the moment for the rite has come. Sending his retainers out of sight, the Count, taking up the momentarily dropped thread of his aria, gives excited expression to his resolve that Leonora shall be his or no one's:

14

and notwithstanding the urgent need for immediate action Ferrando and the others repeat his sentiment at leisurely length. Di Luna and his crew are never anything more than stock figures of melodrama, but musically this is melodrama in Verdi's most vigorous middle period style.

The overlong episode ends with the Count taking cover with his retainers to await the moment for decisive action. From inside the convent a chorus of nuns is heard exhorting the postulant Leonora to renounce the world and find enduring peace in the bosom of the Church; the incident would be mightily impressive were it not for the unfortunately comic turn Verdi has given to it by the ejaculations of the hidden Count, Ferrando and the retainers, calling on gods and men to witness that these things shall not be. Our gravity returns when Leonora enters, accompanied by Ines, to the accompaniment of a series of those volleying chords in the orchestra that were a favourite device of Verdi's to establish an atmosphere of tragic presage. Leonora, in accents of sincere feeling, bids her confidante not to weep for her, for her soul will soon be at peace. As she turns away to go to the altar the Count rushes forward, crying that the only altar deserving of her is that of Hymen, and that he has come to make her his. But just then the Troubadour appears, and the stage is now set for the big ensemble that is to end the act. Leonora expresses her amazement at this unexpected turn of events in a melody:

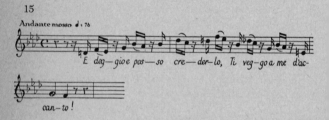

15

Andante mosso ♩ = 76

E deg—gioe pos—so cre—der-lo, Ti veg-go a me d'ac-can-to!

("Can I believe I see you once more? Is it a dream, some marvellous enchantment?"), that does not ring quite true; but it gives Verdi the material for the launching of a fine ensemble, in which the Troubadour and the Count hurl vigorous defiance at each other, Leonora pours out her joy in an exuberant repetition and expansion of No. 15, Ferrando and the retainers warn the Count that the hand of heaven is manifest in all this, and even the nuns congratulate Leonora on having escaped the convent through this providential reappearance of the lover she had supposed to be dead. When the furious Count draws his sword to attack his

126

rival he is overpowered by Manrico's followers, headed by Ruiz. Again a big ensemble is built up, and it looks as if this is to be the end of the act; but Verdi has a more telling effect in reserve for us. He suddenly checks the choral flood in full torrent and lets us hear for a moment or two the voice of Leonora alone, singing of the ectasy of reunion with her lover: then the other principals and the chorus join in a final four bars of fortissimo comment, and the curtain falls.

6

The third act brings us, as the penultimate act of all plays should do, to the vital turning-point in the action. Azucena is now the centre of interest.[1]

Manrico has gone to Castellor, taking Leonora with him. The towers of the fortress are visible in the distance; the foreground of the stage is occupied by the camp of the loyalists, the tent of the commander, Count di Luna, being distinguishable by the banner that floats above it. A vigorous orchestral and choral introduction shows us some of di Luna's soldiers preparing for the imminent battle by playing dice, while others, more professionally minded, are bracing themselves at the bidding of Ferrando for the assault on Castellor that has been ordered: "grandioso" is Verdi's marking for the martial chorus in which they declare their eagerness to fight and their confidence of victory:

16

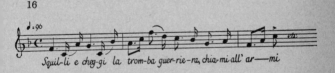

Squil-li e cheg-gi la trom-ba guer-rie-ra, chia-mi all' ar——mi

Laurels and loot, they are convinced, await them in abundance. The *entrain* of this marching-song is irresistible even today.

Di Luna is about to indulge himself in dreams of the recovery

---

[1] For the first scene of this act Verdi wrote a series of ballet numbers for the Paris production of the opera. These do not appear in any of the scores except the French, and the spectator is not likely to meet with them in any ordinary performance.

of Leonora and victory over his rival when Ferrando brings him the news that some of the soldiers have captured a gipsy woman whom they suspect to be one of the enemy's spies. (It is, of course, Azucena, on the last stage of her journey in search of Manrico.) She is brought in with her hands tied, and is interrogated by di Luna. She is a gipsy, she tells him, wandering as is the way of her race, trying to find, if she can, a son who had left her. When she discloses that she has come from the Biscayan mountains dim suspicions arise in the minds of the Count and Ferrando. These suspicions are confirmed when, in an unguarded moment—not knowing to whom she is speaking—she half admits knowledge of the burning, years ago, of a child whom the Count now declares to have been his brother. Ferrando thereupon denounces her as the daughter of the sorceress of that old story. Her bonds are strengthened, and when, in her despair, she calls on heaven to send her "son Manrico" to her aid the Count exults in the prospect of a double vengeance on his hated rival. The voices are built up into an impressive ensemble, the whole scene, indeed, being musically one of the finest in the opera. It ends with Azucena being taken away by the guards, and with the withdrawal of the Count to his tent, followed by Ferrando.

The next scene shows us Manrico and Leonora in colloquy in a hall in Castellor, with Ruiz in attendance; the latter is soon sent away to prepare the garrison for the assault on the fortress. Leonora sees nothing but gloom in the omens for her marriage to Manrico, and he tries to inspirit her with an aria, in Verdi's most serious vein, in which he assures her that, if it should be his fate to fall in the coming battle, his last thoughts shall be with Leonora, for whom he will wait in heaven. The soft pealing of an organ in an adjoining chapel recalls them to the realities of the moment; and they are about to enter the chapel to be wedded when Ruiz rushes in with the news that Azucena has been seized by the enemy and is now being led in chains to a pyre already lighted. It is his mother, Manrico informs the astonished Leonora; and frenziedly he orders Ruiz to prepare for an immediate sortie in the hope of rescuing her. His first duty, he tells Leonora, is to this most affectionate of mothers; the pyre his enemy has kindled has lit a fire in him that cries aloud for vengeance:

17

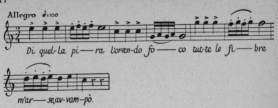

This rousing episode has always been a favourite with operatic tenors, particularly those who feel sufficiently sure of themselves to finish on a high C. Ruiz having returned with a number of soldiers, Manrico bids a final farewell to Leonora and makes an imposing exit to trumpet tones in the orchestra.

7

The spectator of the opera has now to assume, in the absence of any direct information on the matter, that Manrico had failed in his sortie from Castellor, and that he and Azucena have been brought back prisoners to Aliaferia, where they are both in a dungeon in a tower of the palace. The fourth act opens with an expressive orchestral introduction, appropriately elegiac in tone. Ruiz and Leonora, both heavily cloaked, steal in; here, says Ruiz in a whisper, is the tower in which prisoners are confined, and where Manrico now is. He leaves her to her meditations. She has come to save her lover if she can; for herself she has no fear, she says—glancing at a ring on her right hand which we presume to contain a poison for use in case of need. In an expressive adagio she sighs out her soul to the night and to the captive Manrico; for modern ears the self-conscious coloratura with which the aria is larded takes some of the sincerity out of it.

But Verdi now launches into one of the greatest scenes of the older Italian opera. The death bell tolls, and from within we hear a choir of tenors and basses chanting in broad harmonies and in solemn rhythm the Miserere, the prayer for mercy on the souls of those about to set out on the journey from which there is no return. This is followed by the supreme example of those "volley-ing" chords in the orchestra to which, as has already been pointed out, Verdi instinctively resorted for the suggestion of an atmosphere charged with doom:

18

The persistent rhythm serves as the basis for a moving cry from Leonora, "What solemn sounds are these, sounds of darkness and terror, that halt my breath and make my heart stand still?":

19

Her cry ends in a series of broken sobs in a descending scale:

20

From the tower is now heard the voice of Manrico bemoaning his unhappy lot and thinking of his lost Leonora—"Ah, how slow is the coming of Death to him who longs to die; farewell, Leonora, farewell!":

21

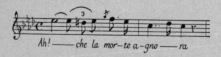

The inner choir breaks in again with its solemn Miserere; and the whole expressive episode is repeated and expanded, with Manrico vowing that he will wait for Leonora in heaven, she promising that she will never forget him, the choir of monks intoning their sombre elegy, and underneath it all the orchestra hammering away with the persistent rhythm shown in our No. 18. These pages of the score have never been surpassed in Italian opera.

As the choral and orchestral mass thins out the voice of Leonora is heard singing once more of a love that Death itself cannot end:

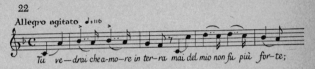

22

Allegro agitato ♩=116

Tu ve—drai che a-mo-re in ter-ra mai del mio non fu più for-te;

All this rings rather less true for us of a later day because of its unnecessary repetitions and the coloratura of some of the writing. It is too obviously the prima donna's showpiece.

Her aria over, Leonora stands aside as the Count enters with a number of attendants to whom he gives the order that at dawn the son is to be beheaded and the mother burned at the stake. They go into the tower, leaving the Count to indulge in a short soliloquy: if he is exceeding the powers entrusted to him by the Prince, he says, his excuse is Leonora's fatal fascination for him. But where is she now? he asks; in vain he has sought for her. Hearing this, Leonora comes forward. In a long duet she pleads for mercy for Manrico:

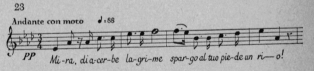

23

Andante con moto ♩=88

PP *Mi-ra, di a-cer-be la-gri-me spar-go al tuo pie-de un ri—o!*

or, alternatively, that he will take her life too. He rejects her appeal; so blind is his hate for Manrico that simple death alone cannot slake his desire for vengeance. As a last resort the desperate Leonora offers herself as the price for the Troubadour's pardon. Having extracted an oath from her to that effect di Luna gives a whispered order to the guard. While his back is turned she takes the poison from the ring and swallows it, muttering "The bride you shall have will be a lifeless one!", and then bursts into a song of joy, welcoming death for herself if only she succeeds in saving her lover's life:

Vi—vrà! Con-ten-de il giu-bi-lo i det—ti a me, Si-gno—re,

while di Luna congratulates himself on his unexpected good fortune. The over-long and too conventionally treated episode ends with them going into the tower together.

8

The final scene takes place in Manrico's dungeon, a gloomy cell half lit by a lamp hanging from the ceiling. Azucena is lying on a rough pallet, exhausted; Manrico sits by her side. The rank air of the dungeon has brought the gipsy, accustomed to life in the open air, near death's door. Verdi is at his convincing best in the opening dialogue between the pair, with Azucena racked with fear of the fire and her son unable to offer her any consolation. To the accompaniment in the orchestra of No. 9 she once more sees, in imagination, her mother being dragged to the stake and burned. This hysterical access is succeeded by a mood of exhausted resignation. In a state between waking and sleeping she indulges herself in a nostalgic dream of a return with Manrico to their beloved mountains:

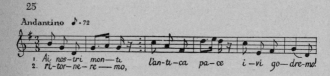

1. Ai nos-tri mon—ti, l'an-ti-ca pa-ce i-vi go-dre-mo!
2. ri-tor-ne-re—mo,

never to leave them again. He endeavours to soothe her, and the tender, quiet-toned duet is one of the finest episodes in the score; Verdi has once again shown a genius for rising to the full musical and dramatic height of his subject after a complacent lapse into much that was merely conventional.

As Azucena drops into a sleep and Manrico is still on his knees beside her Leonora enters with the news that he is free. His suspicions aroused, he gathers that his liberty has been purchased by Leonora at a price, and he refuses to accept a life bought by the passing of Leonora into the possession of his rival. In vain she implores him feverishly to fly without delay; and Azucena, waking from her sleep, breaks into the musical tissue with a poignant repetition of the nostalgic No. 25.

Once more Leonora begs him to fly to freedom, and once more he rejects the suggestion with bitter scorn. His resolution breaks down only when she falls at his feet with a confession that she has taken poison for his sake and already feels the death agony coming upon her. As she is bidding him a last farewell the Count enters and, standing silently on the threshold, realises from what he overhears that Leonora has cheated him. As she falls dead he calls to the guards to seize Manrico and take him to the scaffold. As a last refinement of cruelty he drags the half-awake Azucena to the window to witness the execution. As the axe falls she gives a wild cry of "This man was your brother; now, oh my mother, you have been avenged!"; and the last thing we hear is an agonised cry from the Count, "And I still live!"

Aïda

GIUSEPPE VERDI [1813–1901]

PRINCIPAL CHARACTERS

Aïda	*Soprano*
Amneris	*Mezzo-soprano*
Radames	*Tenor*
The King of Egypt	*Bass*
Ramphis, The High Priest	*Bass*
Amonasro	*Baritone*

1

N November 1869 a new Italian opera house had been opened in Cairo, and Verdi had been invited by the Khedive, Ismail Pasha, to write an opera for it, to be performed in connection with the opening of the Suez Canal. Verdi had refused. In the early part of 1870, when he happened to be in Paris, the offer was renewed and again declined. But a little later his Paris friend Camille du Locle sent him a brief outline of a possible opera subject that at once took his fancy. The sketch, which ran to no more than four pages, was the work of a famous French Egyptologist, Mariette, who had lived and worked for some years in Egypt, where he had been made Inspector-General of Monuments and given the title of Bey. Verdi and du Locle having between them developed the scenario in French prose, the composer's friend Ghislanzoni was called in as librettist. It was planned to produce the new work in Cairo in January 1871. But in July 1870 the Franco-Prussian war broke out and Mariette was immured in Paris during the siege of the city. With him were the designs and costumes and some of the properties for *Aïda*, without which no progress could be made in Cairo. Verdi now felt himself justified in negotiating with the Scala for a first production in Milan, as the terms of his contract with Draneth Bey, the director of the Cairo theatre, authorised him to do; but when the causes of the hold-up were explained to him he waived that right, and *Aïda* after all received its first performance in Cairo, on the 14th December 1871, under Giovanni Bottesini. Verdi had taken advantage of the enforced delay to revise some portions of his work, especially in the second act.

2

He had been even more critical of his librettist than usual during the construction of the text of *Aïda*, not only suggesting a recasting of the words at many points but occasionally demanding lines to fit in to music already composed or sketched. After the opera had been produced he was angered by the frequent criticism that much of the work was "Wagnerian." We know him to have had a profound respect for Wagner as an artist, and there can be no doubt that he had given intensive study to the German master's scores. His letters of this period show him doing some new thinking about the problems of form and texture in opera. He was no longer content with the four-square melodic structures he had inherited from his Italian predecessors and so effectively manipulated himself in earlier works. "Melody," he told one of his correspondents, was not in itself everything: "Beethoven was not a 'melodist,' nor was Palestrina," i.e. "in our Italian acceptation of that term." He no longer thought it necessary for melody to be on all occasions constructed on a pattern of balanced symmetrical phrases; there were times, he held, when asymmetry was called for. Further, more care should now be taken than of old in the fusion of the recitatives with the cantilenàs; the musical disparity between the two should be diminished, and the joins not be too obvious. All this, of course, was "Wagnerian," in the sense that Wagner had long been practising it in his "endless melody." But the charge against Verdi of having succumbed to the Wagnerian "influence" was ridiculous: in the new operatic style of which *Aïda* was the first foreshadowing he was simply following the natural, inevitable bent of his own maturing genius. By 1870 he had developed enormously as a musician; he had a wider and richer sense of harmony, of rhythm and of orchestral

colour, and was master of a new craftsmanship of musical de
velopment." It is true that there is still a fair amount in *Aïda*
of the earlier Verdi, content with the traditional formulae. Bu
for the most part it is a new Verdi that we see. His musica
imagination takes charge of things in a way that it had rarel
managed to do before then: the melodic structure—to conside
that feature alone—was no longer the outcome of a simple addi
tion of limb to limb, but at its best flowed on unbrokenly, evolv
ing not by way of imposed patterns but of inner proliferation. I
is for this reason, among others, that quotations from the matur
Verdi is so difficult. The "melody" is no longer in the parts, o
even—by simple addition—in the sum of the parts, but in th
whole; and we have often to think to the end of a long melodi
line before we can appreciate the subtle interconnection of ba
with bar within it. The "Wagnerism" of the Verdi of *Aïda*, the
Requiem, *Otello* and *Falstaff* is a myth. He had undoubtedly
assimilated certain new procedures which by that time—largely
of course, through Wagner's use of them—were in the Europea
musical air. But the ability to make these procedures his own, to
incorporate them organically into his own artistic individuality
was the result of a long process of silent, subconscious develop
ment in the depths of his own musical being. There is not a page
in his later works that derives, either imaginatively or in the
technical handling, from Wagner; everything bears the unmistak
able dual stamp of "Verdi" and "Italy."

3

The brief orchestral prelude to the first act introduces us a
once to the slave girl Aïda:

1

and in these seventeen bars we see at once the ability of the new
Verdi both to invent an individual melodic line and to "develop"
and inflect and nuance it not in accordance with any stylised
formula of melody but in terms of psychological characterisation;
for anyone who knows the opera as a whole can see in these few
bars the essential Aïda, at once sensitive and timorous. This motif
is followed by one associated in the opera with priesthood—one
uses that word advisedly instead of "priests" of the temple of
Isis, for they are more than conventional stage figures called in
now and then to help the action along:

2

Verdi, as his letters show, visualised them as a kind of inflexible
massed power, against which Radames and the gentle Aïda are
flung and shattered. Conquerors, he remarks ironically in one of
his letters, always attribute their success to the co-operation of
the deity, so he wants Ghislanzoni to model the priests' words at
one point on the famous announcement of the virtuous King of
Prussia after Sedan—"By the help of Divine Providence we have
conquered. The enemy has been delivered into our hands. May
God be with us also in the future!" [1]

The remainder of the short prelude is devoted to a dramatic
opposition of these two motifs; it ends with the Aïda theme dying
out in the highest regions of the orchestra.[2]

The curtain rises on a hall in the palace of the King of Egypt
in Memphis; it is flanked by imposing colonnades. Through a
great gate in the background we see the temples and palaces of
the town, with the Pyramids in the distance. Radames, a young

[1] Or, as an English humorist paraphrased the pious sentiment:
God be praised, my dear Augusta:
The French have come another buster.
[2] At one time Verdi thought of beginning the opera with a more formal
"overture," the manuscript of which is now in the Verdi archives. We may
congratulate ourselves that he finally decided to leave the brief prelude as
we now have it.

Egyptian soldier, and Ramphis, the High Priest of Isis, whose characteristic motif runs thus:

3

are seen in conference. Egypt, it appears, is once more threatened by the Ethiopians, whose hordes have advanced far into the Nile valley. The goddess Isis, says Ramphis, looking meaningly at the officer, has already declared who is to lead the homeland army—one young in years but great in valour; and the High Priest is now on his way to make the announcement to the King. "Oh happy chosen one!", sighs Radames.

The High Priest having departed, Radames, against a background of rousing brass fanfares, lets his imagination play on the thought of himself being placed in command of the army, winning a glorious victory over the invaders, and returning to lay his laurels at Aïda's feet and restore her in triumph to her native land. This is the theme of his famous aria "Celeste Aïda," which is externally like many of the arias of Verdi's early and middle periods, but far above most of these in the sweep of its melody and the varied expression of the orchestral accompaniment.

4

On the conclusion of the aria Amneris, the daughter of the Pharaoh, enters, heralded by one of the main motifs that will henceforth characterise her:

4

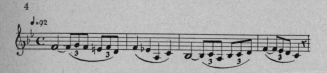

It shows her in her gentler aspect. She is secretly in love with Radames. He confesses to her that he has been indulging himself in the ambitious dream of being the goddess's choice as com-

mander-in-chief of the army, whereupon she asks him insinuat-
ingly whether there is not also room in his breast for a tenderer
emotion and even bolder hopes. He wonders anxiously whether
it is possible that she has divined his love for her handmaiden
Aïda, while Amneris begins to harbour a suspicion that there is
a rival to herself in the field: perhaps it is this Aïda, she surmises
as the slave girl enters and the sudden light in Radames' eyes
betrays his feelings towards her. This episode is dominated by an
agitated orchestral motif expressive of Amneris' jealousy:

5

a passion which bodes ill for them all. She dissembles her real
feelings, however, under a mask of sisterly affection for this
Ethiopian servant of hers. Why is the girl so distressed? she enquires. Because war has been declared and the country will now
be plunged in woe, Aïda replies. Is that all? asks Amneris; is not
her heart ill at ease because of some tenderer, more personal
emotion? The voices unite in an admirably dramatic trio, during
which, to the dismay of Radames and Aïda, Amneris shows more
and more clearly her jealous suspicion of them.

With the entry, to a rousing brass fanfare, of the King, Ramphis,
the other priests, the ministers of the Court, captains of the
guard and others, we embark on one of those spectacular concerted pieces that play so large a part in the opera. At the bidding of the King a Messenger gives the assembly the news that
the Ethiopian army, led by its ferocious, indomitable king, Amonasro, is marching on Thebes, and a great battle is imminent. The
goddess Isis has named as leader of the Egyptian forces Radames
—an announcement that draws an "I tremble!" from the fretted
Aïda, who knows something which none of the others know as yet
—that this Amonasro is her father; henceforth her soul is to be
divided between two loyalties, to her lover and to her father and
her native land. Verdi lapses for a while into his older idiom in
the bouncing melody:

6

Su! del Ni-lo al sa—cro li-do ac-cor-re-te, E-gi—zii e-roi,

to which the King bids them all do or die in defence of their country and its gods. Radames and the others take up the martial strain, while Aïda laments the burden the Fates have imposed on her, and the proud Amneris places the royal standard in Radames' hands. "Return as conqueror!" are her final words to him; and with the others echoing the words in a thundering unison the massive ensemble ends.

All leave the stage except Aïda, who repeats, with sad irony, this "Return as conqueror!" Should that come true, she muses in a recitative, it means that her lover will return to her red with the blood of her kith and kin, in his triumphal chariot the King, her father, in chains. In a more lyrical vein she implores the gods to give the victory not to the Egyptians but to her own people; then, as the sensitive No. 1 sings out quietly in the orchestra, she reminds herself of Radames, asking how it will be possible for her to reconcile these two affections; and she ends with a prayer for help and pity, to music that already foreshadows the appealing pathos of Verdi's Desdemona: "have pity on my sufferings, ye gods; let me die":

7

Nu-mi, pie—tà del mio sof-frir! Spe—me non v'ha pel mio do-lor

As she leaves the stage the curtain falls.

5

The scene changes to the interior of the temple of Vulcan at Memphis. A series of columns, receding in a far perspective, is bathed in a mysterious light. Statues of the gods are scattered about, and sacred emblems surmount the great altar in the centre of the stage; below this is a carpet-covered platform. Incense is burning in golden tripods. This is the imposing setting for the ceremony of the consecration of Radames.

A chorus of priestesses invokes "mighty Phtha, the spirit that animates the universe":

8

the sombre tones of Ramphis and the priests striking in at intervals in solemn chords. Here, and in the final flourish of the priestesses' prayer:

9

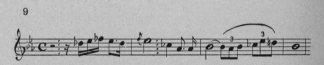

we see Verdi in full possession of new melodic and harmonic resources, creating and maintaining convincingly an exotic atmosphere without a suspicion of pseudo-"oriental" pastiche.

The priestesses perform a sinuous sacred dance in which the exotic colouring is maintained by new scalic and harmonic devices. Radames now enters and goes up to the altar, where a silver veil is placed on his head, and Ramphis hails him as the chosen of the goddess for the task of defending Egypt. The High Priest invokes the blessing and protection of the great god of the land on him, to a strain:

10

that shows Verdi still fluctuating uncertainly at times between his older idiom and his new. On this theme, entrusted to the High Priest, the other priests and Radames, with occasional interpolations, admirably managed, of No. 8 by the priestesses, a great ensemble is built up: it ends with a combined cry of "Mighty Phtha!", and the curtain falls on the first act.

6

In the second act we are first of all taken into a luxurious hall in the apartments of Amneris, where female slaves are engaged some in waving feather fans over her, others in attiring her for the coming triumphal festival. Their song is one of felicitations to Amneris and to the conqueror who is soon to return to them: the refrain of their melody:

11

Vie-ni, sul crin ti pio-va-no, vie-ni, sul crin ti pio-va-no,

and the clinching cadence of Amneris, in which she sighs out the longing of her heart for the return of Radames:

12

Ah! vie —— ni, vie-ni a-mor mio, m'i — neb-bria,

are particularly captivating.

A repetition of the charming vocal vignette is followed by a dance of Moorish slaves, and this by yet another repetition of Nos. 11 and 12.

Aïda enters, to a timid voicing of her motif (No. 1) in the orchestra. Amneris is filled with pity for her in the disaster that has befallen the Ethiopian forces, but at the same time the sight of her awakens the old jealous suspicions in her, and she determines to wrest the slave girl's secret, if there be a secret, from her. She begins with a suave expression of sympathy with her in her sorrow:

13

but when Aïda, deeply moved, speaks ecstatically of the joy and
the torment of love Amneris becomes more and more watchful
of her. In smooth, friendly tones, but with her eyes fixed on the
trembling girl, she professes great solicitude and affection for her,
and by a casual hint at the possibility of the dauntless leader of
the Egyptian army having met his death in battle she betrays
Aïda into an impulsive expression of grief that leaves no doubt
as to her love for Radames. Changing her tactics, Amneris declares that "Radames lives," whereupon Aïda falls on her knees
with a rapturous cry of gratitude to the gods. Throwing off the
mask now, Amneris discloses herself as Aïda's rival—she, a daughter of the Pharaohs. For a moment Aïda is on the point of revealing that she too is of royal birth, but manages to check herself
in time. Humbly, at Amneris' feet, she confesses her love and
implores her powerful and fortunate rival's pity:

14

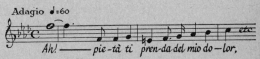

Amneris, almost beside herself, pours out her scorn and hatred
on the presumptuous slave.

The duet is broken in upon for a moment by martial fanfares
and a chorus of triumph from without, to the melody of No. 6;
then it is resumed, Aïda wailing her grief and despair to the gods,
and the exultant Amneris heaping on her contumely and threats.
The scene ends with a repetition of Aïda's piteous appeal to the
gods in the first act (No. 7).

7

The remainder of the second act is devoted to the grand pageant of the return of the victorious Egyptian army. The scene is an avenue leading to the entrance gate to Thebes; on one side is the temple of Ammon, on the other a throne with a gorgeous purple canopy. At the back is a triumphal arch. To rousing martial music the King enters with officers, priests, standard bearers and others, and takes his seat on the throne; Amneris, who has entered after him with a bevy of slaves, among them Aïda, seats herself at his left.

In a succession of vigorous tunes the assembly gives thanks to Isis for the triumph of the Egyptian arms, and the priests are prominent with a four-part chorus based on the motif shown in our No. 2—"Lift up your eyes to the supreme arbiters of victory, and return thanks to the gods for this happy day." Then, to the strains of a stately march:

15

the Egyptian troops pour in and pass before the King: they are followed by dancing girls carrying the spoils of battle, and these by more troops, war chariots, standards, and images of the gods. They are welcomed in another massive chorus, the priests, as before, asserting themselves as a collective entity. When the excitement has been worked up to the utmost possible height the hero Radames enters under a canopy carried by twelve of his officers. The King comes down from his throne to greet and embrace him and hail him as the saviour of his country; and at his bidding Amneris, to the strain of No. 4, comes forward and places on his head the garland of victory. The King having promised to grant the hero anything he desires, Radames asks that first of all the captives shall be brought in: this is done to a renewed professional muttering of thanksgiving to the gods of victory by Ramphis and the priests, to a variant of the motif shown in our No. 2. The dusky prisoners file in under the surveillance of the guards, the last of them being the Ethiopian king Amonasro, in the accoutrement of an officer. At the sight of him Aïda rushes towards him with a cry of "My father!" The multitude cries out in astonishment "Her father!", to which Amneris adds the significant comment "And in our power!"

Amonasro has only time to whisper to Aïda "Do not disclose my rank!" before the King orders him to come forward. "So you are her father?" he says, to which Amonasro replies in tones of quiet dignity, "Yes, her father. I fought like the others: we were conquered: death I sought in vain. My uniform will show you that I defended my country and my king. Fortune was not on our side: at my feet in the dust lay my king, pierced by many wounds. If love for one's country is a crime, all we here are guilty, and we are ready to die. But, oh mighty King," he continues, "show us clemency; today it is we who are at the bottom of fortune's wheel, but tomorrow it may be your turn to lie there":

16

Ma tu, Re, tu si-gno-re pos-sen-te,

Aïda and the captives repeat this appeal; but the priests, true to their character throughout the drama, urge the King to harden his heart and exterminate this rabble. A great choral ensemble is built up on these rival psychological themes, with Aïda joining in the appeal for mercy, Amneris noting jealously the glances of love and compassion that Radames is turning on the Ethiopian girl, Amonasro repeating his warning that fortune's wheel will one day turn against the conquerors, the priests, as usual, clamouring for a comprehensive sentence of death, and the people urging them to show humanity towards the captives. Nothing comparable in dramatic drive and technical craftsmanship to this masterly ensemble, with its fusion of so many conflicting psychological elements into a single musical whole, had ever been seen before in Italian opera.

But even yet Verdi has not exhausted his resources; indeed, so far he has exploited only half of them. A temporary lull occurs as Radames, reminding the King of his promise, asks that the prisoners shall be released. The priests protest against this act of clemency, Ramphis urging that as soon as they are free the vanquished will begin a new war of revenge on their conquerors. To this Radames replies that with Amonasro dead they have no hope of rallying. Then the High Priest stipulates that for greater security they shall at least keep Aïda's father in their hands. With this counsel of prudence the King agrees; and as a further pledge of enduring peace he will bestow on the gallant saviour of the country the hand of his daughter, with whom, in course of time, he will share the government of Egypt. This announcement is greeted with joy by Amneris: "now let the slave, if she can," she cries, "rob me of my love—if she dares!" There follows a fresh chorus of general rejoicing, in which even the priests join. Only Radames and Aïda are dismayed. "What remains to me?" Aïda asks despairingly; "he will ascend the throne, while I can only weep, forgotten!" But Amonasro, drawing near to her unnoticed, quietly urges her to take heart and hope on, for the day of vengeance for Ethiopia will come. Amneris, of course, exults in her triumph, while Radames, in an aside, laments his miserable fate: he has won a kingdom but lost Aïda. Once more a massive ensemble is built up, the act closing in almost universal jubilation.

8

The third act is set on the banks of the Nile. It is night, with a bright moon and many stars. On the summit of some granite rocks, studded with palm trees, stands a temple dedicated to Isis. It is the eve of Amneris' wedding day.

After a brief orchestral introduction that suggests curiously the mysterious silence of the night and the place, we hear from within the temple tenors and basses (in quiet unison), reinforced at the cadences by the soprano voice of a Grand Priestess, praying to the benign goddess who is at once mother and spouse of Osiris, mother also of love, invoking her grace for those who are coming to seek her protection. A boat is seen approaching the shore, from which descend Amneris, Ramphis, some veiled women and a few guards. The High Priest bids Amneris enter the fane and implore the favour, on this her wedding eve, of the goddess who knows all the secrets and the mysteries of the heart of man. She will pray until the dawn, she replies, that Radames will give her all his heart, as hers is now and always will be his. They all enter the temple, to the strains of the chorus of inside worshippers with which the scene had opened.

As the prayers die away into silence the stage remains empty for a few moments, till No. 1 in the orchestra—now presented in such a guise that it blends subtly with the scene, the occasion and the hour—announces that Aïda is somewhere near. When at last she makes her appearance we learn from her lips that she has come there at the wish of Radames. What will he have to say to her? she asks: if a last farewell, then she will seek eternal peace in the dark waters of the Nile. This is the prelude to one of the finest sections of the score, a romanza in which she gazes, in imagination, for the last time on the serene sky, the green fields and the scented shores of her native land, which she will never see again. This romanza alone would suffice to show how far Verdi had travelled as a musician since the days of *Rigoletto* and *Il Trovatore*: the melodic lines are now more delicately drawn, the harmony freer, the orchestral colour more subtly appropriate at once to the psychology of the character and to the milieu; and even when, as he does at one or two points, he makes a little concession, as of old, to the desire of the singer for an opportunity to demonstrate her quality, the vocal difficulties are made so organically part and parcel of the whole melodic line that they never kindle any suspicion of having been put there for simple display's sake, as had been the case again and again in the arias of his earlier days.

9

Amonasro, it appears, has evaded his captors, and now he approaches the astonished Aïda from the cover of the palm trees. He knows that she is here awaiting Radames, on whose love for her he intends to play for his ends and hers. She has the opportunity, he tells her, to avenge herself on her powerful rival the Pharaoh's daughter, and at the same time to restore Ethiopia's fortunes. Eagerly he speaks of the joy of seeing their beloved country again, its odorous forests, its verdant valleys, its golden temples:

17

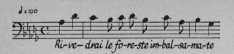

Ri-ve—drai le fo-re-ste im-bal-sa-ma-te

a theme which she takes up with him with even greater ardour. He reminds her of what their land has suffered from the ravages of war, and Aïda's imagination plays ardently on the hope of liberty and peace. The Ethiopians have rallied and are armed, he tells her, and the moment has come to strike the decisive blow. One thing only is lacking to Amonasro's plans—he must know by what route the enemy will march against him. It is certainly known already to Radames, and from him she must worm the secret, playing upon his love for her. She recoils from the suggestion in horror, but he renews the attack still more vehemently, painting a moving picture of the desolation that threatens her land from the Egyptian invaders; and as she still refuses his demands he casts her off from him, calling her no longer his daughter but the Pharaohs' slave.

This brings us to the great climax of the scene. Aïda throws herself at her father's feet, and, to music of a unique poignancy, declares that she is no slave but her father's true daughter, worthy of him and of her country. "Remind yourself," he urges her, in one of the greatest phrases Verdi ever wrote, "that a nation conquered and oppressed can find its salvation in you alone":

18

Pen—sa che un po———po-lo vin-to, stra-zia-to
per te sol—tan-to, per te sol—tan-to ri-sor-ger può.

The long melodic line here is one of the most signal evidences of Verdi's growth as a musician during the years that immediately preceded *Aïda*. His imagination had already sought an expression of the same basic kind in the concluding phrase of Leonora's aria

"Madre, pietosa Vergine" in the second act of *La Forza del Destino* (1862);

19

Non m'ab-ban-do-nar, pie-tà, pie-tà di me, Si-gno-re, deh!

non m'ab-ban-do-nar, ah!———— pie-tà, pie-tà di me, Si-gnor.

("Forsake me not, oh Lord; have pity on me.") The melodic intention and design are essentially the same in both cases. But the earlier line becomes somewhat embarrassed in the fourth bar, while in the critical seventh it dives helplessly down on a broken wing; whereas in the *Aïda* example it first of all soars to successively greater heights in its first half, and in its second descends in complete possession of its vital powers. One can speak here, unfortunately, of the melodic line alone: in harmonic resource, and especially in the management of an accompanying orchestral figure, sharply rhythmed, that takes twenty-eight bars to ascend slowly to a climax as Aïda sings "Oh my country, what a price I am paying for you!", the long episode is the best proof conceivable of the arrival of a new Verdi on the operatic scene.

Seeing Radames approaching, Amonasro takes cover among the palms. Aïda checks Radames' protestations of devotion; she does not doubt his love, she says, but what hope can he have against a combination of the wiles of Amneris, the power of the King, the devotion of the people, and the wrath of the priests? He replies that the two countries will soon be at war again; he will be in command of the Egyptian forces, and when he returns victorious, as he assuredly will, he will confess to the King his love for Aïda and claim her hand as his reward. Aïda's reply is that she has a surer plan to realise their dream of happy union—flight together to a happier land, on the tone-painting of the charm of which Verdi once more lavishes some of the best of his new art.

When the soldier and the patriot in him revolt against her suggestion she turns on him in anger, professed or real, declaring that he no longer loves her, and bidding him enter the temple where Amneris is awaiting him; "and then let the axe fall on me and my father," she concludes. On this his resolution fails him; and in a passionate duet—not in Verdi's best vein—they both revel in the thought of the new happiness that lies before them, and are already about to take flight when Aïda asks by what route they can evade the troops already marshalled for the invasion of Ethiopia. "By the route already chosen for us to march upon the enemy," he replies; "till tomorrow it will be deserted." "And where is that?" asks Aïda. "The mountain gorges of Napata," is the answer; whereupon Amonasro emerges from his hiding-place with a cry of "And there I will post my men—I, Aïda's father and Ethiopia's King!" In the depths of bewilderment and despair Radames cries out again and again that he is dishonoured and lost; Aïda and Amonasro endeavour to calm him; and the latter is on the point of dragging him away when Amneris, crying "Traitor!", rushes out from the temple, followed by Ramphis, the priests and the guards. "My rival!", Aïda exclaims. Amonasro draws his dagger and rushes at Amneris, but as the guards advance on him Radames bids him and Aïda take to flight, and then surrenders himself to the High Priest.

10

The first part of the fourth act is staged in a hall in the King's palace: on the left is a great door leading to the subterranean chamber of justice, on the right a passage leading to a prison in which Radames is confined. When the curtain rises Amneris is crouched, in an attitude of despair, before the door on the left; and writhing in and out of the orchestra we hear the motif of her jealousy (No. 5). She is a complex character, this Amneris, more complex, indeed, than any other in the opera. Her detested rival, she muses, has escaped her, while Radames is awaiting the sentence of the priests on him as traitor. But a traitor he is not, she continues, for though he had revealed the high secret of the war his intentions were to fly—with Aïda. Then, in an access of fury, she cries out that they are traitors all, deserving of death.

But once again her mood changes, and with No. 4 breathing softly in the orchestra we see the gentler side of her nature reasserting itself. She loves Radames, she declares, and if only he could love her in return she would try to save him. At an order from her the guards bring him in. She addresses him in measured, mournful tones:

20

Giài —sa-cer-do-ti a—du—nan-si

The priests, she tells him, are now assembled to pass judgment on him; yet it is not too late for him to clear himself, and she herself is willing to plead with the King for his pardon. To the melody of No. 20 he rejoins that he has been guilty of no treachery: his incautious lips had betrayed him, but there had been no thought of evil in his heart, and his honour is unstained: he is ready to die, for life without happiness and hope would be abhorrent to him.

Passionately she appeals to him to live:

21

Ah! —— tu dei vi-ve-re! Sì, all'a-mor mìo vi-vra-i;

To save him she, who has suffered so much through him, will give up throne and country and life itself. He rejects her offer with scorn. With a reversion to the melody of No. 20 he reproaches her for having separated him from Aïda, whom no doubt she has already slain. She assures him, however, that Aïda still lives, though her father had died in the fighting; but where Aïda now is she does not know. If she saves Radames, will he promise to renounce the girl for ever? This he refuses; whereupon the desperate Amneris declares that he has changed her love for him into enmity, and calls on the gods to avenge her. Death for him, he tells her, has no terrors: gladly will he die for Aïda; and he heaps scorn upon Amneris and her pity for him. As she falls back exhausted the guards enter and take Radames away.

Left alone, Amneris reproaches herself bitterly for having delivered him, in her blind jealousy, into the power of the priests, whose sinister motif (No. 2) accompanies her brief monologue. Soon the white-robed ministers of death, as she calls them in her despair, are seen crossing the stage on their way to the subterranean hall of justice, to the unceasing accompaniment in the orchestra of the inexorable No. 2. "He is in their power!" Amneris moans, "and I it was who delivered him up to them!" From below there comes now a unison canticle of Ramphis and the priests, praying to their gods for their blessing on what they are about to do; and interspersed with their pious phrases are wild laments from Amneris.

From the crypt Ramphis is heard denouncing Radames as a traitor and bidding him defend himself against the charge. To the long and impressive indictment he makes no reply; only the wailings of Amneris punctuate the solemn monotones. Then judgment of death is passed on him—slow death by immurement under the altar he has profaned. As the priests, still to the unwavering tread of No. 2, emerge from the crypt, Amneris turns on them in fury, denouncing them as blood-lusting tigers and heaping curses on them for sending to his death an innocent man; to which their only reply is a reiterated "He is a traitor and must die!" As they disappear from the scene Amneris launches a final curse on them, and rushes out madly as the curtain falls.

11

The final scene occupies two floors. The upper one shows us the splendid interior of the temple of Vulcan; the lower one is a gloomy crypt with long receding arcades, and colossal statues of Osiris, with crossed hands, supporting the pillars of the crypt. Radames is on the steps leading down to the vault; above him are two priests lowering the great stone that is to seal it off. He laments the ending of his days in this dark dungeon, and his separation from Aïda: wherever she is, may she know nothing of the fate that has befallen him! But he hears a groan, and searching the gloom he sees a human form which he soon identifies as Aïda. Sadly she tells him that, anticipating his fate, she had crept unseen into the crypt, there to die in his arms.

From now to the end of the opera Verdi is at the summit of his powers. In passionate but mournful tones Radames laments the extinction, for love of him, of so much beauty and sweetness;

while she, for her part, has an ecstatic vision of their reunion in a world free from all sorrow. From the temple above floats down a chorus of priests and priestesses solemnly invoking, to the strains of No. 8 and No. 9, the mighty Phtha, the informing principle of the universe.

Vainly Radames makes an effort to dislodge the stone that closes the crypt, and the lovers resign themselves to their fate. They sing their Liebestod, a sad farewell to life, Aïda leading off with "Farewell, ye vale of tears, dreams of a joy that faded out in sorrow":

22

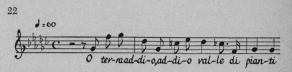

Radames echoes the resigned lament. The chorus break in again with their solemn ritual song, and on the upper level we see a desperate Amneris throwing herself on the stone, imploring, in choked accents, peace for the soul of her beloved Radames. The lovers continue with No. 22, the final cadence of which:

23

constitutes their last farewell to life. Aïda falls dying into the arms of Radames, Amneris numbly stammers again her prayer for eternal peace, the chorus inside the temple invoke Phtha for the last time, and the curtain falls with the mystical Nos. 22 and 23 slowly fading into silence in the highest reaches of the orchestra.

Otello

GIUSEPPE VERDI [1813–1901]

PRINCIPAL CHARACTERS

OTELLO	*Tenor*
DESDEMONA	*Soprano*
IAGO	*Baritone*
CASSIO	*Tenor*
RODERIGO	*Tenor*
LODOVICO	*Bass*
MONTANO	*Bass*
EMILIA	*Mezzo-soprano*

1

T is probable that the idea of an opera based on Shakespeare's *Othello* had occurred to Verdi in the 1860's, though for a long time *King Lear* interested him more. It was not until 1879, however, that the Othello idea was taken up seriously, when the young poet and musician Arrigo Boïto (1842–1918), the cultured son of an Italian father and a Polish mother, came into friendly relations with Verdi after a longish period of mutual misunderstanding. The first-fruit of their collaboration was the *Otello* of 1887, the second the *Falstaff* of 1893. Boïto was enough of a poet to see a great subject imaginatively and to be scrupulous about style, and enough of a practical musician to understand from the inside the many problems involved in the co-operation of words and music in opera; and it is fairly safe to say that without his generous servicing of Verdi we should never have had an *Otello* at all. He skillfully condensed the five acts of the Shakespeare play into four, retaining practically everything that was vital to the action and inserting little that was not, and making a remarkable success of the rendering of many of Shakespeare's best-known lines into Italian.

The poet in him made him at times, of course, more poetical than was necessary for the composer's purposes. He gave himself a great deal of needless trouble to preserve a particular rhyming scheme intact even when the lines in question were divided between different characters. The mature Verdi had no use for these technical verbal refinements, and ruthlessly scrapped them whenever they conflicted with his musical purpose. He would make mincemeat of Boïto's carefully concocted rhyme-patterns, shaping his melodic line to convey the simple sense of the words, so that sometimes an end-rhyme on which the poet had evidently plumed himself finds itself lost, unnoticed, in the middle of a musical line. Verdi, in fact, had outgrown the age-old notion that it was the first duty of a composer to cut and trim each limb of a melody to the measured inches and the neat rhyme-click of the lines of poetry: his new dramatic sense and his great growth as a musical craftsman both urged him on to the creation of long melodic sentences that took the shape not of pre-dictated symmetrical patterns but of a continuous run-on of the notes from the beginning to the end of a given dramatic idea. If in this process the poet's rhymes were swamped, so much the worse for the poet and his rhymes. Verdi was wholly bent now on what he called "la parola scenica"—the diction of the musical stage, which is often quite a different thing from the diction of a poem intended primarily to be read.

It seems to have been Iago who first captured his imagination in *Otello*, and for a time he proposed to call his opera after that character. He probably began formal work at the score about 1884, though there must have been a good deal of quiet sketching before then. The music was completed on the 1st November 1886, and the first performance took place at the Scala, Milan, on the 5th February 1887, under Franco Faccio, with Tamagno as Otello and Maurel as Iago.

2

Providentially, as it happened, certain psychological defects of the Shakespeare drama played right into the hands of the opera composer. A modern reader of Shakespeare sometimes finds it hard to understand how any man of ordinary intelligence could be so blindly credulous of what he was told about his wife as Othello was. Old Thomas Rymer, in a famous passage in his book *Tragedies of the Last Age*,[1] did not mince his words where the bard was concerned. He wrote Othello off as "a tedious drawling tame goose, gaping after any paultry insinuation, labouring to be jealous, and catching at every blown surmize." "Testy Rymer" has been described by at least one Shakespearean scholar as the worst critic who ever lived. Maybe, though there are many other claimants to that distinction. Even a bad critic, however, cannot help being right sometimes; and today we find so acute a psychologist as Mr. T. S. Eliot confessing that no convincing refutation of Rymer's views on the jealousy of Othello has yet come his way.

The problem of Othello's "gullibility" has been dealt with in masterly fashion by the American professor, Elmer Edgar Stoll,[2] who demonstrates in the first place that this—to us—amazing credulity figures again and again in the plays of Shakespeare and his contemporaries, the "motif" evidently being one that the public of that day was prepared to swallow whole,[3] and in the second place that Elizabethan audiences did not look for quite the same things in drama as we do. They laid less stress on "dramatic psychology" and its slow consistent developments than the modern world does, and, as Dr. Stoll puts it, "from beginning to end the Elizabethan dramatic method was founded on speech and outcry." We cease to jib at Othello's endless capacity for credulity when we realise that Shakespeare was less concerned with making the man wholly credible than with making him the excuse for the pouring out of a vast amount of great poetry. Music, in its turn, asks primarily for opportunities to spread its own wings in its own way. And not only does Shakespeare's play of itself provide a composer abundantly with these opportunities for rhetorical expansion, but Boïto artfully provided Verdi with another entirely of his own invention—the "Credo" which he puts into the mouth of Iago in the second act. Here he boldly out-Shake-

[1] 1692; Vol. II, p. 120.

[2] In his *Othello; an Historical and Comparative Study* (1915).

[3] It was older than the Elizabethan age, and it makes its appearance in more than one later drama.

speares Shakespeare. "Iago's don't exist," says Dr. Obispo in Mr. Aldous Huxley's *After Many a Summer*. "People will do everything that Iago did; but they'll never say they're villains. They'll construct a beautiful verbal world in which their villainies are right and reasonable." That may be so; Boïto's Iago perhaps paints himself in colours too uncompromisingly black. But as in doing so he gave Verdi an opportunity and a pretext for writing the "Credo" music, we turn an indulgent eye on his offence against normal human psychology. On this point, however, there will be more to be said when we arrive at the "Credo."

3

Otello does not lend itself well to point-to-point exposition and fragmentary quotation, because so much of it is taken up by big scenes into which Verdi crams a vast amount of musical detail of which no idea can be given by citation of a bit of a theme here and a bit there.

In the opera the whole action takes place in "a seaport in the island of Cyprus"; the period is the end of the fifteenth century. The curtain rises on a quay, on which stands a tavern with an arbour. It is night, and a hurricane, accompanied by thunder and lightning, is sweeping the sea. The quay is crowded with Cyprian citizens and Venetian soldiers, anxiously awaiting the arrival of the commander of the Venetian forces, Otello; among them are Cassio, Otello's lieutenant, Iago, his ensign, a Venetian gentleman, Roderigo, and Montano, Otello's predecessor in the government of Cyprus.

There is no overture, Verdi plunging at once into a lurid orchestral description of the storm at sea, where Otello's ship is fighting for its life, and the inferno in the sky. Boïto indulges himself in a good deal of rich poetic imagery on these subjects, but his labour is mostly in vain, for it is only the general musical effect, not the actual words of the chorus, that counts in performance. At last there comes a great choral cry of "She's safe!", and in a few moments Otello appears on the steps leading up to the quay from the shore. In stentorian tones—the brief passage of eleven bars is perhaps the most difficult tenor "entrance" in all opera; it at once reduces many an otherwise good Otello to something like ineffectualness—he announces complete victory in the recent battle; the Turkish fleet lies at the bottom of the sea. The storm now abates, enabling us to overhear a conversation between Iago and Roderigo. The latter simple-minded gentleman has come from Venice filled with a hopeless passion for the fair Desdemona, and the master villain, confessing his own hatred for Otello, who has passed him over and made Cassio his lieutenant, promises Roderigo full success in his pursuit. Already at the words (in Shakespeare),

> *He [Cassio] in good time, must his lieutenant be,*
> *And I—God bless the mark!—his Moorship's ancient,*

we see Verdi limning the false, plausible Iago in the serpent turns and twists of the melody he puts into his mouth:

Note the sardonic shake on the final "alfiere" ("ensign," "ancient"). The two go out at the back, still talking.

There comes now a lapse into "opera" of the more conventional type. Boïto and Verdi could have gone on quite easily and naturally from here to the big scene in which Iago gradually envelops Cassio in his coils; but apparently before then the audience must be granted a little "relief." So they show the stage gradually lighting up with festal bonfires, coloured lanterns, and so on, and start the chorus off on an elaborate set piece in praise of fire and flame and the similarity of these natural phenomena to the ardours of love.

This unnecessary interpolation out of the way, and the storm having by now died down completely, we can concentrate our attention on a group standing and sitting near a tavern table, among them Iago, Roderigo and Cassio. The action now follows Shakespeare closely. Employing a musical conversation tone of admirable directness and speed, Verdi shows us Iago drawing both Cassio and Roderigo deeper and deeper into his net. He forces Cassio, against his better judgment, to drink with him: his

drinking song—"And let me the canikin clink"—fulfils all the functions of an old-style aria yet is wholly one in substance with the
course of the action, not interrupting it at any point but carrying
it easily on: its vigorous pendant:

2

Allegro ♩=120

Chi al-l'e—sca ha mor-so— del di—ti—ram—bo

has an *entrain* that Cassio and the others find irresistible. There
is a foretaste here, not only in the solo parts but in the choral
ensemble, of the light and easy musical speech of *Falstaff*; and
what is most remarkable of all, while ensembles of this kind in
Otello run to a length rare in the earlier Verdi they do not immo-
bilise the drama but keep it moving steadily forward.

4

As the serpent's coils weave themselves closer and closer about
Cassio, Iago gives Roderigo his instructions; when the lieutenant
is thoroughly and pugnaciously drunk and obviously incapable
of fulfilling the commission brought to him by Montano from
Otello to guard the bastion, Roderigo is to inveigle him into a
brawl. This ends in Montano, who has tried to make peace between them, being sorely wounded for his pains, with Iago hypocritically professing to be anxious to end the fray, and sending
Roderigo off to rouse the town by spreading a rumour of mutiny.
Soon the alarm bell is heard ringing, and the tumult brings
Otello on the scene, hot with anger. He demands to be informed
of what has happened. The wounded Montano, and Cassio, now
sobered, can tell him nothing; Iago also hypocritically professes
to lack all understanding of how the insane quarrel had begun.
By now the turmoil has brought Desdemona from her bed; and
at the sight of her Otello's Moorish blood boils over. To Cassio
he turns with a curt "Thou art no longer my lieutenant." Cassio
lets fall his sword, which Iago picks up and hands to one of the
soldiers, muttering "I triumph!"
Otello having dismissed them all, bidding them see that peace
is kept in the town, everything is now set for the great duet be-

tween him and Desdemona that is to end the act. This begins in exquisite soft orchestral colours as Otello sings of the calm of love that has at last succeeded the dangers and tumults of the day:[1]

His later development of the ecstatic strain is to a skilful adaptation on Boïto's part of a famous section of Othello's speech to the Senate in Shakespeare's first act—

> *She loved me for the dangers I had passed,*
> *And I loved her that she did pity them*:

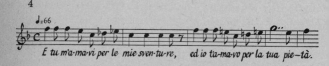

The long and lovely episode was obviously intended to suggest the extreme of quiet happiness under a starlit sky of peace; it should not be bawled at us in the way it too often is by singers who no longer have a mellifluous pianissimo left in them.

The duet ends with a rapturous cry of "A kiss, and again a kiss!", to a motif that will make a poignant reappearance at the end of the drama:

[1] Verdi's dynamic indications are very quiet almost throughout the duet, ranging mostly between *ppp* and *pppppp*. But these must not be taken too literally: as Toscanini has reminded us, the average Italian orchestra of that period was so prodigal of tone on almost all occasions that in order to get a real *pp* Verdi had to write *ppppp* or even, as in one case in the present duet, *pppppp* in a score. One is reminded of Berlioz's story of the singer who always pronounced "poisson" as "poison." The conductor managed to get something like the *ss* out of her only by assuring her that the word was spelt with three s's.

5

and with a last happy glance at the Pleiades and an invocation to Venus the pair go out arm in arm towards the castle, to a final soft breathing of No. 3 by the orchestra.

5

Boïto has thus dexterously condensed Shakespeare's first two acts into a single act of the opera, and now, having disposed of the preliminaries, he can get down in good earnest to the core of the drama—the gradual bringing by Iago of the other main characters into his toils.

The second act shows us a hall on the ground floor of the castle, with two spacious galleries at the sides, and at the back a door opening upon a garden. The serpentine twists and coilings of the brief orchestral introduction:

6

show us Iago's evil mind at work; and when the curtain rises we see him entering and engaging Cassio in conversation.

Verdi's conception of Iago is already suggested in our musical examples No. 1 and No. 6; always the stress is on the smooth-moving, snake-like element in the man's intellectual and moral make-up. If he were an actor, Verdi told one of his correspondents in September 1881—the painter Domenico Morelli, who had sent him a sketch in which Iago figured as a small man in a black costume [1]—and were called upon to play Iago, he would present him as a tall, lean man with thin lips, small eyes set near the nose like

---

[1] Verdi did not object to this: "that Iago should be dressed in black," he told Morelli, "nothing better, seeing that his soul is black. . . ."

a monkey's, his forehead high and receding, the back of the head markedly developed; in manner he would be *distrait, nonchalant,* indifferent to everything, cutting, lightly throwing off remarks good and evil with an air of not attaching the least importance himself to what he was saying, so that if anyone were to accuse him of having said something infamous he would reply "Really? I didn't think it so; but don't let us say any more about it." A man of this type, Verdi continued, could deceive anyone, even, to a certain extent, his own wife, whereas a small, malignant man makes everybody suspicious of him and so deceives no one. That was the Iago, basically evil-minded, unscrupulous, plausible, self-contained, self-controlled, that Verdi set himself the task of portraying in music. He succeeded admirably.

When the curtain rises we see Iago, always to the accompaniment of the twisting No. 6 in one form or another, giving the disconsolate Cassio some advice—he is to work on Otello's feelings through Desdemona. It is the latter's habit to rest at mid-day in the garden with Emilia, Iago's wife; there, then, let Cassio await her. Having dismissed his dupe, Iago, still to the accompaniment of No. 6, embarks upon a soliloquy in which he expounds his own philosophy of life—the famous Credo. A tremendous unison in the orchestra, ending with a sinister shake:

7

prefaces his confession—"I believe in a cruel God who has created me in his own image . . . From some vile germ, some atom, was I generated. Because I am human I am evil . . . Whatever I do or think that is vile was decreed for me by Fate. The honest man is merely a poor actor, whose tears and kisses and glances and professions of honour are only lies. Man is the sport of the evil Fates, from the germ in which his being began to the grave and the worm." At this point No. 7 reappears in a weightier and darker harmonic form:

8

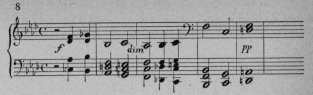

which is repeated as Iago resumes his brooding: "At the end of this farce comes death. And after that? Nothing! heaven is but an ancient idle tale!"

6

The musical idiom changes as Desdemona and Emilia appear in the garden: Iago hurries to the colonnade into which Cassio had retreated, and bids him hasten to Desdemona. This he does, and we see them strolling up and down together, in close conversation, with Desdemona smiling in friendly fashion on the suppliant. Now is the time, says Iago to himself, to bring Otello here; but before he can move to do so he already sees him on his way thither. Taking up a position by one of the columns on the left, he gazes fixedly at the pair in the garden, and, pretending to be talking to himself, mutters, "That I like not!" Otello, having overheard the remark, as it was intended that he should, comes forward and asks him what he means. To the smoothest of music Iago begins to stir up Otello's suspicions—for he has observed that at the precise moment he had appeared, Cassio had taken leave of Desdemona. The episode that follows is modelled closely on Shakespeare's handling of the intrigue. In oily tones Iago asks Otello whether, when he was wooing Desdemona, she was acquainted with Cassio, and if that young man had enjoyed his confidence at the time:

9

Otello's suspicions are soon at boiling point, while the crafty Iago remains cool, feeding the flames with sly insinuations and warnings—"Beware, my lord, of jealousy!":

10

It is the green-eyed monster, which doth mock
The meat it feeds on.

With hypocritical professions of love and loyalty Iago advises the now maddened Otello to delay action until he has proof: let him observe Desdemona well with Cassio, for a single unpremeditated word of hers may either dispel Otello's suspicions or finally confirm them.

Their talk is broken in upon by a chorus in the distance singing the praises of Desdemona, who now re-enters the garden through the great door at the back of the scene: she is accompanied by women and children of the island and Cypriot and Albanian mariners, who come forward offering her flowers and other gifts. Some of them break into song, accompanying themselves on the guzla (which Verdi is careful to describe as "a sort of guitar") and small harps slung across their shoulders; children strew lilies on the ground; some of the sailors present Desdemona with necklaces of corals and pearls. This overlong and dramatically superfluous episode is a blot on the construction of the drama, a sad lapse on both Boïto's part and Verdi's into operatic convention; and what makes it worse is that Verdi's music for it all is in anything but his best vein.

When the chorus has ended, Desdemona graciously kisses some of the children and bestows a purse on the mariners, while some of the women kiss the hem of her gown. The crowd departs, leaving only Desdemona and Emilia at the back of the stage. Desdemona comes forward to the hall and greets Otello—who, with Iago, has been watching the preceding scene—and poet and com-

ɔser take up again the temporarily severed threads of the dra-
ɔatic action. We get back to Shakespeare once more. Desdemona
ɔeads for the restoration of Cassio to Otello's favour. Her inno-
ɔnt importunities end in exasperating him, and when she offers
ɔ bind her handkerchief round his throbbing temples he throws
ɔ down angrily. It is picked up by Emilia. There follows a mas-
ɔrly quartet, in which Desdemona humbly and affectionately
ɔgs forgiveness if she has unwittingly offended, and Otello be-
ɔails his lost illusions, while in the background Iago wrenches
ɔe handkerchief from Emilia's reluctant hand; "now," he ejacu-
ɔtes, "I have them in my meshes, to work upon as I will!"

7

At a sign from Otello, Desdemona and Emilia leave the stage,
ɔgo launching a veiled threat at his wife as she goes out—"Say
ɔthing. Do you understand?" "Desdemona false!", moans Otello,
ɔhile Iago, glancing at the handkerchief before placing it in his
ɔublet, mutters the equivalent of Shakespeare's:

> *I will in Cassio's lodging lose this napkin,*
> *And let him find it. Trifles light as air*
> *Are to the jealous confirmations strong*
> *As proofs of holy writ.*

ɔtello turns on him furiously, reproaching him for having placed
ɔm on the rack as he has done by making him doubt Desdemona.
ɔhe text now follows closely the superb rhetoric in which Shake-
ɔeare (Act III, scene 3) makes Othello bid farewell to every-
ɔing he has done and been:

> *Farewell the neighing steed and the shrill trump,*
> *The spirit-stirring drum, the ear-splitting fife,*
> *The royal banner and all quality,*
> *Pride, pomp and circumstance of glorious war! . . .*
> *Farewell! Othello's occupation's gone!*

ɔis recollection of the glorious warlike past to which he must
ɔw bid adieu is accompanied by military fanfares and by a
ɔarch-like figure in the orchestra:

11

a presumable variant of which will appear later. He threatens Iago
with dire punishment if he fails to prove to him that Desdemona
is guilty. In reply Iago tells him, in smooth, insinuating tones,
how, sleeping in the company of Cassio lately, he had heard the
young lieutenant murmuring endearments in his sleep to Desdemona and crying "Cursed fate that gave thee to the Moor!" This
crazy babbling, of course, Iago points out hypocritically, was only
in a dream; but what if a simple fact should confirm it? Did not
Desdemona once possess "a handkerchief spotted with strawber-
ries?" he asks. "I gave her such a one," replies Otello; "'twas my
first gift." That handkerchief, says Iago, he had seen for certain
yesterday in Cassio's hand. For Otello this is the last faggot on the
flames. Calling insanely for blood he falls on his knees and summons heaven to witness that his hatred for the guilty pair will
never end until he has been avenged by his own hand. This superb piece of musical rhetoric is based on a figure:

12

which certainly seems to derive from our No. 11, though one has
to confess that one can give no valid reason for the affiliation.

Before Otello can rise, Iago too sinks to his knees and, taking
up the strain, vows that until the sun shall cease to shine he will
give himself up, body and soul, to Otello's service. Then the two
voices blend in a duet that ends with a great united appeal to an
avenging God. And so the second act ends, with a credulous
Otello caught beyond hope of liberation in Iago's snare.

8

The setting of the third act is in the great hall of the castle. On
the left is a large colonnade, which joins on to a smaller hall; at

the back is an open gallery. After a short orchestral introduction, which becomes more and more agitated as it proceeds, the curtain rises, showing Otello and Iago. To them comes a Herald, with the news that the watch at the port has signalled the arrival of a galley bringing the Venetian ambassadors to Cyprus. The Herald having been dismissed, Iago begins a fresh assault on the credulity of Otello. He has arranged for Cassio to call on Desdemona again: and Otello, in hiding, is to observe the pair closely. Iago would speak of the handkerchief, but Otello sends him away with a curt "Go; I would forget that!"

Desdemona having entered by a door on the left, a conversation ensues between her and Otello that is one of Verdi's masterpieces of dramatic characterisation. Desdemona is all affection; Otello treats her with all imaginable courtesy, in which, however, we detect a sinister sub-ironic note. Desdemona, in her kind-hearted innocence, at once broaches the subject of the discarded Cassio. Otello asks for her handkerchief, but the one she offers him is not the one he wants to see—one given to him, he tells her, by his mother, who had it from an Egyptian charmer; while in his mother's possession it would secure her the love of her husband, but

> To los't or give't away were such perdition
> As nothing else could match.

The tension of the music increases as Desdemona protests that though she has it not with her at the moment it is not lost, and tries to turn the conversation once more to the subject of the forgiveness of Cassio. Losing control of himself Otello imperiously demands the handkerchief again and again, each time more angrily, and ends by damning her for a strumpet. Wrenched out of her obsession now, she protests her loyalty in accents of the deepest feeling, while Otello, torn between anger and love, raves madly against her.

Suddenly he regains command of himself, and, as Verdi's stage directions put it, his tone changes for a moment from that of rage to one of an ironic calm that is even more terrifying. Reverting to the smooth melody with which their conversation had begun he takes her by the hand and conducts her ceremoniously to the door by which she had entered. There he dismisses her with a final brutal insult; then he returns to the centre of the stage in deep dejection. There follows the great soliloquy that is Verdi's supreme achievement in serious opera. The words are a masterly Italian paraphrase of the words Shakespeare puts into Othello's mouth at a later stage of the drama:

> *Had it pleased heaven*
> *To try me with affliction; had they rain'd*
> *All kinds of sores and shames on my bare head,*
> *Steeped me in poverty to the very lips,*
>
> .　　.　　.　　.　　.　　.　　.
>
> *I should have found in some place of my soul*
> *A drop of patience;*　　.　　.　　.　　.
>
> .　　.　　.　　.　　.　　.　　.
>
> *But there, where I have garner'd up my heart,*
> *Where either I must live or bear no life,*
> *The fountain from the which my current runs,*
> *Or else dries up; to be discarded thence!*
> *Or keep it as a cistern for foul toads*
> *To knot and gender in! Turn thy complexion there,*
> *Patience, thou young and rose-lipp'd cherubin,*
> *Ay, there, look grim as hell!*

9

The first part of the long soliloquy is based on a tiny orchestral figure:

13

that twists and turns, in one astonishing mutation after another, through more than twenty bars of the score. Here, if anywhere, we see how marvellously Verdi had developed as a musical crafts-man in this final phase of his career. Basically his procedure here is the one to which attention has been more than once drawn in our analyses of *Rigoletto, Il Trovatore* and *La Traviata*—he fastens upon a small melodic turn which he pursues with dogged persistence through bar after bar. But in his middle period he had confided the turn to the vocal part, and his unchanged repetitions of it were often so mechanical as to make it in the end ludicrous. But here he allots the figure not to the voice but to the orchestra, and by means of one harmonic and contrapuntal change after another he gives it a new psychological significance each time it recurs, for there seems to be no limit to his resources of deducing B from A, and C from B, and so forth in a single organic process. Nowhere else is he Verdi so "Wagnerian" as in these remarkable pages; yet nowhere else is he so completely, so loftily and profoundly, just Verdi.

The procedure, as we have seen, is one in which the main burden of expression is laid on the "symphonic" developments in the orchestra, the voice part being confined throughout to what is virtually a brooding monotone. Nothing could have suggested better than this monotone the numbness of the man's spirit. But with consummate tact Verdi breaks off the procedure at just the right moment, and launches Otello on a great lyrical flight on his own account at the point indicated by the line

But there, where I have garner'd up my heart,

a flight that finds its culmination in a great soaring and then drooping phrase:

14

as he speaks with infinite regret of the extinguishing of the sun, the smile, that had been his life and his joy.

This melting mood soon vanishes: frenzy takes possession of

him, and as he cries "Damnation! She shall confess, then die!" Iago enters with the news that Cassio has arrived. He places Otello in the colonnade, where he can see without being seen, then runs to usher in his dupe. His speech is once more deceptively smooth; he ends his first sentence—"Come; the hall is deserted; step within, Captain"—with one of his customary sardonic shakes on the third syllable of "Capitano." Well he knows that he is now complete master of the game.

Cassio is in poor condition; his only hope, he says, is in Desdemona, whom he had hoped to find there; and at that name Otello pricks up his ears. Iago leads Cassio up within earshot of Otello, and, affecting a friendly gaiety, as of one man of the world to another, decoys him into speaking of his mistress Bianca. This puts the lieutenant for a moment in merry mood, and he begins to tell of his finding a handkerchief in his room, placed there by some unknown hand. Iago's strategy is to keep Otello on tenterhooks by moving the lieutenant now and then out of Otello's range and bidding him speak softly, so that his words are now and then lost; but when he shows Iago the handkerchief Otello has no further doubts. The conversation is carried on to light-hearted music, so that the episode has something of the effect of a musical scherzo, in an idiom that is an anticipation of some portions of *Falstaff*. Knowing that Otello has seen what he intended him to see and that, as he puts it, the fly is now caught in the web, Iago launches a fast-moving trio, in which we see Cassio lost in admiration of the workmanship of the handkerchief he innocently holds in his hand, while Otello, bemoaning his own tragedy, manages to conform to the rhythm and pace of the other two without any sacrifice of his own musical individuality.

10

Suddenly, as Otello conceals himself again, trumpets sound without and the great gun of the castle booms out, announcing that the Venetian ship has dropped anchor. Iago hustles Cassio away; and Otello, emerging from his hiding-place, asks him the sinister question, "How shall I murder her, Iago?" The crafty villain plays on his frenzy, reminding him of Cassio's brazen display of the handkerchief, and Otello bids him get him some poison, for Desdemona shall die that very night—only to decide a moment later that she shall die not by poison but by suffocation in her bed. As for Cassio, Iago promises to see to him, and Otello makes him his lieutenant from that hour.

Otello now prepares to greet the ambassadors, and sends Iago off to find Desdemona, whose presence he desires in order to avert any possible suspicion. The fanfares ring out once more, and the stage gradually fills with a great crowd, among them the dignitaries of the Venetian republic, the still lovelorn Roderigo, the ambassador Lodovico, noblemen and ladies and soldiers, while Iago has returned with Desdemona.[1] Otello, ostensibly reading a document handed him by Lodovico, watches Desdemona suspiciously, and is goaded to fury when he hears her tell Iago that she hopes to see Cassio soon returned to her husband's favour. Maddened beyond endurance he strikes her, to the general horror —can this be the noble Moor, Lodovico asks, who is the pride and glory of the Senate?

At Otello's command Cassio is brought in, and Otello discloses the contents of the document the ambassador has brought—the Doge has recalled him to Venice, and his lieutenant Cassio is to succeed him in the command of Cyprus; he himself will set sail for Venice on the morrow. He lays a violent hand on Desdemona, who falls to the ground. Helped to her feet by the pitying Emilia and Lodovico, she sings a sorrowful lament for the love she has plainly lost. Her song rises to ecstatic heights as she recalls the days when she was all in all to Otello:

15

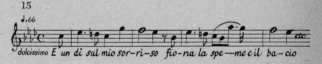

dolcissimo E un di sul mio sor-ri-so fio-ria la spe—me e il ba-cio

Round this strain is built up a massive ensemble, in which not only the chorus but Emilia, Roderigo, Cassio and Lodovico comment, each according to character, on the horror of the situation, while Iago urges Otello to act quickly, before his wrath dies down; he himself will deal with Cassio before the evening is out. Roderigo he counsels to be of good heart: as things stand now,

[1] At this stage of the action Verdi later added a ballet for a production in Paris. This is dramatically superfluous.

Otello will depart on the morrow—and with him Desdemona, whereas if some "accident" should befall Cassio, then perforce Otello would have to remain in Cyprus. For the "accident" to Cassio—at the point of Roderigo's sword—Iago himself will provide.

The huge ensemble ends with Otello being seized by one of his Moorish brain storms. In terrible tones he bids them all leave him. Desdemona gives an appealing cry of "My husband!", but he repulses her with a curse. She is led away, half-fainting, by Emilia and Lodovico, and the crowd breaks up in dismay. Left alone with Iago, Otello is seized by a convulsion as he recalls the episode of the handkerchief, and falls to the ground in a swoon. "My poison works!" ejaculates Iago; and as shouts of "Long live Otello! Glory to the Lion of Venice!" resound without, accompanied by rousing orchestral fanfares, he makes a horrible gesture of triumph over the inanimate body, and, as the curtain falls, cries "Behold the Lion!", with his usual ironic shake on the second syllable of the last word ("Leone").

11

The scene of the short fourth act is Desdemona's bedroom, with a bed, a prie-Dieu, a looking-glass and some chairs. Over the prie-Dieu is a statue of the Madonna, before which a light is burning. On the table is a candle. It is night. As the curtain rises the orchestra gives out softly a plaintive theme:

16

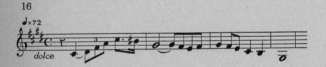

that anticipates the melody of Desdemona's "Willow" song. When this brief prelude has run its course we find Desdemona and Emilia in conversation. The maid would persuade her mistress that Otello seemed calmer when last she saw him. He had bidden Desdemona go to bed and there await him; and now, with a premonition of evil, she is asking Emilia to lay on the bed the white sheets that had been on it on her wedding night, adding

*If I do die before thee, prithee, shroud me
In one of those same sheets.*

Sad and weary, she seats herself before the looking-glass and sings, to the melody of No. 16, of a poor maid of her mother's, one Barbara, who had died of love, and who used to sing a ditty with a refrain of "Willow, willow, willow." That mournful song Desdemona cannot get out of her mind tonight—

Sing all a green willow must be my garland.

She starts as she imagines she hears a knock at the door, but it is only the wind. Voice and orchestra are hushed as she bids Emilia good night; but in an instant there comes from her a passionate cry, as of a frightened child, of "Ah! Emilia, addio, Emilia, addio!":

17

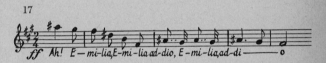

This cry is one of Verdi's masterstrokes of dramatic timing and expression.

When Emilia has left her, Desdemona kneels before the image of the Madonna and prays for herself and for all souls in affliction, for the sinner and the innocent, for those oppressed and for their oppressors—"Pray for us now and in the hour of dying":

18

As her tones die away and she lies down on the bed Otello becomes visible on the threshold of a secret door; he is accompanied by an ominous theme in the depths of the double basses which develops into a kind of long recitative. For some time not a word is spoken. Otello places a scimitar on the table, then halts and stands before the candle, as if in doubt whether to extinguish it or not. His glance falls on the sleeping Desdemona, and he puts the candle out. With a furious gesture he approaches the bed, pauses, raises the curtain, and, to the accompaniment of phrases in the orchestra that are like sobs, looks down for a long time on the quiet figure, and kisses it three times, the orchestra giving out a poignant reminiscence of the "Kiss" motif from the first act (No. 5).

She awakes. He asks her if she has said her prayers, and in sombre tones exhorts her, if she has any unredeemed sin on her conscience, to pray heaven's forgiveness for it now, for he would not kill her soul. She protests that her only sin is that of love for him, and for that she is now to die! He charges her with having loved Cassio, and bids her confess it; he would not have her die perjured. Passionately she demands that Cassio be sent for; but he tells her that Cassio is dead. Despairingly she pleads for life, but now he is beside himself with grief and rage, and he suffocates her.

As he stands motionless, gazing down at her, he is startled by a knocking at the door and the voice of Emilia crying out to him to admit her. When he does so she brings the news that Cassio has killed Roderigo, but—a bitter blow, this, for Otello!—"Cassio lives." From the bed comes the pitiful small voice of Desdemona, declaring "I have been unjustly done to death; I die innocent!" She has died by her own hand, she continues as Emilia hastens to her in terror: "Commend me to my Lord; I die innocent! Addio!" Emilia turns furiously on Otello, whose only reply is the equivalent of Shakespeare's

> *She's like a liar gone to burning hell*:
> *'Twas I that killed her,*

for she had been Cassio's strumpet; that he had had on the word of Iago. "And you, oh fool, believed him?" cries Emilia. She runs to the door, crying despairingly "Help! Help! the Moor has killed Desdemona!"

Lodovico, Cassio and Iago come in, followed by Montano and some soldiers. The raging Emilia turns on Otello, denouncing him as the murderer of his innocent wife. "Not innocent," he says, for he had seen in Cassio's hand a handkerchief he had once given her as the pledge of his love. Disregarding Iago's angry attempt to silence her, Emilia discloses that the fateful handkerchief had been taken from her by force by her husband. "And I found it in my chamber," says Cassio; to which Montano adds, "Roderigo, before he died, revealed to me the infamous wiles of this villain." Otello, sword in hand, turns furiously on Iago, who takes to flight, pursued by some of the soldiers. Lodovico orders Otello to surrender his sword. The wounded Lion answers him with a strange gentleness: "Let no one fear me, armed though I be. This is the end of my journey. Of Otello nothing remains." He turns a pitying gaze on Desdemona, with a heart-breaking cry of "Desdemona! Desdemona! Dead! Dead! Dead!" He has let fall his sword; but now he draws a stiletto from his doublet and stabs himself. His last words, as he falls on the body, are virtually Shakespeare's

> *I kissed thee ere I kill'd thee; no way but this,*
> *Killing myself, to die upon a kiss;*

and the orchestra closes it all with a last poignant reminiscence of No. 5.

La Traviata

GIUSEPPE VERDI [1813–1901]

PRINCIPAL CHARACTERS

VIOLETTA VALERY ("LA TRAVIATA")[1]	*Soprano*
FLORA BERVOIX	*Soprano*
ANNINA	*Soprano*
GIORGIO GERMONT	*Baritone*
ALFREDO GERMONT	*Tenor*
GASTONE, VISCOUNT DE LETORIÈRES	*Tenor*
BARON DOUPHOL	*Baritone*
MARQUIS D'OBIGNY	*Bass*
DR. GRENVIL	*Bass*

1

MARIE DUPLESSIS, the heroine of Dumas *fils' La Dame
aux Camélias*[2] and of Verdi's *La Traviata*, is one of
the few people who have achieved such immortality
as art can bestow on anyone within a few years of
their death. As the reader will be aware, she was the most famous
Parisian courtesan of an epoch that was peculiarly rich in that
fauna. But to see her merely as that is to underrate her. She is
psychologically the most intriguing and the most baffling crea-

---

[1] "Traviata" is the past participle feminine of the verb "traviare," meaning
"to go astray."

[2] Dumas persisted in spelling the word thus until the end of his days. When
it was pointed out to him that there should be two l's he replied gaily that
George Sand before him had spelt it with one, and he would rather write
incorrectly with Mme Sand than correctly with other people.

ture of her type that the modern world has known—"one of the mysteries of our epoch," as she was described by Jules Janin, who knew her well. Abundant testimony as to her strange beauty and her unanalysable charm is to be found in the writings of those of her contemporaries who have left us their reminiscences of her; and no doubt others, such as Liszt, who refrained from doing so—in public—would have grown equally lyrical over her had they written about her.

Jules Janin has recorded the impression she made on him on that day in 1845 when he and Liszt encountered her in the foyer of one of the minor Paris boulevard theatres. Her appearance was so charming, he says, her look so innocent, her manner so natural, "at once bold and becoming," that she gave one the impression of belonging to the highest society. "Her face was serious, her smile imposing; and merely from her carriage one would have deduced that she was, as Elleviou said of a certain court lady, either a demi-mondaine or a duchess." She could be in no company, private or public, bourgeois or aristocratic, without all eyes being drawn to her. Liszt, we are told, after a few minutes' conversation with her sang her praises to Janin with the discriminating enthusiasm of one who was a connoisseur where the other sex was concerned. The young woman—she would be about twenty-one at that time—seems to have been equally impressed by the great pianist, for to Janin she had hardly a word to say. Shortly afterwards Liszt became a visitor at her house.

A critical scrutiny of the Liszt-Duplessis affair in its entirety reveals several errors of time and fact in Janin's famous preface to *La Dame aux Camélias*. With all this, however, we cannot concern ourselves here; it belongs more properly to Liszt biography, which now calls for re-writing at many points. Whatever blunders —or perhaps intentional manipulations or concealments?—there may be on Janin's part does not affect his account of the impression Marie Duplessis made on him at his first meeting with her and later. Liszt was undoubtedly one of her lovers, though his biographers seem to have been unaware of it.

2

Marie was "tall," we are told by Dumas *fils*, who came into her orbit about 1844, and "very slender, with black hair and a pink

and white complexion.[1] Her head was small, her eyes long and
lacquer-like, resembling those of a Japanese, but delicate and
animated; her lips were cherry-red, and she had the loveliest teeth
in the world; she put you in mind of a Dresden figurine. . . . She
was one of the last and the few courtesans with a heart: that, no
doubt, was why she died young. She lacked neither intelligence
nor disinterestedness. She died poor[2] in a sumptuous apartment
that had been distrained on by her creditors. She had an inborn
distinction, dressed with taste, and carried herself gracefully, almost nobly. Sometimes she was taken for a lady of high society:
mistakes of that kind are made every day now." Théophile
Gautier describes her as "a young woman of exquisite distinction,
a pure and delicate type of beauty."

3

She is popularly supposed to have been unable to endure the
scent of any flowers but camellias, and Dumas, in his novel of
1848, says that no one ever saw her with any other flower—that
at the florist's shop kept by Mme Barjon she was known as "la
dame aux camélias," a nickname that has stuck to her. In a preface
of 1867, however, to a new edition of his play—which was later
than the novel—he said categorically that she was never known,
during her lifetime, as "la dame aux camélias": he appears to
imply that this characterisation of her was as much his own
invention as the name he bestowed on her, Marguerite Gautier.
The truth seems to be that she decorated her apartment lavishly

---

[1] On two of her passports, issued at different periods, her height is given
as 1 metre 65 and 1 metre 67, that is to say, about five feet four inches. One
official described her eyes as black, the other brown. A captious critic here
and there wrote her down as thin for her height; "no sculptor," said one of
them, "would have chosen her as a model." The disturbing beauty of her
face no one ever questioned. There exists a painting of her which confirms
the judgment of her biographer Johannès Gros that her face and form were
the purest expression of the "keepsake" type of female beauty in vogue in
the early nineteenth century, fragile, virginal, spiritual, vaporous, expressive
of melancholy and tender aspiration. In order to come as near as possible
to the sylph ideal the fashionable woman of that epoch, so the Comtesse
Dash assures us, ate as little as possible: this practice, combined with late
nights and perpetual excitement, no doubt increased Marie Duplessis' tendency to consumption, even if it did not originate it.

[2] This is not true, as we shall see later.

with flowers according to the season, but disliked the proximity of strong-scented ones, such as roses, which made her feel faint. A camellia she could wear in her corsage without discomfort. Moreover, camellias were the "correct thing" in fashionable Paris circles at the time when Dumas was dramatising her. "La dame aux camélias" was probably just a novelist's licence on his part, on which he sometimes let his fancy play irresponsibly. "During twenty-five days of each month," he says slyly in the novel of 1848, "the camellias were white, but during the other five red; one never understood the reason for this variation of the colours, which I record without being able to account for it." He brings in this change-of-colour motif, as we may call it, at a decisive point in his novel.

The matter is complicated somewhat by his saying that on her monument in the Montmartre cemetery her name—her true name, Alphonsine Plessis—was surmounted by "a crown of artificial camellias affixed to the marble in a glass casket." The solution of this little mystery seems to be that this ornament was placed on Alphonsine's grave some time after her death, when Dumas' drama, which had stirred the sensibilities of all Paris, especially the women, had fixed indelibly in the public mind the poetic image of her as the lady of the camellias. The play was written in 1849, soon after the novel, but not produced, owing to difficulties with the censor, until 1852. Dumas's illuminating preface to it was written in 1867, for a definitive edition of his *Théâtre complet*.

4

To the making of this exquisite flower of a Marie Duplessis there had gone a considerable quantity of mud. We know much more about her now than her contemporaries did; thanks to the reminiscences of many of those who had known her, and to much patient French research among the official archives of the region in which she was born, we are able to reconstruct her short life with considerable accuracy. She was the daughter of one Marin Plessis, a mercer in a small way of business in Nonant, in the department of the Orne, a man of bad character and vicious heredity. His wife, Marie Louise Michelle Deshayes, whom he married in 1821, came from a family of better standing than his. There were two children of the marriage; the second, Rose

Alphonsine—the future "dame aux camélias"—was born on the 15th January 1824. At some date which we cannot fix precisely Marie Louise Plessis had to be saved from the brutalities of her husband by a relative on her mother's side, who obtained for her a post as housekeeper to a certain "Lady Anderson Yarborough," who lived now in Paris, now in Geneva. Apparently the mother never saw Alphonsine again.

The child was put by her father to work on a farm, where, as might have been expected, her singular beauty soon attracted the notice of the youth of the countryside. Finding her no doubt something of a problem her father took, or sent, her to Paris at about the age of fifteen, and left her more or less to her own resources. She appears to have worked for a while in various shops, but soon found a more agreeable scope for her natural talents among the students and small shopkeepers of the quarter. Paris was dance-mad at that time, and Alphonsine was an assiduous frequenter of the dance-halls. An excursion one day to Saint-Cloud with a small tradesman no longer in his first youth ended in her being installed in an apartment in the rue de l'Arcade as his mistress. It was not long before she was filched from him by a young man of birth, wealth and fashion who has been identified as Agénor, Comte and later Duc de Guiche, and later still Duc de Gramont and Prince de Bidache, Napoleon III's Minister of Foreign Affairs. The grisette was now fairly launched in the fashionable world.

She must have been a strange blend of voluptuousness, love of luxury, simplicity and disinterestedness. When the young Dumas first met her she was little more than twenty, and one could see, as he puts it, that she was still "à la virginité du vice." Part of her inexplicable charm lay in what would have been called, in a woman of rank, her high breeding. "She had an inborn tact, an instinctive elegance," said one who knew her well. We have abundant testimony that in the most riotous company she was generally quiet, discreet in her gaiety, speaking little, laughing rarely, with a shade of sadness in her smile, as though in the depths of her being she had a premonition of an early and tragic end. When she chose to talk, we are assured, her conversation could interest the most sober and sensible of men. The catalogue of the sale of her effects after her death listed books by Byron, Marivaux, Chateaubriand, the elder Dumas, Goethe (*Werther*), Molière, La Fontaine, Rousseau (*La Nouvelle Héloïse*), Lamartine, Victor Hugo, Walter Scott, Thiers (eleven vols.), and Rabelais. The few letters of hers that we possess are quiet in tone and sensible in substance. She was no vulgar, flashy gold-digger, and, contrary to popular belief, she "ruined" none of her rich lovers; she merely accepted the luxury in which they voluntarily and gladly indulged her. They were men of the highest Parisian society, on whom crudity of speech or vulgarity of manner would have grated. In her train she had poets, artists, and men of letters; and not one of that critical entourage has a word to say against her on any score. A greater feminine mystery the world has perhaps never known.

One of the legends connected with her is that while she was taking the waters at Bagnères, whither she had gone to escape for a while from the exhausting whirl of her life in Paris, hints of consumption having already forced themselves on her, she met with an old duke who had recently lost, through tuberculosis, a daughter of the same age as hers and resembling her physically; it ended in his taking her under his protection as a second daughter when she returned to Paris. The one element of truth in all this is that there was such a person, and Marie became his mistress in 1844. He was the Comte de Stackelberg, an elderly diplomat— he was approaching his eightieth year—living with his wife at No. 7 of the rue de la Chaussée d'Antin; a generation earlier he had functioned at the Congress of Vienna as Russian ambassador to Austria. He figures in Dumas' work as the Duc de Mauriac. "The legend," Dumas assures us, "of the consumptive daughter whose traits the duke found again in Marie Duplessis is pure invention. The Count, notwithstanding his great age, sought in her not, like Oedipus, an Antigone, but, like David, a Bathsheba." He installed her in a sumptuous apartment at No. 11 of the Boulevard de la Madeleine, with a carriage, jewels, furs and everything else that her luxury-loving heart could desire.

It was while she was living under the protection of this elderly nobleman that the acquaintance with Dumas *fils* began. That story, however, had better be told later, in closer connection with the play and the opera. Of the last two years of Marie's short life there is otherwise not much to tell.

5

At the end of 1845, after her rupture with Dumas, her accredited lover was a certain young Édouard, Vicomte de Perrégaux, who corresponds vaguely to the Comte de N . . . of the novel and the Comte de Varville of the play.[1] On the 25th January 1846 Marie obtained in Paris a passport—in her actual name of Alphonsine Plessis—and early in February she and Perrégaux set out for London, where they lodged at 37 Brompton Row, Kensington. On the 21st they were married at the Kensington Registry Office; on the certificate the bride's age was correctly given as twenty-two, while Perrégaux knocked some sixteen months off his, giving it as twenty-nine. Presumably it was for family reasons that he chose to have his marriage with the *dame aux camélias* celebrated in London rather than in Paris; but why it took place at all is a mystery still unsolved. Nor can we understand why, a little later, in a calm and friendly letter, the original of which has survived, Marie—signing herself "Marie Duplessis"—wrote to him thus: "My Dear Édouard, Of the many things touched upon in your letter there is only one to which you appear to wish me to reply: you desire me to say in writing that you are free to do whatever seems to you good. I told you this by word of mouth the day before yesterday: I now repeat it and sign myself, Marie Duplessis." No doubt there were family reasons at the back of all these moves; but that the marriage was legally valid, and that Perrégaux acknowledged it after her death, is proved by the fact that it was he who obtained permission from the authorities to have her body exhumed and re-interred.

Her vitality and her fortunes began to decline markedly in the spring of 1846. The summer of that year she spent in a feverish search for health and distraction at Spa, Wiesbaden, Ems and

---

[1] His grandfather was a celebrated financier whom the first Napoleon had raised to the Senate and made first Governor of the Bank of France; on his mother's side he was related to the Duc de Tarente. Édouard's father had been created a count by Napoleon. Édouard's elder brother, who came into the title in 1842, entered the French embassy service. Édouard chose the army, without showing any great zeal to carve out a military career for himself. He seems to have been of an amiable disposition, with an inclination to romantic melancholy. Eight short letters to him from Marie have survived and have been published.

other resorts. She could no longer doubt that she was consumptive and that the end could not be far off; and we may reasonably suppose that it was fear of the dread malady that accounted for the general neglect of her by her friends during the last few weeks of her life. When Dumas, in his preface of 1867 to a new edition of his play, described her as dying "poor, in a sumptuous establishment that had been seized by her creditors," he was speaking in relative terms. In the play and the opera she does indeed die in poverty, having come to the end of the sale of all her possessions, with only her maid and a certain Gaston remaining devoted to her to the end. The facts are, however, that although some of her creditors, obviously sensing that her star was setting, were pressing her for payment, and she was realising her possessions to satisfy them, she was far from anything resembling poverty. Her debts at the time of her death amounted to no more than about 20,000 francs; the four days' sale of her effects, which included jewellery, a considerable quantity of clothes, much table silver and porcelain, various objects of art, some elegant furniture, a fine horse, a carriage and a pony, realised more than 89,000 francs. The beneficiary of the estate seems to have been her sister Delphine, who had married one Constant Paquet.

Marie died on the 3rd February 1847, shortly after completing her twenty-third year, and was buried on the 5th.

In the final scene of the play and of the opera, which had to be made as romantically harrowing as possible, the only friend who remains faithful to Marie during her last weeks of agony is the impecunious young "Gaston" who had first introduced Armand to her. There is little reason to doubt, however, that Perrégaux visited her, and certainly he and the old Comte de Stackelberg accompanied her body to its temporary grave in the Montmartre cemetery. It remained there only a few days. On the 12th February Perrégaux bought for 526 francs a "concession" in the new quarter of the cemetery "for the sole and perpetual burial place of Mademoiselle Alphonsine Plessis." Four days later her remains were exhumed and re-buried: her final resting-place bore the simple inscription "Here reposes Alphonsine Plessis, born the 15th January 1824, died the 3rd February 1847. De Profundis."

6

Thanks mainly to Dumas' various prefaces and some scattered references of his in later life to the affair, we know now accurately enough how much in the novel and the play is fiction and how much fact. The reader will remember that the opera, which follows in the main the structural lines of the play, opens with a gay party in Marguerite Gautier's [1] house at which she meets Armand Duval [2] for the first time. In essentials this scene is drawn from life. After a chance meeting at one of the Paris theatres the young Dumas seems to have been taken to the house of Marie Duplessis by a friend who figures in all three versions as "Gaston"; the intermediary was a certain "Prudence Duvernoy" (in the opera "Flora Bervoix"), a former demi-mondaine one of whose windows almost touched one of Marie's; ostensibly in business now as a milliner, she made herself useful as Marie's confidante and woman of affairs, and borrowed money from her which she never had any intention of repaying. The large supper party of the opera owes its existence solely to the usual necessity for big vocal ensembles: at the actual supper the only people present were Marie, Prudence Duvernoy, "Gaston" and Dumas. The future novelist and dramatist was then a boy of twenty-one—the junior of Marie by some six months. An unhappy childhood had woven a thread of romantic melancholy into the texture of an ardent temperament; and there was in him already a good deal of the social moralist—especially where women and the preservation of French family life were concerned—with whom his books have made us familiar. On that fateful evening Marie's interest in him had been stimulated by the revelation that the boy had long worshipped her from afar, and that during her recent severe illness he had several times enquired at the house about her without leaving his name.

We have his assurance in later years that the account of what happened at the supper is not fiction but fact. Marie, suddenly seized with a fit of consumptive coughing, had to leave the table

[1] This is her name in the novel and the drama. In the opera she becomes Violetta Valery.
[2] It will be observed that Dumas' hero has the same initials as Dumas himself.

She was followed anxiously to her room by Dumas: [1] the others were more or less indifferent, having been the witnesses of several previous attacks of this kind. Marie was touched by the young man's solicitude and his love, in which she saw interwoven a troubled pity for her manner of life that betokened a profound understanding of her. For the first time in her febrile career she realised that she was loved for her own sake; and though she neither desired nor conceived it possible to be "rescued" in the sense that he and the world of their epoch attached to that word, she was profoundly moved by and grateful for the delicacy of feeling he showed. Their talk ended in her accepting him as her lover; and Dumas has vouched for the literal truth of the episode in the novel in which, as a symbolic sealing of their compact, she plucked a red camellia from a bouquet of those flowers and placed it in his buttonhole. To his enquiry when he could see her again she replied with a smile "Later; it isn't always possible to carry out the terms of a treaty the day it is signed." "When, then, may I see you again?" Armand asked. "When the camellia has changed colour," was the reply. "And when will that be?" "Tomorrow, between eleven and midnight."

Apparently their rapturous idyll lasted only a few weeks; then the inevitable complications began. Loving and being loved disinterestedly for the first time, Marie dreamed of a *solitude à deux* for a while that summer in the country near Paris, the world forgetting, by the world forgot. As the young Dumas' modest income would be quite insufficient for that purpose, she expected him to leave the financial side of the matter to her. Against this both the lover and the chevalier in him rose in protest. Both Marie and Prudence had tried to make it clear to him that the idyll of young romantic love in temporary seclusion from the world could be only a chord of delicious harmony in the feverish dissonance of Marie's life. That life, she gave him clearly to understand, she could not change; she needed luxury on her present scale, with which Dumas would be quite unable to provide her even in their country retirement, and the whirl of excitement to which she had been accustomed was a physical and moral necessity

[1] In the play and the opera, of course, it is the guests who retire, the vital scene between Marie and Armand having to be played out in view of the audience.

for her if she were to live at all. She told him that as she knew she had not long to live she must live faster than other people. He, for his part, was too young and too poetic, too self-consciously literary, to be able to see the matter with her curious mixture of disinterested idealism and practical realism. He had read *Manon Lescaut*, and Marie's refusal to cut loose the economic tie that bound her to the generous old "Duke"—the Comte de Stackelberg—on whom her very existence depended, and her proposal that Dumas should not concern himself at all with the expenses of their temporary flight into the country, seemed to him a suggestion that he should be another Des Grieux living on another Manon supported by the purse of another M. de B. . . . The young man's jealousy also played its part in the tragic dénouement. Marie made no secret of the fact that she had other and richer lovers whose purses were at her disposal, for the scale of her expenditure went beyond even the liberal allowance of the venerable Comte. It all ended with a frenzied outburst on his part—half common jealousy and wounded amour-propre, half honourable revolt—during which he wrote her a letter that ended their association, though not the pathetic love of each of them for the other.

7

What purports to be this letter is given us, in slightly differing forms, on page 149 of the novel and in Act II of the play: the latter, being the shorter of the two, can be quoted here:

"It does not suit me to play a ridiculous part, even in connection with the woman I love. The moment I left you, the Comte de Giray entered your house. I am not as old as Saint-Gaudens,[1] nor am I of the same disposition. Pardon my only fault, that of not being a millionaire, and let us both forget that we have known each other, and, for a moment, believed that we loved each other. When you receive this letter I shall already have left Paris. Armand." In the novel, the lovers are soon reconciled, thanks to Marie's quiet good sense; she returns the letter to Armand and he destroys it. The course of events in real life was very different.

By a curious freak of fate the actual letter of the real "Armand"

---

[1] A ridiculous elderly character in the play who is led by the nose by the cocotte with whom he is in love.

has survived. It no doubt went to Marie's sister after her death, along with her other possessions, and in due course found its way first of all, apparently, to a collector of autographs, then into the auction room or the catalogue of some dealer in merchandise of this sort. Dumas bought it. In the early 1880's Sarah Bernhardt took up the part of Marguerite Gautier in a revival of *La Dame aux Camélias*; and Dumas was so moved by the memories she brought to life within him at a performance at the Théâtre de la Porte Saint-Martin in January 1884 that he presented her with the letter, enclosing it in a copy of an edition of the novel which by then had become a rarity. The letter, he assured her, "was written by the actual Armand Duval some forty years ago."

It is dated "Midnight, 30 August"; the year, according to M. Gros, can only be 1845, as in August of the following year Dumas was apparently not in France. It runs thus:

"My dear Marie,

I am not rich enough to love you as I would wish, and not poor enough to be loved as you would desire. So let both of us forget—you a name which should be almost indifferent to you, I a happiness that has become impossible for me. There is no need for me to tell you that I am sad, since you know already how much I love you. Adieu, then. You have too much heart not to understand why I write this letter, and too much intelligence not to be able to pardon me for it.

A thousand souvenirs,
A.D."

Whether she replied to this letter we do not know, or even whether she ever saw Dumas again. Be that as it may, the arguments he puts into Marguerite's mouth at her meeting (after the letter) with Armand Duval in the second act of the play are probably the very ones Marie employed to bring Dumas to reason all through the pitiful period of their association: he had enough of the objectivity of the dramatist in him to depict her as his superior in logic, knowledge of the world, good sense and good feeling.[1] As to whether the tragic dénouement came about through

[1] This is the finest section of the play, and perhaps the most important chapter (No. 15) of the novel. It is a pity that not the smallest use was

anything even remotely resembling the action of the play at this point—Marie's silent self-sacrifice to save the "honour" of a respectable family—we need have no hesitation in writing that down as an invention of the dramatist. It is even doubtful whether the rupture was brought about by any lavish expenditure on Marie's part for Dumas's benefit. In the preface of December 1867 to the new edition of the play he says expressly that "Marie Duplessis did not have all the pathetic experiences I have given to Marguerite Gautier, though she would not have shrunk from them. If she sacrificed nothing to Armand, that was because Armand did not wish her to do so; to her great regret, she was called upon to play only the first and second acts of the drama." The whole trouble, culminating in the rupture, seems to have come from the young man's resentment at Marie having other lovers, coupled with the bitter knowledge that he was not rich enough to ensure himself the sole possession of her by supplying her with the means to live to the full the kind of life that had become second nature to her. Of the sincerity of their love for each other, and of his later remorse for his behaviour towards her, there can be no question. We have a precious record of both his love and his remorse in a number of poems, inscribed to "M.D.," that form part of a very rare little volume—*Péchés de Jeunesse*—which he brought out in 1847, not long after her death. Only a hundred copies were printed, and only fourteen of these were sold.

8

It was no doubt to try to forget his sorrows that in the autumn of 1846 he went with his father and some friends on a trip to Spain and North Africa, where he found temporary consolation, as indeed he frequently did in later years, in some lighter loves. It was apparently in Algiers that he heard that Marie was gravely ill; and according to the *Péchés de Jeunesse* he wrote to her that he would return to ask her forgiveness:

> *Je vous avais écrit que je viendrais, Madame,*
> *Pour chercher mon pardon, vous voir à mon retour.*

---

made of this material by Verdi's librettist, for it constitutes the psychological core of the tragedy.

But apparently there was no reply from Marie, who was no doubt by that time too weak and too broken to write; so Dumas continued with the itinerary of the party. On the 4th January 1847 they arrived at Toulon. The father hurried back to Paris to attend to his dramatic affairs; the son stayed on at Marseilles until the 10th February. He was preparing to return to Paris when the news reached him of Marie's death a week earlier. When, a few days later, he arrived in Paris, it was too late either to attend her funeral or to be present at the sale of her effects.

The poignancy of his grief was enhanced by a chance return in the first days of June to the countryside in which he and Marie had spent so many happy hours. He sought relief from his anguish in the writing of his novel, which took him, he tells us, no more than three weeks. The play was written in 1849, but, as we have seen, trouble with the censorship delayed the stage production of it until the 2nd February 1852—five years, all but a day, after Marie's death.

As Verdi was living in or near Paris about the time when Dumas' novel was published we may be fairly certain that he made the acquaintance of the Lady of the Camellias then, and that he felt at once that this was the kind of subject—simple, moving, passionate but not "stagey" as he once put it—for which something within him kept crying out as a relief from the gloom of *Rigoletto* and *Il Trovatore*. When later he saw the play at its first appearance in the Paris Vaudeville Theatre in February 1852 he could no longer doubt that he had found what he wanted; and as soon as the play was published he sent it to his friend Piave to be turned into a libretto for him. Verdi's sketches for *La Traviata* have survived. They show with what ardour he worked at the congenial theme, laying out first of all, as was his general practice, the broad dramatic lines of the opera and then concentrating on the more emotional "numbers." What is musically the finest section of the whole work—the orchestral prelude to the third act—was evidently realised, just as it now stands, in a single hour or two of inspiration.

The new work was intended for the Fenice Theatre, Venice. From the beginning Verdi had difficulties with the casting of the rôles. He could never visualise the plump Signora Salvini-Donatelli as his Violetta, and would apparently have preferred almost any other capable soprano for the part: [1] he even received an anonymous letter warning him of "a stupendous fiasco" if he did not get another soprano and another bass. When he arrived in Venice in February 1853 to take charge of the rehearsals he found a Violetta quite as disillusioning to the eye as he and others had feared, and, in addition, a tenor (Graziani) who had lost his voice, and a baritone (Varesi) who obviously could not work up any interest in his rôle of the elder Germont.

The first performance took place on the 6th March 1853. The audience was favourably disposed towards the work until the middle of the second act, when Varesi sang "Di Provenza il mar" so badly as to set the house against him. With the third act came out-and-out disaster, the spectators, with the expansive figure of Salvini-Donatelli before their eyes, being quite unable to take seriously the doctor's diagnosis that the consumptive Violetta had no more than a few hours to live. "Sorry to have to bring you bad news," Verdi wrote with his customary curt stoical frankness to his publisher Ricordi the next morning, "but I can't hide the truth from you. *La Traviata* was a fiasco. Let us not waste time asking why. It just was." His message of the same day to his friend Emanuele Muzio was even more laconic: "*La Traviata* a fiasco last night. My fault or the singers'? Time will show." And two days later he wrote in the same resigned vein to Luccardi after the second performance: "Fiasco! out-and-out fiasco! I don't know who is to blame, and the less said the better. I'm off tomorrow to Busseto."

9

The legend still survives that the audiences of the 1850's in general jibbed at the novelty of operatic characters appearing in contemporary costumes; but the fact is that in the second production [2] the action had been put back a century and a half, and the costumes were those of the reign of Louis XIII.[3] Nor is there any more truth in the second legend sometimes associated with the fiasco—that the moral susceptibilities of some members of

---

[1] She was the second wife of the great Italian actor Tommaso Salvini.

[2] See p. 191.

[3] In present-day productions the setting of the opera is rightly that of the play—the Paris of the 1840's.

the audience were outraged by the subject of the work. That had undoubtedly been the case in Paris, where Dumas' play was stigmatised in some not normally prudish quarters as "an encouragement to immorality." To see how the sterner moralists of the period regarded Dumas' *La Dame aux Camélias* we have only to turn to Comte Horace de Viel Castel, who devoted a couple of corrosive pages in his diary to the play after seeing it on the 10th February 1852. The purpose of the censorship, he said, had been precisely to protect public morals against such outrages on them as this: "the play is a disgrace to the epoch that patronises it, to the government that tolerates it, and to the public that applauds it." Viel Castel, who knew Dumas *père* and Dumas *fils* well, detested them both. "Alex. Dumas *fils*," he continued, "is a young good-for-nothing to whom, I must say in justice to him, everything has been lacking—domestic education, moral instruction, decency of environment. The only company he has ever seen in his father's house is that of loose women. His father and he have often had the same mistresses and wallowed in the same orgies"; and he records a cynical dialogue between the father and the son that cannot be reproduced in English.

As for the opera, it is evident from the enthusiasm with which it was greeted at its second production that the Italian audience found nothing in the subject calculated to damage anyone's morals. This second production came about through one Antonio Gallo, the proprietor of a music business in Venice, and a great believer not only in Verdi but in the artistic value of *La Traviata*. He took the slighted work in hand, engaged a different company for it, and produced it in his own theatre at San Benedetto (Venice) on the 6th May 1854. It was an instantaneous success, and was quickly taken up by other theatres in Italy and abroad. For the new production Verdi made some changes in the score, mostly in the second act.

It is no disparagement of his work—a remarkable one for its epoch, and still very much alive—to say that the time is ripe for a new operatic treatment of the subject by some dramatist and musician of genius. The old conventional apparatus of the play and of the opera should be scrapped, and the theme treated on fresh lines, as a psychological study not of the fictitious Marguerite Gautier and Armand Duval but of the actual Marie Duplessis and Alexandre Dumas *fils*. Neither the imagination of the mid-nineteenth century nor the musical idiom and technical apparatus of the Italian opera of the period was equal to the task of limning so complex a character as Marie Duplessis in music. One sees her today as a psychological problem of profound interest, an unstable compound of the sensual and the spiritual, complicated, as cases of that kind so often are, by an hereditary tendency to tuberculosis. The borderline between the two temperaments is frequently a very uncertain one, and the merest chance may decide in a particular case on which side of that line the subject's life will be lived. It is impossible to read the effusions of the female saints, with the frequent tinge of the sensuous in their imagery, without feeling that by a single slight turn of the wheel of fate, a single small change in the chemistry of some gland or other, a single abnormality in this cerebral centre or that, the great saint might easily have become a *grande amoureuse*. Conversely, there are psychological grounds for believing that by the merest difference in the blending of the constituents of a Marie Duplessis, and in the epoch and the milieu of the blending, she might have become not a courtesan but a mystic, the knowledge that she was doomed to an early death filling her with a desire not to live more feverishly in this world but to aspire towards spiritual love.[1] Awakened sexually at a very early age and thrown into an environment that accelerated her development primarily along the lines of sex, she was predestined to be what she became. Modern music, with the instruments for psychological probing forged for it by Strauss in his Salome, his Elektra and his Don Quixote, would be much better equipped for the realisation of a character so complex as that of Marie Duplessis than the Italian music of Verdi's days was; it could show the subtle interworkings of the sensual and the spiritual in such a woman in a way that even poetry might find it hard to achieve. Piave and Verdi, even if they had been conscious that an interesting pathological problem existed, had not at their disposal the technical means for stating it. The Verdi of the 1850's could think of no better way of characterising the more frivolous side of Marie's nature than by giving

---

[1] Dumas himself described her as "a virgin of whom a nothing had made a courtesan, a courtesan of whom a nothing could have made the purest virgin."

er a passion for coloratura. No doubt his experiences of the prima
onna of the period had made him suspect that facility in colora-
ura and mental negligibility were interchangeable terms; but
aat naïve way of dealing with the Traviata will hardly do today.
he whole subject should be taken up and thought out afresh by
ome composer of the present day—if he can find the right li-
rettist.

10

Piave's libretto, dramatically considered, is a mediocre piece of
ork, though it is difficult to see how he could have made a much
etter job of it, the operatic conventions of the period being what
ey were. For us today the most vital part of Dumas' play is the
cond act, in which Marguerite quietly lays all her cards on the
ble in her argument with Armand as to ways and means, and we
alise how inevitably the conflict between her mentality and the
ruples and jealousy of her lover must end in catastrophe. This
rt of Dumas' second act is completely ignored by Piave and
erdi. For the rest, while the general structure of the play is
llowed in the libretto, it is psychologically trivialised in the
era at many points simply in order to make it "opera." There
e indications that Verdi himself, in later years, did not regard
e part of Violetta as putting much strain on the intellectual
wers of a prima donna. In 1886 the young Gemma Bellincioni
as suggested to him as a possibility for his Desdemona, seem-
gly on the strength of the success she had had as Violetta. Before
ming to a decision, Verdi wrote to Ricordi, he would like to
e her in some other opera: "one could not judge her by *Traviata*;
en a mediocrity could shine in that work and be very bad in
ery other."

The brief prelude to the opera is based on two themes, each of
hich delineates Violetta. The first:

1

an expressive melody which we shall not hear again until the
ird act, when it will be put to the finest uses: its appealing plain-

tiveness and its tenuous texture characterise the heroine in he
last hours of suffering and resignation. The second theme:

also depicts Violetta, this time as *amoureuse*; we hear it for th
first time in the opera itself in the second act, at the point when
after the crucial scene with Germont *père*, she bids Alfredo a pas
sionate farewell. (See Ex. No. 21.) In the prelude the orchestr
sings the melody twice, the second time with a decorative coun
terpoint of smaller notes intended to suggest simultaneously th
more frivolous side of her character. The composer's intention
are rational enough, but the realisation of them is not always be
yond reproach. Here and there the ornamentation is musicall
rather naïve, suggesting an "air with variations" of a technicall
very rudimentary order; but in the end Verdi's sincerity silence
any criticism we might feel impelled to make on that score.

The curtain rises on the drawing-room in Violetta's house. I
the background there is a door leading to another room; ther
are also two lateral doors. On the left is a fireplace surmounte
by a mirror; while in the centre of the room stands a richly lai
out supper table. We find ourselves in a scene of revelry of th
established operatic kind. Violetta, sitting on a sofa, is chattin
with some of her friends, among whom is Doctor Grenvil, whil
others are hastening to greet some new arrivals, who include th
Baron Douphol and the Marquis d'Obigny, the latter with Flor
Bervoix (Violetta's confidante) on his arm. Violetta rises and goe
to greet the newcomers, promising them and herself an evenin
of pleasure. The general atmosphere of careless gaiety is sug
gested at once by a sparkling melody in the orchestra:

Pleasure, Violetta explains to her friends, is the drug that reconciles her to living.

A new and soberer theme breaks in suddenly on the lively No. 3:

4

as the Vicomte Gastone enters, bringing with him a young man whom he introduces to Violetta as his friend Alfredo Germont—another of her many admirers, he assures her. Alfredo kisses her hand, and greets the Marquis, whom he already. knows.

11

By this time the servants have completed the laying of the table, and Violetta, to the effervescent strains once more of No. 3, invites her guests to be seated. They arrange themselves so that Violetta is between Alfredo and Gastone, with Flora opposite her between the Marquis and the Baron; the others sit where they like. The orchestral texture of the scene is always admirably homogeneous, the transitions from No. 3—which depicts the company as a whole—to No. 4—which relates more specifically to Alfredo—and back again being managed without any break of continuity. It is No. 4 that comes into the foreground as Gastone tells Violetta that she is never out of Alfredo's thoughts; during her recent illness the young man had called at the house every day to enquire after her—"which is more than you did," she remarks maliciously to the Baron, who at once takes a dislike to this young newcomer who is obviously finding favour already in Violetta's eyes. The gay No. 3 ripples out again as she fills the cup of the shy and mostly silent Alfredo. The company clamours for a toast; and the Baron (the company's butt' as well as Violetta's) feeling no inspiration, Alfredo is prevailed upon to try his powers.

The orchestra breaks into a lively melody in three-eight time, to which Alfredo launches a toast:

5

They are to drink to youth and beauty and love, and especially to the bright eyes of Violetta. The company echo his sentiments enthusiastically, and Violetta tells them how happy she is among them, exhorting them to live like her, for pleasure is fleeting and youth soon over. After this, Cupid gets to work quickly, as he always does in the fantastic kingdom of opera. The Alfredo who had been too shy even to leave his name when he called daily to ask after Violetta in her illness is now bold enough to talk to the dashing courtesan about love. For the moment they get no further, for after another bacchanalian chorus to the strain of No. 5 a sparkling waltz is heard behind the scenes:

6

and Violetta, regardless of the fact that the supper has only just begun, invites her guests to join her in a dance in the next room. They accept with alacrity, and are all moving off when Violetta suddenly turns pale—we are not told how this physiological transformation is to be conveyed to the audience—totters a step or two, and is obliged to sit down again. It is just an attack of faintness, she assures them, and bids the others go into the adjoining room, where she will join them shortly. All but Alfredo obey her, the dance music continuing in the orchestra without a break.

Going to the mirror to look at herself she perceives that Alfredo is still with her; and with a change in the waltz strain:

7

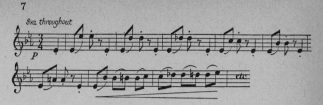

the action takes a new turn. He exhorts her earnestly to give up this feverish life, which will surely kill her. How is it possible for her? she asks him sadly. If she were his, he tells her, he would watch over her and tend her. She cannot believe her ears; is it possible that anyone should feel like that towards *her?* With the lively No. 7 still coming from the adjacent room Alfredo assures her that until now no one has really loved her. She laughs neurotically at the idea that anyone should love a woman like her disinterestedly, and is still incredulous when he tells her that he has done so for a whole year:

8

since the day, indeed, when he first saw her. This is true love, he assures her passionately, to a melody that will frequently appear like a leitmotif later:

9

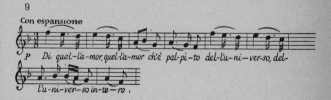

love that is the heart-beat of the universe, mysterious, noble, at once a torment and an ecstasy:

197

10

She answers him in accordance with her character as seen by
Verdi, that is to say, she tells him, soaring into coloratura, to fly
from her:

11

for she herself cannot love, nor can she expect from him a devotion so heroic. She will be frank with him; let him seek another
love and forget her. He replies with No. 10, to which, by way of
emphasising her incorrigible flightiness, she contributes more irresponsible coloratura.

The waltz music is resumed, and Gastone appears for a moment
in the doorway to ask, in his usual carefree way, what the devil she
is doing. Just indulging in nonsense, she assures him, and he
discreetly retires. Turning to Alfredo once more, she advises him
not to speak to her again of love; but as he is on the point of leaving her she halts him, takes a flower from her corsage, and tells
him to preserve it . . . and bring it back to her when it has faded.
That must mean tomorrow, he opines; and she coquettishly
agrees. Still to the accompaniment of the waltz music he swears
once more that he loves her, kisses her hand, and bids her, for
the present, farewell.

12

The dancers, to the melody of No. 3, return and break into a
chorus in which the guests assure Violetta and each other that as

day is dawning it is time for them to leave and replenish their capacity for pleasure by a little sleep. After a great many resolutions and reciprocal assurances to this effect, as was the way in Italian opera finales of that period, they take themselves off, leaving Violetta with the stage to herself for the great scena that is to close the act. It is strange, she muses in a preliminary recitative, how deeply Alfredo's obviously sincere words have engraved themselves on her heart. Would a serious love bring her disaster? She will leave the answer to her throbbing heart, which no man has yet warmed into real life. She has never known the joy of loving and being loved; and shall she turn away from it in disdain now, to continue her present feverish life? Then she launches her famous aria, "Ah, fors' è lui che l'anima, solinga ne' tumulti, godea sovente pingere?" ("Ah, was it he, perchance, whom, lonely in all my dissipations, I so often saw in imagination?"):

12

She recalls the words and music (Nos. 9 and 10) of Alfredo's little song in praise of love. She repeats the whole of this first section of the aria to other words, her mind going back to the dreams she had had of such a lover in her childhood.

For a moment or two she remains silent, lost in thought; then she recalls herself to reality with a cry of "But this is folly, delirium! In the crowded desert that is Paris what can a poor lonely woman hope for? What can she do but seek distraction in the giddy whirl of pleasure?" A coloratura flourish points her final words, and prepares us for the next phase of the aria.

In an allegro brillante:

13

she declares that she will think of nothing but novelty after novelty in the way of folly, confirming her resolve with a flight into coloratura that takes her up to the high D flat. But now there comes a true operatic touch—the voice of Alfredo is heard from beneath the balcony, singing his No. 9 once more, with its No. 10 sequel. The only effect it has on Violetta is to send her off into a repetition of the feverish No. 13; and while Alfredo continues with his canticle to love she surrounds his melody with coloratura more and more brilliant; and the curtain falls with a final assurance on her part that henceforth pleasure shall be the lodestar of her life. Granted that in the operatic world of the 1850's it was in some such form as this that feminine frailty and frivolity had to find expression, the thing could not be better done: a century of familiarity with the aria has not robbed it of the smallest particle of life.

13

But after all this we must confess to a slight feeling of surprise when at our next meeting with Violetta we find that she has done everything which she had vowed so copiously she would never do, even for the affectionate and ardent Alfredo. In Dumas' play the psychological change in her and in the drama comes about quite naturally. At the end of the first act there is no grand scene for the heroine alone: Armand, having received a pledge of love in the form of the flower, says goodbye to Marguerite, who rejoins her guests and encourages them to dance: it is perfectly evident that she is already in love. At the commencement of Dumas' second act we find her broaching to Armand a "combination" that has occurred to her: in a fortnight she will have realised her plan to be free to spend the summer with him in the country near Paris. Armand does not take kindly to the scheme, for the reason that, as he puts it, he cannot reconcile himself to playing the part of a Des Grieux, living with his Manon at the expense of a rich M. de B. . . . Marguerite fences dialectically with the jealous young Armand, and it is arranged that he shall call on her again on the morrow. Left alone, she indulges in a little soliloquy: "Who could have told me, a week ago, that this man, whose existence I did not even suspect, would come to occupy as he does, and so quickly, my heart and my thoughts? Besides, does he really love me? Do I even know that I love him, I who have never been in love? But why deny oneself a pleasure? Why not follow the caprices of one's heart? What am I? A creature of chance; then let chance do with me what it will. What does it matter? It seems to me that I am happier than I have ever been. Perhaps that is a bad omen. We women always foresee that we will be loved, but never that we ourselves will love, and that so profoundly that at the first assault of this unforeseen trouble we lose our bearings."

In the play, then, only a few days have elapsed between the first act and the second. In the opera the first act takes place in August, the second in January of the following year; yet not a word is vouchsafed us in explanation of the change in Violetta's feelings towards Alfredo and towards life in general during those five months. In the second act we are suddenly confronted with a new Violetta, all tenderness and goodness and self-sacrifice, without so much as a coloratura trill or roulade left in her. The stickler for dramatic logic may jib at all this, but Verdi gives us ample musical compensation. This second act of his reveals to us a new Verdi, a fine-fingered musical psychologist.

14

In the second act of the opera, then, Violetta and Alfredo have long been lost in the felicity of their seclusion in the country. When the curtain rises we see a room on the ground floor of their villa near Paris. On the background wall, facing the spectator, is a mantelpiece with a mirror and a clock, and on each side of it a glass door opening on the garden. In the foreground are two other doors facing each other. The room is furnished with chairs, tables, books—and writing materials, the dramatic necessity for which we shall discover later.

After a quiet orchestral introduction Alfredo enters in hunting costume. Putting down his gun, he declares, in an expressive quasi-recitative, that when Violetta is away life has no joy for him. Three months, he muses aloud for the benefit of the audience, have gone by since Violetta turned her back, for his sake, on all her former pleasures and associates, and still she scorns them all; he too is a new man, vivified and purified by her love. In a following aria:

14

he describes how by her love and her always gentle smile she has calmed and strengthened him; their retreat in the country has become a paradise to him.

Annina, Violetta's maid, enters hurriedly, out of breath. Alfredo's questions elicit the information, bit by bit, that she has been to Paris, commissioned by her mistress to sell her horses, her carriages, and what other possessions she can dispose of quickly, for this quiet life in the country has proved very expensive to her. Learning that the amount now required is a thousand louis, Alfredo declares that he himself will go forthwith to Paris and raise that sum; meanwhile Annina must not breathe a word of his intention to Violetta. Pausing only long enough to deliver himself of an aria:

15

in which he reproaches himself passionately for his blindness all this time—Violetta has been his silent protectress against the hard realities of life, and he must wash himself clear of that shame—he rushes out.

Violetta now appears and learns from Annina, to her great surprise, that Alfredo has left hurriedly for Paris but will return before night. Her manservant Giuseppe brings her a letter, which she surmises to be from a business man whom she is expecting, and who was to have been shown in as soon as he arrived. Annina and Giuseppe having left her she opens the letter, which turns out to be from Flora, who, it appears, has discovered the secret of her retreat and now invites her to a dance at her apartment in Paris that evening. They will expect her in vain, says Violetta quietly. Just then Giuseppe returns with the news that a gentleman has called to see her. Assuming him to be the man of affairs whom she was expecting she orders him to be shown in. The visitor, however, proves to be an elderly stranger, who, after making sure that he is addressing Mademoiselle Violetta Valery, announces himself as Alfredo's father. He at once reproaches her roughly for having brought his poor boy to the brink of ruin. Quietly correcting his lapse from good manners in his way of speaking to a lady in her own house, she assures him that he is mistaken in his facts. "He is about to make over his property to you," the father insists.[1] Violetta denies it; Alfredo would never have dared to suggest that, nor would she have accepted anything from him. By way of enlightening him as to the true state of affairs she shows him a paper which proves that it is she who is selling her possessions. Perhaps it is her past that is accusing her? he suggests. The past no longer exists, she assures him; she loves Alfredo, and God has allowed her to cancel out her past by repentance. (Evidently the part she is to play henceforth in the opera is that of the penitent magdalen—always an interesting character in the nineteenth century novel and drama.) Germont, struck by a nobility of soul in her which he had not expected, is now emboldened to ask a sacrifice of her. The happiness of both his children, he says, lies in her hands, for besides his son he has a daughter, pure as an angel:

16

Allegro moderato ♩ = 84

dolcissimo Pu—ra sic-come un an—ge-lo se Al-fre-do ne-ga rie-de-re in
Id-dio mi diè una fi——glia;

se—no alla fa—mi—glia;

whose marriage to a certain worthy young man can never take place unless the stain inflicted on the family honour by Alfredo's association with the courtesan is removed. (Germont is the operatic "heavy father," another type very much in favour in drama

[1] The course of events is made clearer in Dumas: Germont has heard from his Paris lawyer that his son is proposing to make over to Violetta the inheritance he had received from his mother.

and fiction a hundred years ago, the inflexible guardian of family morals. In Dumas he is a highly respectable provincial receiver-general, whose wife had died some three years before the action of the play begins.)

15

Violetta opines that Germont merely wishes her to separate from Alfredo until the daughter is married: that sacrifice would be grievous for her, she assures him, but she is willing to make it. But when she learns that he expects the renunciation to be permanent she is horrified: Germont does not realise, she protests in agitated accents, how deeply she loves his son:

17

Since she has known him, all the rest of the world has ceased to exist for her. And is Germont not aware that she is the prey of a dread malady the inevitable end of which she knows to be not far off? Separation from Alfredo would mean, for her, suffering so great that she would prefer her life to end at once.

The father is full of sympathy for her now, and by way of consoling her he points out that his son is very young, the heart of man is liable to change with the years, and the day will come when he will weary of her—for unions such as theirs have not received the blessing of heaven. His aria:

18

is another illustration of that peculiarity of Verdi's early style to which attention is drawn in our analysis of *Il Trovatore*—a tendency to reiterate the same figure (here seen in bars 2, 4, and 6 of our quotation) till it comes to have an unintentionally comic effect.

Violetta sorrowfully admits the unblessedness of her union with Alfredo, and, seeing that she is weakening, the father presses his advantage home, exhorting her to make an end of this mad dream of hers and save the honour and happiness of his children by listening to what he assures her is the voice of heaven itself. There is a sudden dramatic change from the major key to the minor as Violetta breaks into a wild lament over the lot of women like her, on whom the doors of hope are closed and barred; for even if God forgives them, man has no mercy on them. With tears in her voice she sings a song of resignation that is one of the most moving passages in the work:

19

Andantino

P   Di-te al-la gio—ri-ne   si bel-lae pu —— ra, ch'ar-vi u-na vit-ti-ma

"Go tell your daughter that she shall have a victim whose one comfort in her misery will be that she has sacrificed herself and is ready to die." Equally moving is Germont's reply: "Weep, weep, unhappy one: I know well how great is the sacrifice I am asking of you: have courage, and your noble heart will win its victory":

20

Pian-gi,   pian-gi,   pian — gi   o   mi-se--ra!

She accompanies his efforts at comfort with another mournful reiteration of her willingness to make the sacrifice demanded of her. This whole episode is musically the most moving one of the whole act; we can see that Verdi himself has been profoundly moved, and has drawn upon all that was most finely spun in his own nature to deal with the situation. We feel for Violetta as for a hurt, uncomprehending child: Verdi will never again achieve anything quite like this until the death scene of his Desdemona.

Violetta humbly awaits Germont's commands. "Tell him you do not love him," he advises. "He will not believe me," she replies. "Then leave him." "He will follow me." She asks him to embrace her as a daughter, and as he does so she comes to her great decision. Alfredo will soon be back: let his father be here to console him in his affliction. Telling Germont to go into the garden to await the return of his son, Violetta sits down at her writing-table. She will not tell Germont what her plan is; she will die, and if some day Alfredo learns the truth, let him not curse her memory. The father tries to console her with the prospect of life and happiness, but she reiterates her acceptance of death: she desires only that Alfredo shall know some day that her self-sacrifice was born of her love for him, and that she was his until the end.

16

With another embrace they part, Germont going out by the garden door, and Violetta, with a prayer for strength, sitting down again to write a letter the address of which surprises Annina when she gives it to her with instructions to deliver it herself. Then, to a wailing figure in the orchestra, she writes and seals another letter, which she conceals in confusion when Alfredo enters hurriedly. He sees, however, that she has been writing, and asks to whom. "To you," she replies; but she refuses to give him the letter just then. Alfredo tells her that he is uneasy in his mind because he has had word that his father has come to Paris. He has not seen him, but has had an angry letter from him: still, when his father sees Violetta he is bound to love her. Keeping back her tears with difficulty she begs that she shall not be present when the son and father meet; Alfredo will take her to his father later, when he has explained everything and calmed him, and then she will fall at Germont's feet and all will be well. Meanwhile she begs Alfredo passionately to give her his assurance that he loves her; she ends with the great cry (No. 2) which has already figured in the prelude, but is here heard in the opera itself for the first time: "Love me; Alfredo! Love me as much as I love you! Farewell!": [1]

She runs into the garden. The uncomprehending Alfredo sits down, opens a book, and is wondering whether his father will come now, for it is late in the day, when the excited Giuseppe rushes in with the news that his mistress has gone off in a coach to Paris, and that Annina too has disappeared. Alfredo is not perturbed by this; he assumes that Violetta has gone to Paris to speed up the sale of her property, but believes that Annina will check her. (The reader will remember that he had told Annina that he himself would raise the 1,000 louis Violetta needs.) He catches sight of someone in the garden, and is about to go out to see who it is when he is stopped by a commissionaire, who hands him a letter for a "Monsieur Germont" that had been given him by a lady not far away from the house. Alfredo opens it, reads no further than the opening words—"Alfredo, when this comes into your hands . . ."—, assumes that he has been betrayed, turns round with a wild cry, and finds himself in the arms of his father, who

---

[1] The resemblance has often been pointed out between this melody and the one sung by Lida in Verdi's *La Battaglia di Legnano:*

Many similar "echoes" can be found in his operas; it was not that he was "repeating himself," but simply that he unconsciously employed very much the same basic formula whenever he fell into the same mood. "Fingerprints" of this kind—inveterate *tics* of characterisation—can be found in abundance in all composers.

has entered from the garden. Germont exhorts his son to return and be once more the pride and glory of his home: then, while the despairing Alfredo remains seated with his head in his hands, the father sings the famous appeal to him that cannot quite escape the charge of sentimentality but is still very effective in its proper setting. What has blotted out from Alfredo's mind, he asks, the memory of the soil and the waters of the beautiful Provence that gave him birth:

22

Andante ♩ = 60

P Di Pro-ven-za il mar, il suol chi dal cor ti can-cel-lò? chi dal

cor ti can-cel-lò? di Pro-ven-za il mar, il suol?

where he had been so surrounded by love, and where kind hearts are now aching for his return? [1]

The furious Alfredo is not to be reasoned with: he has surmised, not knowing the full truth, that Violetta has wearied of him and the country and has gone back to Baron Douphol (the Varville of the play), and he can think of nothing now but vengeance. In vain does his father, in another aria in which a little figure resembling that of bar 2 of our example No. 18 is regrettably insistent, exhort him to return to the family that has been mourning his absence, where love and forgiveness await him:

[1] In Dumas' drama, where the whole course of events is more natural than in *La Traviata*, there is no scene between father and son corresponding at all to that in the opera, which was probably inserted only in order that the baritone might be indulged in the luxury of another aria. In the play, Duval *père* has entered from the garden unobserved while the commissionaire was handing Violetta's letter to Armand. The latter reads the first few words of this, gives a cry of rage, and, turning round, sees his father: he throws himself sobbing into the latter's arms, and the curtain falls there and then.

The destination and the contents of the two letters written by Violetta may not be clear to the casual spectator of the opera. In the play everything is clear: Prudence Duvernoy (the Flora of the opera) enters and is given the first letter, to take to Paris. She is astonished when she reads the address—evidently that of one of Marguerite's lovers, Arthur de Varville: she realises that Marguerite is forsaking Armand and returning to her old life.

Assai moderato

PP   No, non u-drai rim-pro-ve—ri; co-priam d'oblio il pas-
sa-to — l'a-mor che m'ha gui-da — to sa tut-to per-do—nar.

(There is too much repetition here—more than the general quality of the music given to Germont *père* can comfortably carry.) The appeal evidently has no effect on Alfredo, who, after his father's final harangue, tears himself away, catches sight of Violetta's letter on the writing-table, opens and reads it, and rushes out with an angry cry of "She has gone to the party! I will have vengeance for this betrayal!"

<h1 style="text-align:center">17</h1>

The next scene takes us back into "opera" again. The actual drama will be resumed—indeed, worked up to its climax—later in this act; but the librettist and the composer have to fill in a certain time-space before that can happen. When the curtain rises once more we see a richly furnished and illuminated gallery in Flora's Paris mansion; for Verdi's Flora is not a mere sponging, cadging confidante-of-all-work, like the Prudence Duvernoy of Dumas' play, but a demi-mondaine in a large way of business on her own account. There is a door in the background, and another on each side of the gallery. On the right stands a gaming-table, on the left a table with flowers and refreshments, and elsewhere chairs and a sofa. According to the score, the second act of the opera takes place in January, the third in February. Dumas' chronology is more in accordance both with the historical facts and with credibility: the first half of the second act shows us Armand and Marguerite still happy in their summer retreat in the country, while the second part relates to a month or so after Marguerite's flight, and the exact time of the third act is the following New Year's day.

Verdi paints in the liveliest colours the revels in Flora's house, where, as the curtain rises, we see Flora herself, the Marquis d'Obigny, Doctor Grenvil,[1] and a few early arrivals engaged in conversation, from which we learn that both Violetta and Alfredo have been invited to the party. If the former comes it will presumably be with the Baron Douphol, in whose company she had been seen by one of the guests the day before. The conversation is interrupted by the entry of a number of lady guests disguised as gipsies, prepared to tell anyone's fortune; after them comes another crowd (among them Gastone) masked as Spanish matadors and picadors. For all this gay, irresponsible bustle, as well as for a little tiff—soon smoothed out—between Flora and the Marquis, Verdi finds appropriate music, if not music of the highest order.

As the men unmask and stroll about or seat themselves at the gaming-table the moody Alfredo enters. He curtly denies any knowledge of Violetta, and sits down to play. Soon Violetta enters, on the Baron's arm. He informs her in a whisper that Alfredo is there, and grimly warns her not to address a single word to him. She gives a cry of distress that, coming where it does and being what it is—the first expression of deep feeling in this scene—is one of Verdi's most telling dramatic effects:

24

("Oh why was I so rash as to come here? Have pity on me, O God, have pity.") Twice in the later course of the scene the same phrase will strike in, with the same electrifying effect.

Some of the guests seat themselves at the gaming-table, others stroll about. An insulting remark by Alfredo about Violetta's treachery towards him nettles the Baron, who suggests that he and Alfredo shall pit themselves against each other at play; Alfredo's extraordinary luck so far, he says ironically, suggests that

[1] Why the Doctor, who has really no part to play in the opera until the death scene in the third act, should appear both in the first and the second, each time in surroundings hardly of a strictly professional kind, is a mystery. Perhaps Piave and Verdi felt that as they had to have a bass of some capacity for the final scene he might as well be made to earn his fee by putting in a bit of work in the earlier scenes, in each of which, however, except for a sentence or two, he merely adds his voice to the concerted pieces.

it is the traditional compensation for being unlucky in love. The game begins, the other guests, including Violetta, gradually leaving the room, only Alfredo and the Baron remaining behind. Not for long, however; Alfredo's luck still holding, the Baron proposes to postpone his revenge to another occasion. They go off to rejoin the others. The orchestra dies down slowly into an ominous silence, then lashes itself into life again as Violetta returns, agitated, breathless. She has sent word to Alfredo to join her, and she is certain he will come, she says, for his hatred of her will have more weight with him than her appeal. When he appears, she beseeches him to leave the house at once, for she dreads a quarrel between him and the Baron. Alfredo refuses to quit the field: if he kills the Baron, he tells her, he will have the satisfaction of having deprived her of her lover and her protector with one stroke. To Violetta's anguished cry that it is *he* for whom she fears, he replies that he will go on one condition—that she will accompany him. This, she says, is impossible; let him leave her and forget her, for she has promised another, on oath, that she will blot Alfredo out of her life. He asks if this other is Douphol; "Yes," she replies, and adds, summoning up all the strength that remains to her, "I love him."

Insane with fury, Alfredo opens the door and calls to the company to return. When they have done so he points to Violetta, who is leaning exhausted against the table, and brutally denounces her: "This woman, for love of me, squandered her money on me, and in my blindness I accepted the sacrifice. But now the time has come to cleanse myself of this stain. I call you all to witness that thus I discharge my debt"—and he flings a purse contemptuously at Violetta's feet. She faints in Flora's arms and the guests turn on him in anger. Meanwhile Germont *père* has entered unobserved.[1] He now comes forward, and, in the noblest heavy-father style, renounces this son of his as unworthy of him. Alfredo's rage has by now spent itself, and he is contrite and broken. A big ensemble is built up, which is hushed for a moment as Violetta, in a feeble voice, reproaches Alfredo for his unkindness, which he would have spared her had he known that what she had done to him she did to prove her love. Time will enlighten him, she

---

[1] That Germont should put in an appearance at the demi-mondaine's house is incredible.

goes on as the ensemble is resumed; and when that day comes
may God lighten his burden of remorse! Finally Germont *père*
drags the distracted Alfredo away, the Baron following them.
Flora and the Doctor take Violetta into the adjoining room, the
guests disappear, and the curtain falls.

18

The third act opens with a prelude for the strings that is the
finest piece of purely instrumental music ever written by Verdi—
a miniature symphonic poem, flawless in every imaginative and
technical respect, with each idea growing so naturally, inevitably
out of its predecessor that the whole seems to be contained in one
great line. It is the sick Violetta that he shows us here, Violetta
nearing her end, a pathetic figure. The prelude is based on two
themes; the first, breathing the purest spirit of emancipation from
this painful world, is that with which the opera had opened
(No. 1). In the second:

25

we have the veritable accent of passion, but now passion purified:
it seems to soar into the skies, then descends in a series of broken
sobs:

26

and at last dies away into tremulous silence.

The curtain rises on Violetta's bedroom, with the bed at the
back, the curtains half-drawn, and near it a stool with a bottle of
water, a glass and various medicines. In the centre of the stage
stands a dressing-table and a sofa, and a little way off a piece of
furniture on which a night-light flickers. In the grate a fire is

212

burning. Violetta is asleep on the bed; her maid Annina, worn
out with watching, dozes by the chimney. The time is seven
o'clock in the morning.

Violetta awakens and asks in a faint voice for a glass of water,
which Annina gives her. At her bidding the maid opens the
shutters, looks into the street, and announces the coming of
Doctor Grenvil, who arrives in time to assist Violetta to rise
from the bed and stumble towards the sofa. All this while the
orchestra has been musing softly upon No. 1; and as the Doctor
is feeling her pulse and Violetta tells him that though her body
suffers her soul is tranquil, for last evening a priest had brought
her the comfort of religion, we hear, for the only time in the act,
a brief pallid reminiscence of No. 25. Grenvil assures her that she
will soon be convalescent, but with a sad smile she dismisses the
assurance as merely the sort of kindly untruth with which doctors
try to hearten the sick. As he is leaving, Annina has a few subdued
words with him and learns that her mistress has only a few hours
to live.

Annina returns to Violetta and exhorts her to take heart, for
all Paris is on holiday, gaily celebrating the carnival; "but God
alone," Violetta interjects, "knows how many unhappy souls
there are in the town today." How much money is there in the
drawer? she asks. "Twenty louis," Annina replies. Violetta bids
her take them and give them to some poor souls, and in response
to Annina's protests that this will leave little for herself she assures her that however little it is it will be enough. Annina having
left her, Violetta takes a letter from her bosom and reads it aloud
in the quietest of tones. It is from the elder Germont: "You kept
your promise. . . . The duel took place. . . . The Baron was
wounded, but is recovering. Alfredo has gone abroad. I myself
told him of your sacrifice; he will return to you to ask forgiveness. . . . Take care of your health. . . . You deserve a better
future. . . . Giorgio Germont." The orchestra accompanies the
reading with a barely audible enunciation of Alfredo's song in
praise of love in the first act (No. 9 and No. 10).

19

She rises, looks at herself in the mirror, and murmurs sadly,
"I wait for him, I wait, but still he does not come! How greatly

I have changed—yet the Doctor bids me hope, while I know I am doomed!" She sings a pathetic little song of farewell to all the lovely dreams of the past:

Her end is nigh, and though no one will weep over her grave and bedeck it with flowers, God will have mercy and forgive her.

Suddenly the air is rent by a bacchanalian chorus from the street in praise of the Fatted Ox of the Paris Carnival. Why did Verdi see fit to introduce this unnecessarily jarring note? Presumably only for purposes of "theatre": he may have been afraid that the audience would find a whole act devoted to a death scene somewhat monotonous, and have felt that in any case Alfredo's entry, which was due shortly, would be more effective set against this noisy background than against the quieter one of Violetta's lament. We must respectfully disagree with him on both counts.[1] When the shouts of revellers have died away Annina returns hurriedly, to prepare Violetta, to the accompaniment of an agitated figure in the orchestra, for the great news she is bringing—the return of Alfredo. The latter follows close on her heels. The lovers embrace passionately: Alfredo implores Violetta's forgiveness, while now she half-believes that death will after all stay his hand. Gently he exhorts her:

[1] It was no doubt in order to get this rather crude contrast of the atmosphere of the death chamber with the noisy, thoughtless world without that he placed his third act during the carnival, instead of on New Year's Day as in Dumas.

to turn her back with him on Paris for ever and seek new health in a happier clime—the thought of which gives poor Violetta strength enough to indulge herself for a while in a certain amount of fioritura. But the emotional shock of her lover's return has been too much for her. She sinks exhausted in a chair, forcing a sad smile and explaining to the terrified Alfredo that it is just a passing weakness and that she is better already.

She calls to Annina to help her to dress. But her strength fails her: she throws the garment down with a gesture of defeat, and gives a despairing cry of "Oh God! I cannot!" Annina is sent off to summon the Doctor again: "tell him that Alfredo has returned and that now I want to live." Then, turning to Alfredo, she tells him that if his coming cannot work the miracle of restoration nothing can save her. Summoning up her last reserves of strength she sings a wild protest against the cruelty of death for one so young as she:

29

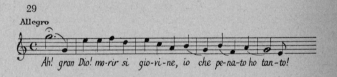

Alfredo, mingling his tears with hers, takes up the passionate, despairing strain, and their voices blend in a duet.

As Violetta falls exhausted on the sofa Germont *père* enters—somewhat superfluously, we cannot help thinking, though Verdi manages to invest the scene that follows with a good deal of pathos. Germont has kept his promise, he tells Violetta; he has come to take her to his heart as his daughter. But she has no illusions left now, she assures the Doctor, who by this time is also of the company; her one consolation is that she will die in the arms of those who love her. At the mention of death Germont becomes wildly remorseful: "I have been a foolish old man! Now, too late, I see the evil I have wrought!" Violetta summons Alfredo to her side, and while the orchestra reiterates one of those figures of volleying chords:

Andante sostenuto ♩ = 56

PPP

which Verdi so often employed as a symbol of impending doom,[1] she takes a miniature of herself from a casket and gives it to Alfredo; it will remind him, she says, of their days of happiness together, and if one day he should meet some pure and tender girl and make her his wife, he can give her this and tell her that it is the portrait of one who is praying in heaven for her and for him. Verdi builds up an impressive quintet, with Germont pouring out his regrets, Alfredo imploring Violetta not to leave him, and she reiterating her pious charge to him in the matter of the miniature.

As her physical forces ebb she becomes spiritually transfigured. While the orchestra breathes the softest of reminiscences of Alfredo's love song (No. 9) she has a momentary illusion that life is returning to her; but at last she falls back once more on the sofa. The Doctor, feeling her pulse, tells the others that the end has come, and a few hammered octaves in the orchestra bring the opera to a close. We cannot help feeling that Verdi could have devised a rather more moving ending than just these blunt octaves: a German composer would no doubt have played for a while in the orchestra on the exquisite No. 1 and No. 25

[1] See the *Trovatore* analysis, pp. 129-30.

Manon

JULES MASSENET [1842–1912]

PRINCIPAL CHARACTERS

MANON LESCAUT	*Soprano*
CHEVALIER DES GRIEUX	*Tenor*
LESCAUT	*Baritone*
GUILLOT DE MORFONTAINE	*Bass*
DE BRÉTIGNY	*Baritone*
POUSSETTE	*Soprano*
JAVOTTE	*Mezzo-soprano*
ROSETTE	*Mezzo-soprano*

1

As I have mentioned elsewhere in another context, the psychological centre of the Abbé Prévost's famous story (1733) is not really Manon but des Grieux: Prévost's own title for the work, indeed, is *Les Aventures du Chevalier des Grieux et de Manon Lescaut*. It is said to have been founded on experiences of the author's own; and whoever the original Manon may have been, it is certain that, as Michelet put it, " the author and the hero are one." The story is told to the supposed narrator of it by des Grieux, and it is through the latter's eyes alone that we see Manon throughout. And the tragedy, when all is said, is far less Manon's than his, because his is the more complex nature of the two.

Massenet's *Manon* was produced at the Opéra-Comique, Paris, on the 19th January 1884, with Talazac as des Grieux and Marie Heilbronn as Manon. Puccini's *Manon Lescaut* followed nine years later. Long before either Massenet or Puccini, however, the subject had been treated twice by Scribe — in a ballet-pantomime in 1830, with music by the future composer of *La Juive*, and in an opéra-comique, with music by Auber, in 1856. This latter work is one of those curiosities of operatic literature which perhaps only Scribe could have achieved. The third act, which takes place in Louisiana, opens with a chorus of negro slaves expressing such sentiments as perhaps no slaves have ever cherished with regard to their master except in opera: " when a slave has a good master he loves to serve him: to defend him and work for him is a real pleasure." Then a young male slave of the name of Zaby obliges the company with what he calls " une chanson du pays." It commences thus:

> *Mam'zelle Zizi,*
> *Mam'zelle Zizi,*
>
> *Un peu d'espoir*
> *Au pauvre noir,*
> *Pitié pour lui!*
> *Le teint n'y fait rien,*
> *Quoique noir, on aime bien.*

But even Zaby and Mam'zelle Zizi are no remoter from Prévost than some of the other characters and incidents of this amazing specimen of the French opera libretto of the 1850's.

2

The libretto of Massenet's work is by Henry Meilhac and Philippe Gille, who have made a very fair job of converting into an opera a story the essence of which defies operatic treatment. In the first place, Prévost presents the librettists with only three full-length portraits — the Chevalier, Manon, and her brother Lescaut. Prévost's Tiberge, the sober friend of des Grieux in his school days and his moral support and prompter of conscience later, is useless for operatic purposes. Neither des Grieux's father nor the men with whom Manon betrays her young lover are anything like full-size studies in the novel, but Meilhac and Gille get out of this difficulty quite well: des Grieux *père* is easily converted into the traditional heavy father of opera (he is first cousin, indeed, to the elder Germont in *La Traviata*), and Guillot de Morfontaine and Brétigny are near enough as makes no matter to some of the older and richer lovers of Manon as sketched by Prévost.

In the second place, the final American adventure of the Chevalier and Manon, which has been included in Puccini's work but omitted from Massenet's, is not good operatic material, in spite of the easy opportunities for pathos which it affords. Librettist and composer lack space in which to set forth in any detail what happened to the young lovers in the New World, as narrated in the thirteenth chapter of the novel. If all they are to be shown doing in America is for one of them to die and the other to be broken-hearted over it, Manon may just as well quit this life at Havre, as Meilhac and Gille make her do, as go to Louisiana for that purpose, as in Puccini: for there is not a word anywhere in Puccini's work [1] to explain just how and why their idyll has come to so sad an end in the neighbourhood of New Orleans, and why they happen to be painfully toiling through the desert on the particular day of Manon's death.

In the third place, many of the effects that are the very essence of Prévost's art are from their nature impossible of reproduction in opera. Take, as an example, the episode that immediately follows the death of Manon, as told by des Grieux:

"For four-and-twenty hours I remained without taking my lips from the face and the hands of my dear Manon. It was my intention to die like that: but at the beginning of the second day I reflected that after my death her body would become the prey of wild beasts. So I resolved to bury her and await my own end on her grave. The weakness due to my fasting and grief had brought me so near my end that it was only by the greatest effort that I could keep on my feet. . . . The soil was sandy, so it was not difficult for me to open it. I broke my sword to dig with, but found my hands of more use. I made a deep grave, and in it I laid the idol of my heart, after having wrapped her in my own clothes so that the sand should not touch her; but not before I had kissed her ten thousand times, with all the ardour of the most perfect love. Once more I seated myself near her and contemplated her for a long time, for I could not bring myself to close the grave.

[1] The only words in the Italian text that have the smallest bearing on the question are Manon's "Ahi! mia beltà funesta ire novelle accende. Strappar da lui mi si volea" (Alas! My fatal beauty has caused new misfortunes. They wanted to tear me away from him [des Grieux]). But not a word of explanation is vouchsafed as to who "they" may be, and what are the "new misfortunes" that have followed in the wake of Manon's charms in New Orleans.

At last, feeling my strength leave me and fearing it would fail me wholly before my task was done, I committed to the earth for ever the sweetest, the most perfect thing that had ever trodden it. Then I laid myself on the grave with my face turned towards the sand, and, closing my eyes in the hope of never opening them again, I invoked the protection of heaven and awaited death impatiently."

It is touches of this kind, incomparable in their simplicity and their pathos, that make Prévost's book what it is: and the things they describe all take place in the soul of des Grieux. It is only through him, indeed, that we know Manon at all. In and by herself, if the truth be told, she is sometimes hardly likable. Certainly the real Manon, complex, in a paradoxical sense, only through her very lack of complication, is not translatable into terms of an art so forthright as music. She is not even immoral: she is simply amoral, not a creature who has forgotten virtue but one who has never learned it and whose constitution makes her incapable of ever learning it. Des Grieux describes her as " a being of a most curious kind. Never had any woman less craving for money; but the fear of lacking it left her without a tranquil moment. It was only pleasure and amusement that she wanted: she would never have desired to possess a sou if pleasure could be purchased without cost. . . . She would have preferred me even with a moderate fortune, to the whole world; but I could never doubt for a moment that she would abandon me for some new B . . . when I had nothing more to offer her than constancy and fidelity." From first to last she is utterly and honestly unable to see either that she does des Grieux any wrong in betraying him whenever his purse is low, or in robbing and deserting, and then callously deriding, some rich lover or other when he has served his financial purpose. So it was that des Grieux could say of her paradoxically after many a betrayal, " Elle pèche sans malice; elle est légère et imprudente, mais elle est droite et sincère." But he at once adds that " L'amour seul suffisoit pour me fermer les yeux sur toutes ses fautes." It is always through des Grieux's eyes that we see her; and we feel more for him than for her. But in an opera next to nothing of all this psychological involution can be suggested. The only thing to be done with Manon is to make her what Massenet and his librettists have done — a charming piece of

feminine frailty, lovable and pitiable both for the Chevalier's sake
and for her own. Massenet in particular, with his unique gift for
expressing certain elements of female sensibility in music, has
produced what is undeniably a masterpiece in its own genre. And
his opera is so purely Massenet and so purely French that we learn
without surprise that certain sapient Paris critics accused him, in
1884, of merely " following in Wagner's footsteps " and of having
" imposed German music on a French subject."

3

The brief prelude (Massenet does not call it an overture) passes
in quick review two or three of the characteristic melodies of the
opera, but without any attempt either to summarise the story by
the sequence of the themes or to construct a miniature symphonic
poem out of them. We get first of all:

the lively music of the fête in the Cours-la-Reine in the third act,
to which is tacked on a suggestion of the graceful minuet — though
now in a much faster tempo — with which that act opens. No. 1 is
repeated; then comes a quiet suggestion of the song of the archers
in the fifth act:

which modulates into des Grieux's passionate invocation of Manon
in act 4:

This is allowed due scope to spread its lyrical wings; but at its
climax it breaks off suddenly, and we get No. 2 once more, this

time rounded off by a curious harmonic progression taken from
the scene on the road to Havre in the fifth act:

It will be gathered from this that no theme positively representa-
tive of Manon herself appears in the prelude; we see her, in truth,
as we do in Prévost's story, only through the eyes of des Grieux,
by the instrumentality of No. 3.

The opening scene shows the courtyard of an inn in Amiens,
with a gateway at the back opening on to the street, some steps
on the right, leading up to a pavilion, and on the left an arbour
with a well and a stone bench in front of it. A little further back
is the entrance to the inn. It is the hour when the coach from
Arras is due. Standing by the pavilion are two rich Parisians, the
elderly Guillot de Morfontaine and his friend Brétigny, about to
dine, they hope, with the three mistresses of Guillot, Poussette,
Javotte and Rosette, who are inside, looking out of the window.
At the moment when the curtain rises all five are appealing mock-
pathetically to the apparently deaf or dead innkeeper to do something to save them from dying of hunger and thirst. They have
almost abandoned hope when he comes out of the inn followed
by scullions bearing a number of dishes in solemn procession towards the pavilion, to a melody as ceremonious as themselves, but
made comical by its sudden changes of volume and colour:

This theme, in one form or another, runs through the whole of
the gay ensemble that ensues. The menu proving to be everything they could have desired, the Parisians joyously follow the
procession of hors d'œuvre and buisson d'écrevisses and poulet
and pâté de canard ("un objet d'art," as the host proudly de-

scribes it) and the vieux vins into the pavilion, the door and windows of which are then closed.

Left to himself, the innkeeper indulges in a sage reflection or two upon the crowd of idlers and sightseers who now begin to filter into the courtyard to see the coach arrive: he himself hurries away to book a place in the coach for the young Chevalier des Grieux, as he had promised to do. Among the townspeople are three gardes-françaises in uniform, one of whom is Lescaut. He tells his two companions to go to the neighbouring tavern and await him there; he himself must stay behind to meet his little cousin Manon, who will arrive by the coach now due. (In Prévost she is his sister). The gaping bourgeois are aptly characterised in a ponderous phrase which accompanies all their chatter:

while Lescaut's motive:

suggests the self-satisfied swagger that never deserts him. Lescaut is the one character in the opera who can become, in performance, just what the actor can make, or chooses to make, of him, stressing chiefly his broad humour, or his rough geniality, or his incurable rascality as the case may be, and according to how much or how little the singer knows of Prévost's Lescaut, or, knowing him, how much or how little he tries to model himself on the original. Generally speaking, however, the players of the part merely reproduce a familiar stage military type.

The place fills with intending travellers and porters carrying their luggage, and soon the coach arrives. There is an amusing scene, which may be paralleled any day (in peace time) at any continental port, everyone having lost his luggage or his porter or both, everyone speaking at once, and everyone wanting to be attended to first. The whole character of the music, which so far has been of the sprightliest kind, suddenly changes as a young girl, who has just descended from the coach, looks at the jabbering, gesticulating crowd in astonishment. It is Manon, on her way to the convent to which her people have consigned her; and her perturbation at this first experience of humanity in the mass is indicated by the hesitating syncopated phrase that accompanies her as she comes into our view:

Lescaut soon finds her, and comments, sotto voce, that her looks do credit to the family. In the prettiest fashion she apologises for her girlish gaucherie: this is the first time she has ever been away from home, and everything she has seen en route has been a wonder to her, she tells her cousin, in one of those chattering bird-like phrases that fall so naturally from the mouths of Massenet's female characters:

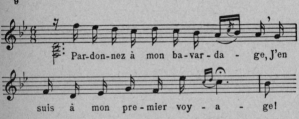

Sometimes, it appears, she could have wept from sheer distress, and we hear once more the timid No. 8; then she makes a sudden transition to young-girlish laughter.

The coach at length sets out again, to the accompaniment of another animated and humorous chorus, leaving no one on the stage but Manon and her cousin. The latter goes out in search of her luggage. Just at that moment Guillot, stepping out on to the balcony of the pavilion to order more wine, catches sight of Manon, and at once loses what the years have left of his heart to her. He goes straight to the point, as is the way in opera: he tells her his name, and assures her that he is rolling in money and would give most of it for a single word of love from her. She laughs at the decayed old amorist, and her laugh is repeated by Brétigny and the others, who have come out on to the balcony to see what is going on. They gaily advise Guillot to come back before he burns his fingers; but he manages to tell Manon, unheard by his friends, that he will have a carriage and postilion ready immediately in which to carry her away. There follows a little trouble with Lescaut, who, returning just then, demands to know what the stranger has been saying to his cousin. Guillot goes back into the pavilion in some confusion, which is increased by the ironic comments of his friends; and Lescaut is about to speak seriously to Manon when one of the guards enters to remind him that the cards and the dice are awaiting him at the tavern. He does not go, however, until he has given Manon a quasi-paternal warning to mind her step, as it were — " Ne bronchez pas " — and to bear in mind that he is the guardian of the honour of the family.

Manon, when she is alone, has a moment of sober reflection: she must put all frivolity out of her thoughts, she muses. Then she remembers wistfully and enviously how well-dressed and opulent-looking Poussette, Javotte and Rosette had been. Still, she says, in another of those typical Massenet phrases that have the natural accent of a spoken sentence:

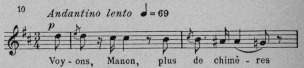

10   *Andantino lento*   ♩ = 69

Voy - ons, Manon, plus de chimè - res

she must leave fancies of this kind behind her at the door of the convent. And yet how seductive is the glimpse she has just had of that other life! While the child is turning all this over in her mind she perceives a stranger, and hastens to seat herself demurely on the stone bench. It is the young des Grieux, not much more than a seminarist yet, whose serious nature is indicated by his characteristic motive:

11   *Andante tranquillo*   ♩. = 63

We learn that he has missed the coach, but that anyhow on the following evening he will be with the good father whom he so loves. But in the middle of his musings he catches sight of Manon, and he feels at once that a crisis in his life has been reached. All through this scene — and indeed throughout the opera — Massenet characterises him admirably. In his most ardent or furious moments the Chevalier never loses his dignity; he is always a young aristocrat of the finest breeding. The spectator will be lucky if he finds the portrait even approximately realised once in a lifetime of opera-going: the tenor with the right combination of appearance, vocal timbre, youth, grace and polish for the part can hardly be said to exist.

Des Grieux approaches Manon respectfully, accompanied by a motive symbolical of the future love of the pair, a motive:

which will reappear in the last moments of the opera, when Manon is dying in des Grieux's arms. Timidly and simply she gives him her name; she is a poor girl, not bad at heart, she says, whom her family are placing in a convent because they suspect her of being too fond of pleasure. " Et c'est là l'histoire de Manon Lescaut," she concludes simply, to the wistful little melody of No. 10. Des Grieux cries out against the barbarity of immuring so much charm and loveliness in a convent, and he has little difficulty in winning her round to his way of thinking.

Just then the postilion who has been told by the infatuated Guillot to await the young lady's orders becomes visible at the back of the stage. A smile passes over Manon's face: here is an opportunity to profit at the expense of the old gallant who had forced his attentions on her. She tells des Grieux of that episode and suggests that they shall use the carriage to fly to Paris together. Des Grieux agrees, and the lovers sing a simple little duet on the subject of the happiness that awaits them in some romantic love-nest or other in Paris:

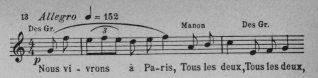

Nous vi - vrons   à Pa-ris, Tous les deux,Tous les deux,

Any lingering doubts that Manon may have as to the prudence or the morality of their flight are dissipated by another burst of merry laughter from the care-free cocottes inside the pavilion. " Ah! how pleasant it must be to amuse oneself one's whole life long! " she sighs; and she rushes away with des Grieux just as Lescaut returns from the tavern, drunk and bankrupt. When Guillot comes out, looking for Manon, he is seized by Lescaut, who takes him for the abductor of his cousin. They get at cross-purposes, to the amusement of the crowd that filters into the courtyard, attracted by the noise; and the amusement becomes universal when the innkeeper tells them that the pretty girl who was here a little while ago has gone off with a young man in a carriage belonging to old Guillot. Brétigny and the three girls try to console Guillot, whose thoughts, however, are now concentrated on vengeance for this perfidy.

4

The second act takes place in a little apartment in the rue Vivienne, Paris, in which the Chevalier and Manon have installed themselves. Des Grieux is writing a letter to his father, telling him how he has met a paragon of beauty and charm, a girl named Manon, sixteen yesterday, whom he proposes to marry. Manon and des Grieux read the letter aloud together: the two main motives of the exquisite scene are the grave one of the young Chevalier, quoted above as No. 11, and a more light-hearted one, symbolical of Manon, that hovers about it caressingly:

and at the same time a little ominously, for Manon is no longer the timid ingénue of the scene at Amiens. The coquette latent in her has come to the surface, and the rippling laughter of No. 14 seems at times almost a mockery of the naïve sincerity of her lover. Already there is in the room a bouquet of flowers the sight of which troubles him somewhat; but she assures him that it was thrown in through the window by an unknown hand, and he believes her.

Lescaut enters, accompanied by Brétigny, also in the uniform of a garde-française. Apparently Brétigny has already managed to cultivate the acquaintance of the pretty girl he had seen at Amiens: he and Lescaut have traced her to her apartment, and his plans for separating her from des Grieux are laid. Lescaut begins by taking a high tone with the Chevalier, but the swashbuckler is soon put in his place. He then explains that, Manon being his cousin, he has merely come to ask whether or not the Chevalier intends to marry her. To satisfy him on that point des Grieux takes him towards the window to read the letter he has just written to his father. Brétigny seizes this opportunity to tell Manon that he has been in communication with des Grieux *père*, who intends to have his son taken away from Paris by force that same evening. At first Manon refuses to countenance the scheme, declaring that she loves the Chevalier, and him alone. But Brétigny cunningly works upon her weakest point: does she prefer perpetual poverty with this young man to a brilliant life with one as rich as himself? By the time that Lescaut, professing himself quite satisfied with the letter, has returned to the other two, des Grieux's fate is sealed. The musical texture of this scene is admirably varied and at the same time unified. Lescaut preserves his own physiognomy throughout, more especially by means of a motive:

that is thoroughly characteristic of his pose of the bluff but honest broker. The ensemble writing is rich in ironic touches. The Chevalier and Manon are musically their now familiar selves; while Brétigny's passion breaks out every now and then in a phrase:

Andante appassionato ♩= 126

Ma - non! _____ Ma - non!___

which, whenever it recurs, stands out markedly from the rest of the tissue.

Lescaut and Brétigny having gone away, entirely satisfied with the state of affairs, Manon and des Grieux are about to sit down to their modest supper when he remembers that he has not yet posted his letter. He begs for an assurance that Manon loves him: he gets it, but the frivolous No. 14 in the orchestra — now somewhat subdued, it is true — hints at the cross-currents in her soul. When he has gone out with the letter Manon sincerely laments her own fragility: then, in a touchingly sad and simple little monologue ("Adieu, notre petite table") she bids farewell to the happiness that has been hers with des Grieux in spite of their poverty, when one glass sufficed for them both to drink from, for then each drank from the other's lips.

Des Grieux returns, heralded by the motive of his love for Manon (No. 12). He tells her of a dream he has had — of a tiny house in the woods, which ring with the song of birds: it will become a paradise when Manon joins him there. But there comes a knock at the door, and an agitated variant of No. 16 (the Brétigny motive) in the orchestra makes clear the significance of it. A mournful "Adieu!" slips out of Manon's mouth almost without her volition. Then, recovering herself, she tells the Chevalier not to open the door, for she does not wish to leave him. Unable to understand her emotion, des Grieux goes out to order the inopportune caller away: he will return to her in a moment, he says, and they will laugh together at her foolishness. But outside is heard the sound of a scuffle, followed by that of carriage wheels. Manon goes to the window and gives a dolorous cry of "Mon pauvre Chevalier!" and the triumph of Brétigny is emphasised by a *fortissimo* statement of No. 16 in the orchestra.

5

The first scene of the third act, which opens with a dainty orchestral minuet that brings with it fragrant memories of the elegant eighteenth century, is set at Cours-la-Reine, where all Paris is enjoying itself. Vendors of all sorts of wares who have established their stalls under the great trees importune the gay crowd that passes up and down to buy. On the right of the stage is a ballroom.

The opening chorus, which makes liberal use of No. 1, is devoted to the cajoleries of the shopkeepers and the replies of the passers-by. A reminiscence of the opening minuet is heard as Poussette, Javotte and Rosette emerge from the ballroom: they are still under the protection of Guillot, but have for the moment evaded him to flirt with younger game. In time they all three pass off the stage, and the chorus is resumed. Lescaut comes into sight with some of the tradesmen pursuing him and pestering him to buy their wares. He is in a good humour, for, thanks to his skill at cards and dice, his finances are flourishing just then. Why economise, he enquires blandly of the universe, when one has a dice-set in one's pocket and knows the route to the hôtel de Transylvanie (a famous Paris gambling resort): [2]

Then, growing sentimental, he sings a "madrigal," in the pseudo-classical style of the period, to one Rosalinde; after which he disappears in the crowd, pursued by all who have benefited, or hope to benefit, by his liberality.

The three cocottes come out of the ballroom again, but happening to run into their elderly protector they scurry away as fast as they can. Guillot is furious, for, as he says, he maintains three of the species in the hope that one at any rate will be faithful to him. While he is in this unpleasant mood he is accosted by

[2] Prévost refers to the place as "l'hôtel de Transylvanie," "where there was a faro table in one of the rooms, while various card games and dice were played in the gallery. This academy was carried on for the profit of the Prince de R. . . . who at that time lived at Clagny. . . ." Modern research has established that the house was that of Franz Rakoczi II, Prince of Transylvania, who, driven from his own territory by the Germans, had to live more or less by his wits in Paris. The house stood at what is now the corner of the Quai Malaquais and the Rue Bonaparte.

Brétigny, who, indulging in his usual irony at his old friend's expense, implores him, in mock terror, not to take Manon from him. This gives Guillot an idea. Brétigny, it appears, has refused to gratify a too fantastically expensive whim of Manon's — to engage the personnel of the Opéra to perform for her at Cours-la-Reine. He, Guillot, will profit by this mistake of Brétigny's to rob him of Manon. He goes off rubbing his hands at the pleasant thought.

To a new theme:

the crowd of bourgeois now celebrate the arrival of a number of elegant Parisian beauties, the queen of whom is Manon, now in the heyday of her prosperity. Brétigny having assisted her to alight from her sedan chair she pours out her little soul in an aria that expresses to the life her frivolity and caprice: naturally No. 14 plays a large part in it. She has everything a woman can desire, she informs the company — beauty, power, horses, adorers: in short, she is the happiest creature on earth. She winds up with a gavotte, in which Brétigny and the other men join her, in praise of youth and spring-time: [3]

Manon and her companions retire to the background as Brétigny encounters an old friend. It is des Grieux *père,* who, we soon learn, has come up from the country to Paris to see and hear his son, now no longer the Chevalier but the Abbé des Grieux, preach his first sermon that very evening. The elder des Grieux, discovering that the former object of his son's affections is the pretty girl pointed out to him by Brétigny, understands now, as he says ironically, how it came about that the latter took so much interest in the moral welfare of the Chevalier. But Manon happens to have overheard the name " Comte des Grieux." She approaches

[3] For one of his Manons, Mme Bréjeau-Silver, Massenet wrote a tricky " fabliau " to take the place of the gavotte in the original score.

the two men, gets rid of Brétigny by a simple pretext, and asks
the Comte for news of the Abbé des Grieux, who, she tells him,
was at one time in love with one of her friends. (Their dialogue
is accompanied by the strains of the minuet in the distance). She
would like to know how the young man had borne the blow of
separation. Has he been able to forget the one who had dealt
it him? Has he suffered greatly? Does he ever repeat her name?
Does he upbraid her? The Comte assures her gravely that his son
has borne all his sufferings in silence; the wound had healed, and
now he has done what men should always do in matters of this
kind — he has forgotten. " Forgotten! " repeats Manon dolorously
as the Comte takes leave of her.

The crowd fills the scene again, among them Brétigny, Guillot
and Lescaut. Guillot plays what he regards as his trump card
against Brétigny — he has brought the ballet of the Opéra to
Cours-la-Reine at terrific expense, simply to please Manon. Everyone runs to see the show; but when the ballet is over and Guillot
turns to Manon for the expected thanks, he learns, to his vast
mortification, that she has " seen nothing." Her mind, in truth,
has been all the time on des Grieux: and as the gay crowd breaks
once more into the melody of No. 1 she calls for her chair and
sets out for Saint-Sulpice.

The second scene of this act opens with the strains of a distant
organ. When the curtain rises we see a parlour in the seminary of
Saint-Sulpice. It is filled with devout women, grandes dames and
bourgeoises, praising the eloquence and piety of the young man
who has just delivered his first sermon: how admirably he had
spoken of St. Augustine and of Santa Teresa! They leave the stage
as the young saint himself enters, accompanied by his father, who
compliments him on his fine performance in a tone of affectionate
irony: the family should be proud to possess a Bossuet of its own!
He tries to persuade his son against the adoption of the priestly
calling. Des Grieux replies that he has experienced in life nothing
but bitterness and loathing; and the orchestra comments mournfully on his words with a tender reminiscence of the love music
(No. 12). The Comte, reminding him that he is still too young to
know much of life, hopes that he will marry some girl worthy of
him and of his ancient family, and find uneventful but solid happiness with her and his children. But the young man's resolution

is not to be shaken. As the Comte takes his farewell of him, he tells him that he shall receive at once the 30,000 livres due to him from the estate of his mother.

When des Grieux is alone he feels old memories surging up within him and troubling the peace of soul he had set himself to win in the bosom of the Church. He would forget Manon, but cannot, he cries in a passionate aria ("Ah! fuyez, douce image"):

Ah! fuyez, douce image, à mon â-me trop chère,

He is summoned by a functionary to the service about to commence in the church; and Manon, who enters the parlour shortly after, obtains permission, by bribing the man, to remain there until the Abbé returns. She muses sadly, the while a Magnificat is being chanted behind the scenes, on the pass to which she has brought both des Grieux and herself, and prays heaven for pardon and a reunion with him. When he returns, and she has uncovered her face and he recognises her, he at first bids her begone. She confesses her fault, but he reproaches her with her perfidy and swears that she has no longer a place in his heart or in his memory. She implores him, to the strain of No. 12, to love her again if he would have her live; then, as is the way with her, she suddenly abandons the note of passion for that of cajolery. In her — and Massenet's — most caressing accents she appeals to him to say whether it is not still the Chevalier's hand that she holds between hers, still the voice, still the eyes of her whom he had once so loved; is it not still his Manon who supplicates:

N'est-ce plus ma main que cet-te main pres - se? N'est-ce plus ma voix?

His resolution begins to weaken. As a distant bell tolls, summoning him to prayer, he makes a last effort to break from her, but

she will not let him go. At last, with a great cry of " Ah! Manon!
Je ne veux plus lutter contre moi-même! " he confesses his undying love for her and folds her in his arms. The passionate No. 12
peals out in the full orchestra as the curtain falls.⁴

6

The setting of the fourth act is the hôtel de Transylvanie.⁵ To
the accompaniment of a feverish theme in the orchestra:

the gamblers stake and lose and win and wrangle, and the
croupiers summon the faithful to their devotions. Among the
crowd that circulates about the tables are Poussette, Javotte and
Rosette, ready and willing, as always, to make the acquaintance
of any man who has been favoured by fortune; as they sagely
remark, while ordinary people win only occasionally, people of
their sort invariably do. Sharpers are everywhere, looking out
for possible victims; and Lescaut, who is in his element in a dubious place like this, has a passing difference of opinion with another
punter as to which of them had won a certain coup. Fortune continuing to smile on him, he obliges the company with a piquant
song, which is accompanied by the clinking of gold at the various
tables — a song in praise of the only goddess he worships, " la
dame de pique " (the queen of spades).

Guillot joins the group, and fatuously assures Lescaut and the
three cocottes that he also, when occasion calls, can " bestride
Pegasus." He has actually, it appears, composed some verses
against the Regent: but as they are too dangerous for the ears of

⁴ The seminary scene was not in the original text. It was suggested to the
librettists by Massenet, whose artistic instinct no doubt told him that the
high-light of the work should be the emotional conflict in des Grieux's soul
between his native seriousness and his passion for Manon, that this conflict
would be most fittingly expressed in an aria, and that the only time and place
for such an aria would be when des Grieux was alone. The original plan of
the opera did not provide any opportunity of that kind.

⁵ This scene also seems to have been Massenet's own idea.

all and sundry, he contents himself with conveying the substance of them to his friends with many eloquent omissions and much gesture. The vain old noodle is mightily pleased with himself, and the others laugh at him under the pretence of laughing with him.

All eyes now turn towards one of the doors, at which the beautiful Manon and her Chevalier are seen entering, to the accompaniment of the melody of No. 18. Guillot cannot conceal his annoyance at the sight of des Grieux, whom he hates for being more successful with Manon than he had been. Lescaut, seeing an opportunity to profit pecuniarily by Guillot's ill-will, draws him aside for a confidential talk. Meanwhile, everyone else being absorbed in play, des Grieux and Manon are left alone in the forefront of the scene. Des Grieux is sad: Manon has quickly run through the 30,000 livres given him by his father, and something within him warns him that he has taken the first step on the road to ruin by accompanying her to the hôtel de Transylvanie. To the passionate melody of No. 3 he opens out his heart to this baffling, perturbing Manon of his, Manon, the siren, the incomprehensible sphinx, with nothing in her heart and her mind but the thought of pleasure and gold, this Manon whom he hates but also loves. She too would love him, she replies, if he would but consent to try to retrieve his fortunes at the faro table. Lescaut, joining them at that moment, adds his counsel to hers — a few lucky coups, and all will be well with the three of them again. The Chevalier turns from the suggestion with horror; but Lescaut whispers in his ear a warning that "Manon does not like poverty": and the fitful No. 22, playing continually round the conversation, gives added point to Lescaut's words. Lescaut confidently promises des Grieux the traditional "beginner's luck": Manon assures him of her eternal love and devotion. The conflict is fought out in des Grieux's soul to the melody of No. 3, which is now built up into a trio.

Guillot approaches them and challenges the Chevalier to a game: he would like, he says, to see whether he is fated invariably to lose to des Grieux. The latter consents and the game is played with ever rising stakes, to the accompaniment of delighted comments, according to their several characters, from Manon, Poussette, Javotte and Rosette. Manon in particular sees in imagination a life opening out to her that will be a continuous shower of gold. Lescaut, for his part, goes to try his own luck at another table, where he soon loses every pistole he had. Des Grieux keeps winning from Guillot, much to Manon's delight, and to Guillot's increasing chagrin. At last Guillot gives up the game, accuses the Chevalier loudly of having cheated him, and leaves the room breathing threats against both des Grieux and Manon.

This scene is dominated musically by the " gambling " motive (No. 22), which continues, in subdued tones, throughout what follows. A loud knocking is heard at the door, followed by a voice outside ordering them to " open in the name of the King." A police officer and several soldiers appear, whereupon Lescaut slips out of the room. Guillot orders the officer to arrest des Grieux and " his accomplice " Manon, both of whom he maliciously begs to observe the completeness of his revenge. Des Grieux, beside himself with rage, threatens to throw Guillot out of the window, but is checked by a word from his father — whose presence in the gambling den, by the way, is not accounted for. The Comte repudiates his unworthy son, remaining unmoved even by the passionate appeal of the whole company to pardon him in consideration of his youth. The scene ends with des Grieux being carried off to prison, at his father's own request; while Manon is taken to the penal institution reserved for women of notoriously scandalous life.

7

The short fifth act takes place at a melancholy spot on the road to Havre. Manon had been condemned, along with a number of other women of bad reputation, to the American plantations: and des Grieux, released from prison, has followed the convoy, which is being escorted by soldiers to Havre, in the hope of rescuing her. A brief orchestral prelude hints at the song of the soldiers (No. 2), which will be heard in full later. Its curious cadence, quoted in our analysis as No. 4, resembles a well-known phrase in Beethoven's " Les Adieux " sonata; hence it has been suggested that Massenet has consciously applied the associations of the Beethoven phrase to the situation in which Manon and des Grieux now find themselves. It may be so, though proof is impossible. The melodic sequence shown in No. 4 happens to be that also of the final bar of the song itself, from which it may conceivably have been derived in the ordinary way. At the same time Massenet plainly attached considerable importance to No. 4, for in the course of this scene he repeats it again and again in every variety of colour.

When the curtain rises, des Grieux is sitting by the roadside, thinking sadly of Manon. He is approached by Lescaut, who has held out hopes to him that somewhere about the spot where they now are an attack might be successfully made on the escort. But, he now informs the Chevalier, at the first sight of the soldiers' muskets gleaming in the sunlight the men whom he had hired for the rescue have proved cowards and deserted them. He tries to excuse himself and his confederates to des Grieux, who dismisses him angrily. But just then there is heard a little way off the song of the approaching soldiers. Des Grieux, in his frenzy, is for attacking them; but Lescaut, who never seems to have much stomach for fighting, counsels another method. He drags des Grieux away as the soldiers enter, still chanting their regimental ditty with its curious instrumental refrain (No. 4). They are thirsty; and while they halt for a while in order to drink, they fall to discussing the odd collection of women whom they have in charge: one of them, it seems, who is already half-dead, does nothing but weep and cover her face when anyone speaks to her. Des Grieux, who, hidden in a bush with Lescaut, has overheard the conversation, gives a mournful cry. Lescaut silences him, and having obtained his purse from him he approaches the sergeant of the troop, of whom, as a fellow-soldier, he asks a favour — to be allowed to speak for a moment with the poor girl whom the soldiers have just been discussing, who happens to be a relation of his. He bribes the sergeant to leave Manon with him for a while, on condition that he brings her back to him in the near-by village before nightfall.

The soldiers, still singing, resume their march and soon disappear — all except one of them, who has been left by the sergeant to keep an eye on Manon and her relation. Lescaut has no difficulty in persuading him to take himself off after the others. Lescaut discreetly follows him; and soon Manon comes slowly into sight, bowed down with fatigue, to the strain of No. 4. She gives a wild cry of " Des Grieux! " as she sees her lover: the Chevalier can answer only with a broken murmur of " Manon! Manon! Manon! " as he takes her in his arms. Their parting duet commences with a new and dark-coloured motive in the orchestra:

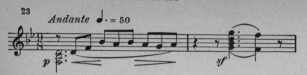

23

Andante ♩. = 50

He tries to comfort her with the assurance that they can escape.
But her strength has gone, and she can only weep and humbly and
affectionately implore his pardon for having brought so much misery on him. He tells her there is nothing to pardon, that his heart
will be hers for ever. As if transfigured, she too promises herself
and him a new and happier life, but with a meaning in her words
which at first he does not perceive. Her mind reverts wistfully to
cherished incidents in their past — their first meeting at the inn,
the coach, the ride to Paris, the letter to his father, their little table
in the rue Vivienne, his black robe at Saint-Sulpice — the orchestra giving out meanwhile the softest of reminiscences of No. 12.

He exhorts her to come with him, but her strength is at a final
end. " I love you, and this kiss is my last farewell! " she murmurs in
a voice that is hardly audible, the orchestra again playing mournfully round her words with No. 12. He tries to re-animate her with
the words of her own appeal to him in the scene in the parlour,
and to the same music (No. 21) — " Is it not my hand you hold in
yours? "; and they take up the melody in unison in a last ecstatic
cry of love. But the final words, " Soon our happiness of old will
come again," are hardly out of her mouth before we hear in the
orchestra a fateful roll in the kettledrums, a soft clang in the tam-
tam, and some faint, irregular pulsations in the plucked strings, as
if Manon's heart had already almost ceased to beat. She suddenly
collapses with a murmured " I am dying: it had to be! it had to be! "
There passes through her failing mind a last reminiscence of the
days before she knew anything of the world and its wickedness (a
faint suggestion of No. 10 in the orchestra); and half-uncon-
sciously she repeats the very words she had used when, in the
courtyard of the inn at Amiens, she had told her simple story to
des Grieux — " Et c'est là l'histoire de Manon Lescaut." As the
Chevalier falls with a despairing cry on her dead body, the orchestra comments on the tragedy with a final recall to our memories
of No. 21.

Carmen

GEORGES BIZET [1838–1875]

PRINCIPAL CHARACTERS

CARMEN	*Soprano or Mezzo-soprano*
DON JOSÉ	*Tenor*
ESCAMILLO	*Baritone*
MICAËLA	*Soprano*
FRASQUITA	*Soprano*
MERCÉDÈS	*Soprano*
ZUNIGA	*Bass*
MORALÈS	*Baritone*
LE DANCAÏRE	*Buffo Tenor*
LE REMENDADO	*Buffo Bass*

1

ARMEN was produced at the Opéra-Comique, Paris, on the 3rd March 1875, and its composer died three months later, in the night of the 2nd–3rd June. Sentimental legends die hard, and that of Bizet's untimely death having been brought about by the "failure" of his opera still survives in some quarters. Whether *Carmen* was a "failure" or not depends on the meaning we attach to that term. It received thirty-five performances during the three months that remained of the 1875 season; that it lay under a cloud in Paris for some time after that can be accounted for by a variety of circumstances not at all uncommon in opera houses, with their changing managements and shifting fortunes. Despite the abuse the work had received from some of the critics the public remained interested in it. When, under a new management, it was revived at the Opéra-Comique under a new director, Carvalho, on the 21st April 1883, there was a general outburst of anger in the

Press and among the public, not because a "failure" had been revived, but because Paris had been so long deprived of what had by this time been accepted elsewhere as a masterpiece. The day before the composer died he had signed an agreement with the Vienna Opera for a production there; and the hard-boiled directors of opera houses do not usually approach a composer for rights in a new work that has obviously proved a "failure."

The first Vienna performance took place on the 23rd October of the same year. Brussels took the opera up in February 1876, St. Petersburg, New York, London, and other towns followed suit during the next couple of years. By the end of 1883 it had attained its hundredth performance at the Opéra-Comique alone, and by 1904 its thousandth there: in the meantime it had consolidated its position all the world over as one of the three or four most popular operas of all time.[1] Camille Du Locle, the director of the Opéra-Comique when *Carmen* was commissioned, jibbed, as many other people did at first, at some of the startling new features of the libretto; but had he regarded the work as a "failure" he would hardly have suggested, as he did almost immediately after the first performance, a new opera by the same composer and the same librettists. Finally, ill as Bizet was in March, we find him working at the plan for an oratorio on the subject of St. Geneviève of Paris; which of itself suggests that the legend of his being crushed by the "failure" of *Carmen* is as much indebted to the sentimental imagination of the authors of it as to the simple facts.

That he was greatly depressed at times after the first performance of the work is undeniable—and quite understandable. He had always overworked a constitution none too strong, teaching and doing hackwork for publishers as well as composing; and the mere proof-reading and rehearsing of *Carmen*, with all the maddening stage and back-stage annoyances inseparable from the production of any new opera, must have been a grievous physical and mental strain on him. The stupidity of many of the critics must also have struck him to the heart. But hundreds of other composers have undergone these vexing experiences without any noticeable effect on the mortality statistics; so we must look else-

[1] By 1951 it had been given some 2,700 times at the Paris Opéra-Comique alone.

where for a reasonable explanation of the depression in which his
friends found Bizet from time to time. He was already a very tired
and sick man; and a long-standing malady of the throat—perhaps
also of the heart—saw the opportunity it had been waiting for and
struck.[1] He would in all probability have died when he did had
the Press notices of *Carmen* been as sensible and kind in general
as, in point of fact, they were imbecile and cruel.

Nor had Bizet's short life been a disheartening struggle for
recognition. Both in the concert room and in the opera house he
had had more opportunities than came to the lot of most young
composers in a not very musical capital in which the competition
was fierce. He was only twenty-eight when the *Pearl-Fishers* was
produced at the Théâtre-Lyrique; it had eighteen performances.
The *Fair Maid of Perth* followed at the same theatre four years
later, with a total of twenty-one performances. The one-act
Djamileh, in 1872, had only a short run, but he himself hardly
questioned the justice of the popular verdict: "the poem," he
wrote to his friend and pupil Edmond Galabert, "is really anti-
theatrical, and my soprano surpassed even my worst fears. For all
that, I am very satisfied with the results obtained." The Press,
though critical, had taken the work with gratifying seriousness;
"never before has an opera in one act been so earnestly, I would
say passionately, discussed." The significant fact is that he had
had the work performed; and he was still only thirty-four.

2

As a composer he had been in search of himself for many years.
There were times when he was tempted to believe that his voca-
tion lay in the field of instrumental music; his symphony in C
major, written at the age of seventeen, a work of great charm,
dashed off in about a month in 1855, must have done something

---

[1] There were other complications. A few weeks before his death he had
brought on severe rheumatism and partial paralysis by bathing in cold river-
waters. On the 31st May he told his friend Guiraud that he had gone deaf in
his left ear. His widow thought the immediate cause of death was a tumour
in the ear on which the surgeons were afraid to operate. His librettist Ludovic Halévy surmised, in his contemporary diary, that Bizet's rheumatism
had suddenly gone to the heart. Paris, of course, was full of rumours: some
people spoke of suicide, others of marital and extra-marital complications,
and so *ad infinitum*.

to confirm him in this belief.[1] An inner voice, however, kept urging him more and more insistently towards the stage. There it was some time before he really found himself—it was not until *Carmen*, indeed, that he fully succeeded in doing so. He had much to acquire by practice and reflection, much dead wood to cut out of himself; and probably no one was more conscious of all this than he was. His published correspondence with Galabert (*Lettres à un Ami*), which extends from 1865 to 1872, throws a good deal of light on his struggle towards self-realisation. Galabert was engaged on an opera the completed sections of which he would send to Bizet for criticism, and we find the latter turning an extraordinarily penetrating eye on his pupil's occasional failures to conceive his dramatic action and his music as an organic whole—and this at a time when Bizet's own operatic practice left a good deal to be desired. As an artist he never had much bent towards the purely speculative—he would never have tried to formulate, for instance, an aesthetic of opera and drama, as Wagner and others have done. He was always the practician, the craftsman concentrating on a particular problem of expression or procedure that confronted him at a given moment. When he made "concessions," as he called them, to the poor taste of his Parisian audience, he did so in perfectly cold blood, and afterwards had no hesitation in pleading guilty to the charge he himself had been the first to bring against himself.

The first impression the casual listener gets from a hearing of *The Pearl-Fishers*, *The Fair Maid of Perth* and *Djamileh* is that of a musician somewhat regardless of the special problems of the musical stage, yielding too readily to the temptation to write delightful music—of which there is an abundance in these three works—for its own delightful sake. That first impression, however, corrects itself to some extent as one comes to know these early operas better; again and again we light upon some touch or other in them that only a musician with the *dramatic* root of the

[1] It was neither published nor performed during his lifetime. The manuscript was one of several of early Bizetiana presented to the Paris Conservatoire by Reynaldo Hahn. In 1933 Mr. D. C. Parker, the author of the first English biography of Bizet (1926, second edition 1951), drew Weingartner's attention to it, and the German conductor performed it for the first time at Basel on the 26th February 1935.

matter in him could have achieved. Still, we are a long way as yet from the Bizet of *Carmen*, the musician always drawing with his eye on the object, and in doing so accomplishing a unique fusion of the lyrical and the dramatic. The change from the musician often using a dramatic situation only as a pretext for lovely music to an artist in whom fine music and dramatic characterisation or dramatic movement are simply different aspects of the same thing, was a curious phenomenon to which we cannot persuade ourselves that we have the key. We can say, if we like, that the final Bizet is a quite natural evolution from the first; but this, true as it is in broad outline, does not answer all the questions we find ourselves asking. There is no unbroken line of evolution observable, nor can we find anything in his letters to suggest that the remarkable change in him of which *Carmen* is the evidence was the product of any willed or desired new orientation on his part, or indeed that he was aware of any fundamental change in himself.

3

Certainly he had always had spells of critical self-examination. A sort of minor crisis seems to have come in the summer and autumn of 1868. In July of that year we find him writing to Galabert, "Nothing new to report. My spirits are low; all black, black, black." The root cause of it may have been physical: he has been very ill, he says—"a very complicated quinsy." But the bodily depression and the following convalescence evidently led, as so often happens with artists, to some soul-searching on his part. "There is an extraordinary change going on in me," he writes later. "I am changing my skin, both as man and artist; I am purifying myself; I am becoming better; I feel it! Come, I shall find something in myself if I search hard enough." In August he develops the theme: "There is going on within me so radical a change, from the musical point of view, that I can't venture on my new manner without some months of preparation. I shall test myself in September and October." For all that, the statement in the text above remains broadly true: there is no conscious, undeviating line of evolution traceable in him even in the field of music drama: three years after the letter just quoted we find him contentedly accepting the libretto of the essentially undramatic *Djamileh*.

After *Djamileh*, on the 17th June 1872, he writes to Galabert, "What gives me more satisfaction than the opinion of all these gentlemen [the critics] is the absolute certainty of having found my path [meaning, one surmises, that he now recognised opera as his true vocation]. I know what I am doing. A three-act work has just been commissioned from me by the Opéra-Comique. Meilhac and Halévy will do the libretto. It will be *gay*, but with a gaiety that permits style." In the same breath, however, he confesses to having "some symphonic projects," a theme that recurs in a letter to another correspondent in which he speaks of the probability of his being asked to write something for the Opéra. The Opéra-Comique commission was to be realised ultimately in *Carmen*, though that subject may not have yet been decided upon. Yet something of the vacillation, the self-doubt, that was characteristic of him all his life at intervals is evident even now. After having got his hand thoroughly in with *Carmen*, early in 1873, he put that work aside in order to write, in the summer and autumn of the same year, a five-act opera on the subject of the Cid.[1] Then, when *Carmen* was probably under way again, he lost interest in it, vowed that he had finished with the stage, and asked the librettist Louis Gallet to provide him with a text for an oratorio on the St. Geneviève subject. And still the indecision persists: he tells his fellow-composer Guiraud that he has lost faith in his capacity to fill an Opéra bill, but believes he can make his mark at the Opéra-Comique, where he hopes to "expand and transform the genre." A man of genius more divided against himself, so little the servant at that time of a daemon driving him inexorably in the direction the Fates had decided upon for him, it would be difficult to find in the whole history of music.

Yet some compulsion there must have been, though he himself was only dimly conscious of it, and that intermittently. It has sometimes been asked, with all respect towards him, whether *Carmen* may not have been just a lucky accident, something the like of which he would perhaps never have accomplished again. The question evades answer, but it persists in obtruding itself. The mere fact that even while under the spell of *Carmen* he could

[1] Seemingly, though completed in his head, not much of this *Don Rodrigue* was actually worked out on paper. The death-blow to the scheme was given by the burning down of the Opéra in October 1872.

seriously think of plunging into oratorio, a genre for which he had never shown the suggestion of any aptitude or any sympathy is of itself calculated to set us wondering whether he was even yet fully aware of what is now so obvious to the rest of the world —that he had a genius of the first order for musical drama, and that he ought now to devote himself heart and soul to developing his capacities in that field.

4

Manifestly a great subconscious change had somehow taken place in him, a remarkable growth both in extent and depth. But what was the meaning of that change? What was the origin of it? Was he himself aware of it, or was it just that he set to work at his latest subject believing himself to be still the same Bizet fundamentally who had written the earlier operas—though of course with more stage experience now—and then found that by the operation of some mysterious psychical chemistry in him he had become something quite different, the talent having somehow developed into a genius? It is generally as the result of a slow change of tissue and temperature within, not through some sudden violent impact from without, that certain highly-strung men have become radically different from what they were: much more must have gone to the transformation of a Saul into a Paul, for example, than hearing a voice and seeing a light one day on the road to Damascus. Various attempts have been made to account for the transformation in Bizet. Outside influences can probably be ruled out. Sentimental musical biography has always been inclined to overrate these in the psychology of a composer—the influence of Schumann's marriage on some of his songs, for instance, or the attribution of the general sunniness of the *Meistersinger* to the change wrought in Wagner's material circumstances by the patronage of King Ludwig. The truth is that in the mysterious complex of forces that we call the artistic consciousness doors open more often by slow silent pressure from within than by sudden assault from without; the poet or the composer simply becomes a different being by an internal metamorphosis of which he himself is unaware at the time.

In the case of Bizet the supreme achievement of *Carmen* seems to have been partly due to the immense good fortune of his coming upon the right subject at the right time. He had always been attracted by the exotic in general and the gipsy in particular; and in the *Carmen* subject he found ready made for him, in Mérimée's great story, a gipsy the windings of whose being he had only to follow in his music curve by curve. But, once again, we feel that Carmen herself might have come to not much more fullness of stage life than his Mab in *The Fair Maid of Perth* had done had there not been an internal change of substance in him by then. Something within him seems to have been impelling him for a long time towards the probing of certain of the darker depths of human nature. There is a hint of a Carmen-José complex *avant la lettre* in his conception of the Myrrha of *La Coupe du Roi de Thule*, who throws an evil spell over the fisherman Yorick. In a letter of December 1868 Bizet is shrewdly critical of Galabert's mis-handling of the scene of the entry of Myrrha: "Had you been describing her in words," he remarks, "you would have done just the opposite of what you have done in the music you send me. This Myrrha is a courtesan of the antique mould, sensual as Sappho, ambitious as Aspasia. She is beautiful, intelligent, and full of charm, the proof of which is the extraordinary fascination she exercises on Yorick. In her eyes there must be that pale-greenish look that is the unmistakeable sign of sensuality and egoism pushed to the length of cruelty." The colloquy between the pair should be supported by an instrumental passage suggest-ing her fascination for Yorick, commencing at the words "Je tremble au seul bruit de ses pas." "The serpent has come, and the bird is half paralysed. . . . This is how I see the situation. Left to himself Yorick is free: he gives passionate, delirious expression to his love, addressing the clouds, the stars. In the presence of Myrrha he is extinguished." Bizet shows how the most can be made of this entry of the enchantress: "she is leaning on the arm of Angus; she comes in slowly, absent-mindedly, as if lost in a dream; her eyes take in all around her, and then settle almost disdainfully on Yorick." We shall find this psychological situation reproduced, in broad essentials, in the first act of *Carmen*.

Perhaps something that had been set going in the depths of him by his brooding upon the problem of Myrrha had been slowly maturing in him in the years between *La Coupe du Roi de Thule* and *Carmen*.[1] On the 1st October 1872 Alphonse Daudet's play *L'Arlésienne* (*The Woman of Arles*) had been produced at the Paris Vaudeville Theatre, with incidental music by Bizet. In this remarkable score we see him at last coming into his own; already he is a master. The dramatic and psychological substance of the play is akin to that of *Carmen* in some respects—Frédéri is fascinated by the Arlésienne (who does not appear in person in the play but is sensed as an ever-present destructive, irresistible force in the background), very much as Yorick had been by Myrrha and Don José will be by Carmen. Moreover, in both *L'Arlésienne* and *Carmen* there is a contrasted purer element, in the former the humble unreciprocated love of Vivette for Frédéri, in the latter the Micaëla who strives, but in vain, to rescue Don José from the clutches of the gipsy siren. Frédéri, unable to square his account between the irreconcilable worlds of pure love and blind fascination, commits suicide by throwing himself from a window of the farm: José kills Carmen and then goes with sombre resignation to meet his own fate.

When Bizet received the commission to write a new work for the Opéra-Comique the Carmen subject appears to have been his own choice. He must have been well acquainted with Mérimée's story long before then; but evidently it was only after his experiences with *L'Arlésienne*—or contemporaneously with them—that it took complete possession of his imagination. Only then was he dramatically and musically ripe for it. Out of this combination of outward circumstances and a new complex of inner forces came the masterpiece that is *Carmen*. It is the most Mozartian opera since Mozart, the one in which enchanting musical invention goes hand in hand, almost without a break, with dramatic veracity and psychological characterisation. The Bizet of the earlier works has here developed a new weight and strength with-

After putting Galabert to work at *La Coupe du Roi de Thule* he decided set the text himself. His score was never completed and little of it has been published; the prelude was performed at a Colonne concert in Paris on the 12th December 1880 under the title of *Marche funèbre*. What remains of the manuscript is in the Paris Conservatoire. For further information regarding the opera the reader must be referred to Mr. Winton Dean's admirable book on Bizet (1948)—indispensable to every student of the composer—and article in the October 1947 number of *Music and Letters*.

out losing any of his old litheness. This is indeed music muscled in the Mozartian way, the fascinating way of the cat-tribe, the maximum of power being combined with the maximum of speed and grace and the minimum of visible effort. The Bizet of the earlier works had been marvellously gifted by the gods with beauty of melody, expressiveness of harmony, and an exquisite sense of colour-values in orchestration. All this endowment was now concentrated, in a heightened form, on a single work.

5

The first performance of *Carmen* took place at the Opéra Comique on the 3rd March 1875, with spoken dialogue, as was *de rigueur* in the genre to which it belonged. After Bizet's death his friend Guiraud rewrote much of the dialogue as musical recitative, some of which was used in the Vienna production of October 1875, in which several extraneous elements suited to the local taste were introduced. It became a sort of opera-ballet, the procession of toreros and picadors (the latter on horseback) in the fourth act being made a pretext for a dazzling stage picture. It was not until 1900 that Mahler succeeded in ridding *Carmen* of these excrescences in the Austrian capital. In 1901 the work was given in the Nîmes arena with the added attraction, for southern eyes, of a real bull-fight, the singing Escamillo being replaced for the time being by an actual torero.

At the first performance of the opera in Paris the Carmen was Célestine Galli-Marié, the first of a long line of famous gipsy heroines.[1] The tenor, Lhérie, seems to have been no more than ordinarily competent, either vocally or histrionically. The Escamillo (Jacques Bouhy) and the Micaëla (Mlle Chapuy) were on the whole better. That the opera should have got off to a rather bad start was in the nature of things. The Opéra-Comique was the favourite haunt of the sentimental bourgeois, who were shocked by the drastic realism of the action and the deplorably low social standing and defective moral sense of some of the characters.

[1] She seems to have been an intelligent woman, who went direct to Mérimée's story for her conception of the part. Oddly enough, in 1864 Victor Massé, the composer of *Les Noces de Jeannette,* had contemplated writing a *Carmen* in conjunction with Sardou; and as his Carmen he had in view Galli-Marié.

particularly the gipsies, and jibbed especially at the uncompromisingly tragic finish, which was out of keeping with the happy-ending tradition of the house. Furthermore, the average patron of the Opéra-Comique was unused to a harmonic idiom so advanced as Bizet's, and puzzled by the seeming "formlessness" of much of the music. He liked to know where he was, with solos, duets and so on of which he could see clearly the beginning and the end: it is significant that the three numbers which drew the most response from the audience were "set" pieces conforming more or less to the accepted patterns—the duet of Don José and Micaëla in the first act, the Toreador's song in the second, and Micaëla's aria in the third. Ludovic Halévy, whose testimony can be relied upon, for it appears in his diary under the date 16th March 1875, tells us that the trouble as regards the general musical idiom and especially the harmony of the work was simply that it took everyone a little time to get inside them. The company had at first found them strange, but in the course of the three or four months during which the rehearsals had lasted had become not only reconciled to them but enthusiastic about them. As Halévy says, the misfortune was that the first-night public had not gone through a similar education.

6

Bizet had as his librettists two seasoned craftsmen of the theatre, Henry Meilhac and Ludovic Halévy: the latter was Bizet's wife's cousin, son of Leon Halévy, the brother of Fromental Halévy, the composer of *La Juive*, who had been Bizet's teacher. Their task was not an easy one, and it is rather surprising that they should have performed it, on the whole, so well. There is nothing dramatic or theatrical about Mérimée's immortal story, which had appeared in 1845. There the story is told in the first person: Mérimée, touring Spain for archaeological and historical purposes, one day falls in with a sinister-looking character who turns out to be a notorious brigand, a certain José, the terror of the countryside. The story-teller does the hunted man one or two little kindnesses and wins his confidence. The brigand, on whose head here is a price, goes off into the mountains, and Mérimée to Cordova, where he falls in with La Carmencita, a gipsy "of a wild and strange beauty," as he describes her; "her eyes in particular

249

had an expression at once voluptuous and fierce that I have never met since in any human glance." Mérimée studies her as a curious case, for gipsies have always interested him. He goes to her home, where she begins to tell his fortune. A man in a bad humour breaks in on them; it is José, who remonstrates angrily with her for a way of life to which he has had reason to object many times before. From her excited gestures Mérimée surmises that she is urging the brigand to cut the stranger's throat; but José ushers him out. When Mérimée returns to his inn he finds that his watch has been stolen by Carmen.

He bothers no further about it but goes off again on his scientific quest. After some months' wandering he finds himself once more in Cordova, where a Dominican Father of his acquaintance, relieved to find that he has not been assassinated, as he had feared, tells him that not only has his watch been recovered but the ruffian connected with the matter, a brigand and murderer known as José Navarro (though actually he is a Basque with an outlandish name which no one can pronounce), is now in jail. Next day Mérimée is allowed access to the prisoner, who is to be garrotted shortly; and now the brigand tells him the story of his life. He was Don José Lizzarrabengoa of Elizondo, a Basque of the old Christian faith: he had been intended for the church, but a quarrel during a game of paume (hand tennis) had led to a fight with lethal weapons, and he had had to flee the country. He enlisted in the Spanish dragoons, soon rose to be a corporal, and was well on the way to becoming a quartermaster when one day he was placed on guard at the tobacco factory in Seville, where some hundreds of girls worked. He was not interested in them, his mind being always on the girls of his own country, with their blue skirts and braided hair.

The story proceeds for a while along the lines of the first act of the opera. José had been punished and degraded for allowing Carmen to escape while ostensibly conducting her to prison. He happens to fall in with her again, when she is the mistress of the colonel at whose door José is doing sentry duty. She upbraids him for so cravenly submitting to his punishment; never could she love anyone of so poor a spirit. Her fascination for him increases, and his mood becomes one of deepening and darkening exasperation. One day he finds her in the company of a young

lieutenant of his regiment who roughly and contemptuously orders the common soldier away. A fight ensues, in which the lieutenant is killed. José is taken away into safety by Carmen, and
soon he finds himself compelled, if he does not want to lose her,
to join a band of smugglers of which she is an active member,
the head of it being one Dancaïre. Time goes on, José becoming
more and more exasperated by the refusal of Carmen to confine
her affections to him. One day he learns that she is actually the
wife now of the ugliest of the smugglers, a repulsive ruffian known
as Garcia the One-Eyed: this adds fuel to his jealousy. The smugglers are caught in an ambush; most of them take to their heels,
only Carmen, José, Garcia, Dancaïre and a fine young fellow
named Remendado being left. In their headlong flight through the
mountains, under the fire of the soldiers, Remendado is wounded;
and Garcia callously disposes of him by shooting him through the
head.

7

So it goes on for a long time, the net of jealousy and enforced
crime closing ever more closely round José. At last a grand
smuggling *coup* is in train, in which it is the business of Carmen
to draw an English officer whom she has befooled in Gibraltar
into a trap in the hills. A quarrel over cards leads to José killing
Garcia: Dancaïre's cynical comment on it all is "To the devil with
love affairs! If you had asked him for Carmen he would have sold
her to you for a few piastres." So now only Dancaïre, Carmen,
José and two or three more of the band are left. Dancaïre is killed
in a surprise attack by the soldiers, and José himself is wounded
and has to hide in a wood. Carmen nurses him back to health and
then takes him with her to Granada. He implores her to make an
end of this life of outlawry and crime and go with him to the New
World; but, as usual, she pours scorn on the idea. Another grand
smuggling scheme is on foot; she means to see it through, and José
must work with her or lose her. He discovers that in Granada she
has made the acquaintance of a noted picador named Lucas, of
whom she characteristically proposes to make use for her own
unscrupulous ends. He is a man, she tells José, whom it will be
easy for her to handle; he has earned a good deal of money in the
bull-ring, and one of two things must happen—either they will

get possession of this money, or she will inveigle him into joining their band.

The picador leaves for Malaga, and José continues his work as smuggler. (It was at this late point in his career, we now learn, that he and the teller of the story had first met.) One day Carmen goes off to Cordova. All José's jealousy boils up in him again when he discovers that there is to be a bull-fight there. He follows her and finds her on a bench in the arena. It falls to Lucas to play the first bull; it charges him, unhorses and crushes him. José takes Carmen away and once more implores her to go to America with him and there lead a decent life. He is very weary of killing her lovers, he tells her; it is she whom he will kill next. But now she is in a fatalistic mood; she had long foreseen the end, she says— "me first, then you." He goes to mass. On his return he finds Carmen gazing into a bowl full of water with melted lead in it, absorbed in one of her gipsy incantations. He takes her away on his horse and makes a last appeal to her: her reply is "Yes, I loved Lucas for a while, but perhaps less than I did you. Now I love nothing, and hate myself for having loved you. . . . I will follow you to death; but I will never live with you again." They are now in a solitary gorge. He pulls up his horse, and Carmen jumps to the ground. "Is it here?" she asks. "You wish to kill me, I can see. It is decreed; but you will not make me yield." He pleads with her abjectly, but she is immovable. She will fence with him no longer, she says, tell him no more lies: as her *rom* he has the right to kill her; but free she was born, and free she will die. He draws his knife, hoping at least that he can make her afraid. "But that woman was a demon," he tells his listener; her only reply was to take from her finger a ring he had given her and throw it into the bushes. Then he loses control of himself and stabs her twice with the knife that had killed Garcia: she falls without a cry. He remembers that she had told him once that she would like to be buried in a wood. He dug a grave for her with his knife and laid her in it, placing beside her the ring and a small cross: then he galloped straight to Cordova and gave himself up at the first guard-house he came to.

8

As will be seen from this swift summary, Mérimée's story covers a much larger extent of space and time than the opera. This was the first of the difficulties the librettists had to face. In the nature of the case, most of what gives the story its unique impressiveness—the atmosphere of unrelieved gloom, the slow inexorable transformation of a decent young Basque boy into the bandit and murderer of the after years—has had to be sacrificed. It is true that José is a different being in each act of the opera; the librettists have managed this very well, and Bizet's genius has heightened their every stroke. But music is always a voracious devourer of stage time; and it was inevitable that a great deal that goes to the mental and moral make-up of the Don José of Mérimée should have to be sacrificed to the peculiar exigencies of opera.

Then there was the difficulty that always attends the transfer of an action from the book page to the theatre, where everything that happens has to do so before our eyes in the person of someone or other. In Mérimée there are really only two characters—Carmen and José—; Lucas, Dancaïre and Remendado each receive only a few lines of mention. But a full-scale four-act opera with only two characters is unthinkable; and so not only had the more or less negative Lucas to be enlarged into the very positive Escamillo, and even Dancaïre and Remendado made to play their musical part in the whole, but an entirely new character had to be invented in the person of Micaëla. In the story we are conscious of the purer, happier, more innocent Basque background of José's youth only by way of hint and inference, as we are, in another way, of the sinister Arlésienne.[1] It is dimly conceivable that the authors of an ordinary play on the *Carmen* subject might have managed to present in symbolical form the antithesis between the

---

[1] At the beginning of José's story of his life he says, "I am a Basque and of the old Christian faith. I was intended for the Church and forced to study for it; but it profited me nothing. I was too fond of paume, and that was my undoing. When we Navarros play at paume we forget everything else. . . ." Meilhac and Halévy manifestly thought it of importance that the audience should know all this, for in the spoken dialogue between José and the lieutenant in the first act they reproduce Mérimée's text almost verbatim. But the dialogue does not appear in the vocal scores now current.

world of trickery and crime in which the later José finds himself trapped and his nostalgia for the Basque environment of his youth; certainly this could have been done in a spoken drama with incidental music on the *L'Arlésienne* pattern. Even in opera— though hardly in that of Bizet's day apart from Wagner—a musical-dramatic tissue might somehow have been woven in which all that Micaëla stands for could have been suggested without bringing her on the stage in the flesh. But in the French opera of the eighteen-seventies this was an impossibility. For purely technical and practical reasons alone there had to be a female voice contrasting with Carmen's; and so the creation of a Micaëla was a sheer necessity. "Contrast" of more than one kind has indeed been thus effected; over against the dark gipsy, for instance, as the incarnation of hard unscrupulous reality, there was now posed a regulation stage blond ingénue symbolising virtue. The librettists and the composer could not have done otherwise than they did: but while admitting that what they did achieved every possible effect of theatrical "contrast"—like the two constrasting subjects of a symphonic movement—we cannot help feeling that the Micaëla of the opera remains something of a lay figure, a *dea ex machina* to be pushed forward when required and afterwards withdrawn without any further or deeper concern with her on the librettists' part or ours. It is only the music that Bizet has given her that keeps us interested in her while she is on the stage; when she is not, we are inclined to forget about her.

Escamillo, as we have seen, is entirely the librettists' creation, and a legitimate one, a development of the merest hint given them in Mérimée's Lucas, the picador Carmen's interest in whom takes her to the bull-fight and so brings about the final tragedy.

9

The overture to the opera is of the simplest and, at first sight, the most innocent kind. Bizet had no thought of making it in any way a symphonic epitome of the characters and the dramatic action: there is no hint in it, for instance, of either José or Micaëla. It is with the animated theme of the music associated with the entry of the bull-fighters in the last scene of the work that he chooses to begin. (See our example No. 32.) On to this he tacks, in an abrupt modulation from the key of A major to that of F major, the refrain of the Toreador's song in the second act; it is played the first time piano, the second time fortissimo. (See musical example No. 17.) Another nonchalant key-leap brings him back into A major and a repetition of the arena music with which he had begun. Then, in the final twenty-seven bars of the short prelude, he introduces his Carmen, whom he impresses on our imagination once for all in a theme, in which the interval of the augmented second is prominent, that stands out commandingly in the 'cellos, a clarinet, a bassoon and a cornet [1] against an ominous string tremolando:

1

Whether we are to regard this theme as representing Carmen the actual woman, or, as some contend, the Fate of which she is the instrument, is an interesting subject for debate but finally immaterial to the dramatic issue. As the motif develops, the augmented second characteristic of it defines itself more and more clearly as part of the chord of the diminished seventh, that has always proved itself so useful in suggesting the sinister; and it is on a double-fortissimo chord of the diminished seventh that the overture ends—or rather remains suspended, arrestingly, questioningly, in the upper air.[2]

The curtain rises on a square in Seville. On the right is the great tobacco factory, employing some hundreds of women, of which Mérimée has given us so interesting an account. On the left is a military guard-room, in front of which is a small covered gallery elevated slightly above the ground by two or three steps.

[1] Not a trumpet, as in the modern miniature orchestral score. Bizet wrote for cornets, not trumpets, throughout *Carmen*.
[2] As Henry Malherbe has pointed out, the *Carmen* prelude follows the same plan as that of *L'Arlésienne*, (a) the theme of the bullfighters paralleling that of the "Marche de Turenne," (b) the Escamillo motif that of the Innocent, (c) the *Carmen* motif that of the Arlésienne.

Near the guard-room we see a rack holding the dragoons' lances, adorned with red and yellow banderoles. Along the back of the stage stretches a bridge. Grouped about the guard-room are a dozen or so dragoons of the Almanza regiment; some are sitting and smoking, the others leaning on the balustrade of the gallery; among them is the brigadier Moralès. Citizens are strolling about, each intent on his own affairs. Moralès and the others join in a charming chorus the burden of which is the pleasant spectacle afforded the idle observer by this endless ebb and flow of Seville humanity: note the piquant accentuation of the chorus and the orchestral bass ascending step by step—this latter a favourite procedure of Bizet's:

2

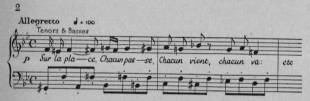

To the accompaniment of a tripping little melody in the violins Moralès draws the attention of the others to a new arrival. It is Carmen's antithesis Micaëla, complete with Basque blue skirt and hair in braids; and she is evidently a stranger in the place, for she comes in hesitantly and, sighting the soldiers, a trifle apprehensively. They gallantly place themselves at her disposal. She is in quest of a brigadier, she explains, a certain Don José; and the orchestra limns her sufficiently for the time being in a modest little motif:

3

They know him, they tell her, but he does not happen to belong to their company, though he will be putting in an appearance shortly, at the changing of the guard. The hand of the matured

Bizet is already apparent in this short episode; as in Mozart, the music is all ease and charm yet everywhere germane to the characters, the words and the situation. Micaëla politely declines their pressing invitation to wait for the brigadier in the guard-room, despite their assurance that due respect will be paid to her there. She will return later, she says—"when the guard coming on duty has relieved the guard going off," she adds, singing the words, with a delightful touch of quiet irony, to the tune to which they themselves had formerly sung the words. Moralès and the soldiers take their rebuff philosophically, and, to the strain of our No. 2, they resume their former occupation of watching the crowd with amused eyes.

At the end of the page of the opera we have now reached the reader will find, in the French scores in current use, the instruction to "join up to No. 2." If he takes any notice of this—in all probability he does not see it, but turns over as a matter of course to the next page—he will be puzzled to discover that this is headed not "No. 2" as he expects, but "No. 3." If he retraces his steps he will find that "No. 1" is the overture, while the scene we have just been describing is marked "No. 2," at the end of which he is now rather surprisingly invited to "join up to No. 2." The explanation of the mystery is that in the original lay-out of the opera there came, between the scene we have just been analysing and the next one—the chorus of street urchins—an extended episode in which, to the great amusement of Moralès and the soldiers, a young wife, promenading on the arm of her elderly husband, is pursued through the crowd by a young lover, who finally manages to slip a letter into her hand. All this was omitted when Carvalho re-staged *Carmen* in 1883, and taken out of the published score; the primary object of the librettists seems to have been twofold—in the first place to give the player of the part of Moralès an opportunity to exhibit his vocal powers in three stanzas of song, in the second place to help fill up the necessary stage time between the exit of Micaëla and the arrival of José. The complete text of the episode, together with the directions as to the miming of it, is easily accessible today in the imprint of the *Carmen* libretto in the collected works of Meilhac and Halévy.

10

We are a fairly long way as yet from even an adumbration of the Carmen-José tragedy hinted at in the closing bars of the overture. The makers of the work have decided, not without reason, that there ought to be a slow approach to this by way of light relief and local colour; and both are liberally supplied in the episode that now follows. In the distance is heard a military cornet fanfare: the new guard is on its way. The retiring guard take up their lances and line up before an officer; and soon the relieving company comes into view, to the strains of a march in the high-piping tones of the piccolos:

The incoming guard is followed by a number of small boys—Meilhac and Halévy's instructions to the producer are that they shall be "as tiny as possible"; later come José, the lieutenant Zuniga, and the dragoons with their lances. While the new and the old guard line up smartly in front of each other, the urchins, marching with exaggerated military discipline, sing their own praises in a delightful chorus to the melody of No. 4; and at the end of the usual ritual of the changing of the guard, the saluting, and all the rest of it, they strut out with the departing troop with the same air of self-importance with which they had entered. Meanwhile Moralès, before leaving the scene, has had time to get in a word with José. He tells him that a young girl in a blue skirt and with her hair in plaits has been enquiring for him. "It must be Micaëla!" exclaims José, after the violins have repeated softly the tiny motif (No. 3) that had accompanied her entry. (We should probably regard José's remarks as a private expression of surprise rather than a piece of information for Moralès' benefit; otherwise it is difficult for us to understand why the news of Micaëla's unexpected presence in Seville should be taken so nonchalantly by José. We shall see in a moment that it was necessary for the librettists' purposes that Moralès should give José this information before he leaves and that he should be overheard by the lieutenant of the incoming guard, a pretext thus being provided for the later talk between José and the lieutenant in which the former manages to give the audience a sketch of his early life.)

The real significance of Moralès announcement and José's curt comment on it comes out in the scene that follows next in the opera, but not so clearly there as in the original libretto. In the former all we get is this brief conversation in recitative between José and the lieutenant of the new guard, Zuniga:

Zuniga: Is not that big building opposite where the girls who make cigars work?

José: It is, sir; and assuredly a flightier lot are not to be found anywhere.

Zuniga: They are pretty, I suppose?

José: I know nothing about that; I don't concern myself with gallantries of that sort.

Zuniga: I know well what occupies *you*, my friend . . . ! [here the orchestra gives out a reminder of No. 3] . . . a charming young girl of the name of Micaëla, in a blue skirt and with her hair in plaits. What do you say to that!

José: I say it is true, that I love her. As for the work-girls here and their beauty, judge for yourself; here they come.

Whereupon there begins the "chorus of the cigar-makers," in which the townspeople take part, for these damsels, as Mérimée explains in considerable detail, are one of the sensations of Seville.

11

But in the original libretto the spoken dialogue between José and the lieutenant had run to much greater but by no means unnecessary length. The former favours Zuniga with much more information about the girls: it appears that there are some four or five hundred of them, and as they discard most of their garments when at work—the younger among them in particular—men are not allowed to enter the factory without permission. To the lieutenant's question "Are they pretty?" José replies with a careless laugh, "I suppose so; but to tell you the truth I am not quite sure, for although I have mounted guard here several times I have never looked very closely at them. As a matter of fact these Andalusian women rather frighten me. I don't quite understand them—always joking, never saying a sensible word." Zuniga remarks quizzingly that perhaps José prefers blue skirts and plaits down to the shoulders—from which it becomes clear that he has overheard Moralès' parting words. José admits the soft impeachment; blue skirts and plaits, he explains, are the marks of the girls of Navarre, and mention of them reminds him of his native land. He regales the lieutenant with a short chapter of autobiography, in very much the words that Mérimée puts into his mouth in the prison. He is Don José Lizzarrabengua, he says, a Navarro of the old Christian faith, and there follows the account of his training for the Church and of the game of paume with its unfortunate sequel. He had been forced to flee the country and enlist as a soldier in Spain. His father was already dead; so his mother had followed her son and settled a few miles from Seville with little Micaëla [1]—an orphan whom his mother had adopted and who is inseparable from the old lady. (This Micaëla is only seventeen years old, a detail which producers and singers should do their best to live up to.) José's story having ended, the lieutenant remarks drily that he understands now why the young man does not know whether the cigar-girls are beautiful or ugly. Just then the factory bell tolls. "In a moment," José tells the lieutenant, "you will be able to judge for yourself. As for me, I am going to make a chain to hang my *épinglette* [priming-iron] on."

It will already be suspected that Guiraud did Bizet no great service in general in substituting recitative for much of the spoken dialogue of the original text, and more particularly in cutting down this conversation between Zuniga and José (which occupies two-and-a-half pages of the Meilhac-Halévy text) to the few lines of dialogue in recitative given on page 429. The longish conversation between the pair is really necessary in order to acquaint the audience with the pre-history of the Basque José, to explain how

---

[1] There is nothing of this, of course, in Mérimée: it was an invention practically forced on the librettists once they had decided to create Micaëla. It serves to account for the Navarre girl now being within such easy distance of Seville, and provides an explanation for her being at present in the town, as the bearer of a message from José's mother. Her convenient residence in the neighbourhood further explains her being able to penetrate to the smugglers' haunt in act three in order to sing an aria that is no more than the soprano's due—for this is opera.

he comes to be in Seville, and to emphasise the native simplicity of the young soldier who is soon to be entangled in the web woven for him by the Fates with Carmen as their instrument.[1]

The lunch-bell has brought the usual crowd of idlers into the square to see the girls erupt from the factory. Even the soldiers come out of the guard-room: of them all, only José remains indifferent, concentrating placidly on his chain. A number of infatuated young men go through what is evidently the established ritual of laying their hearts at the girls' feet, in a charming little chorus of tenors in unison, the harmonies and modulations of which are just pleasantly piquant to the ears of today but no doubt were a bit of a problem to the typical Opéra-Comique audience of 1875: we see Bizet at work here with one of his usual devices—switching the harmony into a seemingly remote key, poising for a moment on an alien chord, then serenely and surely making his way back to the main key of the piece.

As the cigar-girls saunter across the stage nonchalantly smoking their cigarettes—somewhat unfeminine behaviour, one imagines, in respectable Paris circles in the 1870's—the basses among their young admirers [2] comment on their saucy self-assurance in a little unison chorus; then the girls break into a song in praise of the cigarette; in the lazy curl and glide and swaying syncopations of the music we seem to get the aural equivalent of the floating patterns of the smoke:

5

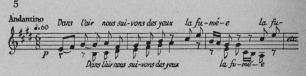

---

[1] At the top of the page (of the present score) on which the chorus of the cigar-girls begins there still remains the direction, "Cue [i.e. for the resumption of the music after the spell of conversation]: 'Quant à moi, je vais faire une chaîne pour attacher mon *épinglette*.'" These are the final words of José to the lieutenant in the Meilhac-Halévy text; they do not of themselves make sense in the score, where the brief conversation in recitative ends with José's "There goes the bell, and now you will be able to judge for yourself," and the direction is given to "run on to No. 4 (the chorus)." In the Italian-German score the "cue" is omitted.

[2] In the original text it is the soldiers.

Bizet develops the vocal and orchestral ensemble with the finest art. The scoring of the episode is a miracle of delicate suggestion —muted strings, sustained harp chords, wood-wind, and muted first violins and violas playing softly with the lulling syncopations of our No. 5 etc.

The young men have no sooner commented on the regretted non-appearance of la Carmencita when she enters, with a bouquet of cassia in her corsage and a flower of the same species in the corner of her mouth: she is accompanied in the violins by a new version—expressive now not of Fate but of Carmen herself—of the motif given out at the end of the overture (No. 1):

6

It is punctuated now by full-volumed staccato chords in wood-wind and brass. The motif is repeated frequently during what immediately follows—an appeal from the young men (tenors) to be informed when she will begin to love them. Her opening words—"I do not know: perhaps never, perhaps tomorrow"— are a magical musical stroke on Bizet's part, the key-shift in the second half of the phrase and the sudden drop from forte to piano being curiously impressive:

7

In the score she is instructed to address these words to the men "after a rapid glance at Don José." But this is surely a plain mis-direction: she has not been on the stage a minute, and so far has been besieged by her eager young adorers. It is difficult to suppose that she has no sooner burst out of the factory than she fastens her eyes on the brigadier sitting apart from the others on the left of the stage, whom she has never seen before, and vows by implication to love *him*, if ever, perhaps tomorrow. Meilhac and Halévy's directions were quite different: "Enter Carmen . . . accompanied by three or four young men; they follow her about, surround her, speak to her; she coquets with them. José raises his head; he glances at Carmen, then sets to work tranquilly again at his chain."

12

"But not today, that is certain," are her final words before she expounds her happy-go-lucky philosophy of love to her adorers in the famous habanera, the thesis of which is that love is a rebellious bird that comes when it wills, not when it is summoned.[1] Threats and prayers are alike in vain: love is gipsy by nature, recognising no law; and she, Carmen, is a true gipsy whose philosophy is "I will love you whether you love me or not; and if I love you, beware!"

The words of the habanera are almost entirely by Bizet himself. He is said to have composed the piece only because he was importuned to do so, and to have rewritten it a dozen times to suit the caprice of Galli-Marié, who wanted an effective show piece immediately after her first entry. The habanera, by the way, is one of the few numbers in *Carmen* that have a Spanish, or at any rate Spanish-American, origin: the tune was the work of one Sebastian Yradier (1809–1865). Bizet, who had been familiar with it for some years, appears to have taken it for granted that it was a folk-song. He has improved considerably on the original. A good deal of ink has been wasted on the question of whether Bizet ought not to have given a more authentically "Spanish" cast as a whole to his "Spanish" opera; the point having been overlooked that *Carmen* is a French opera set in Spain. We might as well censure Mozart for not having given a more specifically Neapolitan tinge to his *Così fan Tutte* by bestrewing it with specimens of the folk-music of the locality, or disapprove of Strauss's *Elektra* because its music is not in the least ancient Greek but wholly modern German.

[1] The librettists no doubt took their cue from José's remark to Mérimée in the prison, to the effect that women and cats are alike in this respect, they "come not when they are called but when they are not."

The habanera, which is interspersed with ejaculations from the chorus, begins each stanza in the minor but terminates in a refrain in the major:

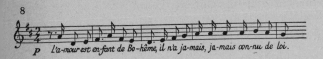

8

p   *L'a-mour est en-fant de Bo-hême, il n'a ja-mais, ja-mais con-nu de loi.*

that is of more direct dramatic significance, embodying as it does Carmen's persistent warning, "If you love me not, I will love you; and if I love you, then beware!"

13

At the end of the song the young men begin again to flock round Carmen and make their appeal to her, but by this time she has lost interest in them. The allegro tempo changes to andante moderato as the Carmen-Fate motif (No. 1) asserts itself in the clarinets, violas and 'cellos, gradually fading out in an interval of a diminished seventh that is like a question mark. Evidently a crucial point in the drama has been reached. The stage directions in the score read thus: "Carmen looks at the young men who surround her, then turns her eyes on Don José. She hesitates, takes a few steps towards the factory, then returns and goes straight to José, who is still engaged on his chain. She takes a cassia flower from her corsage and throws it at him." According to the libretto there comes "a moment of silence" *before* this piece of dumb-show. But obviously the silence should come *after* her approach to José. No specific provision is made for it in the score, but the place for it is clearly after the interval of the diminished seventh in the 'cellos referred to above. This is followed by a silent fermata in the orchestra which the conductor should force upon our attention: it is during this moment or two of complete silence in the orchestra and on the stage that Carmen's fateful resolution is taken; and the precise moment of its taking is when the cornets and trombones strike in with a single brusque staccato dissonant chord.

Then comes the brief dialogue that does not appear in the current scores, and for which we have to turn to the libretto:

Carmen: What are you doing there, my friend?
José: I am making a wire chain to hang my *épinglette* on.
Carmen (with a laugh): Your *épinglette!* Upon my soul! Your *épinglette,* pin-maker (*épinglier* [1]) of my heart!

It is then that she throws the cassia flower at him. It strikes him between the eyes; he rises angrily, and it falls at his feet. The factory bell rings for the second time—the summons to return—and the stage empties, Carmen and the other girls going into the building, Zuniga and the soldiers into the guard-room, to a derisive repetition by the sopranos of the habanera refrain, "L'amour est enfant de Bohème" (No. 8), while the orchestra accompanies the general exit with a sweeping melody and mocking reiterations of No. 1:

9

The gipsy poison has begun to work.

Guiraud now steps in with a short scene in recitative (numbered No. 6 *bis*) in which José muses upon the audacity of Carmen and the pungency of the scent of the flower she has hurled at him; then Micaëla appears. In the original the spoken text is rather longer, though to the same general effect; it is only during this soliloquy that José picks up the flower, not, as in the ordinary French vocal score, during the short orchestral postlude that accompanies the emptying of the stage. He repeats Mérimée's tag about the similarity between women and cats, and smiles at Carmen's effrontery. It is only when he smells the flower that we detect the beginning of a subtle change in him: "assuredly if there are sorceresses," he remarks, "that woman is one of them."

For the time being, however, she is swept out of his mind by Micaëla, who returns to tell him that she has come with a letter and a message and a small gift of money from his mother. There

[1] The play on words—*épingle,* pin, *épinglier,* pin-maker, *épinglette* (priming-pin for a gun), is necessarily unproduceable in translation. In Mérimée there is an added touch of insult: "Ah!" says Carmen, "the gentleman makes lace, since he has need of *épingles*"; and the onlookers laugh at the mortified soldier, whose blood rushes to his face, but who can think of no retort.

follows a tender duet, the most significant section of which, for
the analyst, is that in which she delivers the mother's message to
her son:

10
Allegro moderato ♩ = 88

Et — tu lui di-ras que sa mè-re Son-ge nuit et jour— à l'ab-sent,

whom she has pardoned, for whom she prays day and night, and
whom she hopes to have restored to her soon. Micaëla has been
further commissioned to convey a kiss from mother to son. José's
heart is flooded with tender memories of his village home and
native land. A shadow darkens the picture for a moment as he
thinks of "the demon whose prey I had nearly become," and
Micaëla asks anxiously what is the meaning of his words. But he
brushes the question aside and the tender duet is resumed. Micaëla
is leaving Seville that evening and will be with his mother on the
morrow; she is to assure her that her son will always be worthy
of her; and José sends a return kiss by way of a pledge.

14

The scene that follows the departure of Micaëla is a condensation of the original text; José reads his mother's letter—to an
expressive quiet breathing of No. 10 in the strings—promises to
obey her exhortations, and vows he will marry Micaëla; and he
dismisses "the witch and her flower" with a shrug of the shoulders.
But just as he is about to remove the flower from his tunic there
comes a hullabaloo from inside the factory, from which the girls
soon pour out in great excitement; "it was la Carmencita!" some
of them are crying. The noise brings the lieutenant and some
soldiers out of the guard-house. There ensues a masterly musical
ensemble, in which every feature of the animated episode is
dexterously hit off—the ceaseless cackle of the women and the
vain attempts of Zuniga to make himself heard. As to what had
happened to cause all this uproar it appears that there are two
schools of thought among the women, some siding with Carmen,
others with her antagonist Manuelita; there had been an inter-

change of contumelious repartee between these two ornaments of the factory, ending in a reciprocal pulling of hair.

When at last the lieutenant can make himself heard he sends José into the factory with a couple of soldiers to find out what it is all about. They return with Carmen, the orchestra accompanying her entry with the broad melody that had formerly accompanied her exit. The cackling mob of women having been shooed to the back of the stage by the guard, José reports that the matter is rather more serious than had been thought at first. Among some three hundred excited women in the factory he had found one screaming blue murder and asking for a confessor; a cross had been scored on her cheek with two knife-cuts; standing opposite her was la Carmencita, who "said not a word, but ground her teeth and rolled her eyes like a chameleon." He had accordingly "asked mademoiselle to follow him." For a moment it had looked as if she wanted to resist; "then she became resigned, and followed me as meekly as a sheep." This is the whole truth, on the word of a Navarrais, he concludes. At the word "Navarrais" Carmen turns round quickly and fixes her gaze on José: evidently a line of action has suggested itself to her—she will work on the young man's sympathies by pretending that she is a compatriot of his. This little point cannot be too clearly brought out in the stage action; but it is completely frustrated by the omission of the lengthy spoken dialogue and the substitution for it of a few bars of recitative, after which Carmen begins a nonchalant "Tra la la la," followed by the words, "You can cut me, you can burn me, but not a word will you get out of me. I defy everything, fire, steel, and heaven itself. My secret is mine, and I will keep it well; I love another, and will avow it with my dying breath":

11

The melody to which these words are sung was taken by Bizet from one current in Spain, to which Sarasate (who had been a fellow-student of his at the Paris Conservatoire) may possibly have introduced him: Bizet, however, has decidedly improved on the original.

The words themselves have a rather curious prehistory. They were taken by the librettists almost verbatim from *Les Bohémiens*, a prose translation by Mérimée of a poem (*The Gipsies*) by Pushkin which tells of an alien youth, Aleko, who elects to live among the gipsies, with one of whom, Zemfira, he falls deeply in love. One day he is perturbed to hear her singing, half to herself, a wild song of her tribe in which a wife addresses her husband in this wise: "Cut me in pieces, if you will, burn me; I fear neither knife nor fire. I hate and despise you; I love another, and will die loving him. . . ." Like Carmen she prizes liberty before all else, and soon the inevitable catastrophe comes—she ceases to love Aleko and gives herself to another lover. Aleko surprises them and kills them both, the gipsy girl, like Carmen, defying her jealous murderer to the end—"I fear you not; I scorn your threats! Assassin, I curse you! I love another, and loving him I die." [1]

15

Carmen, still to the strain of No. 11, treats with brazen effrontery the attempts of Zuniga to make her behave herself, even going so far as to threaten another of the women with bodily assault. The soldiers finally drive the excited crowd off the stage, and Zuniga calls for a rope to bind the dangerous Carmen's arms. Quite politely he sends her off to prison, where the jailers, he says, will be able to form their own opinion of the quality of her gipsy songs. He consigns her to the custody of José. Left alone with him she switches off her impertinence and becomes as mild as milk. She persuades him to loosen the rope, which is hurting her hands; he does so, but his manner remains professionally aloof. Once more we have to pass the recitative by and resort to the original text to understand fully what happens next. As in Mérimée, Carmen begins with an unblushing attempt at bribery; she offers to give José a piece of the *bar lachi*, a magic stone one fragment of which will make all women fall in love with him. Finding that this does not work she tries another line. She has gathered that he is a Navarrais; she now asserts herself to be a

[1] Pushkin's poem was drawn upon by Rachmaninov for his early one-act opera *Aleko*.

native of Etchalar, which is only a few miles from José's birth-place, Elizondo. According to her story, in which of course there is not a word of truth, she had been abducted by gipsies and taken to Seville, where she has been working in the factory with the object of saving enough money to take her back to her poor mother, of whom she is the only support; the Spanish women hate her because she is a Navarraise and proud of it.

José tells her bluntly that he does not believe her story, that everything about her, her mouth, her eyes, her complexion, testi-fies that she is a gipsy. Thereupon she frankly confesses that she had been lying, and changes her strategy once more. Yes, she is a gipsy, she admits; but all the same the soldier will do whatever she asks, because he loves her, one proof of which is that he has kept the flower she had thrown at him: it is useless to throw it away now, she continues as he makes an angry gesture, for the charm has already worked. He forbids her to say any more. Very well, she replies; but if she is not allowed to speak she can at least be permitted to sing. There follows a tiny musical episode that has been the subject of some comment, the meaning of which, however, is perfectly clear if we follow the guidance of the librettists' text. José's angry ejaculation, "Do you hear me? Speak no more! I forbid you to speak!" is clinched by a furious gesture in the orchestra, terminating in a single peremptory fortissimo F minor chord. But instantaneously the mood of the music changes, the explanation of this being afforded by the stage direc-tion in the original text after Carmen's "You forbid me to speak? Very well, I will speak no more"—"She fixes her gaze on José, who recoils." It is obviously to this psychological turn in the action that the short orchestral passage that follows the F minor chord relates: a quiet, insinuating melody first in the violas, then in the violins, supported by an occasional pizzicato string chord: [1] Carmen's glance and José's recoil mark the first under-

---

[1] It is often said that Bizet knew nothing of Wagner's music later than *Lohengrin*. This is hardly credible. In 1871, in a letter to his mother-in-law, he had praised Wagner's music to the skies. By the mid-eighteen-seventies the scores of *Tristan*, the *Meistersinger* and much of the *Ring* had been pub-lished; and we ask ourselves whether it is at all likely that so passionate an admirer of the German composer as Bizet was would have been content to let his acquaintance with him terminate with *Lohengrin*. In the case of our

12

Moderato

mining of his defences. As Bizet himself had said to Galabert à *propos* of Myrrha and Yorick, "the serpent has come, and the bird is half paralysed."

With an enharmonic change, the A flat of the last bar of our No. 12 now being treated as G sharp, the music makes towards the new key of F sharp. Three bars suffice for this harmonic shift; then, over the characteristic seguidilla rhythm:

13

Carmen sings the captivating seguidilla, with its piquant fluctuations between major and minor:

14

Allegretto ♪ = 160

PP Près des rem-parts de Se-vil —— le,

Chez mon a—mi—Lil-las Pas-tia,

At Lillas Pastia's tavern near the gates of Seville, she sings, she will dance the seguidilla and drink manzanilla, but not alone. Her new lover will accompany her there; lovers she already has in plenty, but now she is José's and José hers. Distractedly he bids her be silent, but she protests that she is singing only to herself, thinking only of a certain officer, not a captain, not even a lieu-

example No. 12 the later-Wagnerian filiation is surely obvious. Nor is it the only instance of the kind in the *Carmen* score.

tenant, merely a brigadier, whom she is capable of loving to her heart's full content. In vain the bird struggles in the net; when José stammers his protests it is to the intoxicating rhythm of her song that he does so; he sees things now only through Carmen's eyes, his blood beats now only to her pulse. Finally his defences collapse: "I am like a drunken man," he cries; "if I give myself up to you will you keep your promise, Carmen? You will return my love?", and he unfastens the rope that binds her hands. Her reply is a reiteration of the seguidilla, ending in an exultant "Tra la la la."

The atmosphere changes, and we have the feeling of coming down to realistic earth again, as Zuniga comes out of the guard-room with the order for Carmen's committal to prison; he is entirely the soldier, concerned with nothing but the unpleasant but necessary practical business in hand:

15

Carmen sits down demurely, her hands, now quite free, behind her back. To José she says *sotto voce*, "On the bridge I will push you as hard as I can. Fall down; the rest leave to me." Non-chalantly humming the refrain of her habanera, "L'Amour est enfant de Bohème" (No. 8), she places herself between the two men. By now the crowd has come upon the stage again, though the soldiers keep it at a distance from the protagonists. When Carmen and her escort reach the bridge her habanera suddenly merges into a derisive reiteration of No. 15 in the orchestra as, to the amusement of the crowd, she gives José a push and runs. He pretends to fall. Carmen throws the rope over the parapet of the bridge in triumph and disappears, while as the curtain falls the factory girls surround Zuniga and burst into peals of mocking laughter.

16

In the second act we see Bizet really getting into his stride as a musical dramatist; for every smallest turn in the action, serious or humorous, he will now find the right music.

Before the rise of the curtain there comes a short orchestral entr'acte in which he makes use of the theme of the unaccompanied ditty that José will sing later (see No. 20) on his way to the tavern of Lillas Pastia, after spending a month in prison for his connivance at Carmen's escape. There seems at first sight no very logical dramatic reason why the song should put in an appearance now; but, as Henry Malherbe has pointed out, it is subtly apposite to the occasion. Its scoring has throughout a burlesque tinge, with its predominance of clarinet and bassoon colours, its trills, and its drum-taps marking the rhythm: and the general dynamic effect, with its gradual decline to a quadruple pianissimo at the finish, is that of a march-past. Bizet is artfully preparing us for a second act in which the military will play a considerable part, and that not a very dignified one. It is in a sense light relief, but light relief of a curiously appropriate kind.

José's assignation with Carmen in the first act had been at Lillas Pastia's tavern that stands near the city gate: it is a regular meeting-place of the band of smugglers of which Carmen is now one of the leading lights. It is also the resort of some of the army officers, who obviously come there, as on the present occasion, to enjoy the company of the gipsy girls, a couple of whom we see dancing as the curtain rises, while the others are smoking cigarettes with the officers, for dinner has just ended. The music of the dance is a lively affair, with the melody mostly given out at first by the flutes in thirds over a pizzicato accompaniment in violas and 'cellos, many piquant key-shifts, and an orchestral texture in which cymbals, triangle and tambourine play an occasional part:

16

Carmen, sitting apart from the others, has for companion the lieutenant, Zuniga, to whom, however, she seems to be paying little attention. Suddenly she rises and breaks into a *chanson bohème*. This song of hers, descriptive of the intoxication of gipsy song and revel, sets the dancers in swift motion again, while in her cadences Carmen is joined by two of her companions, Frasquita and Mercédès. After the final mad dance Carmen sinks panting on to a bench. Then, in the original text, the others fall into a discussion, in ordinary speech, of the situation of the moment. Lillas Pastia is anxious to close for the night, for the magistrate, it appears, is none too favourably disposed towards him, though he professes not to know why. Zuniga tells him pleasantly why; it is because his tavern is known to be the resort of all the smugglers of the neighbourhood; and he hazards the guess that the real reason why Lillas Pastia wants to put up the shutters now is that he and his contraband friends have some business to discuss. However, as he has no desire to get the tavern keeper into trouble with the authorities, he suggests to the girls that they shall go off to the theatre for an hour or so with him and his companions. At a surreptitious sign from Pastia they politely decline, Frasquita and Mercédès acting as their spokeswomen. Zuniga then appeals to Carmen, but her refusal is uncompromisingly blunt.

He thinks he can account for her manifest animus against him, and in doing so he makes the audience acquainted, as it has a right to be, with what has happened since the curtain had fallen on the first act. The authorities had sent to prison for a month, as in duty bound, the soldier who had obviously assisted Carmen to escape, and who had been suitably degraded. This seems to be news to Carmen, who repeats after him in serious tones, "Degraded and imprisoned?" She is rejoiced to learn, however, that the peccant soldier had been released the day before. "If he is free," she cries, "all is well"; and with a flourish of her castanets she advises Zuniga and his friends to make themselves scarce as soon as possible. They resign themselves to their brusque dismissal; but before they can depart there comes from off-stage a joyous chorus of welcome to the most skilful and intrepid of toreros, one Escamillo, who is on his way to the tavern accompanied by a torchlight procession of his admirers. The situation being explained to the soldiers, Zuniga and Moralès, blandly ignoring the local licensing regulations, gallantly declare that they will stay where they are and drink a toast in the torero's honour; and the lieutenant, going to the window, invites Escamillo, in spite of Lillas Pastia's protests, to join them within. All this is very skimpily treated in the recitative that Guiraud has substituted for the spoken text.

17

Zuniga having greeted the new-comer courteously on behalf of them all and proposed the toast of "the great art of tauromachy," Escamillo thanks him in half-a-dozen words, and then, without more ado, plunges into the famous "Toreador's Song"— a splendid piece of swagger against which the voices and the eyebrows of purists have long been raised in vain.[1] He gives us a colourful description of the thrills and dangers of the bull-ring, including the occasional overthrow of a picador, the scattering of the banderilleros, the panic of the spectators, and even a realistic and most effective imitation of the roar of the maddened bull—or such, at any rate, it appears to be—in a low G flat in the trombone and double basses. Yet even in these perilous circumstances, it appears, the torero should remember that a pair of dark eyes are fixed on him all the time, and that the loving owner of them is waiting for him. This constitutes the theme of the refrain of his song: [2]

17

It is taken up vigorously by the whole company after each verse. At the conclusion of the song the enthusiasts crowd round the hero, shaking his hand and drinking his health. Shortly before

[1] Bizet is alleged to have thought so little of the Toreador's song that he remarked to the conductor, "Well, they want muck; here it is!" If he really thought it "muck," why did he afterwards give it so prominent a place in the prelude to the opera? The truth underlying the traditional story appears to be that Halévy wanted an "aria" at this point and sent his proposed verses to Bizet, who, after jibbing for a while, at last set the lines to music and handed the whole thing over to Halévy with the ironic remark, "Voici ta saleté!" In any case, no one with any sense of humour and any knowledge of the artistic temperament takes rough-and-ready remarks of this sort seriously: they are spoken with a smile, and should be taken with one.

[2] Bizet's marking for the refrain—"Toréador, en garde"—in both verses is "avec fatuité." He also directs it to be sung quietly, not bellowed at us, as is the way with baritones.

the exuberant end of the ensemble there comes an extraordinarily impressive series of cadences by Frasquita, Mercédès, Carmen and Escamillo on the words "L'Amour":

18

during the last two of which, according to the stage directions, Carmen looks intently at Escamillo and Escamillo at Carmen; the latter's low D flat has a curious clinching quality.[1]

The spoken version of what immediately follows is more illuminative than Guiraud's condensation of it in recitative. In response to a renewed appeal from the worried Pastia the company begins to break up; and as it thins out, Escamillo finds himself close to Carmen, who has apparently captivated him at first sight. The remainder of the scene is carried on in spoken dialogue. Escamillo asks her name, and learns that it is Carmen or la Carmencita, whichever he prefers. Gallantly he declares that it is her name he will speak, according to torero custom, when he kills his next bull. And what if he should say he is in love with her? he asks. She replies that she has no objection to this, but that he can dismiss the notion that she will love him in return. In that case, he says, he will wait in hope: her careless reply is that there is no law against waiting, and to hope is always pleasant.

Moralès and Zuniga now try once more to persuade Frasquita and Mercédès to depart with them, but at another sign from the tavern-keeper they decline. The two officers take their second rebuff in good part, but Zuniga tells Carmen *sotto voce* that he will return in an hour, after the roll-call. She advises him pointedly not to, but he only reiterates his promise; then, accompanied by Moralès and the others, he joins the cortège that is to escort Escamillo home, and, to a repetition in the orchestra of the refrain of the Toreador's song (No. 17), the stage gradually becomes

[1] For some unimaginable reason or other these magical bars are sometimes omitted in performance. I have been told of one conductor who did not even know they were in the score, and had to have them pointed out to him. Perhaps they were crossed out in the theatre score he was using.

empty of all except Pastia, Carmen, Frasquita and Mercédès. "Why were you so anxious to get rid of them?" Frasquita asks Pastia, "and why did you motion to us not to go away?" He explains that he is expecting Dancaïre (the leader of the smugglers' band) and Remendado, to discuss with them "affaires d'Égypte," which is the smugglers' euphemism for their contraband activities. The two worthies in question have been waiting outside for the departure of the crowd. Pastia now opens a door and signs to them to come in; and when they have done so he closes the doors and the window-shutters, and they all settle down to business. Remendado has a strain of irresponsible humour in him which Dancaïre has to check from time to time; the librettists no doubt felt that the habitués of the Opéra-Comique were entitled occasionally to a little comic relief. Dancaïre's news is that they have just come from Gibraltar, where a ship has unloaded some English goods which it is the intention of the band to intercept somewhere in the mountains. To this end they need the assistance of the three girls, not, as Carmen laughingly suggests, to carry bales, but because this is one of the situations in which the natural talent of the female of the species for lying and bamboozling will be of inestimable value. The discussion is carried on in a quintet (Frasquita, Mercédès, Carmen, Remendado, Dancaïre) of incomparable verve and musical wit.

18

At the end of it Frasquita and Mercédès say they are willing to set out with the smugglers at once, but Carmen demurs. While the orchestra carries on with the basic melody of the quintet she explains, to the general horror, that *she* cannot accompany them because she is in love. Remendado and Dancaïre remark ironically:

19

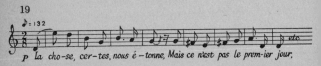

p La cho-se, cer-tes, nous é-tonne, Mais ce n'est pas le prem-ier jour,

that this is no new experience for her; all the same, where business is concerned love must take second place. All through this scene it is clear from the words and the music that these are comic opera smugglers, not taking themselves or their profession too seriously; and we feel that José could afford to throw in his lot with them without undergoing anything of the slow moral degeneration of the José of Mérimée's sombre tale. But in the main we can regard the second act up to now as a sort of dramatic scherzo, designed for the light relief of the audience. Matters, so far as the smugglers are concerned, will take on a more serious tinge in the third act.

Carmen, to the strain of No. 18, replies in the same vein of polite irony; thanks to the genius of Bizet, these smugglers and gitanas, for all their bad upbringing, have perfect manners. In the present instance, she assures them, business will have to come a bad second to love. The others, in another light-footed ensemble, appeal almost plaintively to her better nature; but she is immovable. For the full understanding of what immediately follows we have to by-pass Guiraud and the current score and glance at the original spoken text. Dancaïre makes the mistake of throwing his weight about as leader of the band, entitled to obedience: this of course calls out all that is most rebellious in Carmen's nature, while Dancaïre aims a kick at Remendado, who has mistakenly tried to be facetious once more. To the general dismay Carmen declares that she cannot join them until tomorrow; for tonight she is expecting a man she loves—the poor devil of a soldier who had been put in prison for doing her a service, and whom, a fortnight ago, as Frasquita now discloses, Carmen had tried to liberate by sending him a loaf of bread in which was concealed a gold piece and a file, of neither of which, however, had he availed himself.[1] "You see," says Dancaïre scornfully, "your soldier was afraid of further punishment: tonight too he will be afraid. It's no use your opening the shutters to see if he is coming; I wager that he won't." "You will lose your wager," Carmen retorts; and at that moment José's voice is heard in the distance, singing (unaccompanied) a buoyant little canzonetta in dialogue form:

[1] All this is as in Mérimée. It is important for the light it throws on José's psychology at that stage: he knows that the file will set him free in a few hours, and divines that it has come from Carmen; but he declines to use it because his honour as a soldier forbids; "desertion seemed to me a great crime," he tells his interlocutor in his last hours.

"Halt! Who goes there? . . . A dragoon from Alcalà. . . .
Where are you going, dragoon from Alcalà? . . . True and faithful I come where my loved one calls me! . . . Pass then, my
friend! . . . Affairs of honour, affairs of love, these mean everything to dragoons from Alcalà!":

20

In the Meilhac-Halévy text it is "Almanza"; but that means
nothing so far as the drama is concerned, while "Alcalà" means
a great deal. In Mérimée's story the loaf containing a file which
was brought to José in prison is described as "un pain d'Alcalà";
and in a footnote Mérimée explains that "Alcalà de los Panaderos"
(Alcalà of the Bakers) is a small town not far from Seville famous
for the delicious quality of its rolls. For us who know our Mérimée, therefore, the reference to Alcalà in José's song on his way
to the tavern has a certain dramatic meaning: Carmen, and she
alone, knows at once that it is José who is approaching. The unfortunate thing is that there is nothing in the text to make this
clear to the audience—which, no doubt, is why in the Meilhac-
Halévy imprint of the text José is made to come from Almanza.

During the first verse of the song Dancaïre, Remendado, Carmen, Frasquita and Mercédès have thrown open the shutters
to observe the singer. The smugglers like the appearance of this
new admirer of Carmen's and opine that he would make a valu-
able recruit for their band. She half agrees with them, but for
the moment can think only of her love for him,[1] so she answers
evasively. Obviously the time is approaching when she and José
must be left alone on the stage for their big scene; the librettists'
way of effecting this is to make Dancaïre chase Remendado out
for a remark unusually fatuous even for him, and for Frasquita
and Mercédès to follow the pair to make peace between them.

[1] This is made clear enough in the spoken dialogue, but not in the score.
Gipsy honour demands that a debt shall be repaid.

All this while José has been drawing nearer and nearer, and his timing is excellent; he manages to make a most effective tenor entry on the last note of his song, a prolonged high G.

19

The dialogue that follows the meeting of the pair is compressed by Guiraud into a few bars of recitative, after which Carmen dances a gipsy *romalis* for José. In the lengthy spoken dialogue, however, a good deal is said that it is necessary for us in the audience to know. José, we learn, has only just been released from prison. Carmen asks him why he had not made use of the file to escape: he replies in the words of Mérimée, that his honour as a soldier forbade him to desert, while the gold piece he now returns to her with a noble gesture. With this unexpected wealth in her possession she summons Pastia and bids him prepare a feast—a detailed later episode in Mérimée being thus condensed and brought within the orbit of the second act of the opera. José tells her of his degradation in rank, which, with all the rest of his punishment, he bears gladly for her sake. She becomes for a minute or two quite kindly and likeable, paying off her debt, as she says the gipsies always do, by pressing on José the oranges and bonbons that Pastia has brought; she herself gormandises like a happy child. She tells him that his lieutenant and other officers had been there a little while before, that she had danced a *romalis* for them, and that the lieutenant had vowed that he adored her. As José shows signs of jealousy on hearing this she promises to dance for him also. In a somewhat similar scene on another occasion in Mérimée, as no castanets are available she breaks a plate and makes do with the two pieces of china. But this, of course, would not do in opera; so the librettists, after first of all making her, quite unnecessarily as it turns out, lose her castanets and then break a plate, find the operatically indispensable castanets for her—they have been on the table all the time!

José having seated himself where she has indicated she performs a dance for his sole benefit, humming a constant "La la la" and marking the rhythm with her castanets. But soon there are heard, from a distance, the cornets sounding the retreat; and Bizet combines the military call with the melody of Carmen, in this fashion:

21

The sound has been too faint as yet to attract the notice of Carmen, but the soldier in José is sensitively aware of it. When he draws her attention to it—for now it has come nearer—she is at first merely amused and resumes her dance. But when she realises —the retreat sounding more and more insistently—that José is bent on obeying the summons of duty her fury knows no bounds. In a magnificent piece of musical rhetoric she vents her rage and scorn on him: she has been dancing for him, and now he would leave her at the call of "duty"—for by now he has taken up his cartouche-box and put on his sword-belt. Blind with rage she at last throws his shako at him and bids him begone. His mournful humble protestations of his consuming love for her and Carmen's torrent of abuse are admirably differentiated by Bizet without the smallest loss of unity of musical tissue. At last, as proof of his love, José takes from his tunic the flower she had thrown at him in the first act and shows it to her: he has kept it on him all through his imprisonment, where it has been his one consolation for all he has suffered. A very different José now from the one who had sung of his boyish love for little Micaëla—for the character of the man is now developing subtly in the imagination of Bizet,— he tells her, in the Flower Song, how he had kept this cassia flower in his prison, breathing in its perfume night and day, for it brought Carmen close to him. At times he had cursed the fate that had brought her into his life; yet for all that his one desire had been to see her again.

The Flower Song is unusual in its structure; it flows on, page by page, with hardly a repeat of phrase, weaving an unbroken musical web. It has practically nothing of the symmetries of pattern of the conventional opera aria. In this respect it has a few notable older and newer confrères: the *Marseillaise* is another of these continuous melodies, while songs like Strauss's *Seitdem dein*

Aug' and Wolf's *An die Geliebte* belong to the same non-repetitive or hardly repetitive type. The ending of the Song is a sore trial to any tenor. First of all there comes, to the words "Et j'étais une chose à toi," a slow ascending scale that culminates in a long-held high B flat; and the marking for both voice and orchestra is pianissimo! The passage, while psychologically veracious, is undoubtedly a technical blunder on Bizet's part, for it leaves the ordinary tenor confronted with only two alternatives, each of which is fatal to the intention of the phrase—he must either sing it fortissimo, or, if his artistic conscience will not permit him anything but a pianissimo, resort to an anaemic falsetto. Now in 1869 Bizet had censured Galabert for having written a phrase for the Claribel of *La Coupe du roi de Thule* expressive enough in itself but inconveniently high in the vocal register; "How can you expect anyone," he had asked his pupil, "to enunciate distinctly at this exceptional pitch and at the same time produce a smooth, sweet, unforced tone?" Yet in 1875 we find the admirable theoretician flying in the face of his own sound precepts!

Nor is he entirely happy in the phrase that follows—the final cadence of the Song:

where the curious brief evasion by the orchestra (the high woodwind) of the key of D flat not only makes any departure from the pitch on the tenor's part all too evident, but even today has an air of calculated oddity. To the ears of the Opéra-Comique audience of 1875 it must have been a puzzle and a trial.

20

Carmen is sobered by José's confession of devotion. When the brief orchestral postlude to the Song has come to a quiet and

expressive end she mutters on a low D flat—a most effective touch,
this—"No, you do not love me!", and then launches one of the
most curiously enigmatic passages in the whole work, in which
the six-eight rhythm seems at variance with, and yet is subtly
inwrought with, the melancholy of the words. The gipsy is overcome by nostalgia for the mountains, whither, she says, Josè
must follow her—to the mountains, where both will be free of
the pressure of other lives on theirs, where José will carry her on
his saddle with no officer to give him orders, no retreat to obey,
where they can breathe the divine air of liberty. José is drawn
into the stream of her song and her thought. For a while he is on
the point of succumbing; then the soldier in him asserts himself
once more, and he begs her despairingly, in a splendid phrase in
which passion and despair contend for the mastery, to have pity
on him, for follow her he cannot:

23

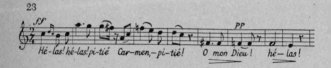

Hé-las! hé-las! pi-tié   Car-men,—pi-tié!   O mon Dieu !   hé—las!

(This moving cry appears to be one of Bizet's own touches; the
words do not appear in the Meilhac-Halévy text.)

At last he manages to shake off the fascination; recalling his
honour as a soldier he tears himself from Carmen's arms. Thereupon her mood changes: she tells him she hates him, and furiously
orders him out. He bids her a sad farewell for ever; but just as he
reaches the door a knock is heard. "Keep silent!" Carmen whispers to José. The door opens, and with a confident cry of "Holà!
Carmen! Holà!" Zuniga enters. Catching sight of José he addresses an ironical reproach to Carmen—"A misalliance! Taking
up with a common soldier when you might have had an officer!"
Roughly he orders José to make himself scarce, and when he
twice refuses the lieutenant strikes him. Swords are drawn and
bloodshed seems imminent; but at a wild cry from Carmen the
smugglers and gipsies pour in, and the great finale begins.

At a gesture from Carmen, the lieutenant is seized by Dancaïre and Remendado and disarmed. A masterpiece of musical irony follows; Carmen politely condoles with Zuniga for having had the bad luck to arrive at an inopportune moment, and Dancaïre and Remendado, with their pistols pointed at his head, take up the polished argument; they are all under the necessity of leaving the tavern at once, and the lieutenant will be good enough to accompany them—"just a promenade," Carmen tells him. Zuniga, not to be outdone in politeness, assures them that no one on earth could resist such potent arguments as theirs, but, still apparently in the best of humours, he advises them to have a care later. The menace beneath his polished phrase is admirably hit off by Bizet in three bars of trills in the strings—even the double basses joining in—that are like the hissing of a pit of serpents, but serpents with Chesterfieldian manners:

24

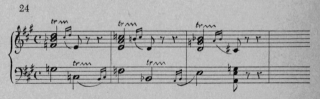

"War is war," replies Dancaïre philosophically, "and now have the goodness to come along with us quietly." The lieutenant is conducted out by four of the gipsies, each presenting a persuasive pistol at his head. Then, as the company takes up joyously the strain of Carmen's paean to liberty, she herself has a quiet word with José. "You will be one of us henceforth?" she asks. With a sigh he answers, "I have no choice!" She comments drily that though the reply might have been given with a better grace, it will do; and the whole company, turning to José, assure him, still to the strain of Carmen's previous appeal to him, that no life is finer than theirs—an open sky, a wandering life, and above all the intoxication of liberty.

José is now fairly in the net: henceforth he will be, as regards his outer life, a smuggler, an outlaw, and as regards his inner life the slave of Carmen's whims and passions. Necessarily the opera cannot depict for us in such grim detail as Mérimée could permit himself the slow disintegration of the man's soul, his inevitable drift from crime to crime, the mad jealousy aroused by Carmen's amorous caprices: but for all that the librettists, with Bizet's help, have done very well. It is really José, not Carmen, who is the psychological centre of the drama, just as in Prévost's story it is Des Grieux, not Manon Lescaut, who should claim our main attention and sympathy; for it is the men who go through one psychological transformation after another, whereas the two women are basically the same from first to last. Carmen is the same Carmen in each act of the opera, while, thanks almost entirely to Bizet, José is a different being each time we meet him. So pronounced is the difference between the José of the first act and the José of the last that even vocally they seem to call for different types of voice and style—an agreeable lyric tenor for the first act, a powerful dramatic tenor for the fourth.

21

As is his way, Bizet places an orchestral entr'acte between his second and third acts. This is an exquisite miniature, with much melodic dialoguing and interwining between the wood-wind instruments. It was originally intended for the *L'Arlésienne* score, where its pastoral quality would have been quite in place. There has been much discussion as to its appropriateness here in the opera: some critics have censured it as having no justification at all on dramatic grounds; others have welcomed it as bringing with it a momentary contrast to, and relief from, the gradually darkening atmosphere of the tragedy. Both are right in their way; neither can be confuted because there is no common ground for argument between them. The only sensible thing to do seems to be to accept the entr'acte for the lovely delicate thing it is and not enquire too closely into its dramatic relevance.

The concluding E flat major chord of the entr'acte is continued for a couple of bars in the orchestra after the curtain rises. The scene is "a wild and picturesque rocky place in the mountains: the solitude and the darkness are complete." A few smugglers are seen here and there lying on the ground, wrapped in their cloaks; gradually others become visible, carrying bales of merchandise. In the orchestra we seem to see and hear their cautious, laboured movements, to sense an air of secrecy and danger in all they do:

25

Note the steady step-by-step tread of the bass (in this case violas and 'cellos) so characteristic of Bizet. This sense of slow wary movement as the smugglers exhort each other to be on the alert becomes intensified in the pianissimo orchestral accompaniment to their chorus:

26

and reaches its climax in a series of descending chromatics in which they sing "Take care not to make one false step":

27

The atmosphere lightens for a moment as the three women, with Dancaïre, Remendado and José—for he is irrevocably one of the smugglers now—unite in a sextet; then the sombre No. 26, No. 27 and No. 25 are resumed. The ensemble ends with a general cry of "Take care! Take care!" that tapers off into a meaningful pianissimo.

In the text proper there follow now some pages of spoken dialogue. Dancaïre addresses the band; anyone who wishes to sleep can do so; he himself, taking Remendado with him, will reconnoitre their chances of getting the goods into the town. There is a breach in the wall at one point at which an official will be keeping guard: Lillas Pastia has assured him that the man will be in their pay, but they must not be too confident. Meanwhile some of the gipsies have lit a fire at which Frasquita and Mercédès seat themselves while the men wrap themselves up in their cloaks to sleep. José seizes the occasion to have a few words of explanation with Carmen. They have evidently quarrelled recently, and he is anxious to make peace. She is unfriendly and hard: she loves him less than she had done, she says, and if he continues to pester her it will end in her not loving him at all, for her liberty means more to her than the love of any man. He speaks sadly of a village only a few miles away in which is an old woman—his mother—who still believes that her son is an honest man. Carmen scornfully advises him to go back to this mother of his, for the smuggler's life plainly is not one for such as he. When he threatens her she replies, "Perhaps you will kill me? Very well! I have often read it in the cards that you and I will die together." With a clack of her castanets she turns her back on him and seats herself near Frasquita and Mercédès, where she watches in silence their consultation of the cards. José, after a moment's hesitation, walks away and stretches himself on a rock.

All this is replaced in the score by a few pages of recitative, into which, at the mention of José's mother, there is introduced a reminiscence in the orchestra of our No. 10 from the first act, and, when Carmen hints that José should leave the band, another of our No. 1; and after she has suggested that some day he may kill her, with the added reflection that after all Fate is master, she makes her way to the card players.

22

The scene of the cards is an enchanting musical vignette, giving not only our ears but our spirits a grateful relief until Carmen shall step into the forefront of the action again and spread a sinister cloud over it. Her two companions are reading their fortunes in the cards. Frasquita sees a romantic young lover who carries her off on his horse into the mountains, where he becomes a famous chief with a hundred men in his service: Mercédès is wooed by an elderly lover who marries her, loads her with gold and jewels, and then, most considerately, dies, leaving her his sole legatee. Twice the prattle of the girls is rounded off by a charming duet:

28

in which they exhort the cards to tell them truly who will love and who will deceive them.

The duet dies away in an orchestral postlude based on the final bar of our last musical example; and this, by a stroke of genius, Bizet instantaneously metamorphoses into the typical Carmen motif (No. 6):

29

For Carmen, who so far has been watching the two girls, has now begun to turn the cards herself. "Diamonds! Spades! Death!" she mutters; "I first, then he. Death for both of us!"; and she points to the sleeping José. Still throwing the cards she muses sombrely, over a throbbing orchestral accompaniment, on the infallibility of this mode of divination—if your fate is settled you may cut the cards hopefully twenty times, but the pitiless answer will be always the same—death! So nothing matters; she will be fearless to the end. Her gloomy monologue terminates in a cadence of extraordinarily tragic power; but the words are hardly out of her mouth before Frasquita and Mercédès, wholly absorbed in their own game, break in with their light-hearted No. 28; and this time Carmen weaves through the bright texture her own dark thread of foreboding.

By now Dancaïre and Remendado have returned with the news that the breach in the town wall is guarded not by one official but by three. The women cheerfully profess themselves capable of dealing with these in their own way, whereupon José turns furiously upon Carmen. Dancaïre roughly orders him to put his jealousy in his pocket, for this is neither the time nor the place for it; daylight is almost on them, and they must act. José is left behind, posted on a rock from which he will have a good view of the country all around; his task is to guard such of the bales of merchandise as the smugglers are leaving behind them for the present. This bit of spoken dialogue—not provided for in the recitative in the score—is essential to the spectator's understanding of what happens a little later; for Dancaïre's final words to José are, "You will be able to see if we are followed: if you should sight anyone, you have my permission to deal with him in the appropriate way."

All except José now make their exit in the best of spirits, singing gaily, in a rousing ensemble, of their confidence in their ability to handle the douaniers if occasion should arise: the orchestra continues the vigorous strain for a little while after their departure.

As the stage will be wanted in a minute or two by Micaëla for her aria it is now necessary for the librettists to get José off the stage as plausibly as they can. So they make him follow the smugglers out, examining as he does so the priming of his carbine, presumably to make sure that if a minion of the law should appear he will be able to deal with him according to Dancaïre's instructions. The next thing we see and hear in the score is Micaëla, after a brief orchestral prelude and a recitative, breaking into her aria. How has the simple girl managed, the spectator asks himself, to find her way in the dark with such certainty to this wild place? The opening words of her recitative are hardly sufficient explanation: "This is the usual resort of the smugglers. Here I will find him, and discharge without a tremor the duty laid on me by his mother." But in the text proper she appears dialoguing with a guide, who, in reply to her expression of surprise that there are no smugglers there, explains that they have just left, but will return soon for the remainder of their goods. Micaëla, he says, is to keep her eyes open, for it is the custom of these gentry to leave a sentinel somewhere, and if he sees her the consequences to her may be awkward. He congratulates her on the courage she has so far shown, even when they had found themselves in the middle of a herd of savage bulls in the charge of "the celebrated Escamillo." (This is the librettists' rather innocent way of

preparing us for the bull-fighter's popping up a few minutes later.)
Since Micaëla is bent on staying where she is the guide takes leave
of her; he has accompanied her thus far, he says, only because
she has paid him well, and if she should need him again she will
find him where she had hired him, in the inn at the foot of the
mountain. And so, invoking all the saints of paradise to protect
her, he leaves Micaëla to her fate and her aria, the first section of
the latter being devoted to assuring herself that her courage will
not fail her, the second to a resolve to confront the evil woman
who has caught her José in her toils and rescue him if she can,
and the third to a *da capo* repeat of the first section, with a final
prayer to heaven for its protection.

She drops into plain prose as she catches sight of José on a rock
not a hundred feet from her; she calls to him, but apparently he
has not seen her and does not hear her. He is looking at someone
in the opposite direction, at whom he fires; whereupon Micaëla,
declaring that she has "presumed too much on her courage," flies
in terror, and we see no more of her for some time.

23

What we do see now is Escamillo, studying his hat, which has
a bullet hole in it: "an inch or two lower," he nonchalantly informs us, "and it would not be I who would be fighting the bulls
I am taking to the Seville arena!" José comes into view with a
drawn knife, and Escamillo introduces himself—a toreador from
Granada. José has heard of him, and gives him a friendly hint
that it might have been better for him to have stayed in Granada.
Escamillo agrees in principle, bulls, seemingly, being less dangerous than smugglers bearded in their lair, but points out that he is
obeying the call of love. The woman he adores is a gipsy, a member of the smugglers' band, a certain Carmen, who at one time
had been in love with a soldier whom she had befriended; Carmen's liking for him, however, had not lasted six months. All
this—and the discovery on Escamillo's part that the "soldier"
was the smuggler now standing before him—leads of course to a
quarrel, during which, while José loses command of himself,
Escamillo remains invincibly polite and ironic. As regards the fight
with knives that follows, the score and the Meilhac-Halévy text
take different lines. In the former the end comes quickly:

Escamillo's knife breaks, and José is about to finish him off when Carmen and the others enter. In the latter there are two stages to the combat. First of all José is at the mercy of Escamillo, who magnanimously grants him his life. As he remains defiant the fight is resumed: this time Escamillo slips and falls, and Carmen arrives just in time to save him. There is no good reason operatically for all this: one round of the fight, we feel, is enough, more especially as Bizet is in the main not at the height of his form in this episode. He finds himself again, however, in the grave phrase in which Escamillo thanks Carmen for having saved his life. Politely, as usual, he promises José to resume their combat at the first convenient moment.

At this point Dancaïre intervenes: there is no time for any more of this bickering just now, he says, for business calls them. He bids adieu to Escamillo, who courteously invites them all to the bull-fight at Seville, where he will do his best to earn their approval; "anyone who loves me will be there," he adds with a glance at Carmen. The smouldering José makes a furious gesture and is about to attack Escamillo again; but the toreador waves him aside, in a telling passage in which the calmness of his words and manner contrasts with the veiled menace of the orchestra:

30

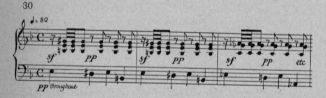

Bizet's handling of this episode has been throughout a remarkable fusion of the dramatic and the musical.

Escamillo departs with great dignity to an expressive slow reminiscence in the orchestra of the refrain of his song in the second act (No. 17), this time in the lower key of D flat major and with richer harmonies.[1] José, menacingly, but with outward self-restraint, warns Carmen that he has reached the limit of the

[1] Once more we may be permitted to wonder why, if Bizet regarded the Toreador's Song as "muck," he should put it here to such gravely expressive use.

suffering he can bear on her account; but she merely shrugs her shoulders and walks away. The others are preparing to depart when Remendado catches sight of an interloper. He drags forth Micaëla, at the sight of whom Carmen not unnaturally ejaculates, "A woman!" Equally natural, in the circumstances, is José's enquiry, "Micaëla, what are you doing here?" Gravely, once more to the melody to which, in the first act, she had delivered his mother's message to him (No. 10), she implores him, in his mother's name, to return with her. Carmen harshly advises José to obey the summons, for at heart, she says, he is not one of them. "So that you may be free to join your latest lover!" he retorts; "no, I will stay, even though it costs me my life":

31

f Dût-il m'en coû-ter la vi—e, Non, Car-men, je ne par-ti-rai pas!

This is one of the finest psychological strokes of the whole score; in this single cry of his we already have the José of the last act, the man goaded beyond endurance, capable now of anything. "The chain that binds us," he continues, "will endure until death. You do not love me? What matters that, since I love you, and I am strong enough to rule you? I hold you in my hand, accursed woman, and I will force you to submit to the destiny that links your life with mine." His frenzy rises; we hear No. 31 again, this time more urgently, in a higher key. There is a general cry of horror; in an agitated ensemble the others, Micaëla among them, exhort José to save his life by flight. His spirit breaks only when Micaëla, to an expressive change in the texture and the colour of the music, tells him quietly that his mother is dying, and with her last breath wishes to pardon him. "Let us go," he cries wildly to Micaëla; and then, turning to Carmen, "You have your way. I go —but soon we too will meet again." The sinister Fate theme (No. 1) is heard for a moment in the wood-wind, then dies away into silence, and in the distance is heard the voice of Escamillo singing once more the refrain of his Song in the second act (No. 17)—"On your guard, toreador! and in combat remember that two dark eyes are fixed on you, and that love awaits you." Car-

men impulsively makes as if to follow the call, but José menacingly bars her path. The smugglers set out on their journey to
the accompaniment in the orchestra of the march-like motif to
which they had come on the scene at the beginning of the act
(partly shown in our example No. 26), and the curtain falls.

24

An animated orchestral entr'acte in Spanish-Flamenco style,
abounding in piquancies of melody and rhythm and in those
swift transitions from major to minor in which Bizet delighted,
prepares us for the ebullient gaiety that is to characterise most of
the fourth act: [1] evidently all Seville is thinking of the coming

---

[1] In 1920 a Spanish musicologist, Rafaël Mitjana, in his history of Spanish
music in the *Encyclopédie de la Musique et Dictionnaire du Conservatoire*,
alleged that this prelude to the fourth act was derived from a polo (a variety
of Spanish song and dance) in a comic operetta of 1804 by Manuel Garcia,
El Criado Fingido (The Feigned Servant). (Garcia himself used to sing the
tenor parts in his own works). This particular polo, said Mitjana, became so
universally known in Spain that it was ultimately regarded as a folk-song;
and Bizet, believing it to be such, "made use of it for the famous prelude to
the fourth act of *Carmen*. I have never seen any mention of this curious
analogy, which, however, as regards the opening phrases and even the con-
tour of the preliminary bars [in the orchestra], leaps to the eye, and proves
how well the brilliant young composer had 'documented' himself before
writing his immortal masterpiece."

Far from the "analogy" between the two pieces "leaping to the eye" it
is barely apparent to anyone but Mitjana. For one thing, Bizet's prelude is
all movement and fire (it is marked allegro vivo), while Garcia's polo is an
andante serenade of the feigned servant to his inamorata. The melodic line
of the prelude resembles that of the polo at scarcely any point. There is indeed a slight similarity between the third and fourth bars of the short orchestral prelude to the polo and the long rippling figures that Bizet inserts
every now and then between the limbs of his melody; but little Spanish
clichés of this sort he could easily have picked up anywhere in the course of
his investigations into Spanish music. He must often have discussed that
subject with his friend the great singer Pauline Viardot, who was Manuel
Garcia's daughter. Furthermore, during the war of 1870/1 he spent some
time in Bordeaux, where he is known to have taken an interest in Spanish
music and story.

Henry Malherbe has justly argued that if Bizet had knowingly made use
of a Garcia original for his prelude he would have said so in a footnote at
the relevant place in his score, as he did in the case of the Yradier habanera.

bull-fights. When the curtain rises we see, according to the stage directions, "an open place in Seville, with the walls of an ancient bull-ring in the background; the entry to this is covered by a long curtain." [1] Edgar Istel has pointed out how easy it is for stage designers and producers to misunderstand this; it is difficult to imagine the murder of Carmen taking place in a public square. In Spain they know better; in a Madrid production, says Istel, the setting showed "a small narrow space between the horse-stables and the bull-ring, through which the *Cuadrilla* (the company of fighters) proceeds to the ring. . . . When it has disappeared the space is closed off laterally by a heavy cross-beam so that it now forms a sort of pen, from which there is no escape for Carmen—a kind of symbol of destiny inescapable."

An animated orchestral prelude and a following chorus show the populace eagerly awaiting the opening of the courses, with fan-sellers, orange-sellers, programme-sellers, water-sellers, cigarette-sellers and so on pressing their wares on the crowd. Among the latter are Zuniga and two other officers, one with Frasquita, the other Mercédès on his arm. Zuniga, in a brief interlude of spoken dialogue, asks the girls where Carmen is. She will be here soon, Frasquita replies, for Escamillo is performing today, and where he is, Carmen will never be far away. She is more infatuated with him than ever, it appears; as for José, he had been seen in the village where his mother lived; an order for his arrest [as a deserter], had been issued, but when the soldiers arrived he was no longer there. "If I were Carmen," Frasquita comments, "I would not feel very comfortable about it all."

The short colloquy is broken in upon by joyous cries from the crowd as the Cuadrilla makes its appearance, with lances flashing in the sunlight and sombreros held high in the air. After the toreros come the alguazils (the constabulary), and later the banderilleros and the picadors—all to the gay tune with which the overture to the opera had begun:

[1] It may just be mentioned here that after Bizet's death some theatres, following in the footsteps of the Vienna production, began the fourth act with a ballet, drawing upon *The Fair Maid of Perth* and *L'Arlésienne* for their musical material. This is an intolerable insult to Bizet's dramatic sense: there is no place in the tragedy for the irrelevant antics of ballerinas.

(Note once again, in bar 5 of this quotation, the sudden key-shift that always gives such vigour and elasticity to Bizet's style.)

A group of children pipe a satirical greeting to "the alguazil with the ugly face," and the men join in with them with a cheery cry of "Down with the alguazil!" Similar greetings fall in turn to the lot of the chulos, the banderilleros and the picadors; till at last the star of the occasion, Escamillo, enters, accompanied by Carmen, gorgeously arrayed; for Escamillo the uproarious welcome takes the form of a choral delivery of No. 17.

Suddenly the mood changes as Escamillo addresses Carmen quietly but passionately: "If you love me, Carmen, soon you shall be proud of me." To the same warm melodic strain she replies, "Yes, I love you, Escamillo, and may I die if I ever love anyone but you."

25

Escamillo disappears from our view, acclaimed enthusiastically by the crowd, which pays its respects also to the alcalde (mayor), who makes his majestic entry into the arena accompanied by alguazils and followed by the Cuadrilla. But the "march," as the text styles it, that accompanies their exit is not imposing, as we might have expected, but curiously, deceptively quiet, for now Frasquita and Mercédès seize the opportunity to approach Carmen and warn her to be on her guard, for José is there, lurking among the crowd. She replies calmly that she has no fear of him; she will remain and face him.

To another brief outburst of the rousing No. 32 the crowd pours into the arena, Frasquita and Mercédès following it. José, whom the thinning-out of the crowd has made visible, and Carmen, whose motif (No. 9) is heard for a moment or two in the violins, then in the violas, are now alone. They begin their last colloquy in sombre tones, Carmen telling him that she had been warned that he was near and that her life was in danger, but she had scorned to fly. In humble, appealing tones:

33

Moderato ♩=96

No—tre pas-sé— Car-men, no—tre pas-sé— je l'ou—bli-e!

he implores her to forget, as he is willing to do, all that is past and begin a new life with him elsewhere. He is asking the impossible, she replies; Carmen has never lied, and between José and her all is ended. The temperature of the music rises as José, in one of the most poignant expressions in all opera of blended love and grief, implores her to let him save the woman he adores. But she is inflexible: in low, level tones she tells him that she knows that he will kill her, and then, in a sudden access of passion, declares that whether she lives or dies she will never yield.

"There is yet time," he repeats; but in vain. "Then you no longer love me?" Her answer is a tranquil "No"; nothing, indeed, in this remarkable scene is more admirable than Bizet's avoidance of the temptation to let Carmen step out of her present character; she never meets storm with storm, but is always stoically resigned. As he repeats still more passionately his distracted appeal to her, her refusals become more sombrely fatalistic. He promises now to remain a bandit for her sake, to do anything she asks of him, if only she will not leave him: but her unvarying reply is, "It is useless. Carmen will never yield. Free she was born and free she will die!" At this point the crowd in the arena, to the accompaniment of No. 32, hails the approaching triumph of Escamillo. Carmen makes a joyous gesture and moves towards the entrance, but José intercepts her. The contest between them is resumed, this time with more desperation on both sides, José maddened by the thought that it is Escamillo who is the rival for whom she is abandoning him, Carmen reiterating that even in the face of death she will cry to the world that she loves the toreador.

There comes another exultant cry from within the arena, and the emotional tension reaches its highest point in a series of thunderous statements in the orchestra of the Fate theme (No. 1). José's reason snaps: for the last time he asks Carmen if she will follow him, and for the last time she refuses; herself now a raging fury, she tears from her finger a ring he had once given her and throws it away. This is the last straw; with a cry of "Accursed woman!" he strides towards her just as fanfares and voices are heard from inside the arena acclaiming Escamillo's triumph and the crowd begins to make its way out. It is at the entrance to the bull-ring that José catches the fleeing Carmen and stabs her. By now the crowd has debouched upon the stage, and as No. 1 thunders out again for the last time in almost the full orchestra José throws himself upon Carmen's body with a great cry of "It was I who killed her! O my Carmen, my adored Carmen!" And that is all: letting the tragedy speak for itself, without any further comment of voices or orchestra, Bizet and his librettists wisely bring the curtain down at once.

Eugen Onegin

PETER ILYICH TCHAIKOVSKI [1840–1893]

PRINCIPAL CHARACTERS

TATIANA	*Soprano*
OLGA	*Contralto*
MME LARIN	*Mezzo-soprano*
EUGEN ONEGIN	*Baritone*
LENSKY	*Tenor*
PRINCE GREMIN	*Bass*
TRIQUET	*Tenor*

1

CHAIKOVSKI conceived the idea of an opera based on Pushkin's *Eugen Onegin* in May 1877. Apparently the first section he set to music was the Letter Scene in the first act. The work was complete in every respect by February 1878, though two years and a half later Tchaikovski added an *écossaise* to the opening scene of the second act for a Petersburg performance, and made a few changes in the finale. The first performance was given in the theatre of the Moscow Conservatoire, by students of that institution, on the 17th (29th) 1879. The composer, by the way, gave his work the title not of "opera" but of "lyrical scenes in three acts."

Pushkin, Russia's greatest poet (1799–1837), took from 1823 to 1831 to write his *Eugen Onegin*, a narrative poem, with many digressions, in eight cantos: he himself described it as "a novel in verse in the manner of [Byron's] *Don Juan*."

Eugen Onegin is a young dandy and rake, disillusioned, cynical, blasé in the Byronic manner of the 1820's: "his malady," we are told, "was simply the British spleen transported to Russia." His father having died, and he himself possessing nothing but debts, he leaves Petersburg to visit an uncle in the country; but before he can arrive the uncle dies, bequeathing his estate to Onegin. There the young man, tired of the large towns, their follies and deceptions, settles down and tries to find some new interest in life. He lives almost entirely alone, for those of his neighbours whose acquaintance he has not been able to avoid making bore him.

An estate near his belongs to a young man named Vladimir Lensky, who has been studying at Göttingen, where he had imbibed all sorts of romantic notions, become infected with all sorts of enthusiasms, and developed the habit of poetising about platonic love: he is handsome and rich, but hardly fonder of society than Onegin is. Neither of them is yet twenty. The two young men become fast friends, in spite of, or perhaps because of, their fundamental dissimilarity of mind and temperament. Each acts as a foil to the other, Onegin, from the heights of his superior experience as a man of the world, condescending amusedly to the more ardent, idealistic Lensky. He is especially entertained by the latter's naïve views on love, a subject with which Onegin has long ago finished.

Lensky is engaged to Olga Larin, the younger daughter of a widowed lady who has a small property near by. Olga is a healthy, modest, cheerful girl, with an older sister, Tatiana, who is in most respects her antithesis. She is not beautiful, not brilliant. She is not unsocial, but the fripperies of social life have no attractions for her: she loves solitude and contemplation. She reads Rousseau and Richardson, from whom she has imbibed in full measure the "sensibility" of the epoch.

Lensky persuaded his friend to visit the Larins with him. Onegin is not greatly taken by either of the girls, but of the two he finds Tatiana more interesting than her superficial sister. Seeing them together, friends of the Larins believe they scent the possibility of a "match." Certainly Tatiana herself, at long last, is in love: she reads more novels of "sensibility" than ever, and in her imagination dramatises herself and Onegin. Sleep deserts her. One night, excited and restless, she dismisses her old nurse after having made her bring her pen and paper, and writes Onegin a long letter in which she lays her whole soul bare to him. She sends the letter to him the next day by the nurse's little grandson.

Two days go by without a reply from Onegin. Then he rides over to the Larin house, where he finds Tatiana in the garden. The blasé young man of the world has indeed been "touched with sympathy," as he expresses it, by Tatiana's letter, but for all that he cannot take it or her seriously. His heart has grown too cold in the larger world for that. He compliments her on her charming sincerity, and says he will meet frankness with frankness: he would not wish to beguile such candid naïveté. If he were a marrying man he would marry her. But he is not: the most he can feel for her is a brother's affection. She will fall in love again, he assures her. But if she does, perhaps he may give her a piece of advice that will be useful to her: she should cultivate more self-control, for the next man to whom she so imprudently pours out her inmost self may not be one like himself. She returns to the house on his arm, his cold words burning into her like a fire. She becomes silent, falls ill, and is intensely unhappy. Onegin, for his part, also retires within himself, striving to make the growing burden of life more endurable by means of exercise, games and good living.

In the following winter Lensky persuades his friend to visit the Larins again on the occasion of Tatiana's fête day. Onegin becomes more and more bored with these worthy provincials, and determines to revenge himself on Lensky for having brought him there. For no reason that anyone can discover he pays such attention to Olga that Lensky leaves the party in a fury of jealousy, gallops home, and sends a challenge to his friend by the hand of one Zaretski, a worthless gambler, bully and one-time duellist. The bored Onegin accepts the challenge without anger and without compunction: the silly affair is a nuisance, but as it is he must see it through. Lensky, paying what may be a last visit to Olga, finds that she is really as simple and innocent and as much in love with him as ever. He spends the night before the duel in sleepless torment, writing a poem on the vanishing of his golden youth and his forebodings for the future. (Pushkin's reflections at this point on the unfulfilled promise of Lensky as a poet have a melancholy interest for us in view of the fact that he himself was killed in a duel a few years later, in his thirty-eighth year.)

Lensky is killed by Onegin. The amiable, superficial Olga soon consoles herself: she marries a lancer and leaves the village in which she had spent all her life till then. Onegin also goes away for some years. When we meet him again he is twenty-six, a wanderer on the face of the earth, unhappy, unquiet, trying vainly to forget the tragedy of Lensky. As for Tatiana, left more then ever alone by the departure of Olga, her thoughts gradually begin to turn again in the direction of the strange, unapproachable, yet attractive Onegin. She goes to his deserted house and turns over some of his books; and as she reads the comments in them the baffling workings of his mind become a little more comprehensible to her. By way of distraction for the suffering girl her mother takes her to Moscow one winter. She is not a success in society: the frivolity of it wearies her, and the gallants pronounce her provincial. But an honourable gentleman of middle age, Prince Gremin, who has sensed the exceptional quality of her nature, falls in love with her and marries her.

One night Onegin is persuaded by someone or other to accept an invitation to a ball. There he sees Tatiana, who, matured now and happy, has shed all her provincialism and developed into a calm, dignified woman of the finest breeding. He learns from the Prince's own lips that she is his wife, and that they have been married some two years. When Onegin is introduced to Tatiana there is nothing of the embarrassed provincial girl of their former acquaintance about her: she greets him with perfect poise, and leaves him after a formal word or two. There begins for him now a period of agitation such as had fallen to Tatiana's lot in the days gone by. He finds himself madly in love with her. He haunts her house and anywhere else where he is likely to meet her — a gloomy, distraught figure; while she is invariably tranquil, courteous, the self-possessed mistress of the situation. He writes letter after letter to her, recalling their past, pleading his unhappiness and begging for her love. She does not reply. But one day he calls on her and finds her reading one of his letters and weeping: for the moment she has reverted to the Tatiana of long ago. They talk of the past. She was young and foolish then, she says: now she can see everything more clearly. He had wounded her cruelly by his frankness; but today she can only thank him for it. She would prefer even his old cynical coldness and sarcasm to the lawless love he now demands of her. In herself she would gladly give up her present riches and enviable position for the old house and little garden of her girlhood, and for the golden days when happiness seemed for a moment to be approaching her, then turned aside and passed her by. Now her lot is fixed and her determination immovable: she

still loves him, but he must give up all thought of ever making her
his. With that she turns on her heel and leaves him — as does the
author of this "novel" in verse, after another three stanzas of semi-
humorous reflection. Pushkin thought more than once in later years
of continuing his seemingly incomplete tale, but wisely decided
that after all the best possible ending was the "half-close" — to
employ a musical term — in which he had left Onegin suspended in
his eighth canto.

2

The action of the opera follows so closely that of the original
poem that detailed analysis of Tchaikovski's work is almost superfluous, except to indicate at this point or that how the composer
has dealt with the subject in terms of his own special medium.

The short orchestral prelude is entirely devoted to the presentation, in one form and another, of a motive always associated later
with Tatiana:

It is typically Tchaikovskian in its drooping lines.

The opening scene shows us the Larin garden, with the house
on the left. It is evening. In the background is a hedge, beyond
which the village, with its church, is visible. Mme Larin is sitting
under a tree, engaged in preserving fruit: the elderly nurse,
Filipievna, is helping her. Tatiana and Olga are singing a duet,
which becomes a quartet as the two older women take part in it.
The girls' song takes Mme Larin back to her own young days, when
she used to read Richardson and behave, like all well-brought up
Russian girls of that epoch, with appropriate "sensibility." The
nurse agrees with her that those were the good old times, when
Mme Larin was young and impressionable and society was distinguished by its elegance. We gather that Mme Larin's sensi-

bility had brought her rather near danger at one time, but that she
had escaped it by throwing herself heart and soul into her duties
as wife and mistress of a household.

Behind the scenes is heard a chorus of peasants, singing, as they
approach the house, of the joy of abandoning work at the harvest
for a while. They have come to present the family with the last
sheaf. At Mme Larin's request they sing and dance in true Russian
style, to a melody which will be familiar to many concert-goers in
other connections:

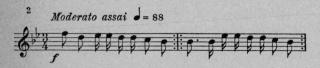

Meanwhile Tatiana and Olga have ascended to the terrace of the
house, whence they survey the pleasant, friendly scene.

Tatiana, who, as usual, has a book in her hand, tells her sister,
to the expressive strain of No. 1, how these songs of the people
transport her in fancy far away. Olga smiles at her passion for day-
dreaming; as for her, the only effect these country melodies have
on her is to make her want to sing and dance herself. Dreaming
has no charms for her, she assures her mother and Tatiana; why
spend the night in tears when each day is so bright? Her little
song is charming enough, but there is just a little too much of
Tchaikovski in it for it to be quite as care-free as Olga intends
it to be.

Mme Larin having dismissed the harvesters with thanks, she
turns with some concern to Tatiana, who, as is generally the case
with her, is absorbed in her book; this particular one, according
to her, describes the sorrows of two lovers in such affecting fashion as to move her to tears. Her mother is trying to impress it on
her that life is not like novels when a coach is heard approaching.
Olga's fiancé Lensky is coming, and with him his neighbour Eugen
Onegin. At the mention of the latter, Tatiana, greatly agitated,
would leave the company, but the others persuade her to remain.
The two friends enter. Lensky introduces Onegin, and the mother
leaves the two young couples together.

A brief quartet follows: Onegin asks Lensky which of the two

girls is Tatiana. His frankly critical opinion of the blond Olga is
that she is a trifle colourless both physically and mentally — she
reminds him, he says, of a Vandyck Madonna. He finds "the other
one, the dark silent one," rather more interesting, though he admits he is speaking more as a poet than an ordinary individual.
Tatiana is at the same time ill at ease and happy, for in this
Onegin, with his distinguished manners and his strong self-
containment, she finds the incarnation of her romantic dreams.
Lensky's quiet comment on it all is that he could imagine ice and
flame matching each other better than these two who have just met.

Lensky goes apart with Olga, with whom he indulges in a warm-
hearted little duet, the poetic theme of which is that to lovers the
separation of a day is like eternity:

Meanwhile Onegin casually engages the embarrassed Tatiana in
conversation: his manner throughout is polite but cold. Does she
not feel bored in this out-of-the-way spot? he asks her. She assures
him that her whole pleasure is in reading and dreaming in the
garden, to which he replies, with a touch of superior irony, that
she seems too much inclined to indulge her imagination: he himself, he says, was at one time very much like her in that respect.
They are still on this somewhat awkward footing when Mme Larin
reappears to summon them all in to supper.

The second scene of this act shows us Tatiana in her simply-
furnished bedroom, lost in meditation before her glass. Feeling
sure that she will not sleep, she asks Filipievna to tell her one of the
stories that used to sooth her when she was a child. The nurse begins instead the story of her own wooing and marriage, long, long
ago. The music here, of course, is in the Russian national vein:

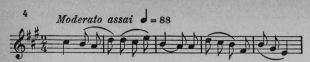

which contrasts markedly with the motive of Tatiana (No. 1), which plays a large part in this and the following scene.

Flinging her arms around her, Tatiana pours out her soul to the old nurse: she loves, she says, and suffers:

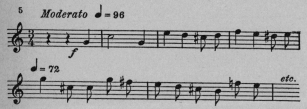

She bids Filipievna bring her pen, ink and paper and then leave her; for in her innocence and inexperience of the world she is resolved to write to Onegin, to say to him what she had not strength to say when he was present. Thus begins the famous "Letter Scene," which is one of the masterpieces of musical-dramatic psychology. The main motives of it are (*a*) the agitated No. 5, (*b*) the theme that accompanies her decision to write the letter:

(*c*) the feverish orchestral figure that accompanies the hurried putting of the glowing words on paper:

(*d*) the melody of her assurance to Onegin that she had never loved anyone before, that her destiny had been to wait for her total fulfilment in him:

(*e*) the grave strain to which she asks him whether he comes to her now as guardian angel or as tempter:

and (*f*) the melody accompanying her decision to give her life to him, whatever may befall, for she is alone, helpless, misunderstood, and will go under if he does not see how she suffers and rescue her:

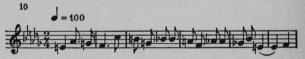

The music models itself faithfully on every nuance of the fine poetry: this suffering, this self-doubt, this self-torment, was something that Tchaikovski well understood.

She seals the letter with a passionate cry to Onegin not to misuse the trust she places in him. The nurse finds her dreaming by the window as the day dawns, and, at Tatiana's urgent request, sends her little boy with the letter to Onegin. As the curtain falls, Tatiana buries her head in her hands, sunk in thought.

The next scene — a short one — shows us a different part of the Larin garden from the one we saw at the commencement of the opera. In the background a chorus of girls is singing a pleasant little song of the Russian folk-type. Tatiana enters in great agitation: she has seen Onegin coming. She wonders what his answer to her letter will be, and half regrets having sent it. She hangs her head in confusion and apprehension as he approaches. As usual he is completely self-possessed, formally polite, but ice-cold. "You wrote to me," he says to her without preamble, "and opened out your soul to me. I honour you for your candour, which rekindled in me, for a moment, a spark that had long died out in my breast. But I cannot flatter. I will be as open as you have been." Then, in that conversational tone which Tchaikovski always had at such easy command in his songs and operas:

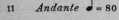

11 *Andante* ♩ = 80

he assures her that had fate destined him to be a husband and a father he would have recognised his ideal mate in Tatiana. But he was not born for happiness of that or any other kind. He is not in harmony even with himself; harmony with another is quite impossible. He can love her as a brother, but no more. The future will justify him in what he is now saying: love, in a maiden's life, is nothing but illusion, deception. His advice to her is to learn to know herself and to hold her romantic feelings in check; for inexperience such as hers generally leads only to disaster. He holds out his hand. She gives him a long, imploring look, then takes his arm as if in a dream and allows him to lead her away to the others.

3

The first scene of the second act takes place in a room in the Larins' house, where a ball is in progress in honour of Tatiana's birthday.

The short orchestral prelude is mostly based on the motive (No. 9) of Tatiana's passionate appeal to Onegin in her letter. As the curtain rises this merges into a waltz:

12 ♩. = 80

to which the guests sing a chorus in praise of a life of pleasure in house and field. Onegin dances with Tatiana, to the admiration of the older ladies, who scent a wedding in the offing, though they do not by any means approve of Onegin, who, we learn from their chatter, has the reputation of being unmannerly, a Freemason, and too fond of wine. The young man, happening to overhear them, resolves to punish Lensky for having brought him to so boring a place by dancing with Olga and so making him jealous. The waltz music runs through the whole of this episode.

At the first opportunity that presents itself Lensky seeks an explanation with Olga. She does not take his indignation seriously, and to show him that he is upsetting himself and her about nothing at all she goes off again to dance with Onegin. A momentary mild diversion is brought about by an elderly Frenchman, Monsieur Triquet, who, somewhat to Tatiana's annoyance, persists in singing some couplets in her honour, couched in the formal terms, poetic and musical, of a French genre that was beginning to be old-fashioned even in Russia at that time. M. Triquet having retired, overwhelmed with the compliments of the company on his charming couplets, the master of the ceremonies leads off a mazurka with Tatiana. Onegin appropriates Olga, and Lensky watches the pair in increasing trouble of soul.

The dance over, Onegin rallies his friend on being "as gloomy as Childe Harold." At first Lensky answers him quietly; but his anger mounts in face of Onegin's cold cynicism. Not content with the conquest of Tatiana, he says, his friend must needs take from him now his own bride, turning her head only to laugh at her later. Onegin's loftily ironic attitude infuriates Lensky still further. The quarrel at length attracts the attention of the other guests. Realising how seriously his friend has taken this trifling matter, Onegin tries to convince him that he is exaggerating the importance of it all; but finally, seeing that it is hopeless to reason with him, he shrugs his shoulders and says no more. Lensky, now beside himself with rage, challenges Onegin before them all. The scene ends with a big finale, in which Lensky laments this sorry ending to his golden dream of love. Onegin, serious and noble at last, regrets that he has tried too far this good friend whom he sincerely loves, and the rest of the company comment on the affair in their several

ways. Though Onegin admits to himself that he is in the wrong
he cannot refuse the challenge; and his temper rising dangerousl
as the maddened Lensky calls him a seducer without honour, h
hurls himself on him. The guests separate the two men. Lensk
rushes out, followed by Onegin; while Olga, the innocent caus
of all the trouble, falls in a faint.

The next scene takes place in a lonely spot by the river. It i
early morning, and the countryside is deep in snow. Lensky an
Zaretzki arrive for the duel; and while the latter paces impatientl
up and down awaiting Onegin, Lensky sits in moody meditatio
under a tree. At length his second goes off to talk with the mille
whose mill stands by the river bank, and Lensky launches into
melancholy aria, bemoaning his vanished youth and his lost hap
piness, and looking forward with foreboding to the result of th
coming duel. The situation is of a type that always called out wha
was most characteristic in Tchaikovski's genius; and the aria, whicl
ends with a cry of passionate love to Olga, is one of the finest thing
he ever wrote:

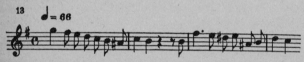

It is an almost constant succession of those falling phrases of whicl
Tchaikovski was so fond, corresponding as they did to his ow
wilting spirits on most occasions of life.

Onegin arrives with his servant Gillot, who carries the pistol
While the two seconds are discussing the ritual of the duel, Onegi
and Lensky, in a short duet in canon form, lament the sad tur
their friendship has taken; honour requires that one of them shal
now kill the other. The two men take up their positions, and a las
thought of Olga (No. 3) flits through Lensky's tortured mind
Zaretzki gives the signal, and Onegin, firing before his opponen
kills him. He runs to the dead man and makes a gesture of horro
and despair, while the orchestra gives out a last mournful remi
niscence of No. 13.

4

The third act opens in a fashionable house in Petersburg, wher
the guests are dancing to a polonaise:

In the gay company, but not part of it, is Onegin, sunk in gloom, regretting his twenty-six wasted years, and still haunted by the memory of Lensky. Travel has failed to still the voice of conscience; and now, in sheer desperation, he is seeking forgetfulness in society again. Tatiana enters and seats herself on a sofa, where, to a gracefully-flowing accompaniment in the orchestra:

various guests come and pay their compliments to her. Onegin can hardly believe his eyes, so lovely, so dignified now is the one-time provincial maiden. From Prince Gremin he learns that she is now the latter's wife; and the good Prince breaks into a song in praise of love:

16

the sober musical terms of which are psychologically quite in keeping with his age. In Tatiana, he assures Onegin, he has been fortunate enough to find the one good and true thing in a world of hypocrisy, treachery and lies. As he presents the young man to his wife there wells up from the orchestra the melody of No. 5. The pair exchange only a few conventional words, Onegin being deeply moved, Tatiana calm: then, to the accompaniment of No. 15, she moves away on her husband's arm, pleading fatigue. Onegin follows her with his eyes, lost in wonder at the transformation that has taken place in her. Can this be the Tatiana, he asks himself, to whom he had once given a schoolmasterish lesson

in conduct, down there in the country? And what is this strange
emotion he now feels at seeing her again, and so changed — dejection? repentance? wounded vanity? And again he realises that it is
none of these, but love, such love as he has never known or understood before; and Tchaikovski gives a curious musical point to this
realisation by making him announce it to the same melody (No. 6)
as that to which Tatiana, when writing her letter, had made the
same discovery within herself. As Onegin goes out, perplexed and
troubled, the dance music is resumed and the curtain falls.

The final scene takes place in Tatiana's boudoir. An orchestral
introduction, based on what seems to be intended as a partial translation into the minor:

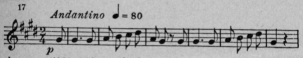

of the song (No. 16) in which Prince Gremin had spoken of his
quiet happiness in Tatiana's love, no doubt aims at showing us the
reverse of that picture: Tatiana's happiness, perhaps we are to
understand, is less complete than his, for at the core of it lie memories of a dead self which she can never cease to mourn in secret.

She enters with a letter in her hand — a letter from Onegin,
announcing that he will call on her. She looks forward with some
apprehension to the interview, for she feels that it will disturb the
peace of soul which she has won for herself by so many hard fights
against fate. While she is musing thus, he appears at the door.
Seeing that she is weeping he rushes to her and throws himself
at her feet. Mastering her emotion, she bids him rise, for she has
an explanation to make to him. Gently she recalls to him, to the
melody of No. 17, the day when, an inexperienced country girl,
she had poured out to him the naïve confession of her love and he
had crushed her with his cold cynicism: yet through it all he had
behaved like a man of honour. She was despised then because the
world did not understand her. But why does he pursue her now?
Is it because, thanks to her husband, a man of worth and distinction, she has wealth, power, social position? Or is it in the hope of
boasting of a conquest of a kind on which the vulgar world will
felicitate him? If he really knew her he would pity her, for cold
reason is her only shield in the fight that is now going on within her

heart. "Alas!" they both sing, "how near to us was happiness once!" But honour, she tells the wretched man, now binds her irrevocably, and he must leave her. He pleads to be allowed to be where she is, if only to die in happiness and peace. The confession is at last wrung from her that she loves him, and he clasps her in his arms. But she frees herself instantly, and, in spite of his anguished appeals not to cast him off, she repeats that honour holds her fast to Gremin, and she will not be false to it. With a last mighty effort she summons up strength enough to bid him adieu for ever, and leaves him crushed and hopeless. With a final cry against the hardness of his fate he too rushes out as the curtain falls.

Tchaikovski had no great range of dramatic characterisation: he could not transport himself easily into more than a few psychological types of more or less his own fundamental cast. Hence a certain monotony in his operas as a whole, in spite of fine moments in each of them. But in *Eugen Onegin* we get the best of him as a musical dramatist, because each of the main characters is to a great extent himself. They are all, in this way or that, defeatists; and for defeatism and frustration Tchaikovski could always find convincing musical expression.

Boris Godounov

MODEST PETROVICH MOUSSORGSKY [1839–1881]

PRINCIPAL CHARACTERS

Boris Godounov	*Baritone*
Feodor	*Mezzo-soprano*
Xenia	*Soprano*
The Nurse	*Mezzo-soprano*
Shuisky	*Tenor*
Stchelkalov	*Baritone*
Pimen	*Bass*
Gregory (Dmitri)	*Tenor*
Marina Mnischek	*Mezzo-soprano*
Rangoni	*Bass*
Varlaam	*Bass*
Missail	*Tenor*
The Hostess	*Mezzo-soprano*
The Idiot	*Tenor*

1

WHEN the Tsar Ivan the Terrible died, in 1584, he was succeeded by the pious Feodor, who was in turn succeeded in 1598 by his brother-in-law, an able and ambitious boyar of Tartar origin, Boris Godounov. Ivan had left behind him also a young son, Dmitri, by a non-legal marriage. This boy was murdered, in his ninth year, in 1591, and the instigator of the crime was believed in some quarters to have been Boris. The latter died in April 1605, after having named his young son Feodor as his successor. During the last year or two of Boris's life a claim to the throne of Russia had been put forward by an adventurer calling himself the genuine Dmitri — the child, he alleged, had escaped the assassins — but who seems to have been a renegade monk named Gregory (Grishka) Otrepiev. This pseudo-Dmitri found plenty of willing supporters of his pretensions in Russia, where neither the strict rule nor the Tartar origin of Boris was in his favour; and he was backed also by Russia's hereditary enemy, the King of Poland, and by the Pope of Rome, Gregory having prudently recognised the Roman Catholic as the one true church when he put forward his claim to the Muscovite throne. After the death of Boris, the pseudo-Dmitri advanced with his Polish allies on Moscow, where he had himself proclaimed Tsar, after having married Marina Mnischek, the daughter of a Polish magnate, the Voyevode of Sandomir. After a very short reign Dmitri was murdered in a popular uprising engineered by Prince Vassili Shuisky, who succeeded him as Tsar.

We have a contemporary account of most of these happenings in a report by a Dutch merchant then resident in Moscow, which was translated into English and published in London in 1607. The title of it is " The Reporte of a Bloudie and Terrible Massacre in the Citty of Mosco, with the fearefull and tragicall end of Demetrius the last Duke, before him raigning at this present." From this we learn that after his death Dmitri was publicly condemned and his memory degraded by his successor. It was "alleadged that he had been a shauen and graduated monke, whose kinsmen, sisters and brothers were yet liuing, that is, his father in lawe, and his owne mother. . . ." These people took an oath that " his name was Gregorie . . . and that he was a Monke of this Cittie in the monasterie of the Castle: men say, that in his youth he was very diligent to reade and write, and delighted much to peruse and reade Histories and Chronicles, hauing sometimes serued in the Patriarkes Court, for a Singing man and a Musitian, euer carefully obseruing whatsoeuer might further his intentions. . . ."

We have also a contemporary portrait of Shuisky, which the reader will do well to keep in his mind when he is listening to the opera: it was drawn by a Scotch soldier, Captain Gilbert, who had been a member of Dmitri's foreign bodyguard. It shows us Shuisky very much as Pushkin and Moussorgsky have painted him, a cool, smooth, artfully dissembling intriguer, hiding his ambitions under a mask of modesty and humility. " The Nobles," says Gilbert, " cast lots foure times to receiue a Successor, as it were, by diuine sentence in lot-oracle: in euery of which times the lot fell vpon Suiskey . . . he modestly refusing and enforced by constancy of the various lot to accept that Scepter; whereof others thinke him as ambitious, as was modest Boris before him. Howeuer, he hath left his name and memorie written in as blacke inke as either Boris or Demetrius, if Reports bee true, which say that he proued a wicked Prince, partly by poison, partly by the Tartars, making away all whose bloud might by Nobilitie threaten a probabilitie of their prouing his Corriuals." [1]

2

So much for the historical background of Pushkin's drama of 1825. The history of Moussorgsky's opera, which was based on that work, is rather more complicated.

Building mainly upon Pushkin's play, with a little assistance from ancient Russian chronicles, Moussorgsky wrote the music of his opera between October 1868 and about May of the following year: the scoring was done between the summer and the mid December of 1869. The score that is known to most opera-goers today by the title of *Boris Godounov* is an arrangement not of this score of 1868, but a later one, by Rimsky-Korsakov. But between the making of this and the original composition of the work a good deal had happened, the full details of which have come to light only during recent years.

Moussorgsky submitted his work to the Directorate of the Imperial Theatres in Petersburg in the summer of 1870, but it was rejected. Thereupon the composer made sundry alterations in abridgements of, and additions to, his score between about April 1871 and July 1872, when the orchestration of this second version was completed. Three scenes from this version were given in the Maryinski Theatre, Petersburg, on the 5th February 1873: a performance of the work as a whole — though with certain cuts — followed on the 27th January 1874 in the same theatre. The vocal score of this version was published about that time. This score later became very scarce; but several of those who possessed a copy of it kept up for many years a fire of criticism against Rimsky

[1] The reader will find these and several other interesting contemporary documents in Sonia E. Howe's book *The False Dmitri* (London, 1916).

Korsakov for his "mutilations" of Moussorgsky's original. In the Rimsky-Korsakov score (first edition 1896, new edition, with some restorations of matter previously omitted, 1908), the order of the episodes in the last act is this: (1) the so-called Revolution Scene in the forest near Kromy, in which the people rise against their oppressors; (2) the triumphal entry of Gregory as Dmitri; (3) the lament of the Idiot; (4) the meeting of the Douma and the death of Boris. When the piano score of 1874 became generally available in a modern re-issue (about 1925), it was found that the "original" order of the closing scenes was (1) the death of Boris, (2) the Revolution Scene in the forest. The feeling was general that not only was this the authentic but it was the better ending: many admirers of the opera had come to regard the Russian folk as the true protagonists of it, and it was held to be most fitting that they should have the last word — to say nothing of historical accuracy. The case that had been slowly built up against Rimsky-Korsakov for so many years in certain quarters seemed now to be complete: the conclusion appeared obvious that the opera had been made to close with the death of Boris partly for the sake of the players of that important part, partly because the average audience does not like the "hero" of an opera to disappear before the very end has been reached.

In 1928, however, the *true* original score was published, i.e., the opera as it had been in Moussorgsky's manuscript of 1868–9: and it was now seen that, apart from sundry other differences between the various scores which need not be gone into here, the original settings of the last act were (*a*) the Square of the Cathedral of St. Basil in Moscow, where the disaffected people give vent to their grievances and the Idiot pours out his lament over Russia, (*b*) the Council Meeting in the Kremlin, at which Boris dies. (There was no Revolution Scene in the forest in this first version).[2]

We are thus confronted by some pretty problems. Putting the Rimsky-Korsakov version on one side for a moment, which of the other two has the right to be regarded as *the* "authentic" score,

---

[2] Some of the best things in *Boris Godounov* were originally written for an opera on the subject of Salammbô: Moussorgsky began work on this in 1863, but did not complete it. A list of passages from it that were incorporated in *Boris Godounov* will be found in Robert Godet's book, p. 144. (See *infra*, p. 317 note.)

with the best claim to performance today? Had the scheme of 1874 been the work of some unauthorised adaptor, the claim of that of 1868–9 would be beyond question. But the 1874 arrangement was, after all, the composer's own. It is now held that Moussorgsky altered his score under semi-compulsion, in order to obtain a performance. To some extent that is true; but it is none the less true that the alterations are his own, and that some of them suggest strongly that between 1869 and 1872 he himself had come to take a different view of his subject from the one with which he had begun. A certain school of thought insists that the "true" *Boris* is the first one, which has the prior, if not the only, right to performance today. But the trouble is that each of the three scores, that of 1868–9, that of 1874, and that of Rimsky-Korsakov, has merits of its own and defects of its own. It is impossible to set forth in detail here all the divergencies between even Moussorgsky's own two scores. Each of them has certain qualities of dramatic construction or psychological characterisation which the other lacks, each of them has its special musical excellencies or shortcomings. Perhaps some day a kind of compromise or synthetic *Boris Godounov* will be constructed out of the two "original" scores — which, of course, will mean discarding certain pages in each of them, if only to keep the performance within reasonable time-limits. But there will still remain the problem of Rimsky-Korsakov's re-writing of some passages which he regarded as amateurish in their Moussorgskian form, and the further one of his scoring. The former problem is a technical one which mainly concerns musicians only; but the latter concerns the general public as well.

There can be no question that Rimsky-Korsakov's brilliant orchestration has played a large part in making the work the theatrical success it is. The faithful contend that Moussorgsky's own orchestration, even when it strikes the listener as a trifle colourless, should be retained purely and simply because it is Moussorgsky's, on the theory that it was in terms of colours such as these that he saw his characters and their milieu. But that again is in the last resort a question which, fortunately, does not call for detailed discussion here. The one fact that really concerns us in practice is that *Boris Godounov* is now inseparably associated, in the theatre, with Rimsky-Korsakov's arrangement and especially with Rimsky-Korsakov's orchestration. Whether the public could in time be induced to accept *in toto* one or other of the two actual Moussorgsky versions in place of the Rimsky-Korsakov one it is impossible to say. Certainly our experience goes to suggest that only a long series of performances could effect, by sheer repetition, this radical change in the public mentality; and as the public, by all appearances, will attend only an occasional performance of one of the "original" versions, regarding it merely as a historical curiosity, we seem to be penned within a vicious circle. As, therefore, the Rimsky-Korsakov version is the one which the average opera-goer will hear on ninety-nine occasions out of a hundred — though even this is cut to some extent in the ordinary performance — it is that version we shall analyse here.[8]

3

Moussorgsky had to compress and re-arrange Pushkin's play considerably, for the episodes of this are so many, and mostly so short, that an integral stage performance of it would involve no less than twenty-four changes of scene. The spectator must bear in mind that the action of the opera covers the space of some seven years. The opening scene, in which the populace is seen awaiting Boris's decision to accept or decline the throne of Russia, takes place in the early part of 1598: the next scene, that in Pimen's cell, belongs to 1603, the Polish scenes and Dmitri's march into Russia to 1604, and the last scene to 1605.

Ivan the Terrible's little son Dmitri had been murdered in 1591, while Feodor was on the throne. Modern historians acquit Boris of that crime. But it seems to have been laid to his charge at a very early date, and by the time that Karamzin's History of Russia came

[8] I wish to make it clear beyond all possibility of misunderstanding that I am not taking this side or that in the matter. The problem of the three *Boris Godounovs* — for the Rimsky-Korsakov score certainly comes into the picture at times — is far too complicated a one for detailed discussion here. The reader who is interested in it can examine the scores for himself and read the specialist literature on the subject, beginning with Victor Belaiev's booklet *Musorgsky's 'Boris Godunov' and its new version* (Oxford University Press, 1928), and Robert Godet's *En Marge de Boris Godounof* (1926). Some of the differences between Moussorgsky's first and his second plan will be mentioned in the following analysis. The reader must decide for himself between these first and second thoughts of the composer. The problem for the theatres is a purely practical one.

to be written, in the early nineteenth century, it had acquired what may be called official sanction. Pushkin took the story over from Karamzin without any question, and it must of course be accepted as fact by the spectator of the opera, for the real tragedy of Boris — a "Russian Macbeth," as he has been described — is the haunting memory of his crime.

The Prologue takes place in the courtyard of the monastery of Novodievich, near Moscow. It is packed with people who have gathered, more or less by official command, to implore Boris Godounov to ascend the throne, now become vacant through the death of the Tsar Feodor. Moussorgsky took this scene over, in its essentials, from Pushkin's play, in which Boris is depicted as artfully making his acceptance of the throne more palatable to the people by a prolonged pretence of reluctance to assume in name an office which he had long exercised in fact. In Pushkin, what is going on in the mind of the as yet invisible Boris is made clear to us by the comments of the cynical, scheming Prince Shuisky; but this character does not function in the opera till later. In Moussorgsky, the leading character in the opening scene is the Russian people, which we see, in all its simplicity, being dragooned into expressing its free vote for Boris. The "national" atmosphere is defined at once in the phrase upon which the brief orchestral introduction is based:

There is never anything conventional about Moussorgsky's choruses. They are not the ordinary choruses of opera, inserted to make an imposing mass effect at this or that climactic point of the action. They have a psychology of their own, which comes out both in the ensemble utterances and in the numerous little individual comments that break through the main tissue every now and then. When we first see the crowd in *Boris Godounov* they are being hustled and browbeaten by the police to make them show a trifle more ardour and spontaneity in their supplications to Boris. They dutifully throw themselves on their knees and begin to drone out the appeal demanded of them:

2

Moderato ♩ = 92

f Why dost thou a - bandon us, thy folk, O father?

and manage, in the end, to work themselves up to a pitch of frenzy
that satisfies even the constable who is busy with his cudgel among
them. But as soon as he has gone away they revert to their former
uncomprehending apathy, asking each other what it is all about,
dropping into gossip about their own little affairs, and some of
them, the women especially, coming near to scratching each other's
eyes out. When the police officer returns, however, and threatens
them again, they fall on their knees once more and repeat their
supplication to Boris (No. 2) for all the world as if they meant it.

Stchelkalov, the Clerk of the Douma, enters, and, as in Pushkin,
announces that Boris has still not yielded to the prayers of either
the Douma or the Patriarch. Stchelkalov has only some thirty bars
to sing, but Moussorgsky, with his curious faculty for characterising people or situations that would appear insignificant to most
other musical dramatists, has made him not only a personality in
himself but the voice of a Russia too inarticulate to find its own
self-expression. "Woe to our Land!" he cries; "pray ye to God
that he may send comfort and help in this the hour of its need, by
enlightening the soul of the weary Boris!"

Just then there is heard in the distance a chorus of Pilgrims singing a fervent appeal to heaven for protection for the Russia that is
so grievously tried, within and without. Soon the Pilgrims enter,
distributing amulets among the crowd, whom they exhort to take
up ikons and the holy emblems and go to meet the Tsar. Their
voices die away in the distance again as they enter the monastery
that stands on one side of the Square, there to make their appeal
to the widow of the deceased Tsar, the sister of Boris, to add her
entreaties to theirs. The curtain comes down slowly on a strangely
impressive scene.

We next see the courtyard of the Kremlin. In the background is
the Red Staircase which leads to the Tsar's apartments — the
Terem. In the space between the Cathedral of the Assumption and
that of the Archangels is a mass of kneeling people. The air is pul-
sating with the clang of bells, great:

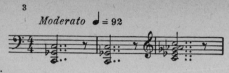

and small:

Boris has yielded, and the boyars are on their way in solemn procession to the Cathedral of the Assumption. Shuisky, from the steps of the Cathedral, cries, to the sound of trumpets, "Long live the Tsar Boris Feodorovich!," and the people take up the cry in their own way. Their choral melody:

continues through most of what immediately follows. The crowd is kept in line by the officials as the imposing procession moves on; and at last Boris himself appears.

As he does so the character of the music changes and the brilliant colour dies out of it. Boris, as in Pushkin, speaks to boyars and people of the sadness he now feels at having yielded to their prayers. His soul is filled with fear and foreboding for himself and for Russia. Invoking the blessing of heaven on him and it, he bids his people first kneel in prayer before the tombs of the great departed Tsars, then feast as his guests. Once more the procession passes on to the Cathedral, with the bells pealing out, the mob breaking ranks and the police restoring order, and the Homage Chorus (No. 5) preserving its own essential outlines at the same time that it fuses harmonically with the tones and overtones of the bells:

To shouts of " Glory to the Tsar! " Boris enters the Terem as the curtain falls.

4

When it rises again for the first act, the time, though not stated in the scores, is supposed to be some five years later. The venerable monk Pimen is seen writing by the light of a lamp in his cell in the monastery of the Miracle in Chudov; he is adding the final page to his chronicle of Russian history. A wandering figure in the bass accompanies graphically the slow passage of his pen across the parchment:

Some day, he muses as he halts in his labour for a moment, his record will come to light again before the eyes of some industrious monk, who will in his turn take up the task which he himself is about to lay down; and bending once more over his table he sets himself to write down the last sentences of his work.

Near him lies the young monk Gregory, asleep. He wakes with a cry: for the third time he has dreamed the same disturbing dream, which he now tells to Pimen. He had seen himself climbing the stairs of a tower, from the topmost height of which Moscow had appeared to him like an ant-hill: the squares below seethed with crowds who pointed up at him and broke into jeering laughter: overcome by shame and terror he had fallen headlong, and so awakened. The placid old monk bids him cool his young blood with prayer and fasting: even he, old and schooled by life as he is, sometimes dreams of wild happenings, battles and feasts and follies of all kinds, in which he had taken part in years gone by — for he had known the great Tsar Ivan the Terrible and his court

in all their splendour, and sat at banquets and fought against
Lithuanians under the walls of Kazan. Gregory envies him these
rich experiences and his memories of them, and laments his own
crabbed life as a poor monk. But Pimen recalls to him how many
Tsars, weary of the world, had been glad at the last to exchange
their vain pomp for the peace of the monastic life — among them
the great Ivan himself, whom he had seen sitting in this very cell,
shedding tears of remorse. His son, the gentle, pious Feodor, had
transformed his palace into a cloister; when God had called him
to Him his chamber was filled with sweet odours, and his face
shone like the sun in its glory. But after that, God was wroth with
Russia, and had sent it for its present Tsar a Tsar's assassin.

How old, asks Gregory, was the little Tsarevitch Dmitri when he
was murdered? In Pushkin's play Pimen tells him the whole story;
Moussorgsky omits most of it from his version of 1874. Pimen himself was in Uglich when it happened. He had been wakened by
the tolling of an alarm bell. He followed the excited crowd to the
palace where the body of the slaughtered boy lay. The mob had
already captured and executed three suspected men, who, before
they died, confessed their crime and named Boris as the instigator
of it. The child was only seven years old. That was some twelve
years ago, so that had he lived he would be the same age as Gregory and would now be Tsar; and at this point we hear in the orchestra the first quiet hint of a theme which will be afterwards always
associated with this Dmitri, and with Gregory as the false Dmitri:

It is with this sad story, says Pimen, that he has closed his chronicle, the continuation of which he commends to his young companion.

The matin bell tolls, and the voices of monks are heard in
prayer outside. Pimen extinguishes his light and leaves the cell.
He is escorted as far as the door by Gregory, who pauses there,
however, to apostrophise Boris, whose crime, he says, will one day
meet with the general condemnation of men and the punishment
of heaven.

The scene changes to an inn on the Lithuanian frontier. The words of the Hostess's charming little song, wholly in the Russian folk manner — "I have caught a drake" — were found by Stassov in a collection of songs for children. The song is broken in upon by voices outside; they are those of two wandering monks, Varlaam and Missail, a couple of engaging sturdy rogues and vagabonds who manage to combine piety with mendicancy and both with deep drinking. The burden of their chant at the moment is that if any rich believer shall be pleased to give — through them — an alms for the building of a new church, God will reward him a hundredfold.

The holy men enter with a blessing on the hostess and her house. They are accompanied by Gregory, whom they have fallen in with en route and about whom they are a trifle doubtful. He is in secular clothes. All they have managed to learn about him since he joined their company is that he is anxious to get to the Lithuanian frontier; till then, as he now assures them once more to a minor version of the Dmitri motive (No. 8), there will be no peace of mind for him. Recommending his own cheerful philosophy to the worried young man, Varlaam, having refreshed himself with the hostess's wine, launches into a lusty song about the fighting at Kazan, at which forty thousand Tartars were slain:

the text of which was another of Stassov's finds.

While the men of grace are getting drunker and drunker, Gregory takes the Hostess aside and asks her how far he is from the frontier. He can get there by nightfall, she tells him: but he will have difficulty in passing the guards, for it appears that someone has escaped from Moscow, and orders have come from the capital to detain and search all travellers. But there is another road into Lithuania besides the highway, details of which she gives the rather frightened Gregory. She has barely finished when a captain enters, accompanied by some guards, and interrogates the three men. Gregory does not seem to him to be worth bothering about, as his wallet is empty. In the oiliest of professional whines Varlaam protests that he and his pious brother in the Lord are also poor, for Christian folk, alas, are stingy nowadays. But the captain keeps looking at the old ruffian suspiciously: the fugitive from Moscow, he has been told, is a heretic monk, and Varlaam seems to him to fill that part of the bill to perfection. As the captain cannot read, and Varlaam thinks it prudent to deny that he has any learning himself, the warrant is handed to Gregory. " An unworthy monk," he reads out, " of the monastery of Chudov, Gregory Otrepiev, a heretic tempted by the devil, after trying to corrupt his holy brethren has fled towards the Lithuanian frontier, where, by order of the Tsar, he is to be arrested." " And hanged," adds the captain with gusto. Gregory says that there is nothing about hanging in the warrant; but the captain sagely remarks that the hanging is implied, for what is meant is not always put in writing. To oblige him, Gregory continues his reading with " to be arrested and hanged." Coming to the description of the fugitive, he reads this out, looking meaningly at Varlaam all the time, as " about fifty years old, of medium height, baldish, grizzled, fat, red-nosed." The guards at once fall on the sturdy monk, who, no doubt recalling his prowess at Kazan, throws them off and threatens them with his clenched fists. In presence of the danger that menaces him his scanty early schooling most opportunely comes back to him; bit by bit he manages to spell out the actual words of the warrant — " about twenty years old, medium height, reddish hair, one arm shorter than the other, a wart on his nose and another on his forehead." He goes up to Gregory, takes a good look at him, and says " You're the man! " But before any of them can lay hands on him, Gregory, unsheathing a dagger, escapes through the window.

5

The second scene of the act is the Tsar's apartments in the Kremlin. Xenia, Boris's daughter, is weeping over the portrait of her dead lover, to whom she sings a moving little song. The young Tsarevitch, Feodor, is poring over a large volume. The old Nurse, who is busy with her needlework, tries to comfort and distract the little Xenia by singing her a song in the folk-vein about a gnat and other insects, the words of which were taken from the collection of children's songs already mentioned, as were those of the "hand-clapping game" that follows — in which, while Feodor sings the tale of a hen, a pig and a calf and sundry other farmyard fauna, he and the Nurse clap their hands on the first beat of each bar. The song comes to a summary end as the Tsar enters. He too tries, in grave and tender words, to comfort his daughter in her sorrow, and then dismisses her and the Nurse.

The book which Feodor has been studying so eagerly is an atlas of Russia, in which he now proudly points out to his father all the leading features of the kingdom. Boris, after a word or two of kindly encouragement, gives vent to the gloomy thoughts that oppress him in a fine aria, "I have attained to highest power." (In Pushkin this monologue occurs in an earlier and different scene). It is six years, he muses, since he became Tsar; they have been six years of care and calamity and disappointment. His daughter has been bereaved of her lover: plague and famine have devastated the land, and in spite of all he has done for his people they lay their misfortunes at his door: the Poles conspire against him: his nobles betray him. And worst of all, his crimes haunt him night and day; always he sees the bleeding body of the child he had murdered, his staring eyes, his hands raised in a plea for the mercy that was denied him. The realistic climax of the aria strikes terror through us, giving place to pity as the broken man murmurs, "O God, in Thy grace have mercy on me!"

From behind the scenes there comes a confused noise, the cause of which he sends Feodor to discover. A boyar, entering to announce that Prince Shuisky craves an audience, whispers in the Tsar's ear the bad news that has come from secret agents — that many of the boyars, among them Shuisky, are conspiring against the Tsar with his Polish and other enemies. Just then Feodor returns, and, apologising for troubling his father with his own trifling affairs when he has more weighty ones of his own to occupy him, tells him at considerable length the story of a tiff between his parrot and the old Nurse Nastasia. Boris congratulates him on the charming way he has explained the uproar he had been sent to investigate, adding, somewhat inconsequently, that "this is the fruit of learning, which gives wings to the mind," and expressing the hope that some day he may see his son rule Russia in his stead. Then Shuisky enters.

This scene is perhaps the weakest in the whole opera from the constructional point of view. There is no valid reason why Feodor should be present throughout Boris's long monologue, " I have attained to highest power," with its bitter self-communing and its confession of the crime of years ago. As we have seen, in Pushkin the magnificent monologue takes place much earlier — anterior, indeed, to the scene of Gregory and the friars at the frontier inn; and the Tsar is alone, as dramatic and psychological probability demands that he shall be, when he indulges in it. Why then does Moussorgsky keep little Feodor on the stage all through this and much of the following scene? The only conclusion we can come to is that having the boy on his hands as a historical character he had to do something with him operatically. Xenia had had her little scene, and the Nurse — as also the Hostess at an earlier stage — had been allowed to sing at moderate length. Obviously, then, the player of the part of Feodor would also have to be given something or other to sing in addition to his few lines in the " hand-clapping game," and this was the only possible place for it in the whole opera; for the third act takes place in Poland, and in the fourth, Feodor appears only when his father is dying at a meeting of the Douma. Moussorgsky's handling of the part of Feodor in this particular scene in the second act nowhere makes sense. He gets the boy off the stage, during the few words exchanged between the Tsar and the messenger, under the pretext of sending him to discover the cause of the uproar " off," which pretext in its turn becomes a pretext for letting him explain it all in the song about the parrot. But there may also have been at the back of Moussorgsky's mind the vague idea that the boy ought not to be present — as he is in Pushkin — when the messenger enters with the grave news of the conspiracy of the boyars; for a little later, when Shuisky happens to mention the names of the true and the false Dmitri, Boris insists on the boy leaving them before he can learn any more.[4]

[4] Moussorgsky never improves matters by departing from Pushkin. In the play, it is not until Shuisky's revelation that the Pretender who has appeared in Poland claims to be the true Dmitri that Boris gives orders for the closing of the Lithuanian frontier. The Tsar had issued no such orders when Gregory had fled from the monastery. Why, indeed, should he do so? At that time he knows nothing whatever of the monk. In Pushkin it is not the Tsar but the Patriarch of the Church who, having heard of the flight of the renegade, gives instructions for him to be captured and sent to do perpetual penance some-

Feodor, apparently, must not know of the awkward report that is spreading through the country that the Pretender is the real Dmitri, falsely supposed to be dead, yet he is allowed to listen to his father's confession of the murder of the child and to be a witness of his soul-destroying remorse! In Pushkin, Feodor remains in the room during both the report from the messenger and the first part of the scene with Shuisky. The latter, at the beginning of the interview, suggests that the boy be told to withdraw, but Boris replies that " the Tsarevitch may learn whatever Prince Shuisky knows." It is only later, when Shuisky mentions the danger to the throne in the current belief that Gregory is the Tsarevitch Dmitri, that Boris bids his son leave him. That makes sense, in Moussorgsky as in Pushkin; but it does not make sense in the opera to have a father anxious to keep from his son the terrible truth of his guilt in the matter of the murder of Dmitri, after he himself had laid it bare to him in an earlier scene!

The modern producer generally side-steps the absurdity of having Feodor present during the Tsar's agonised confession of his crime by getting the boy off the stage before Boris commences his monologue. But that Moussorgsky fully intended Feodor to be on the stage during the confession is proved by a letter of his to Stassov in 1871, in which he says, " The villainous Tsar Boris has now an arioso. . . . The words have been stitched together by my own exalted self. And since to watch and listen to the remorseful outburst of a villain for any length of time is both disgusting and depressing, a crowd of nursery-maids suddenly breaks into the room shrieking out some unintelligible gabble; the Tsar drives them out and sends his son to enquire what makes the women howl. In the boy's absence Prince Shuisky enters and whispers some secret information in Boris's ear. After he has been got rid of, the Tsarevitch returns, and the Tsar questions him "; after which comes the story of the parrot.[5] But in making these changes in his first plan (in 1871) Moussorgsky either failed to perceive the damage he was doing to the dramatic verisimilitude of the scene or was indifferent

where: the Patriarch, indeed, expressly tells his informant (the Abbot of the Chudov monastery) that there is no need to report the affair to Boris, in spite of the fact that Gregory is known to have been babbling about his some day being Tsar in Moscow.

[5] Oscar von Riesemann, *Moussorgsky*, p. 189.

to it. We feel that he would have done better to keep more closely than he has done to Pushkin's scheme in this and one or two other places. Was he influenced to some extent in the present instance, one wonders, by the naïve desire to get in the song of the parrot by hook or by crook, having heard that it was in the reign of Boris that the first parrot came to Russia?

After this little excursion let us return to the point at which Shuisky enters.

Boris, who, from the reports of his spies, knows the Prince for the smooth, perfidious schemer that he is, begins to upbraid him for his hypocrisies and treasons. But Shuisky warns him that he has grave news for him — a Pretender has appeared in Cracow, backed by the King of Poland, the nobles, and the Pope of Rome; and the danger to Boris lies in the fear that the Russian populace may accept this man as the true Dmitri. It is at this point that the agitated Tsar orders Feodor to withdraw — a command, as we have seen, which makes complete sense in the story as a whole as told by Pushkin, but makes something less than sense as Moussorgsky has seen fit to handle it. As soon as Feodor is out of hearing, Boris tells Shuisky to see that the Lithuanian frontier is closed at once. Then, his nerve already beginning to fail him, he asks the Prince whether he has ever heard of dead men rising from their graves to trouble Tsars who have been chosen by the voice of the people and anointed by the Patriarch. When he had heard of the death of the child, he says, it was Shuisky whom he had sent to Uglich to search the matter out. Will the Prince now swear that the body he saw was that of Dmitri? If he lies, he will meet with a punishment so dreadful that Ivan the Terrible would have shrunk from imposing it. Thereupon Shuisky tells him how for some days he had watched the body of the murdered child, laid out in the cathedral with the corpses of thirteen people who had been slaughtered by the mob; and while in these corruption had already set in, the body of the child was still whole, and his face as tranquil as if he were only sleeping.

The crafty Prince has thus poisoned Boris's soul while professing to heal it: he has certified that it was the body of the Tsarevitch himself which he had seen stretched out in the cathedral, with a deep gash in his throat, yet he has hinted that a miracle had happened and the child was not really dead. Boris dismisses Shuisky, who, as he goes, glances back maliciously at his victim. Boris is choking. An ominous chromatic figure in the orchestra:

hints at the storm raging in his brain. Moussorgsky now departs considerably from the Pushkin original. In the latter, Boris says, after a moment of weakness, "So this is why for thirteen years my dreams have been haunted by this murdered child!" Then he masters himself by a mighty effort. Who is this new enemy of his? he asks. A mere name, a shadow! He blows on the phantom and it vanishes! Not this shall wrest the succession from his son! He will go on his way cautiously, but without fear, heavy though his heart is. But in Moussorgsky he becomes the quintessence of all the Macbeths of life or literature. His guilty conscience pictures the murdered boy before him in the room, his throat dripping blood; the ghastly figure creeps towards him, quivering and groaning. "I am guiltless of thy murder!" cries Boris. "Not I! Not I! It was the people's will! O Lord my God, Thou who desirest not the sinner's death, show me Thy grace! Have mercy on the wretched Boris!" It is on this last broken cry of the crazed man that the curtain falls, after one of the most tremendous scenes in all opera. Moussorgsky has added curiously to the horror of the storm in the Tsar's brain by introducing the chiming of a big clock that stands on the left of the stage. That chiming clocks were probably first known in Russia in the reign of Boris was yet another discovery made by Stassov and Moussorgsky in the course of their researches in the Petersburg Public Library. Moussorgsky's genius for realism has enabled him to make the most moving psychological use of this effect.

6

The third act does not appear at all in the first score of the opera: it was added by Moussorgsky in 1871–2, presumably as a necessary step towards obtaining a performance, for one of the objections urged against the work as originally planned was that it contained no outstanding female rôle.

The actual Gregory, whom from this point onwards we shall for convenience' sake refer to as Dmitri, won the love of one Marina Mnischek, the daughter of a Polish notable, the Voyevode of Sandomir. The third act of the opera opens in Marina's apartment, where her maidens are amusing her with their songs as she sits before her mirror. Moussorgsky employs in this act the rhythms of the cracovienne (in 2/4 time), the mazurka, or the polonaise (both in 3/4 time), to establish the Polish atmosphere. The song of the girls in praise of Marina's beauty is of the cracovienne type, while she herself answers them mostly in the 3/4 rhythm. She is not interested, she tells them:

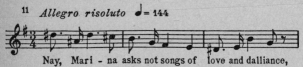

11 *Allegro risoluto* ♩= 144

Nay, Mari - na asks not songs of love and dalliance,

in ditties of the conventional kind; her preference is for warrior songs, tales of conquering heroes making the name of Poland resound throughout the world. And when the maidens have been dismissed she sings of the dullness of her life before this brilliant adventurer from Russia came into it, this Dmitri, chosen by heaven to punish Boris and take his throne from him. She is ambitious for herself: she means both to persuade the Poles to espouse his cause and to make him fall in love with her, for she is weary of lovers of the ordinary sort. Already she sees herself, in imagination, on the throne at Moscow, decked in jewels, a crowd of admiring boyars at her feet. It must be confessed that these audacious sentiments lose much of their force in the stereotyped dance rhythm in which Moussorgsky has seen fit to couch them.

She is interrupted by the entry of the Jesuit Rangoni, a character of Moussorgsky's own invention. He laments the poverty and neglect that have fallen to the lot of the Roman Church in Poland, and exhorts Marina, if she should go to Moscow, to make it her first duty to convert the Russian heretics to the one true faith. She protests that a less exalted mission would be more to her taste. But he insists. Her beauty, he says, has bewitched this alien Pretender; she must now play her cards in such a way as to enslave him utterly and then use him for the Church's ends; nor need she be too scrupulous as to the means she employs, so long as the purpose is attained. When she has him in her toils, she is to extract an oath from him to work as the Church directs. The proud, stubborn, self-seeking Marina turns angrily on the Jesuit; but he cows her by asserting his claim, as the messenger of heaven, to be the keeper of her soul.

There is nothing of all this in Pushkin — no character corresponding to Rangoni, indeed, though there are a few lines of dialogue at one point between Dmitri and a Catholic priest, in which the former promises that in two years' time "his people" and all the Eastern Church will submit themselves to the Holy Father in Rome.[6] Marina, of course, is a historical character.

The second scene of the act shows us the garden of the Mnischek castle at Sandomir. It is moonlight, and Dmitri is waiting by the fountain in obedience to a whispered word from Marina. He sings his love for her in passionate terms. Out of the shadow creeps the Jesuit Rangoni, accompanied by the oily, snake-like motive:

which we have already learned to associate with him in the preceding scene. He assures the young man that Marina is truly in love with him, though she has to suffer much from those about her at the court for having bestowed her affections on him. Rangoni so works upon him that he loses what we may perhaps call his inferiority complex as a conscious impostor and swears that he will win Marina, make her his queen, and deal as they deserve with the

---

[6] In Miss Howe's book will be found an English translation of the Pretender's letter of the 24th April 1604 to the Pope, written in Polish and rendered into Latin by the Jesuit Sawicki. In this the false Dmitri, professing to be anxious for the salvation not only of his own soul but that of all Muscovy, embraces "the immaculate and ancient doctrines of the Roman Catholic and Apostolic Church," and declares himself willing, if God should make his cause prosper, to use all his endeavours, when he has ascended his "hereditary throne," to assist the Russians to see the light as he has been fortunate enough to see it.

arrogant Polish nobles who despise him. The crafty Jesuit asks, as his own reward for his services, only to be allowed to follow Dmitri wherever his fortunes may carry him, as his spiritual counsellor and father. This Dmitri promises; then, on the advice of the Jesuit, he conceals himself among the trees as a number of guests pour out of the castle, Marina among them. To the strain of a polonaise the Poles discuss the march on Moscow that is in contemplation, or pay their compliments to Marina.

At last they all re-enter the castle, and Dmitri, alone once more in the garden, gives free vent to his hatred of the Jesuit, who, he thinks, has deceived him with regard to Marina, for he has seen her on the arm of an elderly Polish nobleman. The incident has stung him to assert himself as, seemingly, he had never done before. He will now, he declares, don his armour, mount his steed, and lead his forces into battle for what he calls the throne of his fathers. This resolution is symbolised by a bold motive in the orchestra:

which will be used with fine effect in the last act.

At this point Marina enters. Dmitri pours out his heart to her, but she at once gives him to understand that a return of his love is impossible on her part unless and until she sees him enter Moscow as Tsar; and once more we wish that Moussorgsky could have found some better method of differentiating the two characters musically than making Marina say everything she has to say in a 3/4 rhythm that is too obviously labelled " genuine Polish." He tries to bring her round to another way of thinking, but she answers him only with irony and scorn: the upshot of it all is that he can have her with Moscow but not without. In the end she insults him beyond endurance, calling him just what he is or has been, an impostor and a menial. This angers him; however mean his station may have been hitherto, he swears, he is the rightful Tsar; and to the proud melody of No. 13 he tells her how his cause is daily gaining strength in every quarter. On the morrow he will march to Moscow; and then, when he is crowned Tsar, he will look down on her in pride and contempt as she crawls towards his throne, mocked by all.

Hereupon follows the "love-duet" proper, in which Marina abandons the Polish dialect for a more international musical idiom. She protests that it was only her great love for Dmitri that had made her reproach him and seem to cross him as she had done. She confesses that she loves him, and the scene ends with their falling into each other's arms. As they do so we catch a glimpse of the crafty Rangoni, who has been spying on them a little distance away. It is the general practice of the theatres today to omit Rangoni from the opera altogether, which is a great pity; not only because without him there is no particular dramatic point in bringing Marina into the story at all, but because the spectator who has not made the Jesuit's acquaintance in the preceding scene misses entirely the subtle point of the downward-gliding chromatic passage heard in the orchestra (No. 12) as Dmitri and Marina embrace. It symbolises the triumph of the Roman Church over them both.

The whole Polish episode is managed much better in Pushkin. It is clear there that no one in high circles believes Dmitri to be anything but an adventurer: they know that in Russia he is regarded merely as a renegade monk with a bad reputation, while on his first entry into Poland he had been for a time a servant in the house of Prince Vishnevetsky. In Pushkin's garden scene Dmitri himself, annoyed by Marina's declaration that politics and ambition count with her for more than love, admits frankly that he is an impostor. For a moment Marina is shamed at the discovery of how she has lowered herself, and stunned by the blow to her ambitions. It is only when Dmitri's fighting spirit revives, when he swears he will yet drive Boris from his throne and then despise Marina, that something of respect for him is reborn in her. But there is no love-making. She tells him frankly that he can send for her when he is Tsar, but not before, and then leaves him. After she has gone he says to himself that women are craftier and more treacherous even than Tsars or Jesuits. He does not trust her, and regrets having given her such a hold on him as he has done by his confession. But at any rate his mind is at last made up. He will waste no more time at the court of Poland: tomorrow he marches against Boris. All this makes sounder dramatic stuff than most of what Moussorgsky has given us in its place. But, as we have seen, the third act did not exist at all in the first form of the opera. It was inserted mainly in order that the work should have a leading soprano as well as a leading tenor and a leading bass; and once she was admitted she was obviously marked out for a love-scene with the tenor.

7

But Moussorgsky's fourth act more than makes up for any short-comings in the third.

The scene is a clearing in a wood, with the town walls of Kromy in the distance. A crowd of vagabonds rushes in, dragging with them a captured boyar, Kroutshov, bound hand and foot. They place him on a big fallen tree trunk in the middle of the stage, and there gag and plague and insult him, wreaking on this upholder of Boris the traditional hatred of the Russian peasantry and prole-tariat for their overlords. As it is not fitting, they say, that a boyar should be without a mistress and a cudgel, they install a toothless, mumbling, coughing old crone by him and put a whip in his hand, the while they sing a chorus in derision of him and of the Tsar and salute him with mock honours:

Praise to our nobleman, servant of Tsar Boris,

Their orgy of malice is interrupted by the village Idiot, who is surrounded by a crowd of teasing boys. He is a pitiful figure, clothed in rags, with an iron saucepan on his head. Seating himself on a stone he sings a song which, perhaps, only Shakespeare among the poets could have matched for its pathos — a vacant, meaningless, yet heartbreaking song of cats crying in the moonlight, and he, the poor fool, praising God and hoping the weather will keep fine:

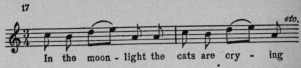

In the moon - light the cats are cry - ing

The boys torment the poor simpleton and rob him of his kopeck, whereupon he sets up a dismal howl.

Our attention is distracted from him by the voices of Varlaam and Missail behind the scene, singing of the evils that have descended on holy Russia because of the Tsar Boris:

Dark is the sun and dark the moon,

Stars are e - clipsed in the heavens a - bove,

As the couple approach the stage the crowd builds up an impressive choral ensemble, voicing the hope of the people for a better time with the coming of their liberator, the new Tsar, the chosen of God, the Dmitri who had been saved from the assassin's knife.

The chorus rises to a climax with wild cries of " Death to Boris! Death to the murderer! " Then comes a sudden calm, and from somewhere in the wood there come the voices of two Jesuits, Lovitski and Tcherniakovski, partisans of Dmitri, singing in unison, " Domine, salvum fac Regem Demetrium Moscoviae, Regem omnis Russiae." But Varlaam and Missail seem to resent this professional competition; they incite the mob against the Jesuits, who are dragged into the wood to be hanged.

Then martial music in the orchestra heralds the approach of Dmitri's troops. They are followed by Dmitri himself on horseback. He is greeted with cries of joy by the crowd as he tells them that he, the lawful Tsarevitch of all the Russias, will protect them against Boris, and exhorts all who are for him to take part in his coming victory. This he sings to the accompaniment of the typical Dmitri

motive (No. 8), which now receives a prouder form. He rides off
to trumpet fanfares behind the scenes, followed by the crowd and
by the two Jesuits — who, it turns out, have not been hanged after
all — chanting a lusty " Deo Gloria! " The stage is at length empty
except for the Idiot, who, still seated on the stone, laments prophetically the coming of woe unspeakable on the poor starving
Russian folk. The curtain falls with a continuous prolongation of
his heartbreaking sobs in the orchestra:

Thus ends a scene that is unique in opera. And dramatically as well
as musically it is almost wholly Moussorgsky's own invention: even
the moving figure of the Idiot, who appears for a moment in different circumstances in Pushkin, must really be placed to his credit.

The setting of the final scene is the reception hall in the Kremlin
in Moscow. (In Pushkin the corresponding scene takes place after
the defeat of the Pretender: it is not till later, after the death of
Boris, that Dmitri attains his objective. This, of course, is in agreement with the historical facts).

A meeting of the Douma is in progress, and the boyars are arranging for a proclamation to be issued, branding the Pretender
as a traitor and threatening with death all who support him.
Shuisky, whom none of them trust, arrives late. He has disturbing
news for them: recently, when leaving the presence of Boris, heavy
at heart because he could see that all was not well with the Tsar,
he had chanced to look back, and had seen him in a pitiable state
— pale, trembling, wild-eyed, muttering strange fragments of
phrases, seeing in his mind's eye the body of the murdered Tsarevitch, and shrinking back with a cry of " Avaunt! " Shuisky is still
repeating this word when Boris himself enters and takes it up
from him.

He is in a semi-cataleptic state, talking to himself for a while as
if unaware that he is not alone. He is no murderer, he protests, and

the lying Shuisky shall meet with atrocious punishment. Then, realising where he is and recovering himself somewhat, he seats himself on the throne, and begins to explain that he has summoned his boyars to counsel him in the difficult time that Russia is now passing through. But Shuisky craves permission to speak: outside, he says, is a pious old man who begs audience of the Tsar, for he has a weighty secret to impart to him. Boris orders him to be admitted: perhaps, he thinks, talk with one so good will lose his soul.

Pimen enters and plunges straight into his story. One evening, he says, an old shepherd, who had been blind from childhood, came to him and told him how he had heard a voice bidding him go to the Cathedral at Uglich and pray at the tomb of the Tsarevitch Dmitri, who is now a saint in heaven, able to work wonders. The shepherd had done so, and straightway his sight had been restored to him. Boris gives an agonised cry of "Help! Light! Air!" and collapses into the arms of some of the boyars. He bids them send for his son and bring the vestments to him. (It was the custom for the Tsars to prepare for death by being received into the Church and submitting to the tonsure).

The frightened little Feodor enters, and, left at length alone with him, Boris bids farewell to him and to the world. He counsels him to be firm and just when he becomes Tsar, trusting few, chastising traitors, defending the holy Russian Church and cherishing his sister Xenia. Upon his children, not upon himself, Boris invokes the protection of heaven. He takes Feodor in his arms and kisses him, then falls back exhausted. Outside are heard the solemn funeral bells and a chorus of church singers praying for the Tsar. "It is the mourners' wail!" says Boris: "give me the monk's robe; the Tsar goes to the cloister!" The boyars return in solemn procession, while the choristers sing of a little child who cried and struggled to be saved from death, and pleaded for mercy, but no mercy was granted him. With his last breath Boris starts up with a great cry of "I still am Tsar! Here " — pointing to his son — " is your new Tsar. Almighty God have mercy on me!" He presses his hand to his heart, sinks back in his chair, and dies.

This ending is Moussorgsky's own. In Pushkin it is the Patriarch of the Russian Church who tells the Tsar the story of the miracle of the shepherd. Boris shows some signs of agitation after hearing this, but makes no comment; and the situation is saved by Shuïsky, who smoothly argues that a time of insurrection, such as the one they are then living in, is not the ideal time in which to test the truth of such tales, or, having tested them, to put them to profane use. He himself, he says, will publicly denounce the Pretender who presumably is the fountain head of all these rumours. In Pushkin's drama, as we have said, the death of Boris does not occur until much later. Boris, taken suddenly ill behind the scenes, is carried in by the boyars, is left alone with Feodor, and dies after giving his son a good deal of sound advice in statecraft on much the same lines as in Moussorgsky's final scene, but at greater length, and without any display of remorse or any hint of terror.

Cavalleria Rusticana

PIETRO MASCAGNI [1863–1945]

PRINCIPAL CHARACTERS

SANTUZZA	*Soprano*
TURIDDU	*Tenor*
LUCIA	*Contralto*
ALFIO	*Baritone*
LOLA	*Mezzo-soprano*

1

AVALLERIA RUSTICANA, which was the first of Mascagni's operas, has also been the most enduringly successful of them the whole world over. Having won the first prize in a competition launched by the Italian music publisher Sonzogno, the work was produced at the Costanzi Theatre, Rome, in the 17th May 1890. It made an extraordinary sensation; Mascagni became famous in a day.

The libretto of *Cavalleria Rusticana* was put together by G. Targioni-Fozzetti and G. Menasci from a short story with the same title by the Italian novelist Giovanni Verga, which had been published a few years earlier; Verga himself made a play out of it later. Neither the matter nor the manner of the tale differs very much from a newspaper report of the evidence in an everyday murder case.[1] Turiddu, a young buck returned from serving

---

[1] This must not be taken as a denial of the effect of the story, still less as a criticism of Verga's art in general, but as a simple statement of fact. Nowhere is he so concise as in *Cavalleria Rusticana*, which runs to no more than about ten pages. As D. H. Lawrence puts it, in the Preface to his translation of this and other works of Verga, "we are here just a bit too much aware of the author and his scissors. He has clipped too much away. The transitions are too abrupt. All is over in a gasp. . . ."

his term as a conscript, is given to swaggering about on Sundays in his bersagliere's uniform under the admiring gaze of the girls of the village. While making love to Santa, the daughter of a local wine-grower, he takes to visiting Lola, the wife of a well-to-do carrier, when her husband, Alfio, is away with his cart and mules. Santa having told Alfio, in a fit of jealousy, what has been going on in his absence, the two men go out one morning to settle the matter in the approved way. Turiddu magnanimously admits that he is in the wrong, but explains that as his old mother had wept copiously over him before he left the house — she had pretended she had got up so early to attend to the hens — he will be under the painful necessity of killing Alfio like a dog. The account of the fight is a charming vignette of rustic chivalry, South Italian style. Alfio scores first with a stab in the arm, for which Turiddu pays him back with one in the groin; and once more he makes it clear that since the pathetic scene in the fowl-house his mother is so constantly before his eyes that it is his plain filial duty to murder his opponent. Alfio bids him open wide the aforesaid eyes, for he is going to be repaid all he has given in full measure. Bent nearly to earth by the pain from his wound, Alfio snatches up a handful of dust and throws it into Turiddu's eyes. "'Ah!' howled Turiddu, blinded, 'I'm done for.' He tried to save himself by desperate leaps backward; but Alfio got him again with another stab in the stomach and a third in the throat. 'That's three. . . . Now your mother can mind the hens.' Turiddu staggered and writhed a little while among the banyan trees, then fell like a log. The blood gurgled foaming from his throat, and he could not even say ' Ah! Mamma mia!' "

The subject appealed as strongly as it did to the audiences of the last decade of the nineteenth century, which had absorbed as much as they could assimilate for the time being of German sentiment in general and Wagnerian romance in particular, by reason precisely of its raw " verism "; and to this verism Mascagni had provided the perfect counterpart in his music, with its forceful if unsubtle emotionalism, its photographic appropriateness to each episode, its obvious melodies — drawn, as it were, with the broad of the thumb, but for all that novel and individual, — and its emphatic orchestral colouring. And that the subject and the music both answer still to something fundamental in the average man is proved by the enormous popularity of *Cavalleria Rusticana* down to the present day. Here and there in Mascagni's other operas there are pages in themselves superior to anything in this, but none of the others holds the unsophisticated listener in so unrelaxing a grip from start to finish as *Cavalleria Rusticana* does. Somehow or other Mascagni's very defects become virtues here. He had never, as a student, shown much liking or much capacity for labour at such refinements of craftsmanship as counterpoint, fugue, and close thematic development. But in the course of his youthful wanderings through Italy as conductor of a small touring opera company he had realised just what the average man wants, and how to serve it up to him. Verdi, who was an old man of seventy-seven when *Cavalleria Rusticana* appeared, got Boïto to play it to him from the piano score. At the third scene he stopped him. "Enough, enough," he said; "I understand." Verdi, as a practical man of the theatre, and with a *Trovatore* and a *Traviata* of his own to look back upon, could see at a glance why the new work had made so tremendous a sensation. Did he, one wonders, also sense prophetically that the composer of *Cavalleria Rusticana* would never rise to an *Aïda*, an *Otello*, or a *Falstaff?*

2

The prelude to *Cavalleria Rusticana* commences quietly with a melody associated later with the peace of Easter Day:

This gradually becomes faster and more insistent till it culminates in a *fortissimo* chord, to be instantly succeeded by a drop into a *pianissimo* statement of the melody to which Santuzza reproaches Turiddu for his cruelty towards her:

This in turn is worked up with a great show of passion. Then comes an episode that made a great sensation in 1890, and is still effective today, long after the first novelty of it has worn off. Turiddu sings behind the scenes a serenade to Lola, a song that is both a eulogy of her beauty and a warning of the danger that threatens them both. Next comes a reminder of the Santuzza who is so tragically concerned in the intrigue:

the melody being derived from her passionate appeal to Turiddu not to desert her in her misery. The prelude, which has been a calculated succession of high lights and low, comes to a close with a last reminiscence of No. 2.

The rising of the curtain is accompanied by the chiming of bells from the church which stands on the right of the stage. It is Easter morning, and the townspeople, to the sound of joyous music from the orchestra:

are passing across the square and disappearing into the church. From behind the scenes we hear a chorus of field-workers singing of the joys of Easter: they come into sight still singing, pass across the stage, and disappear in the distance. The music to the whole of this scene is perfectly in keeping with the Southern milieu; it is graceful, sensuous and fragrant.

The tonality of A major has ruled through it all. This changes to F sharp minor as a brief orchestral interlude hints at the tragedy that is brooding over the place: this is foreshadowed in the sombre motive:

that winds its way in and out of the depths of the orchestra, beneath masses of uneasy syncopated chords. Santuzza meets Turiddu's mother, Lucia, of whom she anxiously begs news of her son. Old Lucia senses that there is something wrong; but before Santuzza can tell her story the cracking of a whip and the sound of waggon bells are heard behind the scenes, and soon the waggoner Alfio enters, accompanied by a number of his cronies. He sings a lively song, descriptive of the pleasures of a calling such as his, and his joy when he returns from his business trips to the home where his faithful Lola is awaiting him. The chorus, after joining in the refrain of the song, melt away in various directions, some of them drifting into the church.

Alfio asks Lucia when he can have some more of the excellent wine that Turiddu brings in from a village in the neighbourhood; and lowering his voice he gives the astonished old woman a hint that her son may not be so far away as she thinks—Alfio had caught sight of him that very morning hanging round his house. Santuzza, by a sign, checks Lucia, who is about to express her surprise at this; and Alfio, who is in no mood for church-going just then, goes his way. From within the church we hear the melody of the " Regina coeli ":

which is taken up by the crowd that gradually occupies the stage, assuming attitudes of devotion in front of the sacred building. Among them is Santuzza, whose voice stands out from the rest in a broad melody:

which is afterwards taken up by them all. From inside the church the worshippers strike in occasionally with cries of "Alleluia."

When the others have left the stage, Lucia asks Santuzza why she had made that gesture of silence in the conversation with Alfio. Thereupon Santuzza tells her whole sad story — how Turiddu had been in love with Lola before he went as a soldier, and how she had married Alfio while Turiddu was away; then, on his return, he had sought Santuzza's love, and, after betraying her, had been caught once more in the net of the wicked Lola; and now, cast aside and disgraced, nothing remains for her but to weep her eyes out:

To the melody of No. 1 she sends the unhappy old mother into the church, which she herself feels she dare not profane with her presence. She will remain where she is, awaiting Turiddu.

Turiddu enters. Santuzza reproaches him with having lied to her — he has not been to Francofonte, as he had given out, for at dawn he had been seen coming from Lola's house. He tries bluff — he will not be made the victim, he says, of her foolish jealousy. But in the full flood of her entreaties and Turiddu's protestations there comes, by one of those swift and pungent dramatic effects so beloved of Mascagni and his librettists, the voice of Lola herself, singing a coquettish little song as she nears the scene. The words die on her lips as she sees Turiddu and Santuzza. She hypocritically asks Turiddu if he has seen Alfio anywhere, and then comments maliciously on the fact that Santuzza seems to be doing her praying in the street. She evidently does not share Santuzza's scruples about entering the church, into which she goes after having infuriated Turiddu by ironically refusing to take him away from his Santuzza. The latter's tears and supplications are now in vain; after an angry scene between the pair he throws her to the ground and rushes after Lola into the church. Santuzza sends a curse after him, and the sinister No. 5 in the orchestra warns us that tragedy is coming.

At that moment Alfio enters. The demented Santuzza tells him

that Lola has just gone into the church with Turiddu. She gives
him the whole story of her own betrayal by Turiddu and his association with Lola. Alfio swears that if she is lying to him he will cut
her heart out; but at last, convinced that she is speaking the truth,
he vows vengeance on Turiddu before the close of day.

As they go out the curtain falls, and the orchestra plays the
famous "Intermezzo sinfonico." The "sinfonico" seems a bit of an
exaggeration, but the Intermezzo fulfils well enough the purpose
for which it was obviously inserted — to give the audience an opportunity to relax for a while from the tension that has been
gradually increasing since the commencement of the opera, and so
prepare itself for the still greater tension that is coming. The short
movement begins by suggesting the Easter atmosphere once more
by means of the "Regina coeli" theme (No. 6), to which there
succeeds a broad melody in octaves, which works up, in the familiar
Mascagni manner, to a hammering climax and then ebbs away
into silence.

When the curtain rises again it is to the joyous strain of No. 4.
The congregation comes out of the church, forms into little groups,
and sings a chorus expressive of the pleasure awaiting them at
home, now that their religious duties have been performed. Turiddu, who has come out accompanied by Lola, goes with his
friends to a nearby tavern, where, led by him, they sing a rousing
song in praise of wine. Soon Alfio enters. Turiddu approaches him,
glass in hand, and asks him to drink with him, but Alfio refuses: to
drink with Turiddu, he says, would poison him. The women of the
party, seeing that trouble is brewing, hurry away, taking Lola
with them. The two men face up to each other like a couple of
fighting-cocks. Turiddu "places himself at Alfio's service"; they
embrace, and the traditional challenge to combat is given by
Turiddu biting Alfio's right ear. Turiddu then becomes repentant
and tearful. He confesses that he is in the wrong, and laments the
fate of Santuzza if he should be killed: but all the same he means
to plunge his knife into Alfio's heart. Alfio coldly retorts that he will
await him in the orchard, then leaves him.

As he does so Lucia enters. Trying to conceal from her what is
afoot, Turiddu begs her blessing, as on that morning when he left
her to be a soldier, and implores her, in a voice broken by sobs,
if he should not return, to be a mother to his Santuzza. The dis-

tracted old woman asks him the meaning of all this. He tries to persuade her that it is the heady wine he has just been drinking that has affected him; but his emotions overcome him. He kisses his mother frantically, bids her a distracted farewell, and runs out. Lucia calls after him in desperation; but her cry is answered only by Santuzza, who enters and falls into the old woman's arms to the melody of No. 8 in the whole orchestra, followed by a suggestion of No. 7. The *ffff* to which the latter ascends is hushed in a second to *ppp;* then, over a sinister orchestral *tremolo,* we hear shouts from the women behind the scenes, " They have killed Master Turiddu! " The chorus rush on to the stage and surround the fainting Lucia and Santuzza as the curtain falls, while the orchestra gives out with its full strength the motive that symbolises Turiddu's fault and its punishment at Alfio's hands (No. 5).

I Pagliacci

RUGGIERO LEONCAVALLO [1858-1919]

PRINCIPAL CHARACTERS

CANIO	*Tenor*
NEDDA	*Soprano*
TONIO	*Baritone*
BEPPO	*Tenor*
SILVIO	*Baritone*

1

EONCAVALLO, like Mascagni, is associated by the average opera-goer with a single work. As with Mascagni, again, the catalogue of Leoncavallo's output is a somewhat melancholy record of aspirations that came mostly to nothing, or next to nothing. The author of *I Pagliacci* seems to have taken some pains as a young man to learn the routine of composition, and up to about the age of thirty he devoted himself to opera-planning on quite a large scale. He began with an opera on the subject of Chatterton. Then he completed the first section, *I Medici*, of a trilogy — to be entitled *Crepusculum* — dealing with the Renaissance; but though this was accepted for publication by Ricordi the production of it was delayed indefinitely. All this while he was glad to earn a miserable living by teaching, and even by playing the piano at café concerts. It was probably the resounding success of *Cavalleria Rusticana* (1890) that induced him to take the score of *I Pagliacci* to the publisher Sonzogno. (It is said that the work had been technically ineligible for the competition instituted by Sonzogno in 1890 because, short as it was, it was in two acts, and one of the conditions of the competition had been that works submitted should be in one act only). *I Pagliacci* was produced at the Teatro dal Verme, Milan, on the 21st May 1892. It was an instantaneous success, and the lucky publisher — Ricordi's rival — now found himself in possession of two of the biggest box office attractions of modern times. It was not long before " Cav. and Pag." became indissolubly linked in the repertory of opera companies all over the world.

The success of *I Pagliacci* led, as a matter of course, to a production of *I Medici* (in November 1893); but the work was such a failure that Leoncavallo never had the heart to complete the two other sections of the trilogy, which were to have dealt with Savonarola and Cesare Borgia respectively. Neither *La Bohème* (1897) nor *Zaza* (1900), in spite of some initial favour, has conquered the opera world. *La Bohème* was hampered from the start by the superior quality of Puccini's score on the same theme (1896); and even the fact that the subject of *Roland of Berlin* (1904) — celebrating the virtues of the house of Hohenzollern — had been suggested to Leoncavallo by no less august a personage than the German Kaiser did not suffice to inspire his muse: the work preceded its gifted imperial progenitor into perpetual exile by about fourteen years. As for the operas, some ten in number, that followed *Roland*, for even the titles of these we have to have recourse to the encyclopaedias.

Leoncavallo was his own librettist, and in *I Pagliacci*, at any rate, he has turned out a highly effective piece of work. The device of a play within a play is of immemorial antiquity, but it never seems to lose its attractiveness or its punch. It has been said that Leoncavallo derived *his* subject from an incident in real life; but if that be so it is merely one more illustration of life's incorrigible passion for imitating art.

2

The action of the opera takes place in Calabria, on the feast day of the Assumption of the Blessed Virgin. A troupe of strolling players (pagliacci) has just arrived in the village of Montalto, where it intends to perform the same night. The opera opens with an orchestral prelude the leading features of which are (*a*) a theme expressive of the restless life of the wandering players:

(*b*) a dolorous melody:

associated later with the grief of Canio; and (*c*) a theme associated with the lover Silvio (No. 7).

At the conclusion of the prelude the mis-shapen buffoon Tonio approaches the audience through the curtain, announces that he is " the Prologue " — in the old theatrical sense of that term — and explains that the play that will be set forth before them that night is no mere creation of fiction but a true story; he hopes that when they see the drama unfolding itself they will remember that even actors are men and women like themselves, passionate, rejoicing, suffering. " I have given you the idea," he concludes. " Now observe for yourselves how it works itself out." And turning to those behind the scenes he calls out " Ring up the curtain! "

The setting disclosed to us is the meeting of two roads on the outskirts of the village. It is three o'clock in the afternoon. Tonio is watching with considerable disfavour the antics of the villagers, who, to the accompaniment of strident and often discordant sounds in the orchestra, are awaiting with delight the coming of the troupe, which they finally welcome in a rousing chorus, with cries of " Viva Pagliaccio! " The loutish Tonio, who seems to have no great liking for the easily amused mob, lies down in the shade in front of the travelling theatre which has already been set up on the stage. The company arrives in a cart. Canio, the proprietor of the show, who is evidently a prime favourite with the villagers, secures silence by a vigorous pounding of the big drum; then, in a speech with all kind of comic underlinings, he invites them to the performance that evening at which they will have the pleasure of seeing Tonio spinning his web of intrigue, and above all the marital furies of Pagliaccio himself, and the fine snare he sets to get his revenge. The crowd accepts the invitation with naïve expressions of delight.

Tonio makes to assist Canio's pretty wife, Nedda, to alight from the cart, but gets a box on the ear from the jealous husband for his pains, at which the crowd laughs once more. The cart is taken off by another comedian of the company, Beppo; the disgruntled Tonio also disappears, in pursuit of some boys who have been making fun of him, muttering, as he goes, "He'll pay for that, the scoundrel!" Canio is invited by some of the villagers to drink with them at the tavern at the cross-roads. Beppo, throwing down his whip, declares that he too will go with them: Tonio, however, refuses Canio's call to him to come as well. He will join them later, he says; at the moment he has to attend to the donkey. One of the villagers humorously advises Canio to keep his eyes open, for it seems to him that Tonio is remaining behind to make love to Nedda. Canio frowns and at the same time smiles at this. Such a game, he assures them, it would be better not to play with him. Tonio, and not only Tonio but everyone else, would do well to remember that the theatre and actual life are not at all the same thing:

Un tal gio - co, cre - de - te - mi, —
è meglio non gio-car - lo con me, miei ca - ri,

If up there — pointing to the booth — Pagliaccio happens to surprise his wife with her lover, he just makes a humorous speech and takes a thrashing, and the audience laughs and applauds:

But, he goes on to say in a changed voice and to the accompaniment of a sinister new motive in the orchestra:

if Canio were to catch Nedda at her tricks in real life, the affair would have a very different ending! Then, recovering himself again, he reverts to his jocular tone of a minute before: "Such a game, believe me, is better not played with me!" Nedda, who has not taken her eyes off him all this time, is greatly perturbed. How much does he really know? she wonders. But surely Canio cannot suspect his Nedda? say the villagers. Of course not, he replies meaningly; he adores her! and he kisses her on the forehead as he leaves her.

The emotional atmosphere of the scene which opened so merrily has darkened sensibly by now. The tension is dissipated by the sound of bagpipes behind the scenes, summoning the faithful to vespers. After an ensemble in which they imitate the ding-dong of bells, and a parting reminder from Canio not to forget the coming performance, the chorus go off to church, leaving Nedda alone on the stage. She muses anxiously for a little while. Suppose the brutal Canio were to discover her guilty secret? Then, being young and romantic, she dismisses these gloomy thoughts and gives herself up, in a lilting ballatella, to the joy of contemplating the birds in their carefree flight through the sunlit air. The situation seems to have been created only to give the prima donna a chance to show what she can do, and the music, with its slender intellectual content, to have been written with the same object.

Nedda's solitude is broken in upon by Tonio, who has heard her song, and, being more of an amorist than a musical critic, has been enraptured by it. For Tonio, in spite of his uncouthness, or perhaps because of it, is in love with Nedda; for him she is the only escape open to him from a world of harsh and ugly reality into one of beautiful dreams. But Nedda has no intuition of the poetry, grotesque and abortive as it is, that lies at the core of the soul of the poor clown who is everyone's butt. She sees only the superficial absurdity of such a creature presuming to be in love, and she makes the mistake of laughing at him, to the accompaniment of a figure of sprightly badinage in the orchestra:

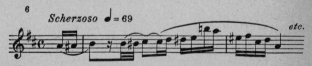

The time and the place for him to talk to her like this, she tells him, will be this evening, when he can grimace to his clownlike heart's content in the comedy. He warns her not to go too far in her derision of him, but she is heartless in her merriment. She goads him into a passionate declaration of his love for her: he tries to kiss her, and she strikes him in the face with the whip that Beppo has left lying in front of the theatre. He goes off mad with rage, swearing that he will have his revenge.

A sensuous phrase in the orchestra:

announces the approach of Nedda's lover Silvio, a young peasant of the neighbourhood: he has left Canio drinking at the tavern and made his way stealthily by a roundabout way through the undergrowth. In a long duet he pours out his love and implores her to fly with him that very night, to which, after some resistance, she consents. They are lost to the world in a slow cadence in close-clinging sixths when Canio enters, accompanied by Tonio, who has seen the lovers together and has run to the tavern to fetch his master. Canio is just in time to hear Nedda promise to meet Silvio at midnight, and to see him escape over the wall at a warning cry from Nedda. Canio pushes Nedda roughly aside and pursues Silvio, but returns baffled. In a blind fury he demands the lover's name, which Nedda will not give him. He is only restrained from killing her there and then by Tonio and Beppo. The latter hurries Nedda into the theatre, while Tonio exhorts his master to be calm, if only for the better securing of his revenge. The show must go on, he says: the people are already beginning to assemble for it: the lover is certain to be there, and is bound, in some way or other, to betray himself. At last he leaves Canio, who, overcome with grief, launches into the famous solo "Vesti la giubba." Pagliaccio, he mourns, is not a man but only an actor, whom the people pay to amuse them: if Harlequin has robbed him of his Columbine he must laugh through his tears, and the public will applaud. His lament culminates in the agonised theme quoted as No. 2. His frame shaken by sobs, he covers his face with his hands and disappears through the curtain of his little theatre.

3

Between the first and the second act comes an orchestral Intermezzo descriptive of the mournful meditations of Canio before the rising of the curtain in his own theatre: it ends with an expansive statement of the theme in the Prologue that had accompanied Tonio's words about himself and his fellows being not merely actors but human beings, of the same stuff as those who laugh at them.

The second act is devoted to the feigned play which soon becomes more real than life itself. In this comedy Canio becomes Pagliaccio; Nedda is Columbine; Tonio is Taddeo; Beppo plays Harlequin.

First of all we see the people thronging to see the play, and Beppo arranging places for them, while Tonio is making a great noise with the big drum. The villagers are first heard in a gay chorus behind the scenes, exhorting each other to hurry, for the play is about to begin. Gradually they take their seats: among them is Silvio, who occupies a place at the front. Nedda, who is going round the benches with a collecting-plate, manages to exchange a few quiet words with him: Canio did not see him, she says, and the plan for flight after the performance still holds good.

At last, after cries and appeals from the impatient audience, the curtains of the booth are drawn aside. We see the sort of poor attempt at a domestic interior that a small travelling company would be likely to carry about — a little room with two side doors and a window at the back: there is a table with two chairs, in one of which Columbine is seated. The orchestra plays a pleasant minuet:

which accompanies Columbine's miming and soliloquising during the opening moments. She is very restless, getting up, walking about, then sitting down again; and she makes it clear to the audience that as her husband Pagliaccio will not be returning until late, she is eagerly expecting her lover. She gives a cry of joy as a guitar is heard preludising off-stage, and Harlequin sings, outside the window, a charming little serenade to his Columbine, who sits at the table once more in a flutter of expectation.

Taddeo, the grotesque servant of this humble establishment, now enters. He has been shopping, and he carries a basket containing his purchases. He falls on his knees before Columbine and makes love to her in the most clownish fashion. He knows she is pure as the driven snow, he says meaningly, while the orchestra gives out a suggestion of the skittish theme (No. 6) to which Nedda had derided Tonio's love-making in the first act. She snatches the basket from him, puts it on the table, then opens the window and gives a signal. The sprightly Harlequin jumps in, carrying a bottle which he deposits on the ground before he kicks Taddeo out. As he goes, Taddeo gives the lovers his mock blessing and assures them that he will keep watch and ward over them. The spectators are immensely amused by it all.

Columbine arranges knives, forks and spoons, and places on the table the fowl that Taddeo had brought in; while Harlequin picks up the bottle from the floor and deposits it beside the fowl. The pair express their naïve pleasure in each other's company in a dainty gavotte, and Harlequin gives Columbine a phial which she is to empty into Pagliaccio's evening drink: when the drug has done its beneficent work he and she will fly together. At that moment Taddeo rushes in with an air of mock terror, to tell them that the husband has discovered everything, and, out of his mind with rage, is looking for them both with a knife. Harlequin manages to escape through the window just as Pagliaccio enters through the door — in time to hear from Columbine exactly the same parting words to Harlequin as Canio had heard Nedda speak to her lover an hour ago: "Tonight, then! And for ever I shall be thine!"

"The selfsame words!" says Canio to himself. Then, with difficulty mastering his emotions, he becomes Pagliaccio again, and to the accompaniment of an expressive new theme in the orchestra:

he begins to play his regulation part in the comedy. He accuses Columbine of deceiving him. She pretends that no one has been with her but Taddeo, whom she calls upon to be her witness: the clown sarcastically assures Pagliaccio that his wife is veracity itself. She laughs in Pagliaccio's face as he demands her lover's name (No. 5). He can bear no more. The mask falls from him: "I am Pagliaccio no more," he cries, "but a man wounded and shamed, and thirsting for vengeance!" Columbine tries to keep the comedy going, but Pagliaccio, as his grief and anger get the upper hand of him, becomes more and more Canio; while the more realistic his acting the more loudly the audience applauds. At last Columbine in her turn also begins to change from Columbine to Nedda. If her husband is so tired of her, she says, with feigned calmness, he can let her leave him, here and now. This infuriates him still further: she shall remain, he shouts, and he will have her lover's name.

With a great effort Columbine steers the play back into its traditional comic vein; no one has been with her, she says with a smile, to the music of the gavotte, but poor frightened, harmless Harlequin. The rustic crowd bursts into a horse-laugh at this, which is checked at the sight of Pagliaccio's frenzy, which is now manifestly more than play-acting. Again he demands the name, and again Columbine refuses it. An ensemble full of dramatic movement is built up. All take part in it — the two leading characters, Harlequin-Beppo, who appears at the back, frightened out of his wits and trying to run away before worse happens, Taddeo-Tonio holding him back, and the audience, realising at last the tragic turn the play has taken, trying to restrain Silvio, who has risen in his seat in uncontrollable excitement. As Nedda attempts to escape into the audience Canio stabs her. Silvio rushes at Canio, who turns on him and plunges the knife into his heart. The spectators seize Canio, who suddenly comes to himself. "The comedy is ended!" he cries out to them in a kind of stupor, as the knife falls from his hand and the orchestra gives out in a thunderous *fortissimo* the melody to which, at the end of the first act, he had sung the words, "Laugh, Pagliaccio, for the love that has been destroyed! Laugh for the grief that is poisoning your soul!"

Elektra

RICHARD STRAUSS [1864–1949]

PRINCIPAL CHARACTERS

ELEKTRA	*Soprano*
CLYTEMNESTRA	*Mezzo-soprano*
CHRYSOTHEMIS	*Soprano*
AEGISTHUS	*Tenor*
ORESTES	*Baritone*

LEKTRA was produced at Dresden on the 25th January 1909. It was the first opera in which Hugo von Hofmannsthal co-operated with Strauss as librettist.

The subject had already been treated, in different styles, by Sophocles and Euripides in their *Elektra* dramas, and by Aeschylus in his *Choephoroi* (*The Libation-Bearers,* the second play of his Agamemnon trilogy). For the roots of the story we have to go back to certain events preceding the Trojan War. Atreus, King of Mycenae, had two sons, Agamemnon and Menelaus. The former had for wife Clytemnestra, and the latter her sister Helena, who was carried off by Paris, the son of Priamus, King of Troy. Out of this there sprang the war between Greece and Troy, which lasted ten years. On the way to Troy the Greek fleet was becalmed at Aulis, for Artemis was wroth with Agamemnon for having killed one of her sacred hinds. To placate the goddess, Agamemnon sent for his daughter Iphigenia and sacrificed her.

After the destruction of Troy and the recovery of Helena, Menelaus, on his journey home, was driven by contrary winds to Egypt and elsewhere, his wanderings lasting several years. Agamemnon returned to Mycenae, where, during his long absence, he had been supplanted in his Queen's affections by Aegisthus. Clytemnestra's hatred of Agamemnon was justified by her as having sprung from a mother's resentment at his sacrifice of her daughter Iphigenia. The Queen and her paramour murdered Agamemnon while in his bath, and Aegisthus reigned in his stead. The great King left behind him a young daughter, Elektra, and a son, Orestes, of whose possible vengeance the guilty pair now live in constant dread. Elektra is degraded to the state of a slave in the palace: the little Orestes had been rescued from death by a faithful slave who placed him in safe keeping at a distance from Mycenae.[1] In due course he returns to Mycenae, where, giving himself out to be a messenger bringing Clytemnestra the welcome news of the death of Orestes, he obtains admission to the palace and slays both her and Aegisthus, as filial duty to the outraged dead required.

It is fundamentally a story of violence, for all the profound moral implications with which the Greek conscience endowed it; and the tremendous expressive apparatus of modern music has enabled Strauss and Hofmannsthal to intensify the violence to an extent that would have astonished and perhaps horrified a Greek. This same apparatus, however, makes possible to librettist and composer a beauty at the very heart of horror that was beyond the scope even of the finest minds of the ancient world.

The opera is in one long act, but analysis of its structure shows that Hofmannsthal's plan has seven main psychological stages, to each of which Strauss gives a different musical cast. It may assist not only the listener in the opera house or on the radio but the home student to have these stages enumerated and summarised here:

1. Elektra. (Pp. 5 to 34 of the German vocal score).
2. Chrysothemis. (Pp. 35 to 59).
3. Clytemnestra. (Pp. 59 to 114).
4. Elektra and Chrysothemis. (Pp. 114 to 161).
5. Orestes. (Pp. 162 to 182).
6. The Recognition. (Pp. 182 to 202).
7. The Vengeance. (Pp. 203 to end).

The emotional climax comes, after a slow ascent from the opening scene, with the despair of Elektra when she hears that Orestes is

[1] In some versions of the story it is Elektra who sends her brother away, looking to him to avenge some day their murdered father. The complex myth, indeed, comes down to us with many variations in detail. The reader will understand that the version here given is the one adopted by Hofmannsthal.

dead. Then the tension relaxes in a long solo in which the avenging fury softens into the tender sister welcoming the loved brother home again; after which the action gradually slips back again into its former atmosphere of hate and strain and lust for vengeance, until, the double deed accomplished, the moral law vindicated, Elektra's *Verklärung* is expressed in a sacred dance.

1. There is no overture, the orchestra launching at once into the arresting motive of Agamemnon:

The setting is the inner courtyard of the palace at Mycenae, which is overlooked by the back of the palace and the servants' quarters. On the left is a draw-well, from which some female slaves, watched by the overseers, are drawing water. Night is falling. Elektra runs out of the house — a ragged, unkempt, hardly human creature, recoiling on herself at the sight of the others, instinctively holding one arm before her face as if to protect herself against them, so used is she to brutal usage:

The orchestra gives out the motive of her undying hate of her mother and Aegisthus:

The maids discuss in fear and horror this almost dehumanised woman who seems hardly more than a wild beast, always sobbing:

and cursing and spitting at any one who tries to approach her. With some of them, fear has long ago hardened into hatred; while one or two are touched with something approaching pity at the thought of the misery and degradation Elektra suffers in the house that was once her father's, lodging with the dogs and eating from the same platter with them. The Fifth Maid, a gentler creature than any of the others, makes no secret of her sympathy with this child of kings who suffers such shame: none of them, she says, is fit to breathe the same air as she. The others turn on her angrily. "Were she my daughter," says one of them, "I would keep her under lock and key"; and we hear in the orchestra the motive of Orestes, who, like Elektra, is the victim of his mother's hatred and fear:

It is when one of the maidservants shows a faint gleam of pity for Elektra that we hear the motive that symbolises her degradation:

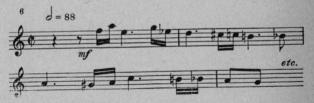

which, as the Fifth Maid speaks of her as a King's child, is linked with the motive of her brother (No. 5). The maids go into the house, from which we hear a cry of "Help, they are beating me!" from the one who alone had ventured to speak a word of love for Elektra and understanding of her.

When the stage is empty, Elektra comes forward and launches

into a fine monologue (commencing with the motives No. 2 and No. 1), in which, in an ecstasy of love and pain, she addresses the shade of the great King who had been so foully murdered. Her imagination darts forward to the day when those who wrought that deed will in their turn be victims raining their life-blood on her father's tomb, along with that of the chargers from his stables and the dogs that once licked his sandals, while she, with her brother and her sister, will dance the royal dance of victory about the tomb. It is a magnificent outburst — most magnificent of all, perhaps, in the figure, symbolising the shade of Agamemnon as avenger of his own wrongs, that rises threateningly from the depths to the heights of the orchestra like a great fist clenched above the house that was once his:

Another theme, which becomes of great importance later, represents the Children of Agamemnon:

It is used here to the words, "Father, leave me not this day alone! Show thyself to thy child as thou didst yesterday, like a shadow in the recess of the wall!" The final stages of the monologue foreshadow the mystical dance to which Elektra looks forward in imagination:

2. As Elektra's last cry of "Agamemnon!" dies away, Chrysothemis enters. This younger sister was designed by Hofmannsthal, as his letters show, to contrast with Elektra as the human with the demoniac. Chrysothemis is as weak through love as her sister is strong through hate. She bids Elektra beware, for Clytemnestra and Aegisthus intend to immure her in a tower into which neither the light of the sun nor that of the moon ever penetrates. Elektra tries to infect Chrysothemis with her own religion of hatred and her lust for revenge. But Chrysothemis shrinks from all this violence. She herself is almost demented with fear; her one desire is to escape from this hag-ridden house, to become the wife of some good man, were it only a peasant, and bear him children:

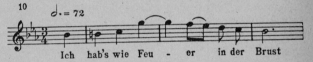

It is because of Elektra that she too is a prisoner in the house, because of the fear that Elektra inspires in her mother and Aegisthus; and it will come to nothing with all Elektra's hopes, for no news ever reaches them of their brother, and meanwhile these years of suffering are breaking down the bodies of the sisters and ageing their faces with care. It is unfortunate that nowhere in the opera does the music of Chrysothemis rise to the height of that of Elektra. Strauss has not Wagner's gift for endowing his second-line figures with the inner vitality, the dramatic veracity, of those of the first line. Gudrune, for instance, says and does very little in the *Götterdämmerung;* but minor character as she is, she is given a characteristic phrase or two that limn her to the life. Strauss's Chrysothemis music is certainly what he intended it to be — a contrast to that of Elektra; but it nowhere carries the same conviction.

From within the palace is heard the sound of hurrying feet

drawing nearer and nearer; and torches are seen in the passage to the left of the door. The Queen, says Chrysothemis, has been dreaming again — this time her dream was that she was being pursued by Orestes, and she awoke shrieking with fright. She is now on her way to propitiate the gods, driving before her the slaves with torches, and the beasts she means to slaughter, and the priests with their sacrificial knives. "Sister, when she trembles she is most terrible. Cross not her path today." Elektra's only answer is that today, as never before, she desires to have speech with her mother. Chrysothemis flies from her in horror.

3. Past the crudely lighted windows figures are seen rushing wildly, driving forward, with resounding whip-blows, a procession of struggling and stumbling cattle. At the broad window Clytemnestra herself at length appears. She is so horrible a spectacle that the Greek imagination, surely, would have shrunk from it. Sleepless nights, remorse, haunting fears have undermined her. Her sallow, bloated face shows up in the lurid light of the torches against her scarlet robe. Her eyelids are unnaturally large, and she seems to hold them open with difficulty. She is covered with jewels, rings, armlets, all of them talismans against evil. She leans heavily on her Confidante, whose dark violet robe contrasts sombrely with hers, and on an ivory staff set with gems. Clytemnestra's train is carried by an Egyptian-looking woman, whose jet-black hair is combed straight back from a smooth yellow face like that of a snake rearing its head to strike.

The music takes on a sombre tinge once more: that allotted to Clytemnestra is full of dragging harmonic clusters of this kind:

which suggest her constant effort to bear up against the load of physical corruption and mental torture that weigh on her by day and by night.

She begins by reproaching the gods for having given her this Elektra for child, this nettle which she cannot endure to touch yet cannot bring herself to exterminate. Gradually, as Elektra draws her into conversation, Clytemnestra leaves the window and comes down with her attendants to the doorway. She turns a deaf ear to their warnings about Elektra. She has come to the end, she says, of what body and spirit can endure, her body rank with disease, her spirit sapped by her dreams and visions. Victims she sacrifices in endless succession, yet no peace comes to her soul. Perhaps this hated and hating daughter of hers may know of a medicine against torture such as hers.

She orders the Confidante and the Trainbearer to leave her, and they go, though reluctantly, into the palace, and with them the torchbearers, so that only a dim light from the windows is left to define the figures of the two women now facing each other in the courtyard. There are simples, could one but know them, for all ills, Clytemnestra tells Elektra wearily. She describes her nights of choking anguish, the evil eyes that seem to watch her as she lies sleepless in the haunted darkness, the sleep that is even more terrible than wakefulness, for in her sleep she dreams. And yet each demon can be appeased if only the right blood be made to flow! There follows a dialogue which, with its swift verbal give-and-take and its wealth of double meanings, harks back to the technique of the Greek tragedy in moments when the action has reached its supreme tension. In each of Elektra's answers to the Queen's eager questions there is a sinister meaning that is hidden from Clytemnestra but perfectly plain to the audience. There are many respects in which the structure of the ancient Greek drama resembles, in essentials, that of the Wagnerian music drama, though the latter has this great advantage, that it can always call on music not only to recall to our memory what has happened in the past but to suggest to our imagination what the future holds in store. To some extent the Greek audience itself supplied this element of backward-glancing and fore-knowing: as every detail of the myth on which a play was founded was known to the spectators, their imagination could always supply what was sometimes designedly left unsaid by this character or that. But opera, with its leading motives that look before and after, and its capacity for supplementing, or even contradicting, in the orchestra what is being said on the stage, is incomparably more potent than any mere verbal drama can be in this regard.

She will slay anything that creeps on the earth or flies in the air to rid herself of her spectres, says Clytemnestra; and Elektra assures her that once the appointed victim has bled under the axe she will dream no more. (Clytemnestra does not know that Elektra has hidden away, for the great day of vengeance, the axe with which Aegisthus had slain Agamemnon). The destined sacrifice, it seems, is not yet consecrated, nor even bound: it still runs free. Clytemnestra demands the name of this beast that must die. It is a woman, replies Elektra. Question after question comes swiftly from Clytemnestra's tongue. One of her servants? A child? A maiden unwed? A wife? Yes, answers Elektra tranquilly, a wife. And what the hour and the manner and the place of killing? At any place, at any hour of day or night. Shall Clytemnestra herself take part in the slaying? No; this time she will not take part in the hunt with net and axe. (According to the legend, Clytemnestra herself had entangled Agamemnon in a net in his bath for Aegisthus to smite him with the axe). Who is to deal the blow? A man. Aegisthus? Elektra laughs contemptuously at the application of the word " man " to one so effeminate and degenerate as her mother's paramour. Will the victim be slain by a member of her household or by a stranger from afar? By a stranger, in sooth, yet one akin to her and to Elektra.

The orchestral texture during this dialogue is an elaborate network of thematic references, with the motive of Elektra's dance of triumph (No. 9) especially prominent.

The two women begin to speak of Orestes, who, Clytemnestra has been told, has lost his reason, and stammers in his speech, and has his abode with the dogs, being no longer capable of distinguishing man from beast. She hypocritically claims to have sent much gold to those into whose keeping he had been given, so that they may treat him as beseems a royal child. Elektra retorts that the gold was sent as a bribe to them to slay the boy, for his mother lives in perpetual dread of his return. As to that, Clytemnestra professes confidence in those whose duty it is to guard her, and turns again to what is uppermost in her mind — the discovery of the one sacrifice that will rid her of the sick terror that haunts her. She reminds Elektra of her power over her and threatens her with chains and hunger if she will not tell her what she so desires to know — what blood it is that must flow that she may sleep once more.

Thereupon Elektra throws off the mask. She leaps out of the shadow and comes nearer and nearer to Clytemnestra, crouching and threatening. She takes up her mother's last words. Yes, blood must flow, but from Clytemnestra's own throat when the huntsman shall have seized her. She sees the slayer creeping through the chambers of the palace till he comes where Clytemnestra lies. He draws back the curtain from the bed. She wakens, and flies screaming: he pursues her through halls and down the great staircase, and she, Elektra, she who has set him on, follows her windings like a hound, heading her off to the huntsman. And at last they come to a shadow in the depths of the darkness cast by a wall: it is Agamemnon, and at his feet the two avengers strike the wretched woman down, but not until she has had time to live in imagination through an eternity of terror and suffering. The axe falls, and Clytemnestra's anguished dreaming is for ever at an end, nor is there need any more for Elektra to dream, for all living things, this load of horror and infamy lifted from them, can now rejoice and be glad.

Clytemnestra stands trembling under the vehemence of Elektra's speech and before the madness in her eyes. But just then lights appear in the palace, and the Confidante runs out and whispers something in Clytemnestra's ear the significance of which she seems not to grasp at once. When she does, her expression changes from one of fear to one of evil joy in triumph. She raises her hands towards Elektra with a menacing gesture. Meanwhile the serving-maids have poured into the courtyard, flooding it with the reddish-yellow light of their torches. Leaning on her Confidante and her staff, Clytemnestra makes her way hurriedly into the palace. During the whole of this episode no word is spoken on the stage, the orchestra alone, with its interlacing motives, carrying on the action and supplying what comment is necessary.

4. Elektra is left alone for a moment, wondering what this sudden gladness on the part of her mother can portend. She is soon enlightened. Chrysothemis comes running in through the courtyard gate, howling, as the direction in the score puts it, like a wounded beast. " Orestes is dead! " she shrieks; and we hear in the orchestra the motive of the Children of Agamemnon (No. 8), but now in the minor. Chrysothemis tells her sister the whole story in her customary three-four rhythm. (See No. 10). Two strangers, an old man and a younger, have brought the news to the palace:

Orestes has been dragged to death by his own horses in a chariot race. A young slave hurries through the courtyard, calling imperiously for a horse, the swiftest that can be had; he must fly with the long-desired news to Aegisthus, who is in the country.

For a while Elektra is stunned: she cannot bring herself to believe what she has heard. Then, recovering herself, she turns to Chrysothemis. They twain, she says, must do it, and here and now. Realising what this means, Chrysothemis shrinks from her sister in horror. She learns for the first time that Elektra has hidden the axe with which their father had been slain, hidden it for the day when Orestes should return and wield it. Now it is for the sisters to kill the Queen and her paramour with it — that very night, in their sleep. Elektra cannot do the double deed alone. Her long sufferings have weakened her: she will need the youthful strength of Chrysothemis to help her. Feverishly she implores that help; let Chrysothemis only give it, and Elektra will henceforth be her slave, living only for her happiness and that of her children. But the weaker spirit of Chrysothemis cannot rise to these heights of fury. With a final cry of " I cannot! " she runs into the house, followed by a curse from her sister.

5. Elektra's resolution is taken: since the others have failed her, she must and will do the deed alone. She goes to a place by the wall of the house, where she begins to dig, noiselessly, untiringly, like an animal, for the axe. After a while she seems to sense that she is not alone. She turns round and sees a figure by the gate, standing out in black relief against the expiring light: a wailing theme in the orchestra (see No. 12) announces him as the herald of woe. He tells Elektra, whom he takes to be one of the serving-maids, that he and another are the bearers of a message which they must deliver in person to the Queen. He tells the whole sad story to Elektra, to the accompaniment of the wailing figure just referred to:

He was the companion of Orestes, he says; they were of the same age. Orestes had perished before his eyes, trampled to death by his own horses. Elektra pours out her unendurable sorrow in one of the most moving passages of the opera. Why has this herald of misfortune come to her? Could he not trumpet the tidings to others, who would rejoice at it? "Thine eye stares at me, and the light of his is quenched. Thy mouth moves to and fro, and his is stopped with earth. Thou livest, and he, who was better and nobler a thousand times than thou, he is dead!"

Gravely the herald tells her that it was meet that Orestes should die, for the gods look with unfriendly eyes on one who rejoices in life as he had done. But Elektra laments once more that the child will never return to the house of his fathers, while those within it live out their foul life in safety and joy, and she herself is hideous and alone, like some miserable beast of the forest. The passion of her grief surprises the herald. Who can she be, he asks, that mourns like this over the death of Orestes and Agamemnon? Is she, perchance, of kindred blood with them? She tells him that she is the fatherless and brotherless Elektra, the oppressed of her mother and Aegisthus. The herald's heart melts within him as he looks on her wild eyes and wasted form. "Give ear to me," he says softly: "Orestes lives!" She bids him, in that case, rescue him before those who hate him can murder him. "By my father's corpse," he replies, "it is for that I have come hither!"

6. "Who then art thou?" she asks in wonderment; but before he can answer, an old servant, followed by three others, comes in from the courtyard, prostrates himself, and kisses the herald's feet, while the other three kiss his hands and the hem of his garment. "The very hounds in the courtyard know me," says the stranger softly, "but my sister not!" She gives a great cry of "Orestes!" and all her savagery falls from her in a moment. The music of the Recognition scene, which now follows, brings us the first grateful relaxation of the terrific tension of the last hour or more. Elektra forgets everything in the bliss of reunion, though Orestes, she fears, is only a vision that may fade away. The music of this great scene is based mainly on the theme of the Children of Agamemnon (No. 8) and a new motive, which may be called that of Elektra's ecstasy:

As in Sophocles and Euripides, she tells her brother the story of her sufferings at the hands of Clytemnestra and her dedication of herself to the one task of avenging her father. Orestes promises her that he will take the expiatory deed on himself, and she blesses him for the relief he has brought her. She becomes the possessed Maenad again as she sings a paean in honour of the man who can do what he has set his hand and his will to do, and on all who help him, who dig the axe and hold the torch and open the door for him. But the figure of an old man with fiery eyes suddenly appears in the doorway. It is the Tutor of Orestes, who bids him be silent, lest they betray themselves to those within before their work be done.

7. A servant with a torch appears in the doorway: behind her is the Confidante, who makes a sign to the two strangers to follow her within. Orestes and the Tutor do so, Orestes, with closed eyes, mastering his horror by a mighty effort. When the door has closed behind them, Elektra, who, on the appearance of the Confidante, had hidden herself in the shadows, runs to and fro like an excited animal again, crying out apprehensively, " They have gone, and I could not give him the axe! There are no gods in heaven! " But from within there comes a shriek from Clytemnestra. " Strike again! " cries Elektra; and there is a second shriek as the shade of the great King (No. 7) seems to rise in all its majesty in the orchestra.

The death-cries of Clytemnestra have aroused everyone. From another quarter Chrysothemis and a number of attendants come running towards the palace; but Elektra, standing with her back to the door, bars their way. They scatter distractedly as Aegisthus appears at the door on the right of the courtyard, shouting to the slaves to bring torches. A strange-looking figure, so wild that it affrights him, takes a torch from its socket, approaches him in the gloom, bows low before him, and offers to light him. He recognises Elektra, and eagerly asks where are the strangers who have come with the news of Orestes' death. They are inside, replies Elektra; they have found a friendly hostess, with whom they now make merry: they are, indeed, not merely expressing their joy in words but proving it by deeds. She accompanies him to the door with a great display of ironical deference; there is even a hint in her movements of the dance that will later celebrate his destruction.

He enters the house. A few moments of silence follow; then Aegisthus appears at a window, tearing back the curtain, and crying "Help! They are murdering your master!" He is dragged away, but reappears at the window, gives another anguished cry, and is torn away again.[2] To his shriek of "Does no one hear me?" Elektra answers jubilantly, "Agamemnon hears thee!" She stands in front of the house, almost insane with excitement. Chrysothemis and the women rush out, and the cry goes up that it is Orestes who has slain Aegisthus and the Queen, and that all within who loved the line of Agamemnon, drunk with joy, are fighting to the death with the slaves of Aegisthus. The women run off, leaving Chrysothemis alone with Elektra, to whom the sounds of slaughter within are heavenly music.

To the motive of her joy at the return of Orestes (No. 13) she sings that her great hour has come, the time for her to lead the dance. But her limbs are heavy, she laments, as she crouches on the threshold, while Chrysothemis, in growing excitement, tells how Mycenae seems transfigured, how men are weeping for joy, and the high gods have endowed them all with a new life. At last strength returns to Elektra. She sees herself as the instrument through which the gods have wrought their tardy justice, and she exults: the gods, she says, to a theme which has already been hinted at in an earlier scene between herself and Chrysothemis:

the gods go their own way through mortals like a sword-blade. She herself had sown the seeds of darkness and reaped a joy above all joys; and now whoso looks on her face must either die or dissolve in bliss. While the happy Chrysothemis runs into the house to embrace her brother,[3] Elektra, in whom reason has snapped through excess of happiness, flings back her head like a Maenad

[2] The Strauss-Hofmannsthal correspondence shows that the poet and the composer had some difficulty in deciding on the details of this episode. Strauss wanted Aegisthus to be killed in sight of the audience. The procedure finally agreed upon seems to have been a compromise.

[3] Orestes does not appear on the stage again after going into the palace.

and breaks into a wild dance, to the strains of No. 13, No. 14 and other leading motives. Chrysothemis reappears at the door, in the midst of a crowd of men and women, and calls to her sister by name. But Elektra bids them all be silent and join her in the dance; and once more motive is interwoven with motive in the complex tissue of the orchestra, till at length the theme of Elektra's hatred (No. 3), that of the shade of Agamemnon (No. 7), and that of Orestes (No. 5) come to the forefront together or in quick succession. As Chrysothemis runs to the door and beats on it with a wild cry of " Orestes! " and the orchestra thunders out for the last time the name of Agamemnon (No. 1), Elektra falls lifeless.

The natural sequel to an Elektra drama in antiquity was one in which Orestes, in his turn, was shown paying the penalty for his offence against the moral law in the murder of his mother. It is interesting to learn that in 1912 Hofmannsthal expressed the hope that Strauss would now write a symphonic poem on the subject of Orestes and the Furies. Apparently the music was to accompany a ballet, the scenario of which Hofmannsthal enclosed with his letter. " Think of Orestes as represented by Nijinsky, the greatest genius among mimes today! " Strauss's reply has not been published; but no doubt he was too full just then of his *Ariadne auf Naxos* to feel much interest in the world of Orestes and the Furies. When, a year or two later, he began to coquet with ballet, it was in connection with the less exacting subject of Joseph and Potiphar's wife.

Salome

RICHARD STRAUSS [1864–1949]

PRINCIPAL CHARACTERS

HEROD	*Tenor*
HERODIAS	*Mezzo-soprano*
SALOME [1]	*Soprano*
JOCHANAAN (JOHN THE BAPTIST)	*Baritone*
NARRABOTH	*Tenor*
HERODIAS' PAGE	*Contralto*

1

HE SALOME story is told in substantially the same way in the 14th chapter of St. Matthew and the 6th of St. Mark. The Tetrarch had married Herodias, "his brother Philip's wife." Herodias, furious at John the Baptist's denunciation of the union, would have had him put to death; but Herod shrank from doing so for the reason, among others, that he "feared the multitude," which "counted him as a prophet"; so John was put in prison. On the Tetrarch's birthday the daughter of Herodias by her former marriage so pleased Herod with her dancing that he swore an oath that he would give her whatever she might ask of him, "even unto the half of my kingdom." At the prompting of Herodias she demanded the head of the Baptist on a charger; and when she received it "the damsel gave it to her mother." In the Gospels there is no mention of "Salome" by name; she is simply "the daughter of Herodias."

The story, with its rich dramatic and psychological possibilities, had been a favourite with artists from at least the time of Rubens. In the 1870's Flaubert made it the theme of a short story, extend-

[1] The accent is on the second of the four syllables of "Jochanaan." "Salome" is accented on the first syllable.

ing the range of the characters and developing the interest of the milieu. Oscar Wilde became interested in the subject in the mid-eighties, probably through some pictures by Gustave Moreau, for whom the story had long had a curious fascination, and the discussion of these in Huysmans' novel À *Rebours* (1884). In Flaubert the instigator of the execution of the Baptist was still Herodias. In Wilde's play the central dramatic action and the psychological motives are a reversal of those in the Gospel story. It is Salome herself who paves the way for her dance, playing cunningly on the Tetrarch's crazy passion for her; and Herodias, far from willing or wishing her to dance for him, for a while does all she can to deter her. All this and more will become clearer to the reader in our analysis of the opera.

Wilde, who was equally at home in French and English, wrote his play, in 1884, in the former tongue; and good as the English version by Lord Alfred Douglas mostly is it lacks much of the special quality of the original. In June 1892 the play got as far as rehearsal in London, only to have a licence for its production refused by the Lord Chamberlain's office. A German production in Breslau in the winter of 1901 was followed by others in several German towns. The drama soon attracted the attention of Richard Strauss, and when, at a performance of the work in Max Reinhardt's Kleines Theater in Berlin, a friend remarked to him "This is a subject for you, Strauss," the composer could assure him that he was already engaged on the music for it. A Viennese poet, Anton Lindner, had sent him a copy of the play and offered to turn it into a "libretto" for him. But the specimens of his versification that Lindner sent him turned Strauss for a moment against the scheme; till one day the idea struck him, "Why not set Wilde's [prose] text very much as it stands?" As soon as he began to do so he realised how greatly superior, even as an opera text, Wilde's original was to anything in the conventional "libretto" line that Lindner or any other stage carpenter could fashion out of it. The subject took complete possession of him; and the score was finished on the 20th June 1905. A remark made by Strauss towards the end of his life seems to justify the surmise that he began by composing the Dance of the Seven Veils and the long closing scene, in which he follows the Wilde text practically word for word, whereas in the rest of the opera there are many excisions.

The Dance was certainly composed with an eye to separate publication and performance in the concert room, perhaps in the event of the opera never being completed or not proving a success. It is an obvious "inset" in the score, bearing a different plate mark from the latter. In the opera Strauss employed the usual numbers to indicate the bar groups for ease of identification in rehearsal. By the time the Dance was reached he had got as far as 247, and 248 does not appear until the Dance is over and the general stage action is resumed. The divisions in the Dance itself are indicated not by numbers but by letters.

2

Dresden was to undertake the first performance of the opera,[1] under Kapellmeister Ernst von Schuch, who had already been the first to give Strauss's *Feuersnot* and was later to have the credit of the premières of *Elektra* and *Der Rosenkavalier*. With the first piano rehearsal trouble began: singer after singer declared his or her part to be unsingable and wished to withdraw, until they were shamed into second thoughts on the matter by the declaration of the Herod (Burian) that he already knew his rôle by heart. Further difficulties arose in the course of rehearsals, the Salome (Frau Wittich) being so shocked by some of the producer's instructions that she cried out, "That I *won't* do; I am a respectable woman." But in spite of everything the opera was produced on the 9th December 1905, and though the wiseacres were confident that it would have a short life, as only one or two of the leading theatres could afford to produce a work calling for so large an orchestra and so many rehearsals, it quickly established itself in the German opera houses, notwithstanding the outcry of the puritans and the bigots everywhere. The clergy were loud in their denunciations of it; and as late as 1918 a proposed production in the Vienna Staatsoper had to be abandoned because of the opposition of an influential Austrian prelate who bore the perhaps not inapposite name of Archbishop Piffl. In New York the work was withdrawn after one performance at the instigation of "a certain Mr Morgan," as Strauss called him.[2]

[1] 9th December 1905.
[2] Strauss has given us an entertaining account of the early vicissitudes of the opera in his *Betrachtungen und Erinnerungen* (Zürich, 1949). The

The German operatic version of Wilde's text was made by Hedwig Lachmann, Strauss, we may take it for granted, indicating the cuts he desired. For the most part these are rational enough, consisting as they do merely of a condensation of Wilde's expansive and luxuriant imagery. This was necessary. For one thing, music generally moves at a more leisurely pace than speech; for another, the cumulative intensification achieved by the poet by a presentation of the same poetic image in varied forms can be done by music in a few pregnant bars; and for a third, the opera, like the play, had to be in one act, and there are limits to the concentration of which either singers or players or listeners are capable.

But the condensation, we feel, has occasionally been carried a little too far. Thus after one of the many attempts of the Page, in the opening scene, to bring reason into the Salome-infatuated mind of the young Syrian Narraboth, there comes, in Wilde, a fairly long discussion, by the two soldiers, "the Nubian" and "the Cappadocian," of the Tetrarch, Herodias, and the gods of various countries. The Nubian tells of the insatiable blood lust of the gods of his people; "twice in the year we sacrifice to them fifty young men and a hundred maidens; but I am afraid that we never give them quite enough, for they are very harsh to us." The Cappadocian fears that in his country there are no gods left: the Romans must have driven them out; the people seek for them in the mountains but cannot find them; they call them by name but they do not come. The soldiers say that the Jews "worship a God that one cannot see . . . in fact, they only believe in things that one cannot see. . . . That seems to me altogether ridiculous." It is *then* that the voice of Jokanaan is heard from the cistern, prophesying the coming of one mightier than himself: "when he cometh the solitary places shall be glad: they shall blossom as the rose. . . ." In the opera the appositeness of this cry from the

---

Kaiser sanctioned a production in Berlin only after the Intendant, his Excellency Georg Hülsen-Haeseler, had had the bright idea of bringing the star of Bethlehem into the sky at the finish, to signify the coming of the three Magi. Strauss has told us that the only opera of his ever attended by the Kaiser was *Der Rosenkavalier*, which the Crown Prince persuaded him to hear—once. The verdict of the royal and imperial mountebank on the work was, "Det is keene Musik für mich."

depths is weakened by the elimination of the preceding conversation between the soldiers, the Nubian and the Cappadocian; Jokanaan's annunciation of *the* new religion comes in quite unmotivated after the Page's despairing appeal to Narraboth, "You must not look at her: you look too much at her."

3

The strange thing is that a dramatist whose mind had no roots in music, and who had not the smallest notion of calling in music's co-operation when writing his play, should have constructed it on lines so very accommodating to music as was the case with Wilde and his *Salome*. He himself, in the *De Profundis* of his last years, made the curious observation that the "recurring *motifs*" of his *Salome* made the play "like a piece of music" and "bound it together as a ballad." By "*motifs*," of course, he does not mean what musicians do by that word; but in a way this remark of his goes to the heart of the matter; his method of insistent repetition not only of dramatic points but also of key phrases has been of cardinal assistance to Strauss in the designing of his musical pattern. Again, the lay-out of the play gave the composer all he could have desired in the way of tensions, relaxations and climaxes. There are three gradual ascents to a climax, each of these latter striking a more stunning blow than its predecessor. The first occurs when Salome conceives her morbid passion for the body of Jokanaan; in her great scena (as our fathers would have called it), for the first time in the opera music is given its head. The second occurs when Jokanaan, after his last opprobrious denunciation of Salome, goes down again into the cistern; this, following on the suicide of Narraboth, is, we instinctively sense, a turning-point of the drama. The third climax comes with the slow crescendo of horror that extends from Salome's cunningly engineered dance to the snapping of the last link of sanity in her brain. All this is of the very stuff that music needs for its own purposes; in each successive climax the composer unleashes more and more of the harmonic and orchestral resources of the art. He seizes unerringly on the smallest opportunity for this deployment of modern musical effect. In the section of Wilde's play that corresponds to the second of the two climaxes just mentioned, all we get is this:

Salome: I will kiss thy mouth, Jokanaan.

Jokanaan: I will not look at thee. Thou art accursed, Salome, thou art accursed. (*He goes down into the cistern.*)

Salome: I will kiss thy mouth, Jokanaan, I will kiss thy mouth.

There follow a few lines of everyday comment by the Soldiers and a short lament of the little Page for his dear dead Narraboth; then Herod and the others come up to the terrace from the banqueting hall.

Our first feeling, on comparing the prose play with the opera at this point, is one of regret that Strauss should have cut out the pathetic little threnody of the Page over the body of Narraboth. This lament is the last fine strand in a delicate minor motif that has been weaving in and out of the tissue of the action from the beginning; and we feel that music could have done so much with it! Nevertheless Strauss was on the whole wise in keeping the Narraboth-Page motif rather in the background throughout, and more especially in denying himself the obvious opportunity for a lament, in music's poignant vein, at the finish of it. Wilde's laconic "He goes down into the cistern" becomes in the opera the legitimate pretext for a purely orchestral interlude in which Strauss plays, first furiously, then in a spirit of sinister foreboding, upon the main motifs of Salome and Jochanaan, for nearly thirteen pages of the score. At the end of it Herod and Herodias come upon the scene, and the drama becomes vocal and visible again.

The outcry against *Salome* on the ground of its "morbidity," "perversity," "immorality" and what not came from people constitutionally unable to distinguish between art and life. The artistically minded man has no more fear as to the possible effects of this "perversity" upon the everyday life of the ordinary citizen than he has of an epidemic of lying and treachery after an evening with Iago or a rise in the domestic murder statistics after a few hours of Othello. Other poets before Oscar Wilde had shown us what happens when the female mind, prone at times to perversities of sexual emotion and hysteria, escapes for a while from the ordinary restraints upon conduct imposed by social convention: we have notable examples of the genre in *The Bacchae* of Euripides and the *Penthesilea* of Kleist. The poets have always been ahead of the ordinary run of mankind in their intuitions, and in the case of *Salome* all that Wilde did was to anticipate some of the darker pages of the case books of the psychiatrists. He himself, in *The Critic as Artist* (1890), had rightly claimed the liberty of the modern artist to probe the darkest and socially most distasteful recesses of the human mind. ". . . There is still much to be done in the sphere of introspection," he makes his mouthpiece Gilbert say in the dialogue. "People sometimes say that fiction is getting too morbid. As far as psychology is concerned, it has never been morbid enough. We have merely touched the surface of the soul, that is all. In one single ivory cell of the brain there are stored away things more marvellous and more terrible than even they have dreamed of who, like the author of *Le Rouge et Le Noir*, have sought to track the soul into its most secret places, and to make life confess its dearest sins."

4

In most of the creations of art that really matter it is not so much a case of the great artist suddenly finding his subject as that of the subject finding him, and that at the right moment. His rôle, at first, has been passive rather than active: forces are at work within him of which he himself is unconscious at the time, or only vaguely conscious. It was so with Wagner when in 1857 he felt an irresistible inner compulsion to lay aside *Siegfried* and embark upon *Tristan*. The ultimate determining cause of this resolution was a vast fund of musical emotion that had been silently accumulating within him for a long time, and for which the saga-world of the *Ring* provided no psychological outlet. He himself has told us again and again that the conception of each of his works was primarily a musical one; the Wagnerian "text" which is still regarded by the generality as a "setting" of a "libretto" was only the objectivation of this vaguely *musical* mood in speech and stage action. By routes less clearly traceable many another musical work has similarly come into being, the subconscious musical urge preceding the reaching out into the world of the concrete. Strauss himself has told us how some of his songs, and those the best, came into being—not through the sudden impact of a poem that struck him as good raw material for a "setting," but through the chance falling into his hands one day of some poem or other that instantaneously crystallised a vague musical mood that had long been stirring dimly within him. He described the psychological process in a communication to Friedrich von Hausegger in 1903, *à propos* of his songs in general. For some time, he said, he would be without any impulse to compose. Then, one evening, he would be turning over the leaves of a volume of poetry; a poem would arrest his attention, he would read it through, it would chime with the mood he was in, and at once the music would fit itself to the words. He had been in an indefinite musical mood, and all that had hitherto been lacking to him for the creation of a song was a poem that would give this mood verbal definition. When this process was in ideal working order a good song resulted: when the process was reversed, or when the poem turned out to be not wholly consubstantial with the mood, he had to call consciously upon the devices of his craft as a substitute for the subconscious urge, and then the results were less good: the song, he himself knew, was made, not born. There are other routes, of course, by which this composer or that may reach the point at which the musical and the verbal impulses within him become fused into one. But the route here outlined is one made familiar to us by all the great modern musicians: the whole, however dimly sensed at first, has preceded the parts. In Pascal's memorable phrase, "You would not have sought me had you not already found me."

Strauss has told us, *à propos* of the genesis of *Salome*, that for a long time he had been dissatisfied with the current operas on Jewish or Oriental subjects, feeling that they were lacking in true eastern colour and fire. In the case of *Salome*, he said, sheer necessity imposed an exotic harmony on him, finding expression more particularly in strange cadences resembling shot silk; at the same time the need for sharp distinctions in character-painting led him to bi-tonality, for it was impossible for him to be satisfied with the simple rhythmical characterisation with which Mozart had achieved such wonders. He recognized, however, that a work like *Salome* was a once-for-all experiment, generated and determined by a particular subject and consequently not to be recommended for imitation by either himself or any one else. He himself was just ripe for such an experiment in 1905. Between 1888 and 1898 he had produced the majority of the orchestral works on which his reputation in this field now reposes—*Don*

Juan, Macbeth, Till Eulenspiegel's Merry Pranks, Also sprach Zarathustra, Don Quixote and *Ein Heldenleben.* (The *Symphonia Domestica* of 1903 already marked a decline in inspiration.) In these remarkable works, and especially in *Don Quixote* and *Ein Heldenleben,* he had endowed the symphonic poem with a new vision and a new language. With opera he had not been so successful. There is a great deal in the high-minded *Guntram* of 1892–1893—written when he was about twenty-eight—that will always command the respect of the thoughtful; but spiritually and musically the work floated mostly in the Wagnerian waters. The *Feuersnot* of 1900–1901 showed him still not in full command of his powers in opera. It was in *Salome* that for the first time he could utilise for dramatic purposes the riches he had mined for himself in the great series of orchestral works, and, indeed, add to them. He was still not wholly at his ease: he could not quite transport himself into such a character as Jochanaan or bring a Herod always to musical life; [1] but Salome herself is a unique creation, and the orchestra performs miracles of characterisation and pictorial suggestion throughout.

5

The opera is scored for a very large orchestra, that includes six horns, four trumpets, four trombones and bass tuba, five kettledrums, an E flat clarinet, a bass clarinet, a celesta, a heckelphone,[2] an organ, a harmonium and a large array of percussion

---

[1] Strauss as a musical psychologist was most at home with characters either emotionally complex or super-charged—such as Salome, Elektra, the Marschallin, Don Juan—or with a bizarre kink in them, such as Till Eulenspiegel, Don Quixote and Sancho Panza. With characters on a normal plane he was less at ease; his Chrysothemis is a good example of this. He could respect his Jochanaan, but could not depict him with perfect understanding or perhaps with complete sympathy. He had a similar difficulty with the virtuous hero of *The Legend of Joseph.* "*Joseph* is not getting on as quickly as I thought it would," he wrote plaintively to his librettist Hofmannsthal in September 1912. "The chaste Joseph himself is hardly in my line, and I find it difficult to write music for a character that bores me; a God-fearing Joseph like this I find infernally hard to tackle. However, I may yet find lurking in some queer ancestral corner of my nature some pious melody that will do for our good Joseph."

[2] A baritone oboe, sounding an octave lower than written, invented by the

instruments. The string specification is for sixteen first violins, sixteen seconds, ten or twelve violas, ten violoncellos and eight double basses. Strauss, however, did not always insist on this huge apparatus, and he tells us of a good performance he heard of the work in Innsbruck with an orchestra of no more than fifty-six.

Singers and producers would do well to ponder what the composer has to say about the right way to perform *Salome*. He disliked the over-emphasis in which most players of the part of Salome think it the correct thing to indulge: what he had seen and heard in the way of Salome writhings and mouthings in a misguided effort to be "exotic" filled him with disgust. "Anyone who has been in the East," he said, "and observed the decency of the women there, will realise that the part of Salome, a chaste maiden, an oriental princess, should be played with gestures of the simplest, most distinguished kind. . . . Her shipwreck on her first contact with the marvellous external world should stir us to pity, not merely to horror and terror." Our Salomes might take this admonition to heart; the Dance of the Seven Veils in particular should not suggest to us, as it too often does, merely the Dance of the Seven Dials. Producers and stage designers and costumiers too should give up the notion that the opera is there simply as an exhibition ground for their own vulgarities and inanities of "effect." All that is required in the way of fury, pathological passion, perversity and madness, Strauss contended, is in the orchestra. It is quite unnecessary, even if it were at all possible, to duplicate all this on the stage. "The acting of the characters should aim at *the utmost simplicity*," he said; the player of the neurasthenic Herod in particular should bear in mind that even in his moments of wildest aberration the oriental parvenu in him makes him try, before his Roman guests, to copy the dignified bearing of great Caesar in Rome. "To rage and rave simultaneously on the stage and in front of the stage is really too much! The orchestra does all that is necessary in that respect!"

There are many recurrent themes in the opera, but they are not used as motifs in the Wagnerian sense of that term; they do not

German instrument maker Heckel in the late 1880's. It has not succeeded in establishing itself in the ordinary orchestra. Strauss must have been one of the first composers to employ it.

change with the changing psychology and experiences of the characters, but remain essentially the same throughout. Each of them, of course, is characteristic of this person or that, and some of them manifestly have a particular psychological application; but it is frequently impossible for us to say whether a given motif used on a particular occasion refers to, say, Salome, or Jochanaan, or Jochanaan seen just then through the eyes of Salome, or Salome seen just then through the eyes of Jochanaan. Broadly speaking, Strauss employs whichever of his many motifs will best suit his general musical purpose at this moment or that. Quotation on the small scale possible in a book like this is difficult; it would often mean not only an elaborate exposition of the complex harmonies but citation in full score, showing the effects produced by the disposition of the orchestral colours. The most the analyst can do is to provide the reader with a few of the more characteristic motifs to keep in his mind as he listens to a performance; but he must remember that none of the passages quoted here have anything like the same sound or the same psychological nuance on his piano as they have in Strauss's orchestra. These quotations have about the same relation to the total tone-complex as a bone or two of a skeleton has to the living man.

6

As in the case of *Elektra*, there is no overture to the opera. There is merely a swift upward run in a clarinet:

1

which at A takes a shape associated in various ways with Salome later; and the curtain rises disclosing a broad terrace in Herod's palace. On the right there is a great staircase, and towards the background, somewhat to the left, an old cistern encased in green bronze. Some soldiers are leaning over the balcony of the terrace. This latter is supposed to be set above the banqueting hall, where, as we shall learn shortly, the upstart Herod Antipas, Tetrarch of

Judaea, is entertaining at dinner some envoys of the mighty Roman Caesar with whom he is anxious to ingratiate himself. In the company also are a number of Jewish zealots who from time to time quarrel violently over sectarian points of doctrine. It is night. Over the terrace the moon shines very brightly.

In the foreground stands a young Syrian, Narraboth, whom Herod has only lately appointed captain of the guard, and a little Page of Herodias, who has a dog-like affection for him. Narraboth's gaze is fixed on the banqueting hall, for he is in love with Salome. "How beautiful is the Princess Salome tonight!" he says: and we hear in the 'cellos a motif characterising his longing:

2

Towards the end of it (bars three and four of our quotation) the bass clarinet strikes in with sombre foreboding. The Page senses something eerie in the air: "Look at the moon's disc," he says; "how strange it looks! It is like a dead woman rising from a tomb." For the infatuated Narraboth it carries a different suggestion: "It is indeed strange: it is like a little princess who has white doves for feet: one might fancy she was dancing." In his enraptured eyes the white moon and the exquisite maidenhood of the little Salome are always one.[1]

7

Suddenly, as the tempo quickens, a horrid orchestral dissonance rends the air, while from the banqueting hall comes a confused uproar; the Jews have lost their tempers and the rival sects are

[1] The character of Salome becomes utterly nonsensical when it is played by a buxom, hard-bitten soprano in the prime of life. The composer, of course, has asked, as composers so often do, for the impossible—"a sixteen-years-old princess with an Isolde voice," as Strauss has expressed it, that can cut through or soar above the heaviest orchestration. But the spectator should try, in spite of all optical discouragements, to see the daughter of Herodias as little more than a child, as yet ignorant of the complex realities of the world.

trying to shout each other down. Oboes and strings snarl and snap at one another:

3

The double bassoon angrily lays down the law, while the double basses insist on their own doctrine:

4

Strauss's direction for the double bass figure (bar 2) each time it recurs is "howling." So the snapping and bellowing and screeching goes on all over the orchestra; we shall hear more of it at a later stage of the drama. The soldiers comment on it all with cynical detachment: "What a din! Who are these howling wild beasts? . . . It's the Jews; they are always like this, quarrelling over their religion. . . . I think it is ridiculous to wrangle about such things." [1]

Regardless of the tumult within, the infatuated Narraboth, who has never taken his eyes off Salome, breaks into a lyrical strain in praise of her beauty:

5

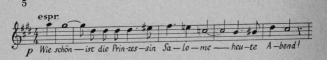

The Page's fears of what is in the air are rising; to a phrase that is often repeated:

[1] Wilde's text specifies the main doctrinal point at issue: "The Pharisees say that there are angels, and the Sadducees declare that angels do not exist."

Du siehst sie im—mer an

he warns the Syrian that it is dangerous to look at Salome so much. But Narraboth merely continues his rhapsody: never has he seen her so pale, he says; she is like the shadow of a white rose in a silver mirror; and once more the anxious little Page warns him that no good can come of this infatuation of his. Meanwhile the Soldiers discuss Herod. He is gloomy tonight, they say; his eyes are fixed on someone, but they cannot see whom. No. 1 in the smooth tones of the clarinet tells us who it is.

As the Page again (No. 6) expresses his anxiety about Narraboth the mood of the music suddenly softens and broadens, and from the cistern the grave voice of Jochanaan is heard, calmly prophesying the coming of One mightier than himself, the latchet of hose shoes he is unworthy to unloose; when He comes the desert places shall be glad and blossom like the rose, the eyes of the blind shall see, the ears of the deaf shall hear. As we have seen, Strauss and his librettist go straight to this point, omitting the discussion by the soldiers, a Nubian and a Cappadocian, of the gods of this country and that. Various themes are allotted to Jochanaan, such as:

7

which often broadens out into the following and cognate forms:

8

Other themes associated with him will be referred to later. They are not motifs in the fullest sense of the word, for such modifications as they are subjected to from time to time are not dictated by any inner change in him, any new reaction to his environment. He is a static character—a personality indeed, but one playing only a passive part in the dramatic action that envelops him. He is ultimately of importance not so much in himself as in the medley of emotions he arouses in the soul of Salome.

One of the Soldiers is for silencing him, for he is weary of this railing fanatic. But the other has a tender feeling for him: he is a Prophet named Jochanaan, he explains, a gentle being, who thanks the Soldier each day when he takes him his food. He comes from the desert, where he was clothed in camels' hair, fed on locusts and wild honey, and had a band of disciples: the Soldier confesses, however, that no one can understand the things he says.[1] The Tetrarch will allow no one to see him. (It is Salome's insistence on seeing him—the insistence of a spoiled child—that generates the whole tragic action of the play and of the opera.)

8

Since the entry of the voice of Jochanaan the music has been subdued in tone and colour. It now suddenly flares up again as the clarinets give out No. 1 once more, and Narraboth, whose eyes have never left the banqueting hall, cries out that the Princess has risen from her seat at the table: she is very agitated; now she is coming out, looking like a dove that has strayed. (Always the poet's imagery insists on her whiteness, her fragility, the suggestion she conveys of belonging to another and less crudely material world.) No. 1 sings out yet again in an expanded form in oboes and violins:

9

Molto allegro ♩ = 76

---

[1] In the play we learn much more about the matter from the conversation of the Soldiers and an enquiring Cappadocian at this point. In this very cistern the Tetrarch's elder brother, the first husband of Herodias, had been imprisoned for twelve years: then Herod sent the death ring to the executioner—a gigantic negro, Naaman, standing on one side of the stage—who strangled the prisoner. No doubt Strauss, for reasons of time-economy, had

as Salome enters hurriedly. When she begins to speak she is not addressing the people on the terrace but communing with herself. She could no longer endure the banquet, she says. Why does the Tetrarch, her mother's husband, keep looking at her so strangely with those little eyes of his that are like a mole's eyes under their twitching lids? How sweet the air is out here! Here she can breathe! and the violins, doubled by the silvery tones of the celesta, give out a suave melody that will become of great importance later:

10

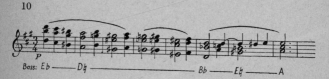

Bass: Eb —— D♮ ———————— Bb —— E♮ —— A

She can stand no more of those Jews from Jerusalem, who tear each other to pieces over their ridiculous observances—here the cackling No. 3 is heard again in the orchestra—or the silent, subtle Egyptians, or the brutal, boorish Romans with their uncouth speech. "How I hate these Romans! How good it is to gaze into the moon, that is like a silver flower, cold and chaste, beautiful as a virgin unspotted!" At one point in her monologue the Page once more addresses an anxious admonition to the Syrian—"Why do you look at her so? Something terrible will happen!"

With a sudden change of key and a slowing of the tempo the deep voice of Jochanaan rings out again from the cistern: "Behold the Lord hath come. The Son of Man is at hand." It rouses Salome from her brooding. "Who was that who cried out?" she asks. "The Prophet," the second Soldier tells her. "Ah!" she says, "he of whom the Tetrarch goes in fear." Narraboth steps forward and asks if he may send for her litter, for the night is fair in the garden. She does not hear him. "He says terrible things about my mother, does he not?" she asks. The Soldier answers evasively;

---

to omit all this, but it is not only of importance to our understanding of the action but has a peculiar significance later, when the dazed Tetrarch, yielding to the importunities of Salome, passively allows Herodias to draw the death ring from his finger and transmit it to the executioner.

and just then a slave enters with a command to her from Herod to return to the banquet. She brushes him aside with a blunt refusal, then asks the Soldier, "Is this Prophet an old man?" Narraboth, sensing evil in the air, urgently begs her to allow him to conduct her back to the hall; but she ignores him, and with a rise of tone asks once more if this Prophet is an old man. No, she is told, he is quite young. Once more the grave voice is heard from the cistern, bidding the land of Palestine not to rejoice because the rod of him who smote it is broken; for from the seed of the serpent will come a basilisk, and its brood will devour the birds.

9

The strangeness of the voice and the enigma of its message impress Salome: she would speak with this man, she says. The second Soldier, in great agitation, tells her that the Tetrarch has commanded that no one, not even the High Priest, shall speak with him. Her only reply is, "I will speak with him! Bring this Prophet forth!" The slave who had brought the message from Herod returns to the hall. The embarrassed Soldiers try to turn Salome from her purpose, but she is inflexible. She goes over to the cistern and peers down into its recesses. The orchestra depicts for us, in a way that no words can do, the horror of what she sees. A prolonged unison tremolo on E flat in the strings, playing *sul ponticello*, is full of grisly suggestion; underneath it some chords in the lower brass suggest the very depths of darkness, and a sombre phrase projects itself serpent-wise in the bass clarinet as Salome says to herself, "How black it is down there! It must be terrible to live in so black a hole! It is like a tomb!" Then she turns upon the Soldiers, and, with mounting anger at being frustrated, again commands them to bring the Prophet out that she may look at him. They dare not, they tell her. In Wilde's play they add a significant line and there is a stage direction both of which Strauss and his librettist unaccountably ignore: "and indeed," they say, "it is not of us that you should ask this thing," whereupon Salome, ejaculating "Ah!", looks meaningly at the young Syrian, of whose infatuation with her she is evidently aware. The little Page, acutely sensitive to what is coming, moans "Oh! what is going to happen? I know that something terrible will happen!" It is a pity that throughout this opening scene of the opera this motive of the Page's love for the Syrian and his apprehensiveness on his account go for practically nothing with the average audience, whereas it should all contribute to the gradual building up of the horror that has been stealing over the action from the commencement.

To the accompaniment of No. 9 Salome now approaches Narraboth and begins to weave her spells about him. He will do this for her, she tells him in cajoling tones, for she has always been kind to him. She wants nothing more than just to see this Prophet of whom she has heard so much, among others from the Tetrarch, who appears to be afraid of him. With increasing distress Narraboth protests that the Tetrarch has forbidden that anyone shall raise the cover of the cistern, and he dare not disobey. With the artfulness of a spoilt child she plays on what she has divined to be his weakness: if he will do just this one thing for her now, tomorrow when she passes him in her litter she will throw him a little flower and smile at him through her muslin veils. "Look at me, Narraboth. Thou knowest that thou wilt do this that I ask of thee."

At last his resolution breaks down: he makes a sign to the soldiers and gives the curt command—"Let the Prophet come forth. The Princess Salome desires to see him." There is a terrifying crescendo and diminuendo in the orchestra, and a triumphant cry of "Ah!" from Salome.

10

The third Soldier goes down into the cistern, and necessarily there has to follow now a brief interval in the stage action before Jochanaan appears, an interval that should contain something that will make it clear to us that the first decisive moment of the drama has arrived, and that it is pregnant with disaster. The poet and the musician achieve this in different ways. Wilde does it through the Page, the young Syrian—and the moon. This last is almost a character in the work, certainly a symbol, and the ordinary opera producer does not sufficiently avail himself of the opportunities with which it provides him; perhaps he has never comprehended them. The aspect of the moon changes with

the psychological changes in the drama. As we have seen, it
figures at the opening as the symbol of super-terrestrial whiteness
and purity, an aspect of it which both Narraboth and the Page
instinctively associate with the young Salome they have so far
known. But now, when the action takes on a definitely darker
tinge, the face of the moon changes, and the Page and Narraboth
are nervously sensitive to it. "How strange the moon looks!"
says the former; "like the hand of a dead woman who is seeking
to cover herself with a shroud." "She has a strange aspect,"
Narraboth agrees, with his dazed mind still running on Salome:
"she is like a little princess whose eyes are of amber. Through the
clouds of muslin she is smiling like a little princess." Then the
Prophet comes out of the cistern. All this in only a matter of a
minute or two in the play.

But the musician has other and far greater resources at his disposal for a situation of this kind than the poet. He can rack our
nerves with orchestral effects that are beyond the capacity of
words; and music, by its reiterations of motifs and metamorphoses
of them, can set our imagination looking before and after in a way
that spoken drama cannot do, though the great Greek tragedians
—notably Aeschylus in the *Agamemnon*—divined something of
the secret of this technique of reminiscence and foreboding in
drama, and made fine use of it.[1] To fill in the time and space
between the departure of the Soldier and the appearance of
Jochanaan, Strauss writes an orchestral interlude, the characters
on the stage being immobilised for a while in tense expectancy.
The sinister depths of the cistern are once more brought almost
visibly before us. One of the Jochanaan motifs (No. 7A) appears
in a relatively new form:

[1] They were helped, of course, by the fact that their drama dealt with
myths and legends the details of which were known to their audiences, so
that a seemingly-casual remark made by a character in the earlier stages of
a play would instantly flash upon the spectator's mind the tragic dénouement
of the story, and vice versa. The opening speech of the Watchman in the
Agamemnon is a case in point. Half in hope, half in dim fear, he is waiting,
as he has done for a year, for the beacon light that will announce the fall of
Troy and the home-coming of Agamemnon. The Greek audience, knowing
the tragic end of the great King, would fill with a more definite and more
tragic meaning that vague suggestion of fear in the Watchman.

11

Salome too has a new theme that will play a large part in the later stages of the opera:

12

and as Jochanaan at last comes up into view we hear over a string tremolo a new motif in oboes, cor anglais, heckelphone and flutes in octaves, expressive of his sense of the dignity of his mission:

13

11

Salome recoils at the sight of him. He comes slowly forward to the melody first suggested in our No. 7, with which the dignified No. 13 soon becomes interlocked. With a new vehemence he denounces both Herod and Herodias, especially the latter, whose abominations cry out to heaven for chastisement. It gradually dawns on Salome that it is her mother of whom he is speaking. "He is terrible, he is truly terrible!" she murmurs, while the clarinets and a solo violin sing softly a melody that will figure largely in the score henceforth:

14

It suggests the curious interest already inspired in her by this Prophet of retribution, the strange fascination he is beginning to exercise over her. His fanatical eyes are especially terrible; to Salome they look like "the black caverns that are the lair of dragons, black lakes played upon fantastically by the light of the moon." And how emaciated and blanched he is! Her thoughts begin to take on a pathologically sensual tinge: "He is like an ivory statue. Surely he is as chaste as the moon! His flesh must be very cold, cold as ivory! I would look closer at him!"

She pays no heed to the young Syrian's despairing entreaties that she will come away. Jochanaan's attention now becomes fixed on her. Who is this woman, he asks, with golden eyes under gilded eyelids? He does not know who she is. He will not know who she is. Let her begone. "I am Salome, daughter of Herodias, Princess of Judaea," she tells him, to the accompaniment of the motif shown in No. 9. To his renewed objurgations of her mother she merely replies, "Speak again, Jochanaan! Thy voice is as music in mine ear. Tell me what it is I must do." He bids her veil her face and scatter ashes on her head and go into the desert seeking the Son of Man. The meaning of his words evades her. "Who is this Son of Man?" she asks him; "is he as beautiful as thou art?" Again he warns her that he can hear within the palace the beating of the wings of the angel of death.[1]

But Salome is now completely dominated by her perverse passion. For the first time in the opera music is given its full wing; Strauss launches Salome upon a long lyrical scena in which she indulges herself in every variety of sensual image in praise of this strange wasted figure: "Thy body is as white as lilies in a field the mower has never mowed, white as the snows on the mountains of Judaea, whiter than the roses in the garden of the Queen of Arabia, than the feet of the dawn on the leaves, than the breast of the moon reposing on the sea. Suffer me to touch thy body!"

Salome sings the opening words of her long monologue— "Jochanaan, I am amorous of thy body"—to the accompaniment of the ingratiating No. 14 in a solo violin and clarinet: it merges, at the words "Thy body is as white as the snows on the mountains

---

[1] "Though the day of him [Herod] who shall die in a robe of silver has not yet come," the play adds. Strauss does not set this line.

of Judaea," into a motif which had better be quoted here in the more extended form it will assume towards the end of the opera:

15

At "Suffer me to touch thy body" we come upon one of those many motifs of the precise application of which we cannot be sure. Obviously derived, in part, from our No. 7, it now steals softly upwards (the marking is "espressivo") in the bassoons and 'cellos:

16

Strauss uses it indifferently to accompany now Salome now Jochanaan.

He repulses her with contumely: through woman came evil into the world: he will not listen to her: he will hearken only to the voice of his God. (Here No. 8 rises majestically in the orchestra.) In an instant her mood changes; now she sees him only as foul and abhorrent. His body is hideous, she declares, as hideous as the body of a leper: it is like a plastered wall in which scorpions have made their nest, like a whited sepulchre full of loathsome things. Graphically suggestive of the transition in her from fascination to repulsion is a harmonic and colouristic transformation of the insinuating No. 14 A:

17

The motif is given to the violins playing "col legno," [1] while the muted violas slither down eerily in two-part harmonies—"like a smear" is Strauss's prescription in the score.

Salome's mood softens again. It is his hair of which she is enamoured, she declares, to the accompaniment of No. 9. It is like clusters of black grapes on the vine-trees of Edom, like the great cedars of Lebanon in whose shade the lions lie and robbers hide; the long dark nights when the moon hides her face are not so black as his hair, nor the forest silence, nor anything in the world. This rhapsody she sings to the motif shown in our No. 10.

Jochanaan, to a combination of one of Salome's motifs (No. 1 A) and one of his own (No. 7 A), bids this "daughter of Sodom" leave him and not profane the temple of his God. This provokes another revulsion in her. His hair is now horrible to her, a mass of dust and mire, like a crown of thorns on his head, a knot of serpents round his neck. With mounting frenzy she tells him, to the accompaniment of a new motif:

18

that it is his mouth she desires, his mouth that is like a scarlet band on a tower of ivory, a pomegranate cut in twain with an ivory knife, and so on, pouring out a flood of images each more

[1] I.e. with the wood, not the hair, of the bow striking the strings. The effect is necessarily peculiar.

corruptly rapturous than the others, while the music lashes itself
into a tempest of passion. "Nothing in the world," she concludes,
"is as red as thy mouth. Suffer me to kiss thy mouth!"

Again he repulses and objurgates this "daughter of lewdness,"
but is impotent to check the torrent. The distracted Narraboth,
who has been watching her with horror, also tries to recall her to
reason, but him too she ignores. At last, tragically aware of the
consequences of having disobeyed the orders of the Tetrarch, he
can bear it no more: he stabs himself and falls dead between
Salome and Jochanaan.[1] The latter exhorts Salome to turn to
Him who alone can save her: He is to be found in a boat on the
Sea of Galilee, talking with His disciples; she is to kneel at His
feet and ask for remission of her sins.

12

The final stage of Salome's great scena is marked by repetition
after repetition, with ever-increasing frenzy, of the words "I will
kiss thy mouth, Jochanaan!" to a motif that will dominate the
last moments of the drama:

19

Molto animato ed appass:

Ich will dei-nen Mund küs — sen, Jo — cha — na — an

Hurling a final curse at Salome and her mother, Jochanaan goes
down again into the cistern to the accompaniment of the majestic

---

[1] In the play, as we have seen, there follows here a passionate lament by
the Page for his dead friend. Strauss omitted this, no doubt for the reasons,
among others, that it would have meant the addition of another leading
singer to the cast, and too long an interruption of the main stage action: it
would certainly have been difficult for the composer to chain the fury of his
music at this point and then, after the lapse of some minutes, unleash it
again. But Wilde, from the dramatist's no less than from the poet's point of
view, was right. The audience should be made to realise, as in the play, that
the death of Narraboth signalises the beginning of the catastrophe that has
been overhanging the action from the commencement. In the opera the
suicide goes for practically nothing; it is doubtful, indeed, whether the
average spectator so much as notices it, for his attention is likely to be concentrated just then on Salome and her final frantic cry of "Suffer me to kiss
thy mouth, Jochanaan!"

No. 13; and Strauss seizes the opportunity, before the entry of the other characters on the scene, to give his orchestra its head once more, the stage action being immobilized for a few minutes. This incandescent interlude is built up of repetitions and contrapuntal combinations of several motifs now familiar to us, in particular Nos. 8, 11, 13, 14, 15 and 19. At last the music dies down into a long shuddering tremolando in the strings, which leads in time into a sudden outburst of the cackling, snarling No. 3 in the wood wind and violins; for now Herod and Herodias and their company have come upon the scene—including the Jews, who are straining at the leash for an excuse for resuming their cantankerous religious debate. That excuse will soon come, owing to an injudicious remark let fall by the Tetrarch.

Herod is a neurasthenic, beset by fears of all kinds, and just now flown with wine: his indecision is curiously suggested by a succession of slithering whole-tone progressions in one instrument after another, including even the bass tuba:

He has come primarily to look for Salome. Where is she? he asks; why did she not return to the banquet as he had commanded? He catches sight of her, but immediately forgets her, for now he is out under the night sky he is neurotically conscious of something sinister in the air. The moon, he finds, has a strange look, "like a naked mad woman seeking everywhere for lovers." Herodias, drily, contemptuously, informs him that the moon is as it always is, just the moon. She would have him go back to the banqueting hall; she particularly resents his looking at Salome as he does. But he orders torches to be brought out, and tables of jasper and tables of ivory; he will drink again in honour of Caesar's ambassadors. He stumbles, finds he has slipped on blood—"an ill omen" —and sees the body of the captain of the guard. How did this happen? he asks querulously; "I gave no orders that he should be slain." The Soldiers tell him of Narraboth's suicide, and he orders the body to be taken away. Suddenly he feels cold; there is a great wind blowing, he insists—as indeed there is in the orchestra—and he hears the beating of mighty wings, a remark to which a fateful significance is given by a quiet upsurge of the Prophet's motif (No. 13) in horns, cor anglais and heckelphone.

He denies that he is sick, as Herodias says: it is her daughter who is sick to death; never has he seen her look so pale. Now his whole thought becomes concentrated on Salome. So far the music allotted to him has been of the declamatory kind, the orchestra supplying the atmosphere of the scene; in general, indeed, the part calls for a great actor rather than an accomplished singer. But now, his wine-cup having been replenished, he becomes for a while fluently lyrical after his fashion as he urges Salome to drink with him:

21

Sa — lo-me, komm, trink Wein — mit mir.

"I am not thirsty, Tetrarch," she mutters in low, sombre tones. He tempts her with fruit; he would like to see her little white teeth biting into it; and a curious figure:

22

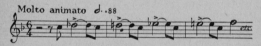

glides in and out in the violins (in octaves) and wood wind. (It will take on a horrible suggestiveness towards the end of the opera, where Salome, with the severed head before her, gloats over the idea of at last kissing the mouth of Jochanaan as if she were "biting into a ripe fruit.") "I am not hungry, Tetrarch," she replies quietly. He renews his entreaties; she must sit beside him; he will place her on her mother's throne. "I am not tired, Tetrarch," is her only reply.

13

From the depths of the cistern comes the voice of the Prophet, announcing that the day he had foretold is at last at hand. Herodias angrily asks Herod to silence this scurrilous fanatic: why does he not hand him over to the Jews, who for months have been clamouring to have him thrown to them? Herod refuses, for this, he says, "is a holy man; he is a man who has seen God." This rouses a tempest among the Jews. No one has seen God since Elias, shouts one. Perhaps, another replies, Elias did not really see God, but only His shadow. In a moment the rival sects and zealots are at each other's throats again, with No. 3 in the fore-front of the fray. Strauss builds up a long ensemble that is an astonishing musical *tour de force*. Dogma is flung in the teeth of dogma, tempers rise, and when the voice of Jochanaan adds fuel to the fire by proclaiming that he hears upon the mountains the feet of Him who shall be the Saviour of the world, and a Roman opines that this must mean Caesar, and some Nazarenes contend that it means "Messias, who hath come" and who has performed miracles in Galilee and is now in Samaria, and the Jews protest that if He is in Samaria He cannot be Messias, for it is not to the accursed Samaritans that Messias shall come, the theological pot boils over.

The turmoil is gradually dominated by the voice of Jochanaan heaping fresh curses from the cistern on Herodias and prophesy-ing a fearful end for her. Herodias, whose demeanour since the beginning of the scene has been for the most part one of dry detachment, for she feels an equal contempt for this drunken husband of hers who was once a camel-driver, for the Romans, and for the Jews, now begins to lose her self-control under this stream of abuse. When the time arrives to act it will find her ready, and it is drawing inexorably nearer. Herod is now obsessed by the desire to have Salome dance for him: if she will, he will give her whatever she may ask of him. Hitherto she has been so sunk in her morbid broodings over Jochanaan that she has hardly noticed Herod; now for the first time she becomes interested in him and his importunities. Herodias, who has all along been ir-ritated by the Tetrarch's unnatural interest in her daughter, urges her not to listen to him. But Salome, now beginning to see her way clear before her, plays cunningly upon the drunken neurotic. She requires him to confirm his promise with an oath. He does so; but in the middle of his feverish appeal to her he shivers, for once more a great chill wind seems to him to sweep across the scene;

"it is as if a huge black bird were hovering over the terrace," he says with a shudder; and once more we hear the threatening Jochanaan motif (No. 13), this time in a suitable and sinister metamorphosis. "Why cannot I see it, this bird?" he asks, "this beating of wings is terrible!" Then suddenly his chill changes to a fever. He calls for water to be poured on his hands and for his mantle to be loosened; he tears from his head the wreath of roses that seems to be pressing on his temples like a band of fire.

At last he can breathe again. Once more he begs Salome to dance for him, and despite her mother's urgent appeal to her she promises to do so, whereupon slaves bring unguents and the Seven Veils and remove her sandals.[1] From the cistern comes the Voice again, asking prophetically who is this [Herod] that cometh from Edom, puffed up with pride in his greatness, but whose gorgeous raiment is stained with scarlet. The now terrified Herodias begs the Tetrarch to go indoors; she will not have her daughter dance, she cries, with the maddening sound of this accusing voice in her ears, and with her husband looking at Salome as he is doing. But nothing now can turn him from his purpose that Salome shall dance for him.

14

The musicians strike up a wild prelude, then, at a sign from Salome, break into a softer strain, and the exotic Dance of the Seven Veils begins:

23

The lulling, insinuating melody is sung by a solo viola. It merges into a sinuous strain in the oboe:

[1] This scene is handled with much greater wealth of words by Wilde. The musician has no need of this verbal elaboration, and does right in pressing on swiftly to the climax.

24

the cadence of which is formed from our No. 1 A, while in the further course of the melody we hear a suggestion (in the minor) of No. 14 A in the clarinet. For a while after this the music is mostly luxuriant arabesque, supported at times by the rhythmically and harmonically striking No. 23. Then a quiet suggestion of the opening of No. 15 steals in, followed by one of No. 19, and this again by a fresh hint of No. 15. The mood and speed of the music change when a broad new theme sings out in the upper strings, lower wood wind and a solo horn:

25

soaring slowly into a great crescendo. Next No. 14 comes into prominence, followed by No. 15 in much the same luxuriant form as it will assume in Salome's closing monologue. Then No. 25, with a new upper counterpoint, steps into the foreground, followed by No. 10 and hints of No. 14.

At this point, according to the directions in the score, "Salome seems for a moment to tire, then collects herself and continues with renewed strength." The music of the final stage of the dance narrows down once more to the semi-barbaric wildness of the commencement. Then comes a last passionate enunciation of No. 15 at breakneck speed, followed by an eerie prolonged shake on a high A in piccolo, clarinet, celesta and violins, with just a hint underneath it of No. 14 A in the flutes, as Salome, according to the score, "pauses for a moment by the cistern like a visionary," her thoughts concentrated on Jochanaan. Then, as the orchestra makes a final convulsive gesture, she rushes forward and throws herself at Herod's feet.

Herod turns triumphantly to Herodias—"You see, your daughter *has* danced for me!"—and he renews his promise to Salome to grant her whatever she may ask of him. There comes another of those long trills—this time on a note high up in the small E flat clarinet, where the tone is particularly cutting—which Strauss so often employs to create an effect of nervous tension; and underneath it we hear a suggestion of the insinuating No. 14 A as Salome, honeying her voice, asks to be given, on a silver charger . . . The eager Herod takes the words out of her mouth: "on a silver charger, assuredly; but what, O sweet and fair Salome, fairest of all the daughters of Judaea? Whatever it may be, were it the whole of my treasure, thou shalt have it." Rising to her feet she says with a smile, "The head of Jochanaan!" Herod recoils, but the revenge-lusting Herodias now commends her daughter's choice. When Salome repeats her demand she insists that her mother's wish counts for nothing with her in the matter: the decision is her own, and she reminds the Tetrarch of his oath. The horrified Herod tries to turn her from her purpose; let her ask of him anything else, even unto the half of his kingdom, but not this. In cruelly hardened biting tones she repeats her demand, once more reminding him of the oath he had sworn before them all. Herodias, now a raging fiend, sees in Salome's demand a proof of her daughter's love for her; she will avenge her mother on the Jewish fanatic who has loaded her with insults. Herod appeals to whatever affection Salome may feel for him, reminding her of his many kindnesses to her, and offering her his most prized possessions, his great emerald, his hundred white peacocks, priceless jewels which even his wife has never seen, a magic crystal in which it is not lawful for a woman to look, the mantle of the High Priest himself, even the veil of the temple sanctuary; [1] but let her not require of him the head of this man, who is a holy man, one who has been touched by the finger of God, and whose death may bring evil on them all.

15

Salome's only reply is a furious "Give me the head of Jochanaan!" "Truly she is her mother's child," Herod mutters helplessly; "let her be given what she asks." Herodias draws the ring of death from his nerveless hand and gives it to the First Soldier: he takes it to the executioner, who goes down into the cistern.

[1] At this there is an outcry of horror from the Jews.

Herod observes that his ring has gone, and wearily asks who has taken it, and who has drunk the wine that had been in his cup: "Surely some evil will befall someone!" Herodias gives a savage cry of "My daughter has done well!"

Salome is now leaning over the cistern, listening intently. For a few tense moments nothing is heard in the orchestra but an insistent dull throbbing deep down in the double basses and bass drum—except for a single high B flat in a solo double bass, repeated sforzando at intervals in the following bars. This extraordinarily grisly effect provoked much head-shaking in critical circles in the early days of the opera. Most people regarded these four notes—if "notes" be a correct description of the sound emitted—as representing the groans of Jochanaan under the blows of the executioner; but in his *Betrachtungen und Erinnerungen* Strauss makes it finally clear that they are intended to suggest the animal half-moans, half-sighs of the crazed Salome athirst for her prey.[1]

To the persistent throbbing of a low E flat Salome asks impatiently why the executioner is so long about his business: if anyone sought to kill her she would cry out, she would struggle, not endure in silence; and a series of pounding blows in horns and kettledrums gives point to her words. At last her straining ears catch the sound of something falling. "The executioner has dropped his sword," she cries: "he dares not kill him; he is a coward, this slave. Send soldiers down there!" She beckons the Page to her and addresses him: "You were the friend of him who died, were you not? Well, there are not enough dead men here. Go to the soldiers and tell them to descend and bring me the thing I desire, the thing the Tetrarch promised me, the thing that is mine!" As the Page recoils she turns in a delirium to the soldiers, bidding them do what she desires.

The tension that has been increasing in the orchestra ends in a great pounding in the bass drum alone as the huge black arm

[1] In a footnote to the orchestral score at this point the composer tells us that the string of the instrument is not to be pressed down upon the fingerboard in the normal way, but pinched firmly between the player's thumb and forefinger, while the bow is drawn across the string in short sharp strokes, "thus producing a sound resembling the choked groaning and sighing of a woman."

of the executioner rises from the cistern, bearing the head of Jochanaan on a silver shield. There is a terrific orchestral outburst as Salome seizes the head. "Herod hides his face with his cloak. Herodias smiles and fans herself. The Nazarenes fall on their knees and begin to pray." These are the stage directions in the play; they are not reproduced in the score, but the observance of them is essential in the opera as in the drama.

16

There comes an immense emotional release in Salome, a strange catharsis of the spirit; and she launches the superb scena that is to occupy the remainder of the score, the recurrent psychological theme of which is her ecstatic cry of "Thou wouldst not suffer me to kiss thy mouth, Jochanaan. Well, I will kiss it now!" The complex musical tissue is woven entirely out of motifs by this time familiar to the reader and which it would be futile to try to specify bar by bar. When she speaks of biting the desired mouth as one bites into a ripe fruit we hear a reminder in the orchestra of the figure (No. 22) that had accompanied the expression of Herod's desire to see her "little white teeth" bite into the fruit he was offering her.[1] Salome's recurrent cry of "I will kiss thy mouth, Jochanaan" is always sung, with mounting passion, to

[1] But we shall hear it again a little later, when Salome says "And thy tongue, that was like a red viper that spat its poison at me—why does it move no more now? It is strange, is it not?"

The more one studies the score the more one is inclined to believe that the final scene was conceived first. Strauss, I imagine, would already have in his mind most of the main motifs of the work, but, as yet, principally as constituents of this superb piece of writing, which is, in essence, a closely and organically knit symphonic poem with a vocal solo. The later allocations of the motifs to this or that passage in the earlier part of the opera was seemingly a matter with him of the suggestion of the moment; thus Strauss's mind, in the episode in which Herod invites Salome to bite into the fruit, would spontaneously revert to the parallel passage in the final monologue. I find this hypothesis more credible than the reverse one—that he *first* invented the "teeth" theme in the episode with Herod and *afterwards* spatchcocked it into the finale; for if the motif were specifically associated in his mind with the idea of "biting into a ripe fruit" why should he employ it a few minutes later, in the closing scene, in the irrelevant context of quite another image—that of the viper's tongue? The true significance of the theme, as we have it in *both* passages in the final monologue, is simply as a

our No. 19, which takes on more and more luxuriant harmonic and orchestral forms.

As has been said already, in this final long monologue Strauss follows Wilde's text virtually word for word, and as it is impossible to quote, or indeed summarise, it all, one can only refer the reader to the play or the score. In the same breath Salome gloats over her fallen enemy and rhapsodises over his fascination for her. He had flung insults at her; now he is dead and she is alive, and his head is hers to do with it what she will, throw it to the dogs or the birds of the air. He had desired only to see his God: "Well, thou hast seen thy God, but me thou didst never see; if thou hadst, thou wouldst have loved me." What shall she do now? She had been chaste, and he had roused her and filled her veins with fire; and "the mystery of Love," she concludes sombrely, "is greater than the mystery of Death."

As she pauses for a while, exhausted, sunk in brooding, Herod mutters, "She is a monster, this daughter of thine!" Herodias tells him that she is well pleased with her daughter, and she will not leave the terrace now. But the quaking Herod insists on her going within. He calls on the slaves to extinguish the torches: he wants neither moon nor stars to look down on him: [he will hide himself in the palace. The torches are put out, the stars disappear; the moon is hidden by a great cloud. The stage is quite dark as the Tetrarch begins to climb the staircase.] [1]

17

Salome now comes into the foreground of the action again. There is a long, nerve-racking shake on a high A natural in the flutes (and, an octave lower, in a clarinet), interspaced with sombre pianissimo chords in the depths of the orchestra and ejaculations of No. 14 A in the oboe and piccolo. Salome finds speech once more, for the last time. "I have kissed thy mouth, Jochanaan:

---

characterisation of Salome's venomous gloating over her vanquished enemy. As such it is mightily effective.

The upshot of it all is that, as I have said, we shall often go far astray if we regard the themes of the opera as "motifs," each with a definite and fixed connotation, in the Wagnerian sense of the term.

[1] The passage here inclosed in brackets does not appear in the score, but it is essential to the staging of the opera.

thy lips had a bitter taste. Was it of blood? No, perchance of love, for they say that love has a bitter taste. . . . But what matters? I have kissed thy mouth, Jochanaan, I have kissed thy mouth." In a final ecstasy of perversity her mind cracks; and Strauss brings in his long-delayed psychological climax in a way possible only to music among the arts. After Salome's final cry the orchestra seems to be preparing to launch another passionate statement of No. 15; but before it has completed its second bar there is an orchestral upheaval that seems to rend the tonal tissue in twain, the upper and lower portions of the harmony asserting themselves in conflicting keys: [1]

26

The spasm is too intense to last more than a moment: the broken Salome has now passed into a strangely mystical sphere in which our everyday concepts of sanity and insanity, the normal and the perverse, cease to have any real meaning. The moon—at the end of the opera, as at the beginning, the silent participator in the action and the silent reflector of the minds of the characters—emerges from the clouds and illuminates her. Herod, on his way out, turns round, and in a spasm of fear and horror cries, "Kill that woman!" "The soldiers rush forward and crush beneath their shields Salome, Daughter of Herodias, Princess of Judaea"; and the curtain falls.

[1] Our quotation shows the passage in merely skeletonised harmonic form. No one who has not heard the opera can have any idea of the shattering force of this clash of keys in the huge orchestra at the point marked with an asterisk.

Der Rosenkavalier

RICHARD STRAUSS [1864–1949]

PRINCIPAL CHARACTERS

PRINCESS WERDENBERG	
(THE FELDMARSCHALLIN)	*Soprano*
BARON OCHS AUF LERCHENAU	*Bass*
OCTAVIAN	*Mezzo-soprano*
HERR VON FANINAL	*Baritone*
SOPHIE	*Soprano*
MARIANNE	*Soprano*
VALZACCHI	*Tenor*
ANNINA	*Contralto*

1

ɪN February 1909 Hugo von Hofmannsthal wrote to Strauss that he had just spent three tranquil afternoons drafting the complete scenario for a new opera. The situations, he said, were broadly comic, the action varied and almost as obvious as in a pantomime; there were opportunities for everything — lyricism, fun, humour, even a small ballet — and two big rôles, one for a baritone, the other for a shapely girl in man's clothes, " à la Farrar or Mary Garden." Place and period, Vienna in the time of Maria Theresa.

This was the first hint of *Der Rosenkavalier*. The musical reader will hardly require to be told that the scheme, " complete " as Hofmannsthal thought it at the time, was modified considerably afterwards: the baritone (Ochs) became a bass, and the true " big rôle " not the shapely girl-boy, not even Ochs, but the Princess. Hofmannsthal was mistaken, again, in imagining that the opera would play only " two hours and a half, i.e., half as long as *Die*

Meistersinger"; *Der Rosenkavalier* is so long an opera that an uncut performance of it is virtually impossible under ordinary theatrical conditions. Strauss fell in love with the scenario at first sight of the text of Act I, though he thought this might prove "a trifle too subtle for the general public," and he foresaw that for parts like these he would need first-rate actors: "the usual opera-singers won't do at all."

He set to work at the music of the first act before the text of the other two was ready, and throughout he kept suggesting modifications of, or additions to, Hofmannsthal's text to conform to the music he already intended to write. Sometimes the poet adopted these suggestions; sometimes he rejected them or improved on them. Strauss wanted "a contemplative ensemble" at the end of the second act, to follow "the explosion of the dramatic bomb-shell." Hofmannsthal did indeed re-write the ending, but not along the lines proposed by Strauss. Three quiet curtains, he pointed out, would be a mistake; and as "contemplative" endings were indispensable in the cases of Act I and Act III, it was only Act II that could terminate in another fashion. Hofmannsthal thereupon outlined the end of the second act very much as we now have it — the intriguing Italian couple demand a fee, Ochs has them turned out, then, excellently pleased with himself, settles down to hum his waltz melody, and so on. The act as a whole, however, was still far from being what Strauss wanted it to be; and he made several admirable suggestions which Hofmannsthal had the good sense to accept. If ever a composer deserves to be regarded as joint author of an exceptionally good opera libretto it is the Strauss of *Der Rosenkavalier:* the reader will find it interesting to follow for himself, in the published correspondence of Strauss and Hofmannsthal, the process by which the text slowly became what it now is. The discussions went on from the early part of 1909 to the autumn of 1910.

Rehearsals began early in January 1911, and the opera received its first performance in Dresden, under Ernst von Schuch, on the 26th January: Margarete Siems was the Princess, Karl Perron the Ochs, Eva van der Osten the Octavian, and Minnie Nast the Sophie.

From the first, some of the German theatre directors jibbed at certain "risky" features of the libretto. Hofmannsthal wisely bowed to the storm he had unwittingly raised: he agreed, for instance, that, as he put it to Strauss, "the Princess shall be out of bed when the curtain rises," and he toned down some of the "coarsenesses" in the words of Ochs's part. Much more than this was required, however, before the work was deemed proper for the chaste ears of the Berlin public. The Intendant of the Berlin Opera, his Excellency Georg Hülsen-Haeseler (son of the Botho von Hülsen who, during his period of office at the same institution, showed such unfriendliness towards Wagner), simply would not produce the work in its original form; and as Hofmannsthal refused to subject the text to a drastic re-modelling, and Strauss no doubt felt that it was not for the composer to do anything of that kind, the necessary changes were made by Hülsen himself. They were many and curious.

The Princess, for Berlin purposes, was made to tell Octavian to conceal himself not "behind the bed" but "behind the screen." Beds, indeed, seem to have been a forbidden subject in the virtuous Berlin of 1911, except by way of escape from something still more shocking. In Hofmannsthal's text, Ochs tells the Princess, by way of illustration of the gracious lack of formality with which certain great ladies used to treat so distinguished a member of the Austrian nobility as himself, that when he called to pay his respects to Princess Brioche the lady made no scruple about receiving him, though she happened to be in her bath at the time, and there was nothing but a screen between them at the interview. Hülsen altered "bath" to "bed." Nor could the bold bad Baron be allowed, in Berlin, to describe himself as in matters amatory "a good hound on a good trail, keen on the scent of any sort of quarry, to right and to left." For Berlin this became "a good wind, turning the weather-vane now left, now right." Towards the end of the first act the Princess tells Octavian that she is going to church. Hülsen, for reasons best known to himself, substituted for this "going to pay a visit." Naïve little Sophie, it goes without saying, was not allowed to tell Octavian that so interested is she in the Austrian book of the peerage that she takes it to bed with her to study titles and pedigrees. In Berlin she was merely allowed to read it quietly in the evenings. After these examples of the purification the text of *Der Rosenkavalier* underwent at the hands of his Excellency Georg Hülsen-Haeseler, the reader will have little difficulty in imagining for himself the whitewashing which some of the more highly-coloured passages in Ochs's rôle received.

2

The scene of *Der Rosenkavalier* is the Vienna of the early years of the reign of Maria Theresa. While Feldmarschall Prince von Werdenberg is away hunting bears and lynxes in the wilds of Croatia, his wife, a lady who is nearing the age at which love calls the·more insistently because it feels that soon the idiom of its call will be no longer understood, is engaged in another species of venery. We see her, when the curtain rises, in her elegant bedroom. The great bed stands in an alcove on the left: near it is a threefold screen. On the other side of the large room are big folding doors leading to an antechamber; at the back, in the very centre of the wall, is a small door. There is a toilet table between this door and the bed, and here and there some easy chairs, tabourets, small sofas, etc.

It is morning: the sun streams in through the half-open window, and the song of birds is heard outside. The Princess, a beautiful, dignified, refined and wholly sympathetic figure, is reclining on a sofa, only one lovely hand and arm being visible to the spectator, peeping from the sleeve of her lace gown. Kneeling on a footstool by her side is the young Octavian — to give him his full name and title, which we shall discover later, Count Octavian Maria Ehrenreich Bonaventura Fernand Hyacinth Rofrano, scion of a most distinguished Viennese family. To the Feldmarschallin he is in particularly intimate moments Quinquin, while for him, in such moments, she ceases to be Marie Therese and becomes Bichette. When the opera opens, Octavian is just seventeen years and two months old; and naturally the inexperienced boy takes his passion for the Princess with the utmost seriousness. The brief orchestral prelude begins with the projection, in successive bars, of themes to be associated hereafter with Octavian:

and the Feldmarschallin:

(The latter is one of those into-the-key-and-out-of-it-and-back-again melodies that are characteristic of Strauss). Nos. 1 and 2 are shown us in a close embrace, as it were; the marking is "tumultuously." At the ninth bar there comes another motive:

which is particularly suggestive of the somewhat exaggerated rapture of the boy in this his first "affair": Strauss has directed that the orchestral playing here shall be *agitato* and with a touch of excess in its exuberance. As the themes are developed, the composer notes in his score that "the working-up is to become positively parodistic."

A change of atmosphere comes with a more tranquil motive in the oboe:

which we shall learn to associate with the Princess in her graver moods; beneath it No. 2a — marked by Strauss "like a sigh" — makes its plaintive voice heard in the clarinet. No. 4 ebbs away into a phrase symbolising the resignation, a kind of *Verklärung*, that will be the only consolation of the Princess in the disillusionment which, she is already secretly conscious, threatens her where her youthful lover is concerned:

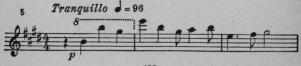

Finally, as the prelude nears its end, the love of the pair finds its simplest yet most heartfelt expression in a broad theme:

upon which Strauss dwells with particular affection.

It is just as we reach this theme that the curtain rises. Octavian launches into a flood of amorous and not always quite coherent babble: the more experienced Princess has greater control both of her emotions and of her verbal imagery. Octavian rushes from one boyish extravagance to another. He closes the window because he cannot bear that the robber daylight shall enjoy with him the sight of his beloved. When the tinkling of a bell is heard he throws himself into a heroic attitude, prepared to defend the sanctuary against all profane intruders. With some difficulty the Feldmar-schallin persuades him to slip behind the screen as the small door back-centre opens, — to admit no more of a danger to their happiness than a little Black Boy in the Princess's service. He is carrying a silver salver with his mistress's morning chocolate on it. With a charming display of ceremony he places the salver on a small table, moves the latter up to the sofa, bows, and trips out again, always with his face turned in the direction of the Princess, who, while all this has been going on, has disappeared behind the curtains of the bed.

She reappears in a light dressing-gown bordered with fur; and when Octavian emerges from his hiding-place she reads him a semi-humorous little lecture on the imprudence of a cavalier leaving his sword lying about in his lady's room as he had done. He takes boyish offence at this, but she easily soothes him, and they sit down, to the accompaniment of a delightful waltz, to take chocolate together. Octavian crows lustily over the Field Marshal fooling away his time in the Croatian forests, while he, a fine young fellow, sits here, also engaged in hunting — what? A cloud passes over the Princess's brow. Let them not talk of the Field Marshal, she says: she had dreamed of him that night. This starts the jealous boy off once more. But the Princess soon hears again, this time in stark reality, the noise in the house which in her dream had accom-

panied the return of her husband. It *must* be the Prince, she says
agitatedly, for the sound came from the back of the stage, whereas
if it were some stranger who had called he would be in the ante-
chamber. Octavian, of course, instantaneously becomes the protective young hero again at the suggestion of danger threatening his
beloved. He draws his sword and runs to the right. She recalls him:
the antechamber, she points out, is by this time full of the usual
morning crowd of callers and lackeys. He makes for the small centre door, but evidently there are people on the other side of that.
The Feldmarschallin at last prevails on him to hide behind the bed
curtains: then she turns resolutely to face whatever trouble it is
that is developing outside.

Suddenly the expression on her face changes from one of apprehension to one of amusement, for the voice she has heard on the
other side of the small door she recognises as that of a country
cousin of hers, Baron Ochs of Lerchenau. She remembers now that
some five or six days ago a letter from him had been brought to
her just as she was entering her carriage with Octavian: she had
put it aside, meaning to read it later, and then totally forgotten it
from that hour to this.

Outside is heard the voice of the Major-Domo respectfully begging the newcomer to wait a moment in the gallery, and a loud
domineering voice replying that a Baron Lerchenau does not kick
his heels about in antechambers in that fashion. But before Ochs
can enter there is a surprise in store for the Princess. Octavian reappears transformed into a serving-maid, in a skirt and short jacket,
and with his hair tied up, as if in a cap, with a kerchief and a
ribbon. Greatly pleased with himself for having conceived this brilliant plan of escape, he curtseys to the Feldmarschallin and explains, in working-class dialect, that he has not been long in her
Highness's service. His words are sung to the accompaniment of
a waltz melody:

7

which will henceforth always be associated with Octavian. The
Princess gives him a quick kiss as a compliment to his cleverness,
and tells him to slip out of the room, go confidently through the

crowd of lackeys, and return to the house in his proper clothes. She then seats herself on one of the sofas, with her back to the door, and begins to sip her chocolate.

But just as Octavian reaches the little door it is flung open, and Ochs comes blustering into the room in spite of the efforts of the footmen to restrain him. He is assuring them loftily that it goes without saying that her Highness will receive him when he catches sight of the pretty young serving-maid, who, not knowing what to do now, stands in confusion by the further wall. Ochs, who, country bumpkin as he is in many ways, has at any rate a theoretical acquaintance with the manners of society, bows three times to the Feldmarschallin in the French style, approaches her with the nonchalance of a man of the world, conducts her to her chair — she had risen at his entry — and in due course seats himself by her.[1] All through the long conversation that follows, however, his thoughts are mainly on the appetising maid, whom, by one device or another, he manages to keep in the room all the time, to the great amusement of not only the Princess but Octavian. The latter, his first embarrassment overcome, plays up to Ochs coolly and impudently, serving him with chocolate and generally acting the part of a minx to perfection. The Princess explains that the girl is Mariandel, her personal maid, fresh from the country, as yet untrained in the ways of the city; all of which makes the child still more desirable in the eyes of the Baron.

Gradually he makes it clear why he has called on the Princess at so early an hour. His explanation is really an expansion of that letter of his which she had neglected to read — an awkward little lapse which it takes all her tact to conceal from him. He has become betrothed, and is now in Vienna to complete the business arrangements precedent to the union. The bride is a certain young Fräulein Faninal. The father is unfortunately not a born aristocrat like himself, though he has recently been raised to the nobility by Her Majesty for his services as contractor for the provisioning of the Austrian army of the Netherlands. The absence of blueness in the family blood, however, is atoned for, in the Baron's eyes,

[1] There is a charming touch, of the kind possible only in music, when the Feldmarschallin apologises to Ochs for having told the servants not to admit anyone that morning, as she had a touch of migraine. The orchestra's sly comment on this is a *pianissimo* breathing of one of the love motives!

by Faninal's riches; he owns a dozen houses and a palace in and about the city, and, the prospective son-in-law is glad to say, the man's health is none of the best.

It appears that Ochs, who has brought a crowd of servants from his estate in the country with him, is putting up at the moment at the White Horse. Before he can enjoy the hospitality of his future father-in-law he must, in accordance with custom, send his bride a Silver Rose; and it is especially in the matter of the selection of the bearer of this token that he has come to ask the Feldmarschallin's advice. She assures him that she is entirely at his service in this or any other matter connected with the marriage. One of the things he most needs is a good attorney to handle the question of the settlements; and the Princess is happy to inform him that her own lawyer generally waits on her about this time in the morning.

The Major-Domo having entered with the information, given with a somewhat bored air, that the antechamber is filled with the usual crowd awaiting an audience, the Baron takes advantage of the Feldmarschallin's preoccupation to ask the serving-maid whether she has ever been out to supper tête-à-tête with a gentleman. The orchestral waltz tune to which he does this:

will be put to piquant use in the third act. When the Princess comments amusedly on the frank way in which her cousin pursues his pleasure wherever he finds it, Ochs plunges into a long and extremely candid exposition of his philosophy in these matters. Compared with him, one gathers, Casanova was an amateur and Don Giovanni a mere débutant. For Ochs has elevated the conquest of women to a science, with different laws for this place or that, this season or that, one feminine physicality or mentality and another. His unapproachable ideal and the object of his professional envy, he confesses, is Jupiter, who had the truly god-like capacity to woo in a hundred male guises. As it is, though, he has a very serviceable strategy of his own for each type of campaign. As he unrolls the lengthy catalogue of his prowess in the lists of

love, Mariandel, who has been listening with the greatest interest
— as the Baron wished her to do — coyly tells the Marschallin that
the gentleman makes her feel nervous.

He reaches the point of asking the Princess outright to give
him the maid to wait upon his future Baroness, for she is a fine
piece of goods: speaking as a connoisseur, he could swear that
she has blue blood in her. The Princess ironically compliments him on his discernment. Such a phenomenon, he assures
her, is not at all uncommon in the exalted circles in which he
moves; he himself, in fact, he adds complacently, has for his
body-servant a young fellow with real Lerchenau blood in him,
as his features will prove when he waits on the Princess with the
Silver Rose. This seems to give the Marschallin an idea. She sends
Mariandel out for a certain medallion: Octavian is a little uncertain as to the wisdom of this, but she assures him sotto voce
that she knows full well what she is doing. The medallion she
shows to Ochs, asking him if the young man portrayed on it —
her own cousin Octavian, younger brother of the Marquis
Rofrano, she tells him — will suit him as Rose Bearer. Ochs is at
once struck by the resemblance between this Octavian and
Mariandel, but characteristically accounts for this by supposing
that the serving-maid is one of the Marquis's by-blows. The
Princess humours him in this notion; it was probably for that
reason, she explains, that she took the girl into her personal
service and now does not want to part with her. She dismisses
Mariandel, who goes out through the folding doors on the right,
giving a last coquettish glance at the Baron, who has kept hard
on her heels till she slams the door in his face.

The truly eighteenth century scene that follows is in the nature
of an intermezzo. An old waiting-woman enters first carrying a
wash-basin, a ewer and a towel. The Princess retires for a few
moments behind a screen which a couple of footmen have
brought forward from the alcove. Two others arrange the toilet
table and a chair in the centre of the room; yet another two fling
the folding doors open wide. It is the hour of the Princess's
levee; and Baron Ochs, who has been visibly upset by Mariandel's
saucy treatment of him, stands aside to watch the motley crowd
that now pours into the room. The Head Cook enters, followed
by a kitchen hand bearing a book of menus, from which the

Marschallin is to choose the dishes for the day. The Princess's Attorney comes in; she presents him to the Baron, who takes him on one side to instruct him with regard to the contract to be drawn up between himself and Faninal. We see also a Hairdresser and his assistant, who, with a becoming sense of their own importance, get to work at the Marschallin's coiffure; a Milliner with the latest styles in hats; a Scholar with a folio; an Animal Dealer with some delightful little dogs and a monkey; a Noble Widow who has come down in the world, and is here, in deepest mourning, to beg the great lady's protection for the three daughters she has with her, all likewise in black; a Tenor (accompanied by a flautist) who has been recommended to her Highness and is in hopes that he will be asked to show what he can do; and finally two very dubious-looking characters, Valzacchi and Annina, intriguing Italians, living by their wits and ready to do any work so long as it is not too honest, of a type well known to the Vienna of the eighteenth century.

Hofmannsthal sets all these puppets simultaneously and successively in the most varied motion, and Strauss skilfully weaves them all into a connected musical tissue. The Marschallin has a good word or a protective gesture for all of them except the Italian couple, from whose furtive attempt to interest her in a surreptitiously printed paper containing all the latest scandal about the fashionable world she turns with disgust. (Valzacchi and Annina always speak in a bastard German of their own). The Tenor, preening himself in the best tenor style, sings, in Italian, an aria that is packed with the conventional poetic "conceits" of the Italian aria of that period. He is getting on quite nicely — the flautist accompanying him on his instrument — until he is approaching the effective top note of his second stanza, when he is shouted down by the Baron. The latter has been having a lot of trouble with the Attorney. He wants the contract for the dowry to include a clause binding Faninal to acquire and convey to him certain properties that used to belong to the Lerchenaus but have latterly passed out of the family. When the Attorney ventures to point out the legal objections to this — the law providing for a *Morgengabe* [2] from groom to bride but not from bride to groom — the Baron flies into a temper which the man of law's

[2] A "morning-gift" from bridegroom to bride on the day after the wedding.

timorous explanations only make worse. Finally he gives such a raucous howl of "Als Morgengabe!" that the poor Tenor has to break off sharply just when he is working up to his "Ahi! che resiste puoco cor," and go off with no more reward for his labours than the gracious permission to kiss the great lady's hand.

While the Hairdresser has been busy with the Princess a courier in a splendid livery of pink, black and silver has entered with a note for her; presumably it is from Octavian. Having read it, she lets the Hairdresser use the sheet to adjust the temperature of his curling iron. A little later there come slouching through the small door at the back the Baron's Body-servant — a strongly built young lout with an expression of stupid insolence, — Ochs's Almoner — a short but sturdy figure, with a wild, gnome-like look, — and his Chasseur, who looks as if he had stepped straight from the farmyard into his ill-fitting livery. The Body-servant has a jewel case of red morocco under his arm. All three of them are to the last degree boorish; after some difference of opinion between them on the question of precedence they take up a position near their master. After the latter's altercation with the Attorney, the Major-Domo and the footman, on a hint from the Princess, clear the room of almost everyone. Of the miscellaneous crowd that had filled it a little while before there remain no one now but the Scholar, with whom the Marschallin exchanges a few words, Valzacchi and Annina. Seeing the Princess engaged, the two Italians steal up to Ochs and offer him their services in any delicate situation that may occur — cause for jealousy, for example, in the case of a young bride: they could keep their eye on such a person, they assure him, from morning till night.

Though the Baron does not anticipate needing them in that way, it occurs to him that the shady couple may be useful to him in another. Do they know a certain Mariandel, her Highness's waiting-maid? he asks. They have to admit that at present they do not, but promise that they soon will. Ignoring Valzacchi's hand, stretched out for a reward, Ochs turns to the Princess, who is now free again. He takes from his Body-servant the case containing the Silver Rose and hands it to the Marschallin. She promises to have it sent at once to the young Count Rofrano, who, she is sure, will have great pleasure in presenting it to Fräulein

Faninal. And now, she says, she must beg the Baron to excuse her, as she must go to church.

Ochs and his servants, the Attorney, the two Italians and the Major-Domo having withdrawn, the Princess seats herself at her toilet table and unburdens her soul of a good deal of perilous stuff that has been weighing on it since she awoke that morning. Her contempt for the woman-hunting, gold-digging Ochs flashes out in a biting phrase or two. And yet, she asks, is not his way the way of the world? Was she not herself taken, like Faninal's daughter, straight from the convent to the altar? And Time, alas, does not stand still. Soon the " little Resi " of that distant day will be spoken of as " the old Princess Resi, the old Marschallin." Where are the snows of yesteryear? How can the gods look on unmoved at the sadness and bitterness of mortal things? For in herself, she feels, she is still the woman she has always been: and if indeed the gods will have it that onward-hurrying life must some day pass her by, why are they so cruel as to make her conscious of it? Would it not be greater charity to hide her tragedy from her too clear-seeing eyes? For the tragedy is less in undergoing this transformation than in being aware of it: and at these words the motive of sadness and longing (No. 4) wells up with inexpressible sweetness in the orchestra.

Her meditations are broken in upon by Octavian, who returns dressed for riding. At once he senses that the Marschallin is in one of her pensive moods; but this he puts down to the fear — for him rather than for herself — she had felt at the possibility of the sudden return of the Field Marshal. In his unthinking youthful high spirits he tries to take up the conversation where it had been broken off by the irruption of the Baron into the room. But he soon discovers, to his dismay, that the woman before him is no longer the Bichette of an hour or two before. He weeps helplessly, pathetically, at her grey musings upon the transitoriness of all this world's joys. But when she goes on to say that some day, sooner or later, he will leave her, he breaks out into passionate protests. She reiterates steadily, " It will come: today or tomorrow you will leave me for one younger and prettier." For Time is ruthless: it flows ever on and on, indifferent to the happiness which poor mortal hearts would fain make eternal, falling silently, inexorably, like the sand in the hour-glass. And the only thing to do is to face one's fate bravely, taking one's happiness lightly when it comes, letting it lightly go when the time for that is reached.

She dismisses the now sobered and wretched boy with infinite loving-kindness, but also with a decision that brooks no answer. She is going to church now, she tells him, and after that she must visit an old bedridden relative: later she will send Octavian word when she will be taking the air, and he can join her in the Prater and ride beside her carriage. Made more thoughtful, in spite of himself, than he has ever been in his life before, he goes out with a quiet " As you wish, Bichette." Hardly is he out of the room when the Marschallin starts up with a despairing cry of " I did not even kiss him! " She rings violently. When the footmen have answered the bell she bids them hasten after the Count and recall him; but they assure her that they had seen him gallop away like the wind. She dismisses them and sends for the little Negro Boy, to whom she hands the morocco case. " Go to Count Octavian," she tells him. " Give him this and say that within is the Silver Rose. He will understand." The child trips away with the case, and the curtain falls with the Princess sitting with bowed head, lost in melancholy thoughts. So ends a scene which, from the moment of Octavian's entry to the fall of the curtain, has few equals in opera for the beauty and depth of its humanism. The closing stages of it are dominated musically by some of the motives most closely associated with the Princess, her sadness and longing in the midst of happiness, and her matured wisdom of life — No. 4, with an exquisite new pendant:

No. 5 in its full *Verklärung*, and a most moving *andante* reminiscence of the passionate No. 6 over a throbbing bass.

3

The second act is played in Faninal's house. We see a great room with a door on the left, a large window on the right, and, at the back of the stage, a centre door leading to an ante-chamber. The corners of this back wall are rounded off by a couple of fireplaces which will play a decisive part in the action later.

The household of the recently ennobled bourgeois is all excitement over the great event in the offing — the arrival of the bridegroom's messenger with the Silver Rose. Faninal's Major-Domo, who has perhaps been acquired, along with the title, to teach the army contractor the ways of high society, is reminding his master that etiquette forbids the bride's father to be there when the Rose Bearer arrives. Faninal accordingly leaves, telling his daughter Sophie that when he returns it will be with the bridegroom — " the Noble and Worshipful Herr von Lerchenau," adds Sophie's duenna Marianne, running the titles over her tongue, all feminine flutters over the honour to the family implied by this marriage.

She and Sophie watch from the window the departure of Faninal's carriage, Marianne almost hysterical with excitement, Sophie doing her best to be sincere in her maiden prayer to heaven that her head may not be turned by her elevation to the aristocracy. Her mother is dead, and she is all alone; may she be as modest and sensible in her new situation in life as in her old, not vain or haughty. But in the end her curiosity gets the better of her dutiful moralising. For she becomes more and more excited as Octavian's couriers, in the street below, are heard calling out " Rofrano! Rofrano! " ever more insistently as the gorgeous coach, the sight of which sends Marianne into an ecstasy of admiration, draws nearer to the Faninal palace. Strauss piles up the excitement in the room and in the street in skilful fashion: the " Rofrano " motive is that of Octavian (No. 7), but in a much more imposing form: the theme, in fact, now develops with a dignity which we should hardly have expected from it the first time we heard it in Act I.

The music works up to a magnificent climax as the centre door is flung open by the footmen, and Octavian enters, a dazzling figure in white and silver: he is bareheaded, and in his right hand he holds the Silver Rose. He is accompanied by a number of his own servants in picturesque liveries of various kinds; prominent among them is a negro carrying his master's hat. One footman bears ceremoniously in both hands the case of the Silver Rose. Behind these servants of Octavian stand those of Faninal's household.

The music suddenly softens as Octavian, with inborn aristocratic grace though obviously not without a certain youthful embarrassment that has a charm of its own, advances to Sophie and hands her the Rose with a little speech couched in the formal terms usual on these occasions: "I have the honor to present to the high-and-well-born bride, in the name of my cousin, Baron von Lerchenau, the Silver Rose, the token of his love." At the mention of the Baron we hear a suggestion of a motive:

which will later be identified with Ochs in his capacity as wooer. Another new theme also heard for the first time during Octavian's little speech:

is to be associated not only with the Silver Rose but with the impression made on each other by Sophie and Octavian at this their first meeting. Its continuation:

which is more specifically connected with the Rose itself, is one of the most salient features of the score, by reason not only of its odd sequences of chords but of its curious tinkling timbre, due to the mixture of flutes, harps, solo violins and celesta. The passage remains, even after repeated hearings, strangely and rather perplexingly alien to the general texture of the work: some listeners never get quite reconciled to it.

The meeting of Octavian and Sophie brings a new something into the lives of both of them. Each of them is at once fascinated and disturbed by the beauty of the other; and from the depths of their hearts youth calls to youth. To each of them comes the same thought — "Never have I lived till today; and may this heavenly vision last to all eternity!" Their ecstasy attains its musical culmination in a phrase launched by Sophie as she savours the fragrance of the Silver Rose, upon which some drops of Persian attar have been sprinkled:

"A rose of paradise, not of earth, it is," she sings; "it is like a greeting from heaven; the perfume seems to tug at my heart." The peculiar melodic turn of No. 13 — the preliminary upward leap, the momentary poise upon the highest note but one of the phrase, followed by a couple of descending triplets — is one which Strauss unconsciously employs more than once in his works for the expression of rapturous emotion: we have the counterpart of No. 13, for example, in a well-known melody in *Don Juan:*

and again in Salome's cry to Jochanaan, "Dein Mund ist wie ein Korallenzweig in der Dämmerung des Meers":

The footman carrying the jewel case hands it to Marianne, to whom Sophie gives also the Silver Rose. Case and Rose are then passed on to the Major-Domo, who goes off with them with much ceremony through the door at the right. Both Octavian's and Faninal's servants all withdraw after three chairs have been placed near the centre of the stage; two of them are for Sophie and Octavian; the other, placed a little to the back and side, is for Marianne, who remains there as duenna.

The world-forgetting emotion of the boy and girl at the first sight of each other has by now burned itself out. They are no longer disembodied spirits predestined to each other from the beginning of time, finding each other by a miracle across interstellar space. They are back in the world of commonplace reality again, and as Fräulein Sophie Faninal and the young Count Octavian Rofrano they feel a little shy and awkward. Octavian discovers that Sophie knows not only his age to a month but can reel off the long list of his baptismal names and titles better than he can himself, for, as she innocently confesses, the Book of the Nobility is her favourite reading. She even knows that among his intimates he is known as Quinquin; and as she utters that word of tender memories the orchestra gives out a soft reminiscence of a passage towards the end of the first act in which the Feldmarschallin had used it. Sophie's transparent simplicity and her ignorance of the world — as shown especially by some of her more naïve remarks about the way she intends to assert her right to precedence after her marriage, and her frank confession that Octavian pleases her more than any man she has ever met — move the young Rofrano deeply.

They are still talking along these lines when the door at the back opens and Faninal enters, ceremoniously conducting Ochs, who is accompanied by a posse of his own clumsy servants. Faninal presents the Baron to his bride. Ochs is, if anything, more completely, more fatuously at his ease than usual, for he can approach the bourgeois world only *de haut en bas.* His condescending familiarity with everyone wins the grateful admiration of Faninal and Marianne; but his coarseness, his animal possessiveness, his frankly expressed view of Sophie as a filly he has acquired and whose points and paces he admires soon bring her to the stage of open revolt. She finds him exceedingly ill-bred; what is perhaps worse, he is pock-marked. With the greatest condescension the Baron deigns to accept a glass of old Tokay from Faninal; then he turns to Sophie and compliments her on being physically the delicate type that appeals to him most. "Just what I would have ordered" would be the modern equivalent of his remarks, which end with a fatuous expression of his satisfaction with himself and his good fortune: "I have all the luck of the Lerchenaus!" And when Sophie breaks away from him with anger and disgust written in every line of her face he approves of her more than ever; these mettlesome fillies are what

he likes best of all the breed! He complacently assures her that
one of these days she will discover what he is to her — as the song
has it, "With me, no room too small; without me, each day too
dull"; and he hums for her benefit the taking little waltz-melody
which, of all the tunes associated with him, characterises him
best:

Octavian, white with rage, at last crushes his wineglass in his
hand and throws the fragments on the floor. He is on the point
of leaving the house without further ceremony when the Attorney
enters, with whom and Faninal the Baron, after a few more
compliments to Sophie on her spitfire charm, goes into the adjoining room to discuss business. His cousin Taverl, he tells
Sophie, will entertain her while he is away. Octavian he assures,
in his usual familiar patronising style, that he is even at liberty
to cast sheep's eyes at the girl if he likes, for the less prudery a
man of the world finds in his bride the better he is pleased.

As Ochs goes into the room on the left he insists on Faninal
following him at not less than the regulation three paces. Faninal
in turn demands the same measure of respect from the Attorney,
and the latter in his turn requires it from his clerk. When the
coast is clear, Octavian and Sophie quickly come to an understanding. Never, Sophie declares, will she marry such a boor as
Ochs: and she begs the help of Octavian as her only friend.
There comes an interruption in their talk that seems dramatically
quite unnecessary. Some of Faninal's female servants are seen
through the door at the back, being pursued across the anteroom
by Ochs's loutish rabble. As one girl in particular seems to be in
some danger, the Major-Domo invokes the assistance of Marianne, who runs off with him into the anteroom to deal with the
situation. The object of all this rather clumsy manoeuvring on
Hofmannsthal's part has simply been to find a pretext for getting
Marianne out of the room, thus leaving the young couple alone
together for the crucial scene.

Now that they are alone and unobserved, the young people
freely confess their love for each other. Octavian is willing to

help Sophie, but first, he says, she must help herself. She must strike a decisive blow not simply for her own freedom but for theirs; and this "Für uns zwei" seems to Sophie the sweetest thing she has ever heard. The long, rapturous colloquy ends in a passionate embrace and kiss. While they are locked in each other's arms, Valzacchi and Annina creep out from the fireplaces in the corners of the room and steal up behind the lovers. Valzacchi seizes Octavian's arms from behind; Annina takes hold of Sophie. Then they call loudly to Baron Lerchenau to come and see the pretty picture.

Ochs comes in, folds his arms with great dignity, and asks Sophie, who meanwhile has freed herself and run to the side of Octavian, whether she has anything to say to him by way of explanation. Octavian speaks for her, though with some difficulty; at last, however, he manages to make it clear to the Baron that Sophie wants nothing more to do with him and certainly will not marry him. As Ochs, too self-satisfied and thick-skinned to take all this seriously, tries to lead Sophie through the centre door to her father, Octavian draws his sword and bars the exit. Ochs by this time does not like the way things are shaping; for if he could be accused of possessing a single virtue it is certainly not physical courage. He gives a shrill whistle, in answer to which his servants come running in. The sight of them emboldens him to draw his own sword. Thereupon Octavian, by this time beside himself with fury, rushes at him and wounds him in the upper arm.

Ochs's sawdust courage at once runs out of him. He sets up a great howl that he is murdered, calls for a doctor and bandages, and orders his yokels to set upon Octavian. But they content themselves with threats: the last thing in the world they want to do is to get within lunging distance of that circling sword. Soon the whole place is in an uproar. All Faninal's servants, male and female, among them Marianne, come pouring in and excitedly discuss the new situation, the main facts regarding which have been given them by the two Italians. The Baron's attendants want to tear up the clothes of the younger and better-looking of Faninal's maid-servants for bandages; but this drastic plan is rendered unnecessary by Marianne and a couple of maids, who run out and return with bandages, basins and sponges. They are all shouting and gesticulating round Ochs, who has been accommodated with a chair in the centre of the room, when Faninal enters with the Attorney and his clerk. The situation is explained to Faninal, who is heartbroken at this insult to so great and good a man as the Baron. He will not listen to explanations from either Octavian or Sophie; the latter, if she does not marry Ochs, will be sent to a convent for the remainder of her days.

Octavian, treating Faninal with scrupulous courtesy all the time, at last takes his leave, whispering to Sophie, as he does so, that she will soon hear from him. As he goes, Marianne marches out with the tearful Sophie; and the excited group in the centre of the stage having broken up we see Ochs comfortably extended on two or three chairs, with his arm in a sling and a doctor fussing round him. The air is rent from time to time with the lamentations of Faninal, who cannot get over the insult to the noble Baron in *his* palace.

Soon there is no one left on the stage but the Baron and his servants. By this time Ochs, having had a generous draught of wine, is feeling that matters after all are not so bad as he thought they were going to be. He can even think tolerantly of the young puppy of no more than seventeen who has defied him, and really affectionately of the little spitfire of a Sophie for the way she stood up to him. He begins to troll the melody of his favourite song (No. 14):

> *Ohne mich, ohne mich, jeder Tag dir so bang,*
> *Mit mir, mit mir, keine Nacht dir zu lang;*

which now expands joyously as he congratulates himself on having " the luck of all the Lerchenaus ":

While he is in this thoroughly self-satisfied mood Annina enters with a letter for him. At his request she reads it to him, for his glasses are not handy. It is from Mariandel, confessing that his charms have enslaved her, though she had thought it prudent to conceal the fact from the Princess; she is free the following evening, and hopefully awaits an answer from the gentleman. (The identity of the writer of the letter is made clear to everyone but the Baron by the Octavian motive (No. 7) accompanying the reading of it in the orchestra). The delighted Ochs bids Annina come to his room shortly with pen, ink and paper, when he will dictate his reply. Ignoring her plain hint that a reward for the messenger would be the correct thing, he dismisses her and gaily trolls his " Ohne mich! " again, which this time the orchestra takes up and expands exuberantly. Annina goes out with a resentful backward glance at him: that stinginess of his will cost him dear before long!

4

There have been a few crudities among the incidents of the second act. There are many more of these in the third act; the librettist's handling of certain points of this, indeed, would hardly be tolerable if it were not for Strauss's music.

The third act opens with a brilliant orchestral *fugato*, played at a great pace and for the most part in a sort of whisper; it suggests that something uncanny is in the air, while suggestions of themes already met with in connection with Octavian, Ochs and the two Italians hint fairly broadly at a coming joke at the Baron's expense. Something of this sort must presumably have occurred to Octavian as soon as, or even before, he had left Faninal's house. For the working out of the practical details of it he must have been dependent on the professional technique of Valzacchi and Annina; and as only some thirty hours or so can have elapsed between the delivery of the letter to Ochs and the opening of the third act, it is evident that in matters of this kind the Italians were quick workers.

The curtain rises while the prelude is still in progress, and though a good deal of action goes on on the stage from that point onwards, it is for a considerable time only in dumb show. The scene is a private room in an inn, with a curtained recess on the left, containing, we are given to understand, a bed, a door leading to another room,[3] a door back-centre, a blind window and a sideboard on the right, and a table laid for two towards the right. There are candlesticks with many candles on this table and elsewhere,

[3] The text-book gives this door as " rechts," but it is " links " in the score.

in addition to sconces on the walls. At the present moment so few of these candles are lit that the room is quite dark.

We soon have a tolerably clear idea of the nature of the plot that has been hatched out against Ochs. Annina is there, got up as a lady in mourning, and putting the finishing touches to her face and costume. Mariandel looks in for a moment, to the tune of No. 7; and to prove to the spectator that she is really Octavian she lifts her skirts — to get a purse which she throws to the grateful Valzacchi — revealing a man's costume underneath, with riding boots. Five "fishy-looking men" — to quote the libretto — enter and are coached by Valzacchi in their parts; at the appropriate moments they are to pop their heads out of trap-doors and secret panels. Candles are hurriedly lit under the supervision of Valzacchi, whose watch tells him that Ochs may be here any minute now. A reminiscence of No. 8, which, it will be remembered, was first heard in Act I when Ochs asked Mariandel if she had ever been out to supper alone with a gentleman, suggests that the Baron has already arrived at the rendezvous.

At last Valzacchi opens the centre door, bowing and scraping to Ochs, who, accompanied by his Body-servant, enters with Octavian on his left arm; the right is in a sling. For a little while past we have been conscious of a pleasant little waltz being played in some other part of the inn:

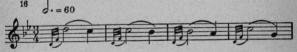

When Ochs hears it he is at first for ordering it to stop, as he had not undertaken to pay for any music; but on second thoughts he decides it may as well continue. He is emphatic, however, on the point of extinguishing most of the candles and getting rid of the fishy-looking men: his own servant, he says, will wait at table.

Soon the room is clear of everyone except Ochs, Octavian and the Body-servant, who brings some bottles from the sideboard and from now on takes an impudent interest in the spectacle before him of the way of an Ochs with a maid. The Baron begins the attempted seduction to an endless flood of waltz music: it is in waltz rhythm also that Mariandel refuses wine — " Nein, nein, nein, nein! I' trink kein Wein! ":

She plays up to him so magnificently that we begin to wonder where Octavian obtained his knowledge of that particular female type. She is by turns amorous, coy, startled and sentimental, this last more especially when the music weaves its soft spell around her; and as she is a good German girl her sentimentality takes, of course, the form of platitudinous philosophising. She discourses quite fluently on the standard theme of Time hurrying by them like the wind, so that soon they two, like the rest of the world, will be no more, passing away unwept, unsung. All this she says to an enchantingly insinuating waltz strain:

These flights of poetry and philosophising, of course, are beyond the prosaic Ochs. Is it the drop of wine she has had that makes her feel like that, he asks with some concern, or perhaps her stomacher pressing on her little heart?

It is as well that Strauss has been able to flood the scene with his delicious music, for the action now and for some time to come is Teutonic farce of a rather poor quality. The barrack-room baiting of the Baron is carried to wearisome lengths. Faces suddenly appear and as suddenly disappear at trapdoors and elsewhere. What seemed to be a blind window is flung open, revealing Annina in mourning, who, addressing him as Leupold, claims Ochs as the husband who had deserted her, and, in the presence of the landlord and others who run into the room to see what all the noise is about, threatens him with all the penalties of the law. She lets loose on him four young children, of ages between four and ten, who caper round him shouting " Papa! Papa! " And even when he is not being tormented in this fashion the Baron is hag-ridden by the resemblance between the face of the Mariandel whom he is pressing so closely to him and that of the vicious boy who is answerable for the pain he sometimes feels in his right arm.

It is Annina and the four children who bring matters to a climax. Feeling that he is going mad under their baiting and the warnings of the landlord that bigamy is a serious matter, Ochs flings open the window and yells for the police to come and "protect a man of quality." Soon a Commissary of Police enters with a couple of constables. Ochs starts off on a confident statement, all in his own favor, of what has been happening, but he soon finds that the Commissary does not take him as seriously as he takes himself. He demands proof that the bald ruffian standing before him — for Ochs, to cool his fevered brain, had some time previously taken off his wig and hung it where now he cannot find it — is really the Baron Lerchenau he claims to be. Ochs appeals for confirmation to Valzacchi, but the latter, after exchanging glances with Octavian, declines to commit himself on that point. The Commissary next wants to know who the girl is. Ochs tries to pass her off as his fiancée, having an innocent bit of supper with him at the inn. One clumsy lie necessarily leads to another under the Commissary's close questioning. The Baron declares the girl to be Fräulein Sophie Faninal. The words are no sooner out of his mouth than Faninal himself enters: he had been summoned a little while before by Valzacchi, at Octavian's bidding, to rescue his future son-in-law, who was in great danger. When the Commissary learns that this newcomer is the Herr Faninal just mentioned, he naturally assumes that the young lady in the case is his daughter. The Baron tries to wriggle out of that by saying that this gentleman must be another Herr Faninal — not the father of his betrothed but a kinsman of some sort; but when Faninal recognises him as his prospective son-in-law he has to abandon that line of defence. The Commissary's next question to Faninal is, "Then this girl here is your daughter?" From that stranglehold there is, of course, no escape whatever for Ochs; and the situation gets still worse for him when Sophie herself arrives. Faninal broken-heartedly exposes the perfidy of her wooer — that rascal standing there with his morganatic wife and his four children; but Sophie is overjoyed at the discovery.

At this point it is necessary, for the later purposes of the action, to get Faninal out of the room for a while. This Hofmannsthal

achieves by making him fall suddenly sick under all the disappointment and mortification of the last few minutes. As he appears
to be on the point of fainting, Sophie and a number of others
carry him into the adjoining room. By this time the Baron has
recovered his wig, and with it something of his blustering self-
assurance. But the Commissary still has some awkward questions
to which he insists on getting an answer. Ochs tries to bribe
Mariandel to support him with a whispered promise that he will
marry her. She repulses him, however, and asks for a private
word with the Commissary. Taking him aside, she evidently reveals the plot to him, for the officer seems vastly amused, especially when, Octavian having disappeared behind the bed curtains, Mariandel's garments are thrown out one by one, and finally
Octavian's head appears through an opening.

The Baron, who has seen something of all this but as yet does
not quite understand it, tries to get to the alcove, but is held back
by the two constables. While he is struggling to get free of them
the Princess enters.

5

At this point of the story a little digression becomes necessary.
The spectator generally wonders how in the name of dramatic
probability the Marschallin turns up in such a place at such a time.
On the face of it it certainly seems to be stretching the long arm
of coincidence to breaking-point. But if the spectator has kept
both eyes open during the scene of the baiting of the Baron he
has probably noticed that shortly after the Commissary's entry
Ochs's Body-servant had run out of the room: and if the spectator
further happens to be a skilled thought-reader he will have
surmised that the man was going to summon the Feldmarschallin. The plain truth would seem to be that Hofmannsthal
had got thus far without himself having any clear idea how the
great lady was to be brought to that somewhat disreputable
hostelry at the critical moment. In the *score* we are told that at the
point of the action just mentioned " the Body-servant, who looks
very worried about the situation, suddenly seems to have been
struck by an idea how to redeem it, and runs out through the
centre door." But this stage direction is not in the German *text*

book; apparently it was an afterthought, which probably only occurred to Hofmannsthal and Strauss when they realised, perhaps at rehearsal, that in the original text the visit of the Princess to the inn had been left quite unexplained.

The stage directions when she enters are a further proof of this. In the text-book these instructions run thus: "First some men in the Marschallin's livery appear, who range themselves in a line. Then the Marschallin enters, the little Black Boy carrying her train." In the score, however, after the words "First some men in the Marschallin's livery appear," there is inserted "then the Baron's Body-servant." A little later we read, in both text-book and score, that "the Body-servant goes towards the Baron, looking proud and pleased with himself; and the Baron indicates that he is satisfied with him." Which is all very well; but for one thing it is highly improbable that the spectator will be aware of this interchange of glances, for naturally all eyes turn to the Princess when she makes her imposing entry, and it is still more improbable that the spectator has noticed the exit of the Servant some time before, or, if he did observe it, grasped the intention of it. Hofmannsthal cannot be acquitted of handling most inexpertly one of the most vital episodes in the development of the action.

One wonders, indeed, to what extent his original scheme for the drama was modified as time went on. As we have seen, when he first broached it to Strauss he spoke of the situations as being "broadly comic" and almost as obvious as a pantomime, with "opportunities even for a short ballet." There is no hint of the tragedy of the great renunciation of the Princess, and, indeed, no foreshadowing of such a character as that set before us in Strauss's score. Hofmannsthal speaks of there being only two big rôles — Ochs and Octavian. The astonishing thing throughout the correspondence, indeed, is the omission, until near the completion of the work, of any reference to the Princess as an important part of the story. In May 1909 Hofmannsthal has no more to say about the plot than this: "The course of the action is simple and intelligible enough for even the least sophisticated public — a fat, elderly, arrogant suitor, favoured by the bride's father, has his nose put out of joint by a handsome young fellow: surely that is the *ne plus ultra* of simplicity!" Even at this stage he could say that the only member of the cast who need be a really gifted actor as well as singer is the Ochs! [4]

We discover from the correspondence that by autumn 1909, after Strauss has actually finished the music to the first two acts, Hofmannsthal is still not ready with the text for the third! One suspects that the published correspondence is not complete; but it is clear enough from the letters we have that Strauss did not like the third act as Hofmannsthal sent it to him in the first place, and insisted on radical alterations in it. Even now Hofmannsthal seems not to have understood his own Princess as we have come to understand her. Still obsessed with the notion that the things that really matter in his play are the "broadly comic" episodes, he actually suggested several cuts in his own text in the more serious scene that follows the Baron's exit in the third act: he could see in imagination, he said, the audience already preparing to leave, and feared boring them by detaining them too long. He "implored" Strauss to "base his composition" on his shortened version of the original text at this point. A glance at the score is enough to show that Strauss refused to adopt the suggestion. It was not until the autumn of 1909 that Hofmannsthal realised, however imperfectly as yet, that in the Princess he had a front-line character from whose psychology effects of the highest pathos could be drawn in the final stages of the opera. That the ending of the work gave him infinite difficulty is clear from a letter of the 23rd April 1910 from the composer, saying that although the score of Act II is already in the engraver's hands he is still waiting anxiously for the concluding text of Act III.[5]

Some six weeks later, Hofmannsthal realises at last that the Princess is not merely a piece of trimming in the story of the boy-and-girl love of Octavian and Sophie but a personality in herself, and a personality of the profoundest human interest. After never so much as mentioning her as an integral part of his "broadly comic" play in the winter of 1909–10, he discovers by

[4] "Strictly speaking it is only the player of the title-part who will need to be a good actor-singer." This proves that Hofmannsthal's first idea was to call the play after the Baron; for his following sentence about Leporello shows that it was a baritone whom he had in mind.

[5] Even at this stage, we discover, it was still proposed to entitle the opera "Ochs."

June of the latter year that now he has reached the end of the work she is the character who matters most! He has had to treat the final scene at some length, he now tells Strauss, because "the figure of the Marschallin must not be deprived of its significance. It is she whom the public, and especially the women, will regard as the leading personality, she to whom their sympathies will go out." Later he enlarges on this theme. Sophie, he says in July, is quite commonplace, just an ordinary sort of young woman; "for real charm of expression and of personality one has to turn to the Marschallin." This character, whom previously he had not thought worth referring to as in any way "principal," is now "the dominating female figure," with Ochs on one side of her, Octavian on the other, and Sophie somewhat in the background. There can seldom have been a more curious example in literature of a character gradually taking such possession of its creator that it evolves silently on lines of its own until he is surprised to find that it has turned out something quite different from what he intended it to be in the first place.

6

And now let us return to our story of the action of the opera, at the point where the Princess enters the room. We in the audience are even more glad to see her than Ochs can be, for, to tell the truth, we have grown a trifle weary of much of the clowning of the last half-hour or so, to which only Strauss's charming music has been able to reconcile us. Ochs having fulfilled his purpose in the play, he is now soon disposed of. At first he is naïve enough to think that the Marschallin will use her authority to put matters right for him; but in this he is soon undeceived. She treats him with studied contempt. The Commissary, who turns out to be a former orderly of the Field Marshal, she handles easily: he soon retires, respectfully leaving the affair in her competent hands. After that, Ochs's star sets rapidly. Sophie returns from the inner room with a message from her father that he never wants to see the Baron again — a sentiment in which, she assures the astonished man, she herself heartily concurs. On the advice of the Princess he leaves the place as quickly as he can. He makes a last desperate attempt to get the situation under control again, to affect to laugh it all off as just a Viennese diversion which he would not on any account wish to spoil, and to get out with some tattered remnants of his Lerchenau dignity still clinging to him. But he is not allowed to leave without a new accumulation of farce about him. The trick of the trap doors is made manifest to him; Valzacchi makes no secret of being an accomplice in the plot against him; Annina removes her mourning cap and veil and wipes the paint off her face; the landlord presents a long bill; the boots of the inn, the waiters, the musicians, and sundry others clamour for tips for services rendered; the four children dance round him again screaming "Papa!"

When at last he escapes, most of the company follow him, the stage being left to the Princess, Octavian and Sophie. Octavian, who has long before this appeared in his proper clothes, has by now got over the shock of the Princess's finding him in such surroundings, but he is vastly mortified and embarrassed. Sophie is broken-hearted; she feels that she has lost Octavian and has been humiliated in the presence of the great lady. It is with some difficulty that the Princess, who has now taken complete command of the situation, induces the awkward, repentant boy to claim Sophie as his own, and Sophie to accept him. For her own part, the older woman bows resignedly to the will of the Fates: "today or tomorrow," as she herself had warned Octavian, the blow was bound to come, and she must bear her chastening bravely. She wins the trust of both of them by her gentleness of manner and nobility of soul. Finally, standing between them, she launches the emotional climax of the opera, the magnificent trio, the opening phrase of which is a stately variant of the almost inane little tune to which Mariandel, not so long ago, had sung her "Nein, nein, nein, nein! I' trink kein Wein!"

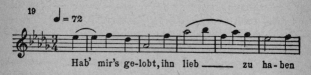

Hab' mir's ge-lobt, ihn lieb —— zu ha-ben

(Why it should be that particular tune that is singled out for the honour of being made the foundation for the splendid superstructure of the trio no one has ever been able to discover.) Each of the characters pursues his own reflections: Octavian is torn between love for Sophie and remorse for the heartbreak he knows to be going on within the Princess; Sophie is too simple to grasp it all, feeling that in some mysterious way the Princess is at once giving Octavian to her and keeping back something of him for herself, and she herself being sure only of one thing, that she loves Octavian; the Princess, as is shown by the insistence of the orchestra on No. 4 to the very end, even after the voices have ceased, resigning herself to her lot, yet finding a certain heart's-ease in the thought that her suffering brings happiness to the boy she has so loved.

When, to the words, " There stands the boy, and here stand I, and with this new love he has found he will be full happy — as men understand happiness! God's will be done! " she leaves the young pair to go into the adjoining room, her going is not merely a stage exit but a symbol of her passing out of the life of Octavian, a symbol poignantly driven home to us in the orchestra, where a final passionate, almost despairing meditation on No. 4a makes way for the more naïve motive of the Silver Rose (No. 11). So wrapped up are the boy and girl in each other that they do not even notice that the Princess has left them. Locked in each other's arms they pour out their love for each other in terms of the utmost simplicity: Strauss has shown fine psychological tact in refraining from putting into their mouths a language of love beyond their years.

While Sophie, the duet ended, is clinging to Octavian for support, the door on the left is opened by Faninal's footmen, who light their master and the Princess into the room. The young couple stand for a moment embarrassed, then make a deep obeisance, which is returned by the older people. Faninal, having touched his daughter on the cheek, conducts the Princess to the centre door, which is flung open by the latter's servants. " Youth is youth," remarks Faninal with paternal indulgence, to which the Marschallin merely replies " Ja, ja!," it being left to the orchestra to describe her secret heartbreak for us with a last tender reminiscence of the music of the closing moments of the first act (No. 4, etc.). When the Princess and Faninal have left, the young lovers repeat, as if in a dream, their simple little refrain of a moment or two before; then they kiss and run off quickly hand in hand, to the strains of the Silver Rose motive. For a few moments the stage is empty. Then the centre door opens and the little Black Boy trips in with a taper in his hand. He looks all round the floor for something which he finds at last, holds it up to our view, and trips out again. It is Sophie's handkerchief, which she had dropped without noticing it.

Index

i

Ernest Newman was born in 1868. Educated at Liverpool College and Liverpool University, he was intended for the Indian Civil Service, but when his health broke down he went instead into business in Liverpool, carrying on musical and literary work concurrently. In 1905 he became music critic of the Manchester Guardian *and subsequently of the* Birmingham Post. *Since 1920 he has acted as music critic for the* Sunday Times *(London). During his long career Mr. Newman has written, translated, and edited numerous books, the most celebrated of which is his monumental four-volume biography* The Life of Richard Wagner *(1933, 1937, 1941, 1946).*

THIS BOOK has been set on the Linotype in CALEDONIA, *a style of type-letter that printers call "modern face." The "modern" part of the classification marks a change in fashion in printing types that took place during the last years of the eighteenth century, under the influence of such "modernizing" printers as Baskerville, Didot, and Bodoni.*

The typographic scheme of the book is the work of W. A. Dwiggins, who also designed the type-face.

V-85	Stevens, Wallace	POEMS
V-141	Styron, William	THE LONG MARCH
V-63	Svevo, Italo	CONFESSIONS OF ZENO
V-178	Synge, J. M.	COMPLETE PLAYS
V-131	Thackeray, W. M.	VANITY FAIR
V-713	Tolstoy, Leo	THE KREUTZER SONATA
V-154	Tracy, Honor	STRAIGHT AND NARROW PATH
V-202	Turgenev, Ivan	TORRENTS OF SPRING
V-711	Turgenev, Ivan	THE VINTAGE TURGENEV
		Volume I: SMOKE, FATHERS AND SONS, FIRST LOVE
V-712	Turgenev, Ivan	Volume II: ON THE EVE, RUDIN, A QUIET SPOT, DIARY OF A SUPERFLUOUS MAN
V-152	Waugh, Evelyn	THE LOVED ONE

VINTAGE BELLES-LETTRES

V-708	Aksakov, Sergey	YEARS OF CHILDHOOD
V-22	Barzun, Jacques	THE ENERGIES OF ART
V-191	Beer, Thomas	THE MAUVE DECADE
V-80	Beerbohm, Max	SEVEN MEN and Two Others
V-75	Camus, Albert	THE MYTH OF SISYPHUS and Other Essays
V-30	Camus, Albert	THE REBEL
V-216	Chamberlain, N. (ed.)	A VINTAGE FOOD SAMPLER
V-64	Evans, Bergen	THE NATURAL HISTORY OF NONSENSE
V-112	Gide, André	JOURNALS, Volume I: 1889-1924
V-113	Gide, André	JOURNALS, Volume II: 1924-1949
V-104	Huxley, Aldous	BEYOND THE MEXIQUE BAY
V-41	James, Henry	THE FUTURE OF THE NOVEL
V-235	Kaplan, Abraham	NEW WORLD OF PHILOSOPHY
V-167	La Rochefoucauld	MAXIMS
V-230	Leedom, William	THE VINTAGE WINE BOOK
V-193	Malraux, André	TEMPTATION OF THE WEST
V-55	Mann, Thomas	ESSAYS
V-232	Mencken, H. L.	TREATISE ON THE GODS
V-34	Montaigne, Michel de	AUTOBIOGRAPHY
V-197	Morgan, F. (ed.)	HUDSON REVIEW ANTHOLOGY
V-54	Nicolson, Harold	SOME PEOPLE
V-24	Ransom, John Crowe	POEMS AND ESSAYS
V-85	Stevens, Wallace	POEMS
V-53	Synge, J. M.	THE ARAN ISLANDS and Other Writings
V-194	Valéry, Paul	THE ART OF POETRY
V-256	Wilde, Oscar	DE PROFUNDIS (Unexpurgated)

A free catalogue of VINTAGE BOOKS will be sent at your request. Write to Vintage Books, 457 Madison Avenue, New York 22, New York.